HOSPITALITY MANAGEMENT

Current Trends and Practices

HOSPITALITY MANAGEMENT

Current Trends and Practices

By

JAGMOHAN NEGI

Director-Professor,

Amity School of Hospitality

&

GAURAV MANOHER

UNIVERSITY SCIENCE PRESS

(An Imprint of Laxmi Publications Pvt. Ltd.)

BANGALORE • CHENNAI • COCHIN • GUWAHATI • HYDERABAD
JALANDHAR • KOLKATA • LUCKNOW • MUMBAI • PATNA
RANCHI • NEW DELHI

Published by :

UNIVERSITY SCIENCE PRESS

(*An Imprint of Laxmi Publications Pvt. Ltd.*)
113, Golden House, Daryaganj,
New Delhi-110002

Phone : 011-43 53 25 00
Fax : 011-43 53 25 28

www.laxmipublications.com
info@laxmipublications.com

Price : **Rs. 250.00** *Only.*

First Edition : 2009
Reprint : 2011

OFFICES

✆ **Bangalore**	080-26 75 69 30	✆ **Chennai**	044-24 34 47 26
✆ **Cochin**	0484-237 70 04, 405 13 03	✆ **Guwahati**	0361-251 36 69, 251 38 81
✆ **Hyderabad**	040-24 65 23 33	✆ **Jalandhar**	0181-222 12 72
✆ **Kolkata**	033-22 27 43 84	✆ **Lucknow**	0522-220 99 16
✆ **Mumbai**	022-24 91 54 15, 24 92 78 69	✆ **Patna**	0612-230 00 97
✆ **Ranchi**	0651-221 47 64		

UHM-9343-250-HOSPITALITY MANAGEMENT-NEG

C—2000/010/08

Typeset at : Sukuvisa Enterprises, New Delhi.

Printed at : Pack Printer, Delhi.

Contents

LIST OF CASE STUDIES

PREFACE

Tourism and hospitality is one of the biggest and most dynamic industries in the world today. In India, the central, state and local authorities are waking up to the fact that this is a major industry that can generate millions of jobs as well as revenue. Colleges, universities, institutions, schools and other educational organizations are expanding their programmes to include courses in tourism, travel and hoteliering.

Tourism, hotel, catering and travel industry comprises a vast number of establishments and organizations, which are directly engaged in the production, supply and distribution of products and services to travellers. Their combined efforts enable people to travel from one location to another. Broadly, these organizations are tourism, transport facilities, hotels and supplementary accommodation, food and beverage services, and other ancillary facilities and services related to travel.

Tourism accommodation comprises a big chain of hotels, motels, lodges, forest lodges, *sarais,* inns, etc. They offer a wide range of services such as accommodation, food and beverages, garage and parking, laundry, florist, swimming pool, valet services, business centres, communication facilities, etc. Hoteliering requires professional and technical skills of a high order and an efficient administrative and accounting framework.

Hotels are generally given star ratings ranging from five to one in descending order, in accordance with the size, location, and facilities provided by them.

With globalization of the economy, international hotel chains are opening new hotels all over the world, creating demand for personnel of international standards to provide the best service, comfort and convenience to travellers. The satisfaction of the customer is the first priority.

The main departments of a hotel are: front office, housekeeping, food and beverages, finance, sales, engineering and security and other miscellaneous services. Each department has a vital role to play for the smooth functioning of the hotel, all aimed at providing customer satisfaction.

This book describes the departmental structure of a hotel and outlines briefly the important skills, tact and managerial tools required in day-to-day operation. It lays emphasis on the control techniques, which are so essential for smooth operation and functioning of the hotel. In addition, topics like security and safety deals with the properties, equipment, guests, customers and employees.

The book is divided into four parts. Part I deals with the management of a hotel. Part II deals with the departmental structure and their operation. Part III explains the miscellaneous departmental services, and Part IV deals with safety and security system for hotels.

— Authors

ACKNOWLEDGEMENT

With immense pleasure, we would like to express our sincere thanks and gratefulness to Dr A K Chauhan, Chairman, AKC Group of Companies and Founder President, Ritnand Balved Education Foundation, Amity University, Shri Atul Chauhan, President RBEF and Founder President, Amity School of Hospitality and Mr Aseem Chauhan, Joint President (RBEF) giving us this rare privilege of working in Centre for World Tourism and Hospitality Research and Development and complete this study.

We would like to express thanks to all those individuals, organizations, hotels, food and beverage establishments, airlines, colleges, universities, institutes of hotel management, who gave assistance and support in the preparation of this book. The lecturing in the Institutes of Hotel Management, Colleges, Universities, Training Centres for Hotel and Tourism programmes, visits and observations at famous international hotel chains and restaurants, air catering establishments and the research and studies conducted at various centers proved very fruitful. The conclusions and results so obtained have been incorporated in the book. Much of the information and knowledge contained in the book has the support of study notes and paper presented at various technical forums.

We take this opportunity to record a deep sense of gratitude towards Mr R R Aiyar, Senior Vice President, Amity University Press whose kind supervision, interest and valuable suggestion went all the way in successful completion of this book.

We express our special gratitude to Taj Group of Hotel, Oberoi Group of Hotel, Maurya Sheraton, various Air Lines and Travel Industries for providing necessary assistance and updating the latest development and technology being practiced in the Hospitality Industries. We are also thankful to our faculty members, Mr Yogendra Singh, and Administrative Staff, for their sincere cooperation. We would also like to express our sincere appreciation to Shri Tek Chand and Ms Abha and other staff and faculty for their support and cooperation.

— Authors

Part-I
The Hospitality Industry

1. Introduction

During the last decade, significant advances have been made by national and international hotel chains. Extensive research carried out in this field reveals that special attention is required in the following areas:

1. Human resources management
2. Marketing strategies
3. Pricing of products and services
4. Training and development, and
5. Use of informational technology

Each organization exists within a particular business environment. To survive, every hotel must carefully assess the changes, development and trends in that environment. This task can best be performed by introducing new techniques such as environmental scanning.

India has vast potential and varied tourist destinations. We require reconditioning of our public policy in hospitality and tourism in the light of implications emerging from policies of prominent economic countries to gain the maximum benefit.

The recently declared policy of the government clearly reflects the growing official recognition of the importance of tourism in the national economy. The areas essential for tourism development are:

1. Consumer protection
2. Diversification of tourism products and transport
3. Inter-governmental cooperation, and
4. Reviewing of the sectoral impact of a wide range of policies

The Hospitality Industry

A dynamic hotel industry is an important ingredient of a healthy tourism industry.

In the context of Indian tourism, maturity is the key to understanding tourism. The region possesses a diverse resource base with tourist attractions ranging from nature trails, forest reserves, etc. to cities, beaches, hill resorts in varied climatic zones.

The economic importance of tourism is universally recognized. It provides million of jobs and ensures a government presence in development and promotional aspects of the industry. Financial assistance comes through a variety of sources including the public and private sector; while most tourism policy is generated at national and sub-national levels.

Growth and decline may be reflected in different areas. Growth is unlikely to be dramatic in some destinations. There may be slow growth, or minor decline reflecting the conditions of a mature market. Growth stages see success associated with capacity increase and competitive pricing, once maturity is reached. The capacity issue changes to one of utility and pricing changes from cost to value. Emphasis on image and promotion becomes over-loaded. There is need for market differentiation in terms of tourism destinations and products/services offered. The consumers need to be seen as discrete groups rather than mass markets. Marketing strategies require greater emphasis on destination systems, with packaging and pricing acquiring more sophistication. These strategies would require greater interaction and cooperation among suppliers and change in developmental and promotional goals of the government.

In the hotel sector, there is an upward trend in the rate of penetration of corporately owned/ operated chain hotels. Many small and privately owned, and government owned chains and hotels with limited resources may thus face a greater difficulty in attracting finance and other resources. Presence of small hotel units is essential in the tourism market. Niche markets require low levels of provision; certain locations may not be able to support levels of demand large enough to satisfy corporately controlled hotels. However, the modern trends in travel and tourism require the presence of a corporate response. Thus, marketing strategies must combine awareness of the market with initiative and knowledge of destination to permit flexibility in manipulating the market variables. In addition, there is an urgent need for better information, more tangible resources of access to market intelligence, and increased funding for promotion and other marketing activities in the global context.

Developing an international perspective is important. Internationalism comes partly from increasingly sophisticated consumers who make comparisons on standards and services internationally. Multinational hotel chains play an important role here. These chains capitalize on some international level markets sectors. These companies can group together to fund initiatives that are difficult to finance on their own. To compete successfully, these chains require knowledge of their competitors' profile while designing their own market strategies. Inclusion on the Internet for larger coverage and a simplified access, at low operating costs requires a hook into a central reservation system, which is possible only to group hotels. Electronic technology provides new opportunities for hotel and destination marketing. Electronic systems may provide information on different property characteristics, including photographs. A vast amount of data can be stored electronically and a customized data could be provided on the basis of the individual inquirer. Cost of use of electronic systems prove to be uneconomical for single properties, but the system is most advantageous for chains with varied packages to sell.

Development and Growth

Travel has been a way of life in India from ancient times. The provision of basic infrastructure like *dharamsalas, sarais, musafirkhanas*, taverns, etc. was a responsibility of the rulers. However, the development in transport and technology all around the world and the increasing needs and

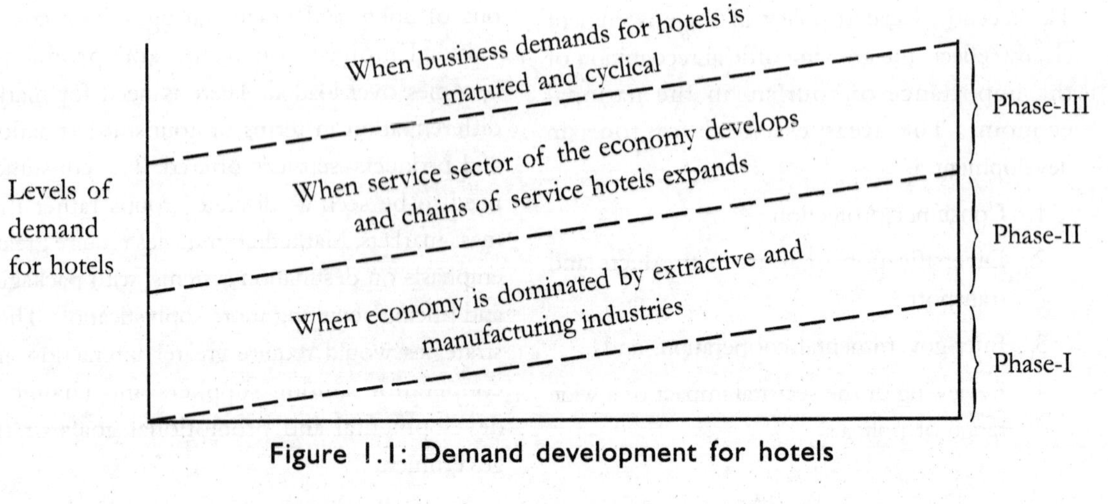

Figure 1.1: Demand development for hotels

Table 1.1: Classification of Tourism Accommodation Facilities

Primary Accommodation

Hotels

International hotels
Residential hotels
Transient hotels
Commercial hotels
Resort hotels
–Summer resorts
–Warm winter resorts
–Cold winter resorts
–The year-round resorts
–Health resorts
Heritage hotels
Budget hotels
Convention hotels
Pilgrim hotels
Airport hotels
Activity-based hotels
–Sports hotels
–Ski hotels
–Boats
Hotels on wheels
–Palace on wheels
–Oriental express
Hotels for children
Lotel
Motel hotels
Boutique hotels
Railway hotels
Yatri Niwas

Motels

Motor hotels
City motor hotels
Roadside motels
Suburb/
Perimeter motels
Tourist cabins
Resort properties

Secondary Accommodation

Travellers' bungalows
Travellers' lodge
Dak bungalows
Forest lodges
Circuit houses
Rest houses
Guest houses
Holiday & Conference centres
Boarding houses
Youth hostels
Hostels
Bed & Breakfast establishments
Paying guest accommodation
Railway retiring rooms
Flats
Chalets
Dormitories
Dharamsalas
Sarais
Holiday houses/Homes
Self-service and self-catering accommodation
Camping grounds
Camping sites
Caravans
Tents
Yachts
Rotel
Ashrams
Community halls
Baraat ghars
Reception/wedding points
Chattis
Musafirkhanas

Intermediary Accommodation

Eurotel
Apart hotel

requirements of various travellers led to the establishment of different types of accommodation units that are significant from the tourism point of view. These units may be classified and structured under the following main categories:

1. Primary accommodation units
   a. Hotel
   b. Motels
2. Secondary accommodation units
3. Intermediary accommodation units

At an international level, most hoteliering businesses have entered a phase of international expansion. At a national level, some of the corporate hotel groups are enlarging their hospitality infrastructure in keeping with the objectives of enhancing international tourism in India. Besides launching a few of new properties across a wide range of tourist destinations, the existing properties are also being upgraded to match modern international standards. The Taj group of hotels, Oberoi hotels, ITC hotels, the Bharat hotels, Clark group of hotels, JP hotels, Hyatt Regency are all set for renovation of existing properties and opening of new hotels. Most of them are undertaking a major re-branding exercise across all their properties to position them in various segments.

Business Demand Development

India is going to be the largest hotel industry in the world. At present, most development is being focussed on economy lodging and hotel resorts. The structure of an economy is the determinant of the extent and pattern of growth in domestic business demand for hotels. In economies dominated by extractive and manufacturing industries, business demand for hotels is relatively modest and cyclical. When the free market service sector of an economy develops and a chain of service business expands nationally, there is acceleration in business demand for hotels. When an economy becomes a full-blown service economy, the rate of growth in business demand for hotels shows and reverts to the cyclical pattern but at much higher volumes.

This could be illustrated by the graph given in Figure 1.1.

India is exhibiting a fast growth in demand. It is unable to match this with a growth in supply. Thus, there is immense scope for further development. However, within the country, there are regions with varied characteristics. Some regions have slow growth in demand and supply and this is likely to continue for some years to come; other areas are experiencing a cyclical recovery and long-term growth in business demand. In some other areas, hotel supply is under-nourished, under-invested and poorly performing, making such areas less attractive for hotel development. Cities like Mumbai, Kolkata, Chennai and New Delhi have stalled the growth of supply due to site starvation and as such no material additions are expected.

Expansion of the Indian Hotel Industry

The rate of expansion of hotel chains in India is being determined by two principal factors:

1. Relationship between demand and supply
2. Availability of capital

The main sources of capital are:

1. Hotel capital
   a. Direct equity investment by financial institutions
   b. Property development companies
   c. Local governments
   d. Local hotel entrepreneurs
   e. Private individuals and syndicates

2. Hotel chain capital
    a. The stock market
    b. Bank debt.

The type of capital, which is available for development of hotels in a region, is determined by whether the hotel is:

a. Self-owned
b. Franchised
c. Managed or
d. Leased.

The pattern of affiliation in hotel varies from country to country. In well-developed economies like UK and Europe, the percentage of owned capital varies from 32 to 80 per cent, franchised from 4 to 23 per cent, managed from 3 to 6 per cent and leased from 9 to 13 per cent. In regions such as Eastern Europe and USA, the percentage for franchised varies from 56 to 71 per cent, managed 21 to 35 per cent, owned 5 to 7 per cent and leased from 1 to 2 per cent. Whereas in Asia, the percentage for managed capital is 75 per cent, franchised 15 per cent, owned 10 percent and leased 1 per cent.

The more the hotel capital is available, the more management contracts and franchises will dominate. The more hotel chain capital is available, the more ownership and leasing of hotels will be dominated by the chains. In developing and under-developing regions, the hotel chains are reluctant to invest their own capital. Investment of hotel chains in these regions relies on individuals and syndicates rather than on financial institutions. In well-developed economies, financial institutions have been active in acquiring equity in hotels and awarding management contracts to major chains, which has helped the hotel industry to become more structured. The hotel chains seeking to become major international operators should adapt to the pattern of capital availability in any region. These chains should generate the flexibility and resources to respond to regional variations in capital availability.

The Indian hotel industry survived the recession and general property slump of the 1990s to emerge in the twenty-first century with new ideas and recognition of new demands. The downward trend in demand and fall in profitability in the nineties had a devastating impact on balance sheets. In order to boost incoming tourism and its contribution to balance of payments, the government introduced the Hotel Development Fund (HDF) scheme which gave grants for building hotels, which exhibited architectural merit.

Economic performance is cyclical in nature, and hotel occupancies have peaks and troughs. Today the prospects for improvement in hotel's profitability seem positive. Levels of growth are likely to increase although the industry is yet to recover fully from the excesses of the last few years in terms of high property values, over supply in certain markets and financial gearing.

The present day customers are more knowledgeable. They are better equipped to make intelligent choices and can easily differentiate between competitive value offerings. Business travellers focus on international hotel brands. For meetings/conferences, buyers opt for the purpose built facilities which provide a suitable environment for corporate debate and recreation. With increasing demand for leisure pursuits the size of market for leisure hotels is on the rise.

The new sophisticated consumer expects specific hotel products for specific needs. Thus, perceived value will be paramount and price awareness will be critical. Only those hotel companies will thrive who would provide a targeted product at a very competitive price. The industry would have to go in for a far higher quality of management than has been the standard till date. Changes in management structure may also be on the cards as drastic changes are expected in both ownership and in property type.

A new generation of purpose-built hotels, international brand budget hotels and recreational resorts is set to emerge. In the intensely competitive market, the product should suit targeted customer groups. Hotels will thus have to acquire knowledge of requirements from a

Case Study 101

A Day in the life of Shri Amar, an Entrepreneur in Hospitality Industry

You will find very few young people who consciously choose to become entrepreneur in the hoteliering business. Shri Amar is one such young and dynamic person. Twenty-five years ago, he fell in love with the food and beverage business. Today, he owns and operates a 200-room hotel and resort in the high mountain of the Himalayas in Uttranchal.

The first job he ever had was in the food and beverage business. He started working part time as a dining room attendant in a large, bustling restaurant chain for Rs. 5 an hour plus tips while still studying for his matriculation examination. He used to set and clean tables and made sure that each customer always had a full glass of water. Within a short period (months), he started angling to become a chef (cook). The prospect of mastering an impressive array of skills in food production drew him to the kitchen. The work was really challenging, demanding, and fast paced, exactly what he was working for.

His first big break came when he got admission in a college for Bachelor's degree in hotel management. Luckily, a small restaurant unit near his hometown suddenly came up for sale. The place had been limping along for years, but Amar always believed that it had great potential. While he had already been accepted at hospitality school, his intuition dictated that this was a once-in-a-life-time opportunity. Four months later, his partner Mr. Kulal and he were proud and slightly nervous owners of a restaurant.

They were both well aware of the fact that they were taking a big risk, but at the same time, they believed it was a well calculated one. As much as they wanted the restuarant, they had agreed not to buy it unless they thought they had a pretty good chance of success. They were well acquainted and familiar with the area. Between them, they had 12 years of experience in the business of food and beverages. The seller Mr. Trilok agreed to hold the mortgage for the first five years. They hired the best people they could find and paid them top money to review the books and inspect the physical plant. They drew up a detailed agreement outlining the steps they would follow in case either of them wanted to terminate the partnership. Both of them were totally committed to the venture and were sure that they were taking a calculated risk. They planned for every eventuality they may face in future.

The first four years were quite difficult for them. Both of them worked long hours and took very little money out of the business.

They exploited every opportunity to make the business grow. Both squared their shoulders and pushed on whenever they encountered a setback.

Case Study cont. ...

Case Study cont. ...

They were fortunate and lucky in that business conditions were generally good, but more than that it was their determination that saw them through difficulties and problems.

Exactly, at the end of fourth year, they took another major calculated risk and decided to sell off the restaurant. They made a good profit and decided to buy a small inn. This time, they agreed from the outset that they would sell off after four years if they could achieve a fairly good profit. They followed the same policies that had made their food and beverage business successful. They watched their costs and made sure that all of their services were realistically and reasonably priced. They never missed an opportunity to promote the business. They delivered what they promised. They went out of their way to hire and keep good staff and employees. They did their homework regularly. They sought the best professional advice but always made their own decisions. They recognised that risk taking was part of their job and profession.

As per their plan, they sold the inn for the price they wanted, on schedule. Mr. Amar then bought his current establishment in the Auli region of Uttaranchal. His partner Mr. Kular decided to go back into the food and beverage business. Both are still good friends and often discuss working together again in the future.

Nobody is born with skills necessary to be a successful entrepreneur. That kind of talent has to be developed. Initiatives, drive, ambition, and commitment are musts. Thereafter come into play the ability to make and exploit your own luck. Being your own boss is a tremendous amount of work. But Mr. Amar would not have it any other way.

The global and domestic environments are intrinsic characteristics of a modern industry. It has become a trend to draw local businesses into the global arena. This is because of the slow growth of the industrialized economics. Companies/corporations having home base in the industrialized economies are being pulled into rapidly expanding foreign markets.

---

sustained commitment to market research. They will require cost disciplines to eliminate waste in both capital and operational costs. In addition to product quality, the new generation hotels will require a critical total management system focussing on creating commitment from staff for a genuine interest in customers. The management will require to spend more time and money on people skills, training and motivation. Reduction of cost on capital and operation front will result in an increase in remuneration, long-term business for the management and various short-term incentives for staff.

The new generation hotel will require an increase in marketing expenditure to build high brand awareness. The hotel will have to run advertising campaigns on television and the national media, the dominant theme being the globalization of hotel chains.

The information superways are set to revolutionize the hotel market system. Hotel beds and facilities can be booked with information on room availability being supplied by literally tens of thousands of travel agents and airline offices across the globe. Direct booking from a desk terminal and interactive television sets at home has replaced the telephone as the routine way of making hotel reservation.

Conferencing on video-phones is common today and guest expect such conveniences in business hotels.

Thus, the pace of change in all sectors of the hospitality industry is very rapid and fast and hoteliering must keep pace as it becomes the world's largest industry on all fronts.

The Concept of Globalization

The rapid expansion of the hotel industry during the past few years has resulted in significant challenges for operators. Through overbuilding, the industry has grown too large. The main focus has been on adding volume rather than value. To ensure prosperity, the industry will have to build on productivity and quality gains that flow from value added competencies and capabilities. High degree of investment and skills in product and process technology are required.

India is emerging as a new business centre and is facing increasing competition for becoming a leading commercial and financial centre. This is a boom period for hotel construction and development opportunities. The government is offering incentives to local and foreign investors to develop tourist facilities.

Privatization and liberalization is leading to a multinational infrastructure. Expansion of international trade and production and manufacturing around the world has increased corporate travel. Thus, there is a growing market for hotel accommodation to facilitate business travel. Service networks comprising hotel corporations and transportation and credit card facilities have made possible this increase in travel all round the world.

Globalization is a process, which establishes worldwide presence of a hotel company. It is perceived to have a standardized impact. Transnational hotel corporations invest abroad, consolidate, introduce brand-marketing practices and seek affiliation with global distribution systems. The global corporation operates without any constraints of national borders or cultural traditions within the host country. It competes in a high potential market. The global corporation is a consequence of several forces such as:

1. Cumulative effect of information technology
2. The development and significance of worldwide media
3. The case of long haul travel
4. The development of capital market
5. The development and application of technologies enable to shift resources rapidly in response to new opportunities
6. The development and application of technologies that seek the simultaneous pursuit of high quality and low-cost in both the product and the production process
7. A clear recognition of the potential for mass markets and global trends

The development of globalization is aided by regional integration and the geographical diversification of corporate activity. The various operations of the global corporation are geared towards a common goal and coordinated by a central plan. These corporations have to face the need to adapt their strategies to meet the particular socio-cultural, economic and environmental needs at the local level in host countries.

One of the central issues of these corporations is how to organize, integrate and manage their activities to respond to the simultaneous need of a global strategic intent and a focus on local conditions, especially the culture, traditions and values of the host community.

With globalization in the hotel industry, domestic hoteliers have to compete with foreign corporations which have penetrated domestic markets. New entrants into the domestic market exert a strong influence on consumer expectations and options. The performance of domestic hotels is greatly affected by the high and consistent service levels and brand names of hotel chains with worldwide operations. Domestic hotel managers need to ask whether their operations are comparable to the world leaders as opposed to the domestic leaders in the hotel industry. These managers will have to seek knowledge outside the domestic environment to ensure effective innovation, skill development and relationship building and to create and sustain competitiveness. The gathering of such information and innovative ideas across borders is called the 'globalization of knowhow'.

The rise of global competition impacts on the manufacturing, and agricultural sectors of national economies which in turn affects national tourism and domestic hotels. Other global industries such as financial services, banking and telecommunications affect the operation and control of specific sectors in the domestic travel system including domestic hotels. The silent revolution of information technology is causing hotel companies to adjust their strategies to compete successfully in the emerging marketplace through global distribution systems. Initially, global distribution systems placed large hotel chains in a position to exploit new technologies, faster than rival hotels. Now the independent hoteliers are able to reach customers worldwide by using superior technology. Globalization strategy is an option even for independent hoteliers. In the past, knowledge about the domestic market was sufficient to survive and technical knowledge was considered to be more important than the management of information. In the present day globalization, to design and sustain competitive advantage, hoteliers have to think about and resolve problems in new ways. The key task of modern hotel managers should be the creation of innovative responses and formulae that fit with new situations, actively adapting the organization to the changes in the outside world.

Assuming that the future of the industry is unpredictable and unstable, the primary challenge for hotel managers around the world is to gain and maintain some degree of control over the direction of their organization. To achieve success in the changing environment, hoteliers need competency in analytical skills and the functional management areas. They have to deal with distinctive market demands, which range from local and regional to global challenges. Therefore to face these challenges, managers should have the following capabilities to develop a global mindset:

1. Flexible management ability and developing organizational ability

Globalization strategy is designed to help managers to compete more effectively. The global or domestic approach masks the complex realities of today's world such as the great disparities that exist between the developing countries in terms of their economic progress and cultural composition, the variances between stable and politically chaotic countries, the dichotomy between thriving and sick regions and communities which have a strong concern for the environment versus places where bad planning has had an adverse effect on tourism. The managers will be involved in asking questions that go beyond their jurisdiction such as:

a. What is the competitive environment like regionally?

b. Who are the competitors in the segment on a global basis?

c. How is the industry structure and the alliance structure in the mid-scale market defined multi-dimensionally?

d. Who is its successful player?

The involvement of the hotel manager at the local level in wider issues will help hotel companies to build a flexible management to respond faster to diverse market needs; develop organizational learning ability that would result in worldwide innovation, and cultivate greater team spirit and thus ultimately achieve greater success.

2. Understand and adjust to opportunities and actions

In a turbulent global environment, hotel companies require strategies that seek to achieve growth and excellence along a continuum which ranges from the global level through the regional and multi-domestic level to the domestic and local level. Similarly the executives require to switch gears to respond more effectively to the changing business landscape. The appropriate hotel strategies and formulation and implementation of an appropriate hotel policy should fit the fabric of the market and should be sensitive to the issues that are significant on a particular geographical level.

3. Cooperative attitudes

In a transnational network, companies will have to cooperate and learn collectively to acquire value creation. There is a need for relationship building between the hotel corporation and its buyers, suppliers, co-producers and distributors and use information technology to speed up the information flow. The partners' goals should be compatible and linked to humanistic values (such as integrity, trust and openness) and business imperatives (such as quality, productivity and essence of urgency). Globalization strategies demonstrate the ability of developing policies and programs with minimal resources. The dual forces and flexibility of these strategies enable hotel managers to ask for specific capabilities before committing to a programme or policy.

4. Multinational and cross-dimensional management

In a progressive hotel organization, serving guests should be viewed as a process integrating all business functions such as accounts, corporate policy, operation, management, marketing and real estate. The managers should not restrict their thinking to within the organization but also outside it. This would mean taking down of departmental or divisional barriers and creating and sustaining value-added service to all customers including suppliers, buyers and employees. This attitude of hotel managers will lead to multi-functional and cross-dimensional management.

5. Demonstrating intercultural sensitivity

In a global market, the customers are different in terms of their cultural needs and expectations. The hoteliers should adapt to these changing needs. They should introduce different programmes aimed at satisfying cultural needs such as:

a. Develop markets cross culturally

b. Employ multilingual employees

c. Accept foreign credit cards

d. Provide translation services and language interpreters

e. Provide currency exchange and proportional materials in foreign languages

6. Contribute in public policy formulation

Travel and tourism is a leading economic contributor in the national as well as international economies. The government sets rules by which the hotel industry operates. Hoteliers should lobby with the appropriate public policy formulating governmental authorities in achieving success. They should cooperate with the industry partners and government in the following areas:

a. Creation of jobs by building the appropriate infrastructure

b. Boosting of export by aggressively marketing their country's international tourism industry
c. Increase in the number of tourist arrivals through leased entry and open skies
d. Taxing the industry fairly and wisely
e. Endorsing national educational campaigns to prepare young people for career opportunities in travel and tourism
f. Fostering cultural and environmental preservation

7. Ethical and environmental values

Environment is a global issue. Hotel business may play a significant role in this area. Pollution does not cease at national borders. It is a transnational issue, acquiring special meaning at the community level, where the negative affects of bad tourism planning become measurable and noticeable. The hotel industry should move from being environmentally conscious to behaving in an environmentally responsible way. A large hotel chain in the country should take responsibility of developing an environmental programme for all hotels with the object of instituting the highest possible standards of environmental responsibility throughout the chain. It requires considerable efforts on the part of the hotel chain. The programme should include formation of environmental committees, environmental audits and consultation from environmental experts. This will help to achieve lowering of costs through waste reduction, energy and water conservation and at the same time build a more positive public profile of the hotel chain.

In addition, the hotel chain could also publish manuals focussing on environmental education. It could be published in various languages and distributed among the hotels and other competitors with a request for their assistance in increasing environmental awareness in the hotel community.

We, in India, require to develop an environmentally responsible behaviour. There should be preconditions for approval of construction by introducing environmental impact statement through governmental regulations. The hotel guests should also be made to become environment conscious. The tourism and hotel industry moves, feeds and accommodates millions of people around the globe every year. Being in tune with the environment is the core of hotel business. The industry must ensure that its growth is environmentally compatible. It is not only right but also makes sound business sense.

8. Preserving heritage and culture

The travellers and tourists are interested in heritage and culture of the destination area. The development of hotels requires to consider both quantitative aspects (*i.e.*, the number of facilities and hotel rooms to be built); and the qualitative aspects (*i.e.*, the type and architecture style of hotel projects). All categories of hotels should make efforts to preserve the sense of place in the communities in which they operate.

9. Enhancing the educational process

In a global economy, the formulation and implementation of strategy implies the need for creating and sustaining value for consumers, corporate stakeholders, and the community.

The hotel managers require upgrading their expertise, if the present incumbents are incapable of meeting the challenges posed by globalization strategies. In an environment of competitive pressure and shortage of skilled labour, the hotel industry should provide incentives to support education, training and research. Hotel companies should be actively involved in the educational process and not just provide financial support. Education and training should be an ongoing agenda rather than a one-time educational exercise.

Kerala Backwaters

Kerala Backwaters

Palm Beach

Resort

Resort

Sitting Area of Std Room

Cruise

Heritage Property

Standard room (Heritage/Palace Hotel)

Standard room (Heritage/Palace Hotel)

Private Charter

2. The Management of a Hotel

Hotel management is a people-centred service business. Therefore, it is incumbent on a general manager to be a leader as well as a manager. Management is defined as getting things done through other people. While a manager is one who arranges resources, a leader is the one who motivates people to get a task done. The principal functions of management are:

1. Plan
2. Organize
3. Direct
4. Control

Hence, arises the important role of a manager to coordinate the above functions and activities in order to achieve a company's organizational goals and targets in tune with its business strategy. The degree to which the functions of management are implemented and the combination in which they are used will depend on the level and position of the manager or supervisor within the hotel.

Functions of Management

1. Plan

'Fail to plan and you will plan to fail.' Therefore, planning in some form or the other is carried out throughout the operation. It is considered as a key function. The senior management team is responsible for a high degree of planning *i.e.*, the production of the hotel business plan, the strategic plan and the annual budget itself. The sales and marketing manager is responsible for planning tactical promotions in accordance with demand. The room service manager handles a computerized yield management system and looks at the patterns of demand and makes decisions on the number of rooms to be allotted to each market segment, and the rates at which these rooms will be sold. All these decisions on a day to day basis may be taken, to greater or lesser extent by the general manager. At the head of the department level, planning revolves around preparing roaster in line, with business forecasts and budgeted wage cost percentage. A reception supervisor plans staff meal breaks, takes into account the peaks of check-out and check-in, as well as allocates daily tasks to the team of receptionists.

2. Organize

The organizational function includes defining the hotel's operating structure or management hierarchy put together by the general manager in conjunction with an operations director and his/her executive team. The degree of complexity will depend on the size of the hotel and its operating procedures. Changing business practices and the increased role of information technology has affected the organizational structure of hotels. Most of the hotels now operate with much 'flatter' organizational structures. Table 2.1 states general guidelines for accommodation and staffing in three different kind of hotels.

3. Direct

Directing can be the prerogative of the personnel and training department in terms of carrying out the hotel's training programmes, which reinforce company culture and enable basic skills and techniques to be communicated at appropriate levels. Direction may also encompass the notions of where the hotel is going, what it stands for,

Table 2.1: Accommodation and Staffing Guidelines for Three Kinds of Hotels

	Hotel A	Hotel B	Hotel C
1. Basic characteristics			
a. Size	Small	Medium	Large
b. Location/type	Resort	Provincial/Commercial	Holiday/Tourist
c. Standard	First class	Economy	Medium
2. Basic dimensions			
a. Bedrooms	52	104	257
b. Beds	78	183	397
c. Employees	61	106	279
3. Employees by department			
a. Reception	5	11	29
b. Uniformed services	7	8	29
c. Housekeeping	12	23	52
(Others)	(37)	(64)	(169)
4. Reception			
a. Head receptionists	1	2	4
b. Receptionists		3	8
c. Bill office clerks	4		7
d. Cashiers		4	5
e. Telephonists		2	5
5. Uniformed services			
a. Hall head porters	1	2	4
b. Enquiry clerks	–	–	4
c. Day porters	3	4	12
d. Night porters	3	2	4
e. Others	–	–	5
6. Housekeeping			
a. Housekeepers	2	4	7
b. Chambermaids	6	9	23
c. Cleaners	3	4	10
d. Linen keepers	1	3	6
e. Others	–	3	6

and what the vision is for the future. Much of this is determined at the corporate level. The general manager and his/her team have a greater role to play in forming a vision. This involves the positioning of a new hotel in the marketplace or in the case of a relaunch, the repositioning of the hotel.

The essential management tools to reinforce culture and enable basic skills and techniques to be communicated include:

a. Employee relations
b. Behavioural interview techniques, and appraisal skills for supervisors and management
c. Statutory training on risk management
d. Fire, health and safety
e. Corporate courses.

A hotel may put its managers, supervisors, and corporate team through a short duration programme for two years. It may introduce managers to the tools and techniques needed to run departmental specific quality circles and cross-functional action teams to teach them how to select projects and use problem solving processes to work through to a solution. Some of the problem solving steps could be as under:

(i) *Identify and select a problem:* A clearly understood statement of the problem and a description of the desired result of solving the problem stated in measurable, observable terms.

(ii) *Analyse the problem:* A rank order listing of causes of the problem supported by data that has been collected and analysed.

(iii) *Generate potential solutions:* A list of all possible solutions, including some wild ideas from 'thinking outside the box'.

(iv) *Select and plan a solution and set goal:* Group agreement on the best way to solve the problem and development of a plan to implement the solution which includes:

- segmentation of responsibilities and due dates
- consideration of others involved or affected by the proposed solutions

(v) *Implement solution:* Implementation of solution according to plan.

(vi) *Evaluation of the impact of solution:* Verification that the problem has been solved or identification of further causes of the problem.

4. Control

Control is crucial to the success of the hotel. It is much to do with setting and maintaining standards, achieving budgets and compiling monthly management accounts. Standard of Performance (SOP) or Standard Operating Procedures should be set up for each department. These should be used as a working document to train new staff and reinforce procedure for existing employees. In a branded operation, the integrity of the brand is important to the success of the hotel. The consistency in that brand must be maintained throughout the hotels. The general manager is the guardian of that brand in his/her unit. He/she is to coordinate the various functions. Leadership is to do with style. The general manager should carry out the role of motivating his/her team to achieve the hotel's/company's objectives. He/she has to balance the resources and the time to best effect. The three 'P' concept as given in Figure 2.1 would greatly help managers to maintain different priorities in equal and balanced perspective.

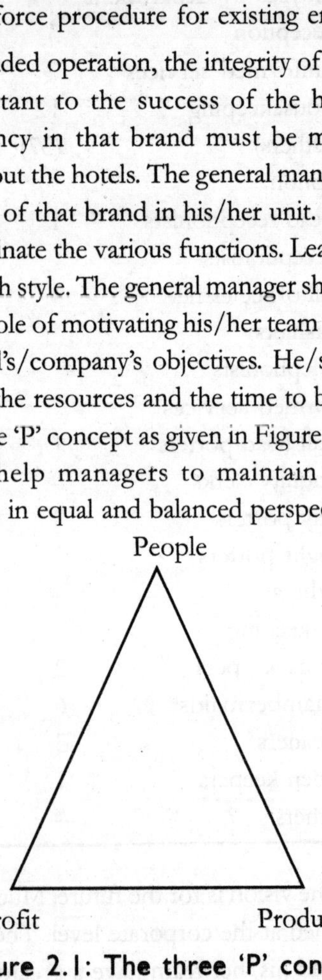

Figure 2.1: The three 'P' concept: triangle of priorities

The triangle of priorities could help the hotel to

reinforce the company's dimensions. Profit is represented by the management accounts and profit and loss statement. Product is assessed by the guests through the use of an in-room Guest Satisfaction Survey (GSS) incorporating therein detailed questions. These could be analysed at the corporate office and returned to the hotel on a timely basis. These questions could be based on core of the key drivers, which could be called from intensive market research as being the main determinants of a guest's intention to return:

a. Check-in speed
b. Cleanliness/servicing of room
c. Value of room for price paid
d. Overall breakfast experience
e. Behaviour of guest clerk
f. Behaviour of bell staff
g. Overall dining experience

The third 'P' (people) is represented by the annual employee opinion survey, in which the hotel staff is asked to comment on all aspects within the hotel. Key employees' drivers are seen as communication, decision-making, reward and recognition, teamwork, and training and development. Results can be presented back to the staff, collectively by each department, and action plans for improvement could be drawn up in conjunction with the staff.

The autocratic style of leadership is an outdated concept. The modern approach is based on consultative and democratic approach. The staff looks to the management to set the culture of the hotel, to create an environment in which they can deliver their contribution to the overall success of the business. The 'People' are at the peak/apex of the triangle. Without people, there would be no managing to do.

An appropriate balance between the three P's is essential to the success of a company's business strategy.

Quality Management

Quality has become one of the most crucial factors for businesses to compete effectively in the today's global economy. Quality mandates a corporate culture in which everyone from manager to worker to supplier is equally committed to produce and deliver high-grade products and services. Many international chains are committed to the training of workers in the areas of quality management in the hope of improving the productivity of their workers and that of the hotel. Developing a strategic quality management training policy is a crucial task for the hospitality firms. The human resources functions such as customer service training and performance appraisal need to be integrated into the quality management scheme. The hotel should turn to quality management practices that focus on the needs of the customer and that support the achievement of product and service quality based on strategies and programmes.

Service quality may be defined as translating the future service needs of customers into measurable characteristics so that product and services could be designed and delivered to give satisfaction or value at a price that the customer will pay. It is a team based approach that involves suppliers, managers, employees and customers. It includes analysis of output methods, e.g. materials, people, work processes and evaluation of products and services, in order to continuously improve the service system.

Service employees need to be developed as service diagnosticians through organization training, support and rewards that empower them to make decisions and respond to customer needs as these arise.

Quality is principally tied to senior management, who decide how work is performed, who create the organization system and the environment necessary to achieve quality. Organization and management elements e.g. communications, reward and recognition, education and training, and leadership are as critical as statistical quality control activities. An organization should be considered as a holistic system undergoing systematic organizational change where organizational strategies, technologies, human resources and internal structures require simultaneous transformation. Quality management without holistic organizational change is doomed to fail. There is a school of thought, which restricts the meaning of quality management to training programmes on statistical quality control, team management, bench marking, quality functional deployment and so forth without calling for change across the entire organizational system.

Principles of Quality Management

In the hotel industry, there is a tradition for training service employees to memorize and abide by standardized operating scripts known as Traditional Training (Script Theatrical Performance Techniques). In this method, a high level of external direction is used where lines (attitudes) must be learnt by rote and mimicry, and changes in scripts are implemented offstage. Yet another technique known as Service Training (Improvisational Theatre) requires the actor to immerse themselves into the moment at hand in order to react spontaneously and appropriately to unforeseen cues from other actors on stage or from the audience. This technique is perceived as personal and satisfying to the audience. The audience sense the drama unfolding as a response to their presence. Creating scripts for training purposes involves consideration of fine aspects of the work processes/jobs that need to be scripted.

(i) *Duties and Tasks:* How many duties or tasks can be scripted for a specific job position?

(ii) *Cross-Training:* How is cross-training affected?

(iii) *Time factor:* How much time will any employee actually spend in scripted tasks? Will the job become too routine?

(iv) *Number of scripts needed:* What is the number of different scripts, any employee will need or is able to learn?

(v) *Nature of script:* How complex is the script? (multiple script levels, main programme and invoked sub-programme)

(vi) *Wording of the script:* How clear is the wording of the script?

Script based training involves memorization with practical drills and tests. Employees are given print manuals specifying exact subroutines for customer service activities such as, greeting customers, using standard probing questions to test customer reactions and offering empathic responses and positive reinforcement to customers with specific phases and body language.

Managers and trainers use these scripts when they have limited confidence in their customer contact personnel. It is a form of insurance that the employee will do what they were trained to do. Using service scripts for training employees have some disadvantages:

a. These scripts are developed based on excessive task analysis of employees' activities and limited observation of these employees in interaction with customers.

b. There is an overemphasis on outcome goods that relate to the completion of job tasks such as registering a customer, or serving an entire group rather than resolving customer challenges and creating hospitality-firm-customer relationships.

c. In addition, there is a lack of attention to customer needs as most scripts are written to an average customer.

d. The very fact that these scripts can cover the full spectrum of customer needs tends to create an operation where service becomes average and not quality-based in terms of rapid response to individual customer requests.

In case of improvisational theatre, the hotel concentrates on improving employee observation skills, diagnosing service problems and improvising quick and workable solutions. This empowers employees to think on their feet and make decisions in front of customer that are customized and appropriate.

The traditional training and service training as discussed above could be shown as given in the Figure 2.2.

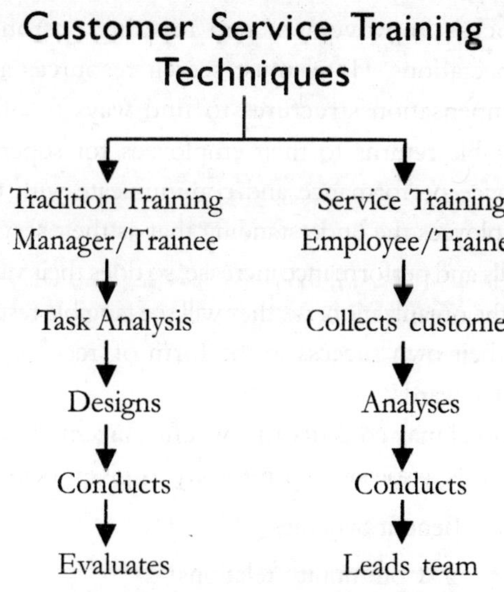

Figure 2.2: Customer service training technique

Service training technique requires substantial organizational commitment to changing the roles of both management and employees of the hotel. Preliminary strategies involve the development of an organizational setting and climate in which customer service training for employees can give key results in customer satisfaction and service quality. The hotel should promote the philosophy that service quality depends on the employees' abilities to respond creatively to individual customer needs in the delivery of service and product thereby establishing one-on-one relationship between service providers and customers. Setting the climate for quality-based service-training will pass through the following phases:

First Phase

In the first phase of service training, a hotel would require five critical activities:

1. Establishing a quality philosophy within the organization
2. Analysing and refining work processes from a customer perspective
3. Manager service training in how to facilitate employees team activities
4. Revising customer feedback systems
5. Reviewing and revising human resources practices

1. Establishing a quality philosophy within the organization

Specific organizational leaders must serve as identifiable champions of the quality based customer service training. They should coordinate the development and dissemination of a statement of quality through all levels of the organization, educating about the hotel's commitment to quality. All statements of quality should use value-based language that is specific, clear and meaningful to all the key players–customers, managers, employees and suppliers. Words should be selected carefully for their ability to build self-esteem, identity and a sense of belonging, urge employees and customers to risk change and develop a sense of purpose.

2. Analysing and refining work processes from a customer perspective

Analysis of service work processes, engaging departmental managers, employees and customers in team-based service, blue-printing and bench-marking activities will form the basis for future job design activities. The analysis must carefully examine:

a. The different contact points that guests have as they enter the hotel.
b. Identify the potential linkages that each employee has with other employees participating in the guests' total service encounter.

It will be of great benefit if all personnel analyse service work processes because all staff levels are then confronted with the need to maximize value-added steps and eliminate rework, operational delays and the need for service recovery actions.

3. Service training of managers and how to facilitate team activity

The hotel should offer a professional development session to encourage managers to learn methods of facilitation to complement later employee training in team-based service diagnostics. This programme should focus on:

a. Individual manager's need for and use of power and status and how this need might interfere with their desire to empower employees.
b. Manager's style of communicating, delegating and coaching employees on the job, and
c. Manager's ability to identify self-esteem and motivation problems exhibited by employees who are faced with increased responsibility for decision making.

Service quality results from a collective approach to problem resolution on the part of key players, rather than from managerial directives alone.

4. Reviewing of customer feedback systems

Marketing techniques, communications, surveys, focus groups and intense service logs may be applied in the pursuit of service quality data. Identifying customer feedback sources and implementing client data collection system in each department requires special attention as customers do not take the time to give their feedback on a regular basis. The feedback data is very useful in subsequent service quality analysis projects.

5. Reviewing and revising of human resources practices

A quality oriented organizational climate, requires revision of current compensation and incentive programmes to establish linkage between reward practices and measure of employee performance in the delivery of quality service to the customer. Thus, former appraisal goals should be aligned with goals of service quality *i.e.*, continuous service process improvement and meeting customer expectations. Hotel must search resources and compensation structures to find ways to offer tangible returns to their employees for superior service performance and communicate with the employees the understanding that as their service skills and performance increase, so does their value to the organization, *i.e.*, they will see tangible results in their own success in the form of recognition and rewards.

A hotel may consider the benefits, incentives and rewards associated with quality as given below:

1. Benefit Schemes
   a. Community relations
   b. Decreased accidents
   c. Increased turnover
   d. Empowerment
   e. Improved morale
   f. Joint enrichment
   g. Job security

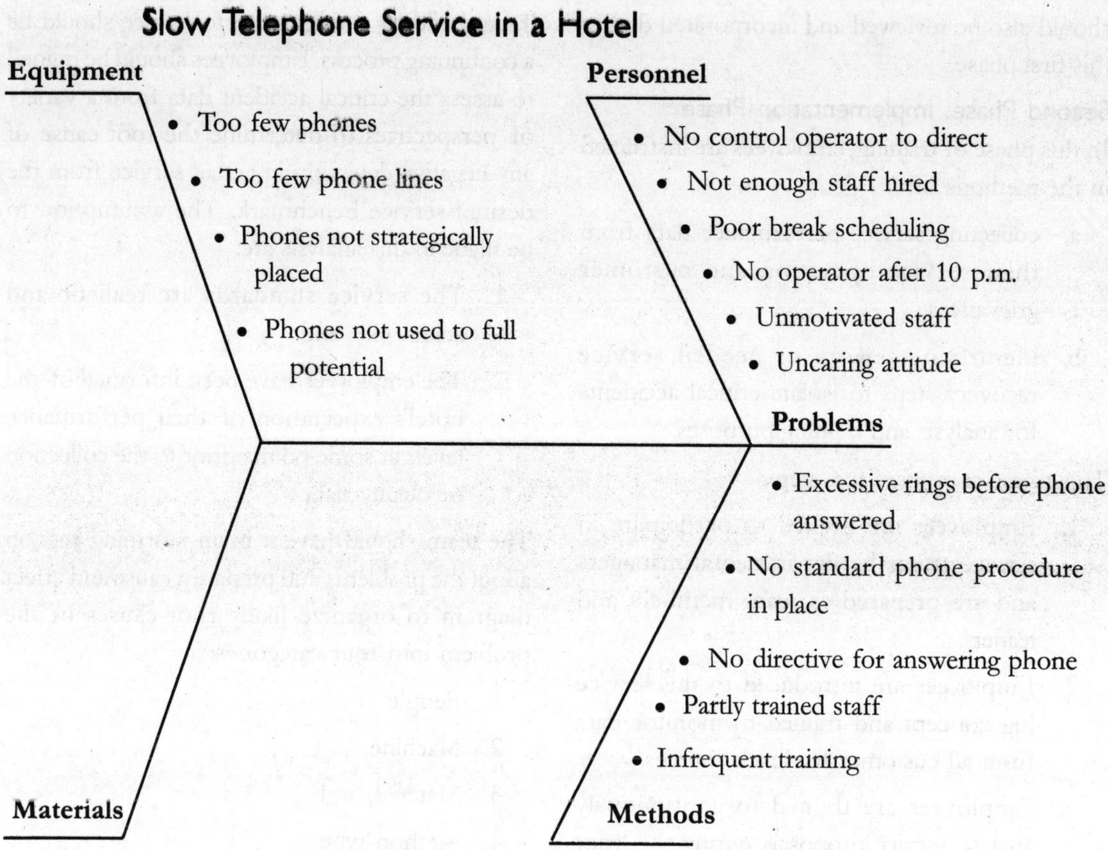

Figure 2.3: Causes and effects of slow telephone service

h. Reduced supervision
i. Self-development

2. Incentive Schemes
   a. Career development
   b. Discounted event tickets
   c. Equitable evaluation
   d. Flexible scheduling
   e. Free travel and dinners
   f. Improved lounge/amenities
   g. Promotion
   h. Quarterly award programme
   i. Training

3. Reward Schemes
   a. Cash bonus
   b. Gain sharing
   c. Health benefits
   d. Pay tied to new skills
   e. Retirement plans
   f. Salary increases.

Hotels, introducing quality management should approach the change process slowly. Sufficient time should be given to the organization to disseminate value statements about quality, train managers in facilitation skills, and create preliminary departmental teams to engage in the source designs and bench-marking activities. Labour interest should also be reviewed and incorporated during this first phase.

Second Phase: Implementation Phase

In this phase of training, employees are instructed in the methods of:

a. collecting service performance data from their service operation and customer grievances,
b. identifying rework or needed service recovery steps to isolate critical accidents for analysis and training purposes.

This phase comprises five steps:

1. Employees are invited to participate in service teams by departmental managers and are prepared as team members and leaders.
2. Employees are introduced to the service log concept and trained to monitor data from all customer feedback sources.
3. Employees are trained to continuously analyse service proposals during the 'root cause analysis' technique.
4. Employees are taught to develop training demonstration and role plays based on 'train the trainer' principles.
5. Employees learn to measure service team performance and provide team level feedback to managers regarding accomplishments.

The service training format prescribes a developmental process where employees become team-mates and co-trainers in a continuous service endeavour. In order to be successful all the above five activities are to be conducted regularly as part of the normal and essential functions of the employee teams. Managers should schedule employees' hours for team meetings and service diagnostics activities on a bi-weekly basis, with monthly service sessions.

Team building and team performance should be a continuing process. Employees should be trained to assess the critical accident data from a variety of perspectives to determine the root cause of any negative deviation in actual service from the desired service benchmark. The assumption to be made in this analysis are:

1. The service standards are realistic and achievable, and
2. The employees have been informed of the hotel's expectation of their performance levels at some points prior to the collection of quality data.

The team should have a brain storming session about the problems and prepare a cause and effect diagram to organize likely root causes of the problem into four categories:

1. People
2. Machine
3. Material, and
4. Method type

This is depicted through Figure 2.3. This diagram represents root causes associated with a deficient hotel service. This analysis aids in the identification of both training and non-training solutions to customer service problems.

The training related problems are analysed and the appropriate team response decides the type of training needed: physical task procedural training or training in department of psychological aspects of service performance, or both. The diagnostic team must follow up with a brief training plan to improve the service problem. Their recommendations may involve any mix of the following physical or psychological skill training objectives:

1. Cashiering techniques
2. Providing information to the customer in a friendly and efficient way

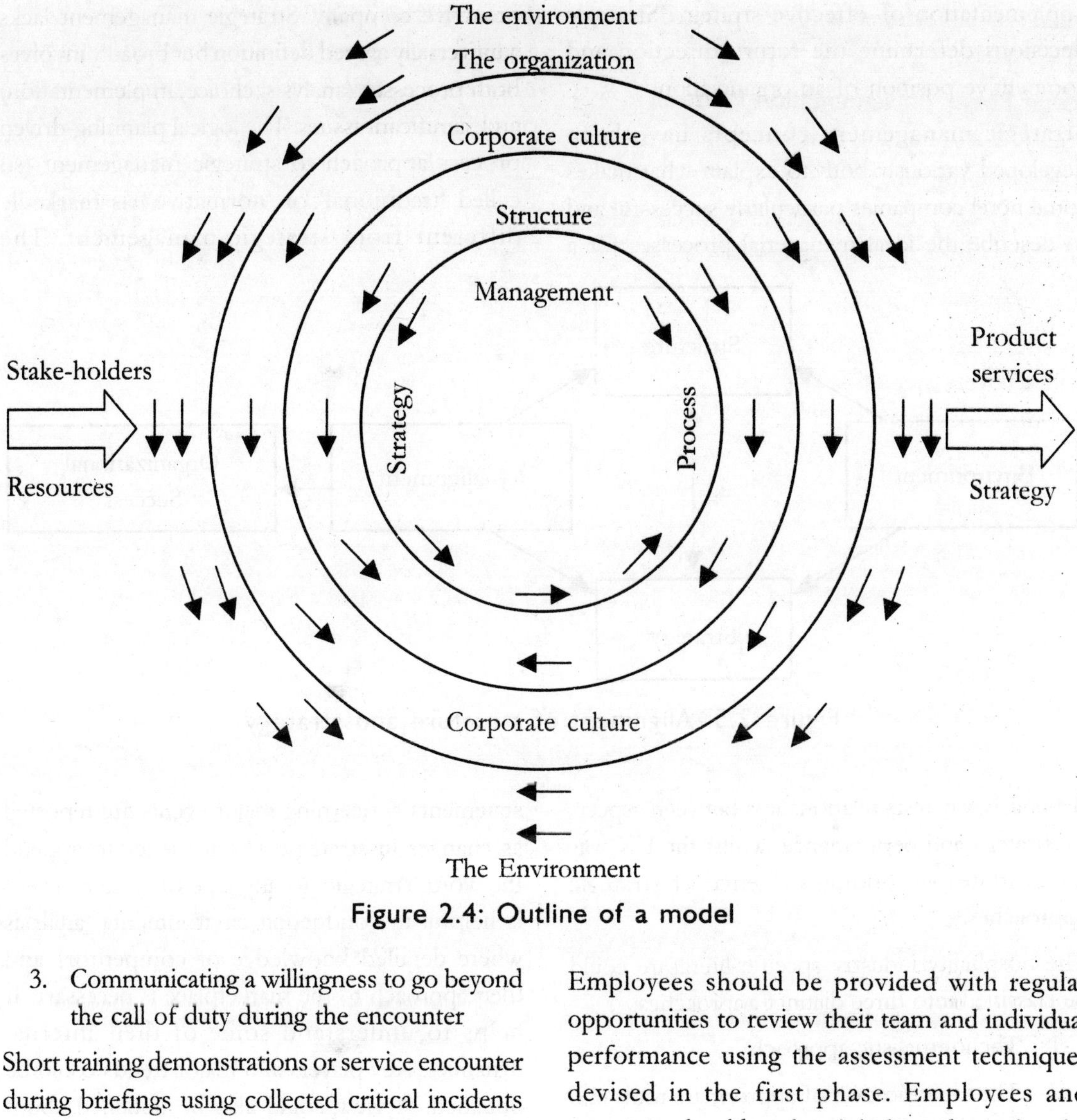

Figure 2.4: Outline of a model

3. Communicating a willingness to go beyond the call of duty during the encounter

Short training demonstrations or service encounter during briefings using collected critical incidents from their own operations should be carried out by designated employee trainers during monthly employee departmental meetings. Existing training and customer service personnel must be identified and integrated into the assignment of responsibilities for coordinating and implementing this employee-led training. The official training personnel could be asked to provide 'train the trainee' programmes to employees who volunteer to lead the training during the departmental meetings.

Employees should be provided with regular opportunities to review their team and individual performance using the assessment techniques devised in the first phase. Employees and managers should analyse jointly to determine the effectiveness of team solutions to service problems. Records should be kept about team contribution in order to track team progress over time. This step is critical to eliciting a greater sense of job satisfaction from employees involved in the service training in hotels.

Strategic Management

Strategic management entails a stream of decisions and actions, which lead to the development, and implementation of effective strategy. Strategic decisions determine the future direction and competitive position of an organization.

Strategic management concepts have been developed variously both to explain what makes some hotel companies particularly successful and to describe the ideal managerial processes for a proactive company. Strategic management lacks a universally agreed definition but broadly involves both processes (analysis, choice, implementation) and significant issues. The logical planning-driven process approach to strategic management (so called 'traditional' or 'normative') is markedly different from strategic management. The American way tests relationships between aspects of strategy and performance, whilst the UK way concentrates on finding evidence of strategic approaches.

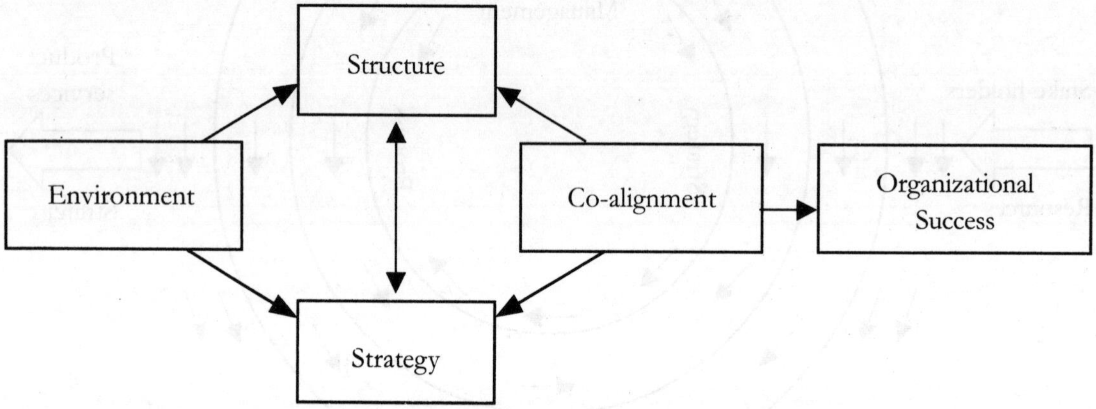

Figure 2.5: Alignment of structure and strategy

The hospitality industry specific literature could be classified into three distinct approaches:

1. The journalistic approach
2. The identification of appropriate tools and techniques, and
3. Applied research.

The Journalistic Approach

The trade press or business sections of newspaper report on strategies. This is in tune with the mainstream opinion that strategic decisions are important, as they are concerned with the scope of an organization's activities. They have implications for change and they reflect the organization's direction in the long run. Therefore, statements concerning major events are reported as changes in strategy. The tendency to append the word 'strategic' to any type of issue or event is helpful in conducting environmental analysis where detailed knowledge of competitors and their approach to the marketplace is necessary. It helps to understand some of their internal dynamics. Key players and major trends could be obtained. A view could also be obtained about the volatility or stability of the industry sector.

Identification of Tools and Techniques

According to this approach academic and management consultants identify appropriate tools and techniques, which might be used in strategic management. This information acts as indicators of the process that an organization uses to plan and implement strategy. It also provides a checklist of indicative behaviour or serves as a test of managerial knowledge and experience.

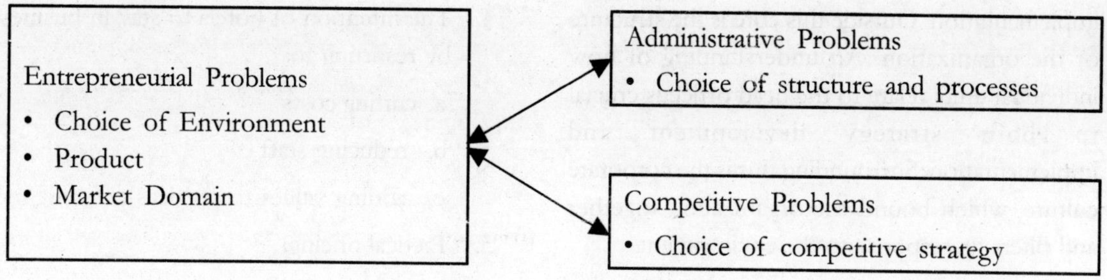

Figure 2.6: Strategic choice model for a hotel

Applied Research

In this approach of applied research, theories or techniques which are held to be valid from a general management perspective are tested through the use of questionnaires to quite a large sampling of organizations or as case study material in hospitality companies. These studies tended to address small elements of the strategic forces, such as environmental scanning, internal analysis or competitive positioning.

How to Structure the Research ?

An ideal and appropriate aid to structuring of primary material for the purpose of research is the building of a model. An outline of the rationale and construction of the model is presented in Figure 2.4.

As given in the figure, the organization is viewed as an open system operating in its environment. This allows an overview of the company, which includes discussion of the environment, a broad consideration of the macro-economic factors, and overview of the Indian hotel industry and the stage in the life-cycle which has been reached. The inputs are stakeholders and researchers–physical, financial and human. The outputs are the products/services provided and the strategy pursued. At the core of the organization is process of strategic analysis, implementation and choice, which are titled as the strategic management process. It is important to have an open mind about how the strategy is managed and look for evidence of adaptation as well as formal managerial planning and

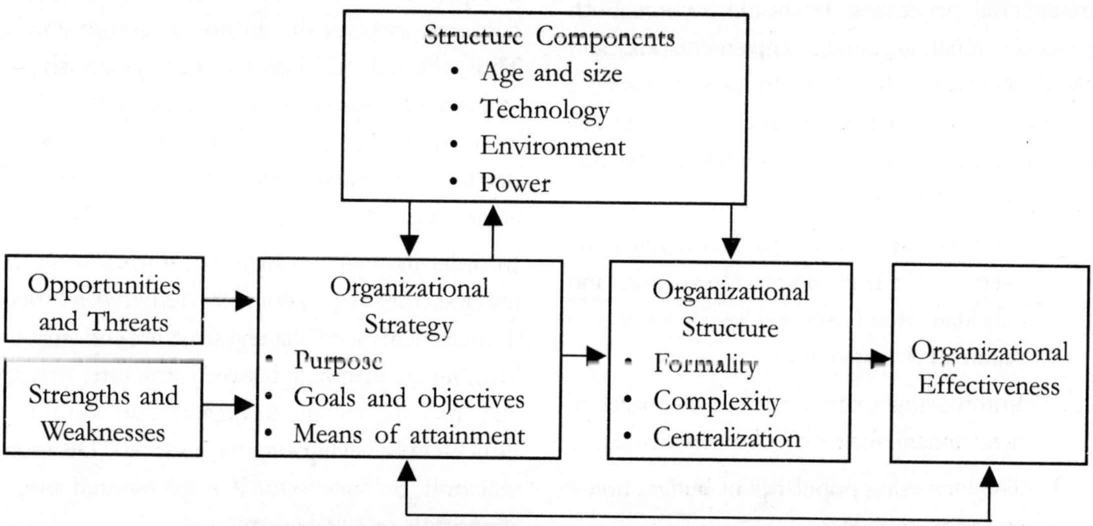

Figure 2.7: Structure and strategy effectiveness model

implementation. Outside this core is the structure of the organization. An understanding of how individual units relate to the head office is crucial to both strategy development and implementation. Surrounding this is the corporate culture, which bound the organization together and filters its response to the environment.

A single company could form the basis of a case study, which could serve the test of a model of strategic management. Because of the complexity of the information, the model is used to structure the information, which comes from a variety of sources, secondary published sources, interviews with key informants and observers. After an initial review of appropriate industry sectors, it could be decided to focus on large hotel companies, operating in the mid-range market.

A critical aspect of top management's work involves matching operational competencies with the opportunities and risks created by environmental change in ways that will be both effective and efficient over the time such resources will be deployed.

Strategic management is developed to make hotel companies successful and to describe the 'ideal' managerial processes. It should involve both processes (analysis, choice, implementation) and significant issues. The hotel industry is facing a competitive and changing marketplace, as well as a highly unpredictable external environment due to the following reasons:

1. The recession which forced corporate hotel users to cut back on travel expenses and subsidiary hotel uses and leisure tourists to reduce their expenditure
2. Fluctuating exchange rate–a powerful determinant factor of overseas demand
3. The increasing popularity of budget hotels and tourists lodges
4. The intention of hotels to stay in business by resorting to:
   a. cutting costs
   b. reducing staff
   c. adding values to services offered
5. Tactical pricing:
   a. special offers
   b. room-only prices
6. Use of franchising and management contracts with a view to growing risk and making profit

In such a scenario the hotel firms must have a proper alignment and match between structure and strategy at the unit level. It will help them in attempting to gain competitive advantage both in terms of increasing customer satisfaction and overall organization. The organization should be structured in such a way as to determine and influence upon business success, particularly when considering decisions and their implementation.

The unit managers should play their role in branded hotels. The unit should be responsible for its business/tactical decision, where immediate action is required. However, the hotel's overall long term corporate policies should not be compromised. Thus, the unit will become more responsive to strategic decisions made by headquarters and will be more proactive with regard to changes occurring in markets and localized and regional environments.

In order to achieve a higher performance in the hotel sector, firms should be required to focus development on co-aligning structure and strategy. Without co-alignment between structure, strategy and the environment an organization will find it difficult in achieving long-term success. Decisions will only be successful if implemented into a supportive or suitable structure.

The alignment of structure and strategy is not a one-time event. The market environment is complex and dynamics. Therefore, a hospitality organization must continually attempt to match its competitive strategies with its organizational structure. It needs to consider both the product and environment to have a thorough knowledge of the situation it faces. The choice of an appropriate competitive strategy will not ensure high performance levels unless the organizational structure is appropriate and fits the strategy. This alignment of structure and strategy could well be depicted through Figure 2.5.

The best alignment of structure and strategy is pursued by a winner who survives at the expense of its competitors.

Varied decisions need to be taken when working in a particular organization structure, as given below:

Structure	Strategy
a. Sample structure (niche)	a. Differentiation
b. Machine bureaucracy	b. Cost leadership
c. Organic	c. Differentiation (innovative)
d. Divisionalized	d. Conglomeration

The following are some of the different organizational structures:

1. Formal organizational structure
2. Complex organizational structure
3. Control organizational structure

Formal structure

It is a structure where rules, procedures, policies and instructions exist. Employees know their role within the organization and therefore work accordingly. Operational strategies relating to simple tasks may operate better within this structure, as there is little room for initiative to unfold.

Complex structure

In this structure the work is divided both vertically and horizontally, allowing employees to operate within different fields according to the amount of specialization and degree of personal expertise within the firm.

Control structure

Within this policy, decision-making authority is delegated to those performing significant functional tasks or a hierarchical decision making. This structure works best when firms are operating in a stable environment, where the product is forced to operate somewhat differently in order to beat off similar competitors. A cost leadership decision will work best under this structure type, as power is controlled by few.

Strategy

For a hotel company to succeed it must match its competitive strategy and its organizational structure according to the realities of the market. Figure 2.6 is a strategic choice model for an organization, which counters the problem that the organization faces in attempting to align structure and strategy within a particular market environment.

Introduction of this model requires that the manager be constantly aware of the environment in which his product is to be positioned. The organization will be required to develop a structure that is supportive of these directions. After considering the external environment, the manager faces the problem of selection of appropriate strategy for his product and market domain. Thereafter the administrative concern needs to be defined. The manager should choose an organizational structure which fits his future decisions. The result of the introduction of this model is an improvement in unit performance.

The hotel firms should define their strategy plans, develop the most appropriate structure that supports these decisions. A 'structure strategy and effectiveness model' could be developed as given in Figure 2.7.

Strategy Development

The first step is to undertake a business 'SWOT Analysis' (strength, weaknesses, opportunities and threats). This will help in developing a strategy which will focus on:

1. Purpose: What you want to achieve?
2. Goals and Objectives: What do you want to do?
3. Means of attainment: How can we achieve?

Thereafter the next step is to consider the most appropriate structure for implementing the decisions. To develop a most appropriate structure for implementing the decision, the following points need to be considered:

1. Formality: The degree to which rules and procedures influence the firm
2. Complexity: The degree of specialization and task variety
3. Centralization: The distribution of authority within the firm's hierarchy

Structures

Structure refers to the means though which strategy implementation takes place. It relates to the organization's effectiveness and performance. Organization structure is determined by the following factors referred to as structural components:

1. Age and Size

In a large organization there are increasing responsibilities, which widens the span of control of managers. Older organizations tend to become more formalized relative to their structured dimensions.

2. Technology

An organization in which the technology is centralized and routine, the most appropriate is the mechanistic structure. When an organization's technology is complex and non-routine, it will require a more decentralized, organic structure.

3. Environment

Organizations that operate in a stable environment tend to have a mechanical nature, while those operating in a dynamic environment need to be flexible and proactive.

4. Power

Power forces within an organizational structure may ultimately affect alignment, and the need to improve performance.

Structural Configurations

These are the final steps in strategy development. Structural configurations are recognized as being increasingly important factors. The degree to which an organization is able to adapt its strategy as well as its structure to a situation will profoundly affect its ultimate performance.

To gain a competitive edge in the market, the hotel company should implement a culture that is better suited to a decentralized structure, permitting unit managers to be flexible and adaptable to their local environment. Each hotel chain should function as a semi-independent property under the chain formula, where unit managers should be allotted responsibility for implementing decisions in their hotels. Then the unit manager will be able to respond positively to any change within the external environment, as well as spend time considering the customers' requirements.

Co-alignment of Structures and Strategy

At the unit level emphasis should be placed upon strategic decisions. Managers of these hotels will have to go beyond implementing budgets and plans. They should engage themselves in strategy formulations, implementation and evaluation. In the past, unit managers were primarily concerned with implementing growth objectives as directed by the corporate and head office. The head office was also responsible for setting guidelines and supporting the managers in their daily roles. As head office staff is reduced, unit managers will have a different role to play. They will be asked to compete effectively at the local level as conditions become competitive. They will have to scan the environment for threats and opportunities and build a strategic plan for their hotels. They will have to become aware of the environmental forces and their effect upon the unit. These changes will make unit managers independent decision makers.

Some of the issues that unit managers will face are:

1. Hotel traditions:
   a. Operating and line management
   b. Food and beverages management
   c. Housekeeping
2. Business orientation:
   a. Accounting and finance
   b. Personnel and training
   c. Audit and control
3. Ancillary function:
   a. Building and maintenance
   b. Computing
   c. Public relations
4. Support function:
   a. Stores and supply purchasing
   b. Fire and safety
   c. Engineering

The difference between corporate and competitive strategy is on a continuous change. Competitive or business strategy focuses on how best to compete successfully within a particular industry/market segment, by developing and maintaining sustainable competitive advantage. Thus, unit managers will become more independent managers who are better placed to interpret and respond to the localized issues affecting their operation. They will focus on generic business and financial issues as well as develop more sophisticated response to customer needs.

The structure developed should encourage managers to take responsibility for their personal development. They should be better equipped to exercise discretion, creativity and flair as they implement strategic decisions made by the head office. They should be able to create and sustain a new, more vibrant business climate in their units so that management teams and staff can adapt to become more responsive and proactive.

The new vision for unit managers and greater responsiveness to alignment will need the support of cohesive and effective work teams. It will need to incorporate staff from all departments, enabling an appropriate structure that helps unit managers to focus their attention on the relationship between the internal organization and the strategies to be implemented. This can be facilitated by concentrating internal efforts on the following areas:

1. Control process: Getting things right the first time
2. Customer focussed culture: Listening to customers
3. Continuous improvement: Exceed the customers' expectations
4. Commercialization: Keeping in touch both upwardly, downwardly and horizontally

The team manager should foster and develop team spirit. This requires special attention to be given to testing and refining the structure. Some of the important structural variables for successful matching of the internal organization at all levels with strategy decision making are:

1. Flexibility
2. Acceptability
3. Empowerment
4. Innovation
5. Team support
6. Opportunities for group decision making
7. Different structures for each department

These variables will enable development of an organization structure that allows the unit to be proactive, generating ideas on how best to alter the unit to meet specified objectives. This will ensure that products are appropriately matched to the continually changing perceptions of the customers. Such initiatives will give clear guidelines to the establishment on how best to satisfy needs, met through individual and team effort. The management should be committed to ensure that the unit structure is ready to align with decisions from both within and above.

Figure 2.8 shows in a diagrammatic form the appropriate way for unit managers to achieve successful structure and strategy co-alignment, to enable all *i.e.*, the organization, the customer, and the employees to adapt.

The unit managers should undertake a more strategic role wherein the process of co-alignment between structure and strategy becomes more important. The manager should assume a proactive stance so that initiatives come from the hotel units as well as the centre. The manager should be equipped to exercise discretion, creativity and flair to implement strategic decisions made by head office.

The challenges a manager will face are a rich array of managerial and entrepreneurial activity initiated and managed at the unit level. A richer and more stimulating set of business and professional tasks will necessitate the alignment between these tasks and the existing structure. These new opportunities are likely to encompass:

1. Business performance
2. Determining projects
3. Strategic decisions
4. Legal complexity

The new vision for unit managers will enable them to be more responsive to strategic decisions made by the head office and be more proactive in aligning situations according to their localized environments. The organization will thus remain competitive.

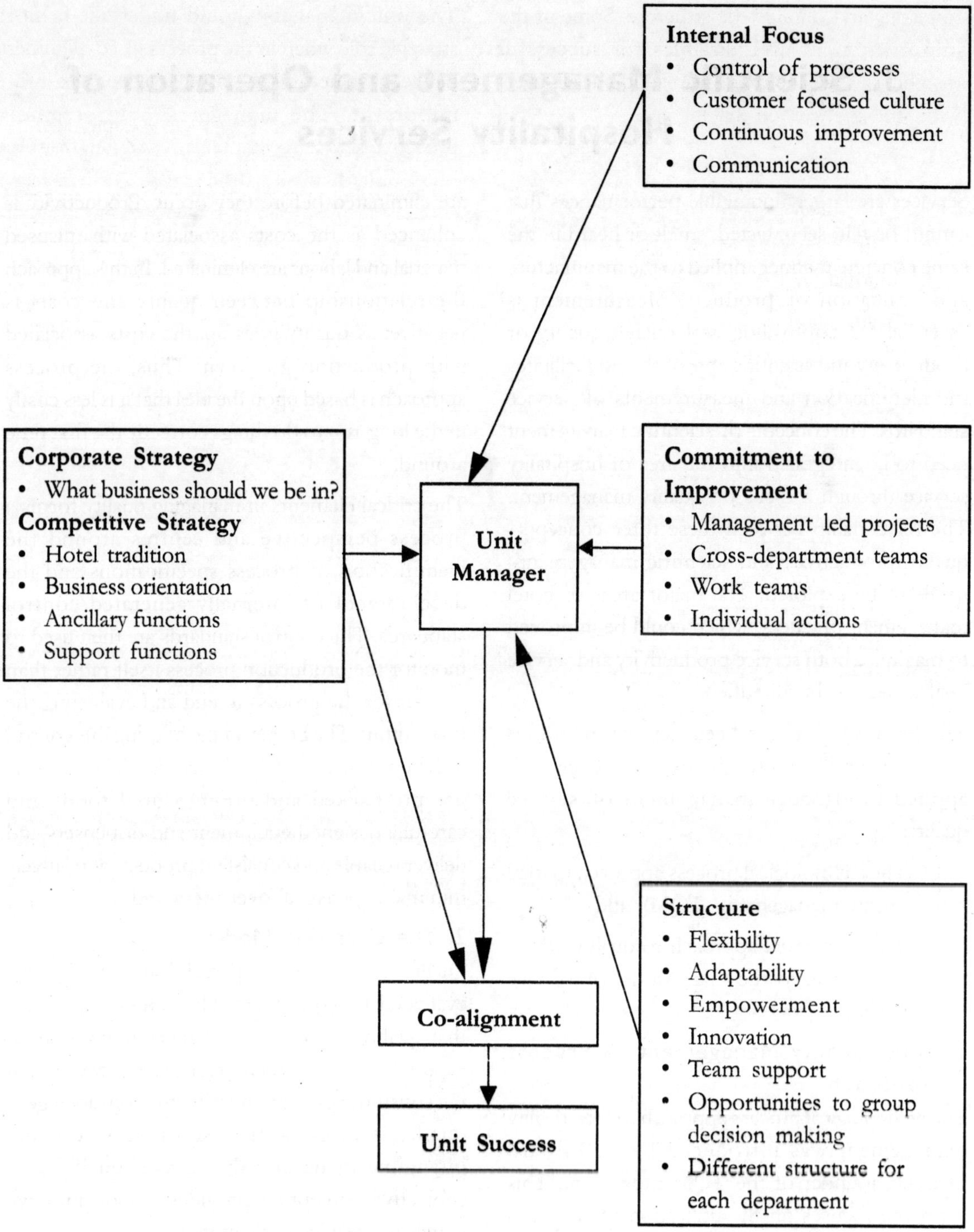

Figure 2.8: Structure and strategy co-alignment for a unit

3. Scientific Management and Operation of Hospitality Services

Services are largely intangible performances that cannot be felt, seen, tasted, smelt or heard in the same concrete manner applied to the manufacture and evaluation of products. Measurement is essential for controlling and raising quality or productivity and scientific approach best facilitates the identification and measurements of service standards. The concepts of scientific management need to be integrated into the area of hospitality service through a focus on quality management. The relationship between these three concepts–quality, productivity and scientific management–needs to be explored. The major areas of hotel management practices, which could be improved to maximize both service productivity and service quality need to be identified.

The term 'Quality' has been defined in various ways. Let us be limited to two approaches as applied to effective management of service quality:

1. The technological process approach to total quality management (TQM), and
2. The user-based approach to quality, which is intrinsic to the Gap Model of service quality.

1. Total Quality Management: A Process Approach

The technological process approach to total quality management was introduced by W. Edward Deming, founder of the TQM movement. This approach focuses on the utilization of statistical controls to facilitate a process that results in consistent and uniform output. It does not use specifications to evaluate finished products. It monitors the production process so that errors are eliminated before they occur. Productivity is enhanced as the costs associated with misused material and labour are eliminated. In this approach the relationship between quality and costs is negative; as quality goes up, the costs associated with production go down. Thus, the process approach is based upon the idea that it is less costly in the long-run to do things correctly the first time around.

The critical elements in managing quality forms a process perspective and centres around the identification of process specifications and the development of internally generated control standards. The control standards are then used to monitor the production process itself rather than waiting for the process to end and evaluating the final output. The best example of using this control technique is the fast food franchising. These outlets use pre-packed and pre-measured foods and carefully designed equipment and dispensers and deliver reliable and consistent products at relatively minimal expense all over the world.

2. The User Gap Model

Quality is a subjective perception which is best evaluated by consumers. This stresses the ideas that quality is a function of meeting consumers' expectations. When there are no gaps between what the consumer expects and what the consumer gets, quality is present. In case of service being intangible in nature, the idea of quality as a subjective perception provides a good intuitive match for service evaluation.

3. Total Quality: An Integrated Approach

Consumer research is necessary to specify exactly what the customer's expectations are. Process control is equally important to ensure that the operation can deliver on these expectations in a consistent and reliable way. Consumers value reliability 'doing it right the first time' over all other dimensions of service quality. 'Doing it right first time' maximizes the customer's satisfaction and simultaneously minimizes the organization's costs. Therefore, this is a core concept in the management of both quality and productivity. When this concept was applied to the art of production, it focused on the identification of the primary tasks involved in making and moving things to determine the best way each task could be performed. It was known as scientific management. A revisiting of the concepts introduced by scientific management may help towards a better understanding of service quality and how it can be more effectively managed.

Scientific Management of Service

Scientific management movement was started with the primary goal to improve the productivity of industrial worker. Frederick Taylor, an expert in Management Science, analysed jobs step by step, eliminating unnecessary tasks and simplifying the critical elements needed to perform job tasks more efficiently.

Most hospitality operators are familiar with the concepts that Taylor introduced. Work simplification and time-motion analysis of jobs is commonly employed in areas of food production associated with hospitality organizations. These scientific management-inspired techniques that work in production have not yet been utilized in the area of service. The traditional perspective is that because services are primarily intangible, they are really not amenable to the kind of hard core task analysis that has worked effectively in enhancing the efficiency of production jobs. Managers in all service industries appear to share the assumption that the characteristics necessary for quality in service delivery are too elusive to measure. They do not analyse the intangible, emotional aspects associated with service delivery.

A scientific approach to the problem of analysing service tasks starts by acknowledging the essential differences between production and service and proceeding from that point. Services are not experienced in the same concrete manner, which applies to products. The intangible association with service is experienced in psychological manner.

The psychological aspects associated with services may be more difficult to measure than purely physical characteristics associated with products, but their measurement is not impossible. Though, one may say that psychological measurement is less precise than the measurement of physical properties. A crucial step in the accomplishment of reliable and consistent service lies in the development of accurate standards for measurement. This step can only begin through a detailed analysis of both the physical and emotional tasks that are an integral part of excellent service.

Intangibility has been identified as the critical characteristics from which all differences between products and services emerge. To quality as a service, the intangible elements in the product/service mix must account for at least 50 per cent of the total service output. Hospitality operators assume that psychological embellishments such as friendliness, caring and individualized attention are desirable across all types of service transactions. The user based service approach to quality, clearly indicates that customer expectations are not homogeneous across the wide range of services that exist. Service operators need to identify the intangible emotional tasks which customers consider relevant and important, depending upon the service being performed. Without this information, it is impossible for service performers to focus on the elements which customers deem critical to quality service.

Attributes of Service

The main intangibles hospitality services associated with hotels, motels, restaurants and some food and beverage establishments may be differentiated as under:

1. Friendliness
2. Care
3. Customer recognition
4. Providing expertise
5. Special treatment
6. Trust
7. Decision responsibility
8. Customer-employee attachment
9. Information needs
10. Relative cost factors

Service employees should be friendly. Appropriate level of friendliness might differ depending on the context and type of service exchange taking place. Some of the attributes of friendliness are as follows:

a. Take time to enquire about personal interests, family, etc.
b. Chat about impersonal topics
c. Exchange a few social pleasantries
d. Give a smile or a nod

Desired level of friendliness could be different for each of the food/service operations and between two types of hotels.

Another intangible attribute of service is caring. This attribute corresponds closely to the idea of empathy. Standards for demonstrating care to customs vary from one hotel to another. When we talk about caring of customer, the employee should:

a. Focus on the physical requirements of their jobs
b. Acknowledge in a friendly manner the customer's feelings
c. Make an extra effort to acknowledge customer's feelings
d. Anticipate customer's feelings and demonstrate concern/support

Being recognized provides customers with ego gratification. This intangible attribute would not be equally important for all hospitality services. The attributes of customer recognition which the customer prefers from hotel employees are:

a. Let me service myself without being acknowledged
b. Acknowledge me as a customer, not as an individual
c. Remember my face
d. Remember my name and face
e. Remember who I am and details about my special needs

Providing expertise is another characteristic of intangible service. Expertise is most often achieved through costly investment in training and selection strategies. The expected level of expertise varies significantly across different organizational types. The employees in this service should have enough expertise to:

a. Know a little bit more than I do
b. Answer questions about product availability, prices, etc.
c. Make general recommendations about a few alternatives
d. Assume legal responsibility for advice and service

Treating customers to specialized service is well recognized. From an operational perspective, the willingness to individualize service may allow operators to maintain a competitive advantage in their respective markets. However, the more individualized the service, the less amenable the operation will be to cost-efficient standardization. Any attempt to specialize services beyond the level expected by customers may be de-functional to an organization's profitability and long-run survival. Most of the customers set different standards for the degree of specialized service they expect when using different types of hospitality services. In this type of service, the employees should:

a. Service customer needs with standard options
b. Make a little effort to satisfy a customer's special request
c. Make a great effort to satisfy a customer's special request
d. Be aware of special needs and meet them as part of normal service

Team Work and Communication

The diversity of operation and culture offers many challenges to the organization, yet at the same time it offers a wealth of opportunity for the operators to learn from each other.

If you can brew beer, why not retail it?

If you can retail beer, why not sell food as well?

If you can sell food, why not give your customer the opportunity to stay overnight?

And so on...

Here it is important to over emphasize the approach to learning. When seeking to learn from another not so much at what your business competitors do, but why they do it. You may be interested in the outcome but more importantly you must be interested in understanding the key to success. The answer is teamwork. You need to understand why a team-based approach can help the achievement of business goals and ultimately benefit the customers, employees and shareholders.

Culture

A buzzing atmosphere is one of the key elements in success of many organizations. In order to create this atmosphere employees need to have a passion for enjoyment. While recruiting, therefore, look for extroverts. Do not interview them. You audition them. Do not try to constrain their individualism and flair, but foster it. Do not ask people to work, ask them to perform.

Let us take the example of performing arts. There exists the occasional genius who can stand alone on a stage and make tears of happiness run down the faces of thousands. Performers need to interact with each other in order to elicit from their audience such feelings of fun and enjoyment. This is certainly the case of employees of good hotels and restaurants. It is a big part of the rationale for a business built on teamwork. To an outsider, the member of different teams, their *raison d'être,* and their relationship to each other will at first appear complex. However, there really is one team, *albeit* made up of members of different sub-groups. The team is the living embodiment of the culture of the hotel.

Motivation and Recondition

Employees are expected to perform at the highest level each and every time they go on stage. What practices and procedures are required to help effect this? Prior to their work each team should have a short period team talk. The team leader should motivate the team. The nature of the team should be such that in a group situation, employees should be able to help each other. The recognition of individual achievement has the maximum benefits when the recipient is within his peer group. Most professional teams readily acknowledge their best players. Thus, recognition of the effort and enthusiasm of both the team and the individuals who make up the teams is essential.

A Sense of Belongingness

An organization should recognize a need to put in place vehicles, which enable their employees to develop a feeling of belongingness. Having recognized the need, the issue is to determine to which group the employee wants to, or should belong. The hotel units could be split across some important brands. Within each brand, there may be a number of regions and within each region, a number of areas. So, with regard to the unit managers, some resource should be put behind creating an area team versus a regional team versus a brand team versus a corporate team. There must be a feeling of affiliation with the brand, the team to which most employees feel they belong. The team building vehicle should be geared towards this. Monthly luncheons for employees hosted by the general manager, short shift meetings, etc. are a good forum for building a feeling of belongingness in the team.

Shared Goals

The sharing of the goal in itself has an ameliorating effect on the team which in turn leads to a higher level of achievement. Teamwork and team spirit should be a consistent theme of corporate communication. The hospitality organization should reinforce that message and make it more of a living reality in the minds of the hotel staff, not least by breaking down the barriers of esteem, status, and implied contribution between:

a. Front line bar staff and those who supported them whether from the kitchen or as cleaners.

b. Full-time and part-time staff

c. House management and their staff

Complementary Skills and Attributes

Research and development and information systems/information technology can easily and quickly identify the correlation between effectiveness and a complementary set of skills and attributes within the project group. Majority of the organizations and employees are still in the category of:

'I will have to go myself'.

Most are in the category of:

'I could do this better, if I had some help. I will ask a couple of colleagues for this support'. There are very few organization employees who have developed the stage of recognising–'This is what I am good at. This is what I am weak at. These are the type of people I will need to work with in order to complete the task.'

Hotels have a lot to learn from project-group-based business, specially their more structured approach to the composition of teams.

Organizational Health Checks

A sound business strategy is based upon real benefit to the customer, the employees and the shareholders. What works for one business may not be appropriate for another. There is a need to measure three things in a business–cash flow, the views of the customers and the view of the employees. There is a need to obtain a three-dimensional perspective and clarity in employees' viewpoints help to achieve them. Employees' views are expressed most vividly in their team environment. Develop means to listen to their views on policies. Hotel team meetings in every outlet every month should be attended twice a year by the area manager. See the colour and feel the texture of the organization by listening to the views of the team, which talks to customers.

Hotel Operation Theories

The principles of hotel operations are based on three schools of thoughts. The 'traditional school of thought' is based around the concept of food and beverage or accommodation management. Each of these is taught as a separate discipline. Most of the ideas have been originally developed by practitioners.

The second school of thought is the 'system view' developed in the 1970s. It is built on the theory of system management. A typical restaurant operation is described and explained as a food service system.

The third and final school of thought is the 'operations management perspective'. The concept is based on the ideas and approaches, which originated in manufacturing and production management. These ideas are now being applied to services.

Traditional Hospitality Theory

This theory was developed in the 1950s when most of the hotel and restaurant operations were similar to each other and used identical technologies. The industry practice was standardized. They practised similar methods and were managed in similar ways. In this approach, operation is seen as a series of steps or stages. In a hotel operation, these stages are identified as:

a. Reservations
b. Reception
c. Housekeeping
d. Cashiering
e. Audit

In case of a food service, these stages could be categorized as:

a. Purchasing
b. Storage
c. Production
d. Service

The introduction of new technologies such as 'cook-and-chill', added some new stages, namely holding and regeneration.

This approach has been used for understanding and teaching hospitality operations management. The typical scheme of work would divide the subject into sessions that occurred at each stage of the operation.

This concept is now outdated. Nowadays there is a tendency to see each kind of operation as unique. There is a vast difference between fast food, cook-chill and air catering and so on. Moreover, this approach focuses on what to do, which is only one level of understanding operations.

Hospitality Systems Theory

During the 1970s, a number of technologies and new methods of working emerged–fast food operations, motels, cook-freeze, microwave cookery and so on. There was a greater diversity of operational activity, which coincided, with the development of Systems Thinking and Systems Theory, originally developed in the 1960s. The theory focuses on modelling activities or operations as inputs, processes and outputs, and identifies the feedback or control mechanisms that enable the system to remain in balance. It seemed an ideal way to analyse the increasingly complex system emerging in the hospitality industry. The systems approach enabled three major trends impacting on the food service industry:

a. Production lining
b. Decoupling
c. Identification of consumer participation

The advantage of the Systems Thinking was that it provided managers and researchers with an approach to analyse what made up an operation and how it worked. The application of this theory emphasized the idea of a hierarchy of systems and subsystems, as well as the relationship between stages in the process and the resources used at each stage.

The systems theory is more analytical than the traditional approach used by hospitality operators. It explains 'how things work'. But it is not managerial. It does not explain why they work in a particular way that they do. It does not explain why specific approaches are the most appropriate for managing cum operation.

Hospitality Operations Management Theory

The third kind of thought is based on Operational Management Theory. This approach can be easily applied to the hotel and food service operations. This theory identifies principles that are common to all operational activity and ways in which specific strategies can be adopted for their effective management. The focus is on the output (key result/areas) of operations. The key result areas are asset performance, employees' performance, customer demand, productivity, service, income and quality.

There are three main components of an operation:

a. The physical assets of the business–building, equipment, financial assets
b. The human assets or employees
c. The customers

Each of these has to be managed effectively. The combination of each of these with one of the others leads to three more key areas. Customer interaction with employees leads to key result areas of service. Decisions about employing physical plant and equipment or employees to perform operational functions constitute an issue of productivity. Customers' entering the physical assets require some kind of transfer of fund, from the customer and hence income. Finally, the combination of assets, employees and customer identifies the seventh and last key area, namely quality.

The application of this theory requires similarity in operation. It is a soft systems approach. For using this technique for teaching hospitality operations, students should be well equipped with transferable operations management knowledge and skills rather than sector specific ones. It draws attention to what they will achieve as managers rather than things over which they will have control.

Integrated Hospitality Operations Theory

This theory is developed on three schools of thought discussed as above. It begins with a view that:

1. All food and accommodation operations were similar and should be managed in similar ways
2. New technologies and processes came along and highlighted that they were increasingly not similar and the differences are growing all the time
3. New ways of looking at operations were devised, centred on systems

This system failed to address issues of performance, which needed a change and the new model was developed focusing on management action.

The three approaches are fundamentally the same, the only difference being they use different ways of expressing the same argument. Each approach explains a complex phenomenon, which make each distinctive and important. Each approach is especially helpful for explaining three different levels of thinking about hospitality operations.

It is possible to identify in the organized complexity of all systems, a series of different levels or hierarchies. Each system has within it a series of subsystems that are complete in themselves. Business organizations consist of several levels–

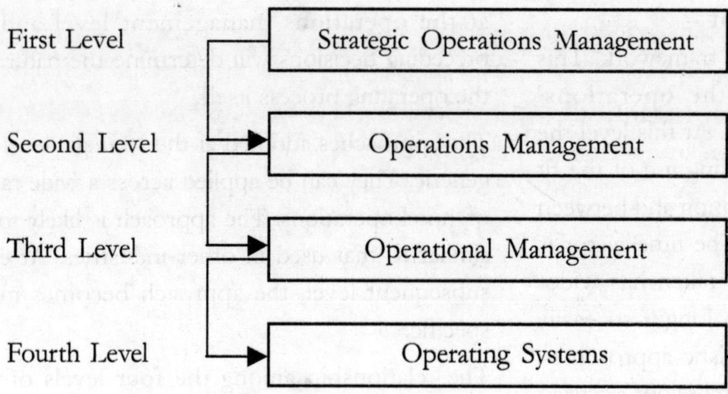

Figure 3.1: A Model framework for hotel organization

individual, group, department, civil, division, and so on. Each level in the hierarchy has its own distinct emergent properties, characteristics that are only appropriate at that level of analysis. The characteristics of one level may have little relevance or meaning at a different level. One application of this analysis to the management task has identified three levels:

1. The operating level or bottom level: It is concerned with accomplishing objectivity effectively and efficiently.
2. The coordinating level or middle level: It attempts to integrate internal activities.
3. The strategic level or top level: It is concerned with relating the organization to its environment and designing comprehensive system and plans.

This pair of ideas, hierarchy and emergence, is the basis of the proposed framework or fourth school of thought in hotel management.

For purpose of understanding hospitality operations, we have four levels of framework as given in the Figure 3.1.

1. Operating System

The diagram given in Figure 3.1 represents an operating system on level four, which includes all specific features of that system. It includes various sections, such as, a call order kitchen, hotel front desk, cafeteria counter, housekeeping section. The emphasis here is on technology and its successful application by users, whether they are back of house employees, frontline workers or the customers themselves. The focus is on process and the continuous management of processes. This in effect is the traditional way of looking at operations, as distinct stages, each operating according to its own rules.

2. Operational Management

This level is responsible for the management of operating systems. It is concerned primarily with ensuring the delivery of predetermined products and services and the control of the operation to meet operating standards. The impact of the external environment at this level is relatively small and the time horizons short. The primary concern is for optimization of decisions that are largely programmable and can be solved by simple computation. For example, the practice of menu engineering looks to optimize the contribution of each menu item through mathematical analysis. The practice of scheduling labour to match predicted demand patterns can also be seen in this light. At this level the emphasis is on managing operating systems effectively and ensuring that researches are deployed effectively. This in effect is the system approval to operations.

3. Operations Management

This is the second level of the framework. This approach is derived from the operations' management school of thought. At this level the manager is concerned with making use of the fit between different parts of operation and between the different key result areas. The time factor is longer and the decision to be taken has wider implications. Decisions are no longer so easily programmed but require a holistic approach to ensure that no unintended repercussions occur in other parts of the system. At this point the focus is on output.

4. Strategic Operations Management

This is the top or first level of hotel operations. The concerns at this level are strategic, taking account of the external environment to make decisions about the long-term future of the operation. This level of analysis emphasizes the distinction between the design stage and the operations stage. These stages are now seen to be located at different levels. The upper level provides the innovation, the design and the direction for the lower level to work within. The middle level provides the constraints within which the lowest level operates through, for example, budgets on operating standards. Therefore, the focus here is on the management of feedback over the long term.

This leads to a second lot of ideas–communication and control. Emphasis is laid on the flow of information provided by lower levels in the hierarchy to the level above. Here the managers make decisions on how to control the operation and to maintain it at a steady state.

As one descends from the hierarchy, the range of possible actions reduces. At the strategic level, the range of possible actions is very wide. Once decisions have been taken at this level, they will constrain the range of possible actions available at the operations management level and all preceding decisions will determine the nature of the operating process itself.

The approaches adopted at the strategic level are generic. They can be applied across a wide range of hotel operations. The approach is likely to be similar to that used in other industries. At each subsequent level, the approach becomes more specific.

The relationship among the four levels of the framework may be summarized as given in Table 3.1.

Table 3.1 identifies each level found in a large hotel organization and the job positions associated with each level. In some hotel organizations, operators may be located at the head office, with the responsibility of an operational system with unit managers and operating management systems vested with departmental heads. In small independent hotel operations, all three systems responsibility rests with one owner. Therefore, the important distinction is what actions and approach managers at each level are using, not what titles those managers work under.

As is clear from the Table 3.1, managers at each of the four levels focus on different aspects of management. This does not mean that unit managers at the operations level should only be concerned with leading; similarly, supervisors are not solely there to motivate. However, emphasis is placed on these roles at these levels.

Now we can also examine the systems focus. The strategic system comprises a framework within which all the four levels operate. At all four levels, there are four sub-systems. Each sub-system is made of input, process, output, and feedback. The system's focus emphasizes the orientation of the management at each level based on this system's thinking. The supervisors at respective departments focus on ensuring that the processes

Table 3.1: Organizational and Managerial Relationship of Framework in Hotel Operations

		Organizational	Management		Time Horizon
		Level	Level	Focus	
Level I	Strategic Operations Management	Organization	CEO/Director	Planning	Medium/ Long term (e.g. 1-5 years)
Level II	Operations Management	Unit e.g. Hotel	Unit Manager	Leading	Short-medium term (e.g. 1 month to 1 year)
Level III	Operational Management	Departments e.g. Housekeeping	Departmental heads e.g. Housekeeper	Organising Controlling	Short term (e.g. one day to one month)
Level IV	Operating System	Section e.g. Reception	Supervisors e.g. Floor Housekeeper	Motivating	Day-to-Day

under their control run smoothly. The departmental heads focus on ensuring that inputs are organized effectively e.g. material ordering, labour scheduling, etc.

Figure 3.2 shows what is the systems' focus at each of the four operations levels.

The organized complexity of hotel operations provides an exciting field of study. It has plenty of practical examples and a wealth of theoretical concepts and approaches. The application of this framework offers a way of making sense of the complexity of the area.

Operational Strategy

The term 'business strategy' may be described as the process by which an organization predicts and responds to its environment. Predict aspects of strategy are concerned with political, economic, social and technological developments. Responsive aspects of strategy address the question of how the organization should act in order to make the best of identified changes in its environment. Responses may take two forms: outward directed activities and inward directed activities. The first one is aimed at optimising the organization's relationship with its market, which is supported by the second one, which seeks to ensure that the organization is in a position to meet the needs of its customers. For example, a marketing programme which aims to establish an image of excellent hospitality service must be supported by an operational programme designed to supply and maintain high quality service.

Operational strategy is a sub-division of business strategy, aimed at providing service outcomes appropriate to market needs and falls under organizational strategies. Operational strategy responds to risks, which can be identified among political, economic, social and technological changes within the business environment. A risk may be defined as the finite probability of a significant harmful occurrence. Business risks are

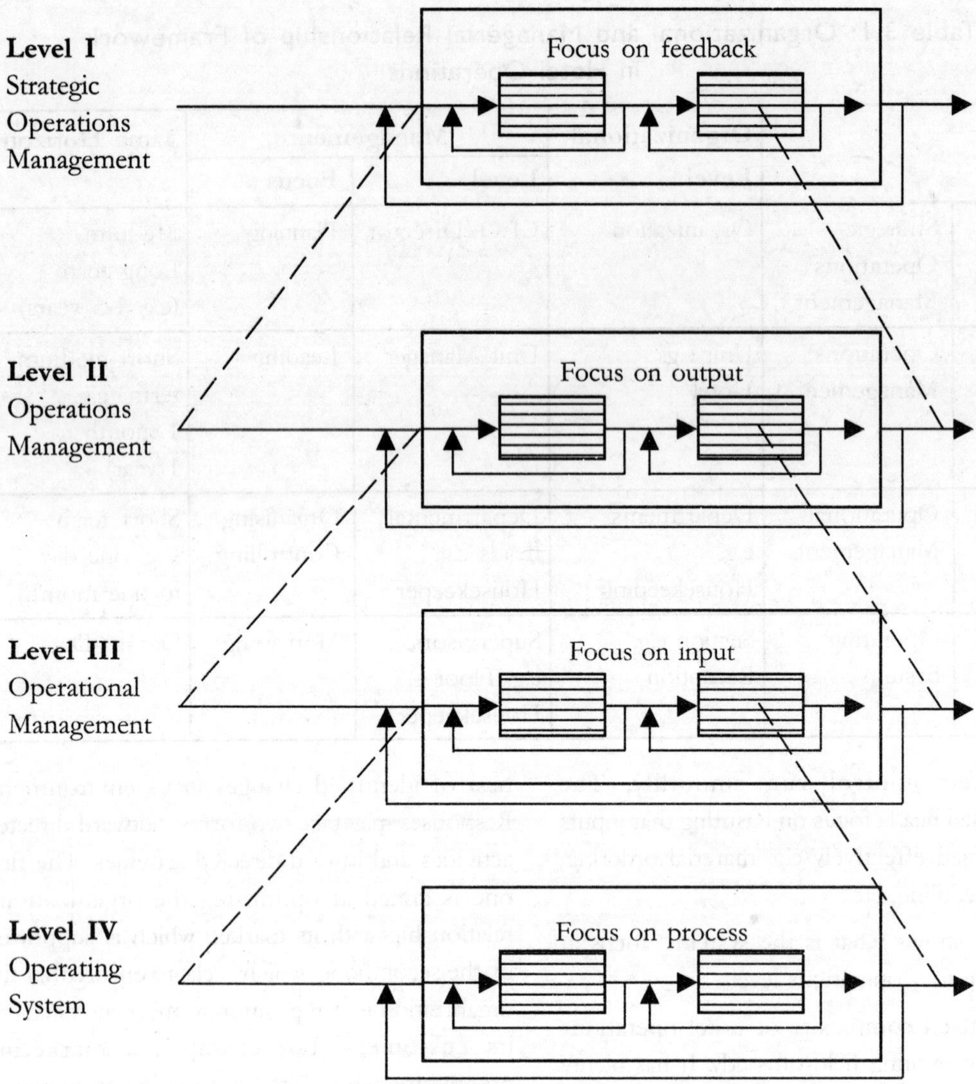

Figure 3.2: Systems' focus at operations levels

potential adverse events which may arise from environmental development. Risk may be interpreted as a matter of losing customers, being overtaken by a competitor or of incurring financial loss through an unwise investment. Operational strategies optimize the organization's response to risk by efficient use of people, materials and capital equipment to deliver service. In addition, operation carries extra risks, e.g. litigation or prosecution in respect of lapses of safety, hygiene or other areas of responsibility.

Hospitality Operations

Hospitality operations represent a spectrum of services, which can broadly be described as restaurants and hotels. In other terms, these are considered to consist of the production and service of food, the reception of guests and the cleaning and servicing of rooms.

Fast food and take-away operations deal with 'goods' while restaurants, which specialize in serving ready-prepared meals, appear near the service end. Hospitality units may be classified using a quantum of 'goods-oriented' and 'service-oriented' operations. This includes a wide variety of possible services, but does not distinguish between hospitality services and other services. An alternative approach is to classify services on the basis of customer perceptions, as transactional or experimental services. Hospitality services may be further classified into those, which fall more towards the 'experimental' end of their brand, and those, which offer a more transactional service. This provides a means of categorising and understanding both the nature of hospitality service and its potential for operational development.

Operational Strategies in Hotel Industry

There is a tendency for hospitality operations to become less formal and less skilled. This is particularly true of food production and food service. The trend has been due to an ongoing shortage of suitably skilled personnel and the desire for increased productivity for flexible output, as well as the availability of even more sophisticated pre-prepared food products. Hotels are developing a unique style of restaurant service, which depends extensively upon sous-vide and other food technologies. This enables the hotel to operate with minimal kitchen brigades and standardized yet flexible menus. Thus, economic, social and technological factors have an impact upon operational strategy. In addition, it demonstrates how operational strategies may be used to minimize legal liability. Legal developments in death, safety and hygiene have focussed increasingly upon the manager's/proprietor's responsibility. The only permissible defence for hotel operations is that of 'due diligence' *i.e.*, the result lies with the said party who has supplied a confiscatory product. The use of almost exclusively prepared products, hotels could shift a substantial burden of legal liability on to the food manufacturers, who must take the ultimate responsibility for safety and quality.

Restaurants show great variation in operational strategy and style. They need to tempt the sophisticated customer by offering a wide variety of different styles of food, most of them ethnic in origin. The operational styles in these restaurants reflect the potential diversity of the hospitality industry. Most of the traditional and Indian style restaurants produce and serve food and use the traditional method values and sty'es for production and service. The service elements in these restaurants are not well standardized. Most of them have buffet service and self-service style.

Fast food and take-away restaurants have reduced and formalized the service elements to a point where it is indistinguishable from retail service. Services in such establishments are unrecognizable in terms of traditional service or waiting skills.

Some restaurants specialize in service and have minimized or eliminated their food production activities. Restaurants have been making extensive use of pre-prepared products–salads, coulis and vacuum-packed, portioned meals, finished sous-vide foods. Advancement in food technology has made possible the decouping of food production service in both space and time. The production aspect can be minimized by having guests cook their own food and there are number of ways in which this can be done. For example, fondue bourgignon consists of pieces of raw steak which diners cook to their own taste in hot oil. Restaurants supply their customers with food to cook on hot rocks or on barbecues. It is also possible to supply only the fire/gas, so that, customers bring their own food and cook within the premises.

Such type of food and beverage establishments could be established at pleasure parks. These establishments/restaurants could reasonably claim to engage in neither food production nor service. However, they fall under the hospitality industry demonstrating the variety of products/service concepts.

Similarly, a traditional hotel is defined as one, which provides guests with accommodation, food and drink. This is an orthodox model of a hotel. New concepts have entered into the hotel business. Therefore, the orthodox concept needs to be modified. Traditionally, a hotel caters for all meals but now you find units offering only breakfast with no provision for restaurants. There are other hotels, which have no restaurants of any kind, with food and beverage service being provided by an independent subsidiary on the same site. Earlier one could not think of a hotel with no accommodation facilities, however, now there are hotels which contract out the servicing of their accommodation, security, and laundry. With such development, operators have to adapt in order to cope with environmental factors. Some examples of environmental factors are:

1. New or changing customer needs e.g. take-aways and fast food establishments, budget hotels, etc.
2. Shortage or unavailability of skilled labours e.g. satellite service units, supplied by central chilled food production units.
3. Effective use of highly skilled personnel e.g. central production units for sous-vide or other high quality long life products, overseen by a top chef.
4. Increasing availability and improved quality of food technology products e.g. all units discussed above and number of products used in fast food outlets or other chain restaurants such as frozen burgers, fish portions, desserts, etc.
5. Need for greater productivity. This is met by centralising production and also by reducing or streamlining service (as take aways or fast food establishments) and by concentrating upon core business.
6. Legal developments: An increasing tendency to place responsibility upon the proprietor with 'due diligence', the only permissible defence.
7. Concentration upon core business: This is the result of innovation discussed above e.g. by decoupling food production services from food and beverage provision.

All the above factors may be equated with an underlying pattern of business risk. Hospitality operations may respond to risk in the following ways:

1. Employing contract services
2. Introducing decentralization and empowerment.

1. Employing Contract Services

Hospitality operations could be rationalized by employing contract services. The various subsidiaries and contractors represent opportunities for hospitality workers, managers and new recruits. Contractors generally provide the hospitality industry with services beyond the scope of normal operations, but these are often closely related to some aspect of the core hospitality business. For example, building maintenance services are clearly related to normal room division activities. Pest control, a part of food and beverage management could also be a contract service. A facilities management company offering contract room servicing could take over the functions of housekeeper and/or room division manager. In addition, there are number of services, which fulfil the needs of guests, but may not be directly related to the operations themselves. Best examples are security services, health and fitness club operators and golf professionals. In hotels aiming specifically at the needs of golfers, the hospitality service may be more attuned to the image of the hospitality product than the 'core' food and beverage or accommodation operations. Even 'core' activities may be put out to contract. Many establishments use laundry contractors and some even contract out the servicing of rooms.

A hospitality operator should choose whether to employ a contractor for a particular area of work or to use in-house (direct) labour. Following criteria could be used for selecting in-house or direct labour:

1. Core activities
2. Needs no specialist or technical skills or knowledge
3. Sufficient manpower/human resources exist within the organization
4. Equipment is already available in house
5. Incurs no risk or legal liability apart from those already likely to be incurred

Following criteria could be adopted for selecting contract services:

1. Peripheral
2. Needs specialist or technical skills or knowledge
3. Insufficient manpower/human resources within the operation
4. Requires specialist capital equipment
5. Incurs specific risks/liabilities (or allows existing risks to be passed on to the contractor)

The decision to employ a contractor could be based upon one of the following three types of criteria:

1. Weighed estimate of costs and benefits e.g. in building maintenance programmes. The cost of purchasing capital equipment or of hiring specialist labour need to be weighed against the importance of a particular job to the operational outcome and the frequency with which it needs to be done.
2. Assessment of operational or general business risk e.g. it may be necessary to employ pest control or security services in order to avoid significant legal repercussions of not doing so.
3. Principal managers may arbitrarily decide to control solely on their core business.

Cost benefit analysis is closely related to legal liability through the concept of risk. It is also possible to assess the value of concentrating upon core business, in terms of diminished likelihood of negligence occurring. The decision between in-house and contract work is a matter of number of factors such as human and capital resources and management competence. Individuals differ in their capabilities, which are related to personal value systems. Therefore, management preference is an appropriate basis for choosing to employ a contractor.

2. Introducing Decentralization and Empowerment

In the hospitality industry, empowerment means permitting frontline staff to take direct action on a customer's behalf. Such a decision allows the service product to be aligned as closely and flexibly as possible to the customer and hence to the market. Individuals are encouraged to focus their talents upon specific customers or customer segments, to do what they do best and to concentrate upon playing their part in the organization's core business.

Empowerment in an organization is accomplished by splitting a large organization into financially independent subsidiaries. It may be accomplished by splitting a company up functionally, *i.e.*, into different functions such as manufacturing and distribution. The split may be market focus *i.e.*, the subsidiaries may take responsibilities for the needs of different customer groups. The different hotel brands represent subsidiary operations aimed at different customer segments. Operating same site facilities–one specializes in accommodation and the other on food and beverage is another example of empowerment.

Decentralization and organizational empowerment are driven by factors such as cost benefit and risk consideration, together with a desire to identify and concentrate upon the core hospitality business. Concentrating upon either accommodation or food and beverage provision brings clear advantages in terms of capital outlay, legal liability and human resource requirements.

Decoupling strategies can be used to split an organization into functional subsidiaries, specialising for example, in food production/food services or accommodation. Chains of fast food or take away establishments are parallel subsidiaries. Many of them add the further dimension of franchising to the decentralization equation increasing independence and hence empowerment.

Operational Performance

The central focus of an organization is how best to manage the business so as to ensure that profits are made and the enterprise is successful over the time. Profitability can be improved in one or more of three ways: by cost reduction, by increasing selling prices and by improving market share. Reducing costs, however, may lead to a decline in standards, thereby weakening market share and putting pressure on the selling price. In a climate of competition, firms can gain greater market share by differentiating their products or services from those of their competitors. In the past, the sale service of competitive advantage of many hospitality units was their favourable location, but now the changing travelling and leisure patterns have demand that operators use customer focussed differentiation strategies in order to survive and grow. Such strategies demand a fresh approach to the way in which firms manage their human resources to improve organization performance. Performance measurement is necessary but is not straightforward in hospitality industries because of the complex nature of the hospitality product. Once a performance strategy is articulated, it is useful for firms to benchmark actual performance against best practice in order to monitor the effectiveness of their strategies.

A strategic model could be used by hospitality and tourism firms to analyse the key factors that affect performance. Let us deal with the basic components affecting performance:

1. Organizational objectives and strategies
2. Strategic human resource approaches
3. Teamwork
4. Performance

Organizational Objectives

Objectives represent the organizational purpose of a firm as perceived by its management. The management uses these objectives to plan its strategies. Organization leaders have three principal functions:

1. To insist that the organization performs according to planned results
2. To develop the internal capability that makes the planned performance possible
3. To integrate job tasks and people effectively

The managers or organization leaders should have a clear vision of redirecting an organization. This task can only be accomplished by taking a strategic and analytical approach towards its internal capabilities. The firm must look to the strategies and goals of its rivals because of increasing competition in the marketplace. An ideal position could be achieved by raising barriers that make a firm's strategy difficult to imitate, by differentiating its product or services so that it is perceived industry-wide as being unique. Differentiation has always been a powerful strategy in the hospitality industry because the core product is broadly similar. Competitive advantage is more easily achieved through the service element. Effective differentiation can stimulate loyalty in customers, who become less price sensitive so that the firms margins and volumes can grow. In a competitive age in order to proceed, the firm must try to keep one step ahead with quality of goods and services.

Strategic Human Resource Approaches

The management should lead the organization successfully. This responsibility can only be achieved through awareness of competitors and customers and human resources, which constitute the means by which goods and services are produced. Management attitudes toward employees may be contrasted in a continuum in which priorities are productivity or people. This could be highlighted as given in Figure 3.3:

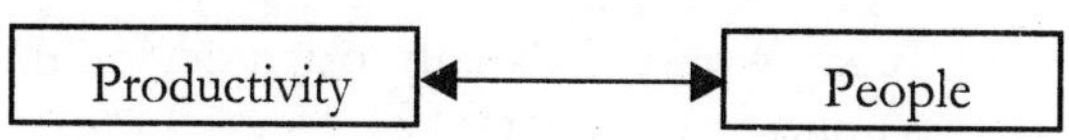

Figure 3.3: Human resources approach

According to traditional theory of Scientific Management as defined by Frederick Winslew Taylor, labour is a factor of production whose work should be exclusively planned and controlled by management. Henry Ford found that economics of scale could be gained by scientific management approach in which employee's skills are less important than production planning.

In contrast to scientific production centered approach there is another approach in which there is a bias towards people as a primary source of competitive advantage. In this approach employees are seen as a key resource through which a firm's products and services, can be differentiated from those of its rivals. This involves a more open attitude in which management must facilitate rather than control and delegate responsibility down the organization. More emphasis is placed upon improving the skills of the employees to make them more productive to the organization, and there is an atmosphere of trust rather than control.

The polarity of these contrasting approaches represents ways in which organizations make use of their employees. In practice, the choice of approach is constrained by two factors–leadership style and organizational size. The leadership style of a manager is affected by both inborn and acquired traits, which may change over time. Many service hotels and owner manager hotels may not be able to adopt this approach. For these small hotels, productivity strategies may be constrained by lack of either skills, financial resources, or the volume of sales, which produce economies of scale. However, a balanced approach is one in which greatest performance is achieved by employee-centered managers who give due recognition to production and treat it as one of their main responsibility.

Teamwork

Hotels require a new style of leadership and management, which focuses on developing workers' skills in a more creative way. More attention needs to be devoted to groups as organizational building blocks, so that, instead of work being done by individuals, it may be assigned to autonomous groups responsible for specific tasks. Higher quality and greater performance is possible from such work teams. Employees feel alienated if they are unable to find self-fulfilment or link their work with overall organizational goals. Thus employees should not be controlled, but should be given opportunities to integrate their personal goals with those of the organization. If employees do not actively seek self actualization at work, then either they may not have been given opportunities to express it, or have not yet fulfilled lower order needs.

The social value of the group is valuable to the human relation approach to management, because it affects the behaviour of the entire organization. A group consists of any number of people who:

a. Interact with one another
b. Are psychologically aware of one another
c. Perceive themselves to be a group

Groups may be set up on a formal or informal basis, either permanently or temporarily. Formal groups form part of the structure that is created by organization managers with the aim of implementing plans and achieving objectives. In a hotel such formal groups are decided according to work function or task, e.g. housekeeping and food-production departments. Alternatively, they may be set up on a permanent or temporary basis as committees, task forces, strategy teams and so on. Proximity to others during the course of work contributes to friendship and association. Informal groups arise in these hotels, as a result of social needs that are not necessarily associated with the work done. These formal groups generate their own culture and values that may conflict with that of the organization, causing resistance to the changes which managers are trying to bring about.

Work teams are more focussed groups that exhibit a unitary perspective. A team has a specific performance objective or recognizable goals to be attained and that coordination of activity among members is required for the attainment of the team goal or objective. A team must possess a definable membership, group consciousness and a sense of shared purpose and must interact in a unitary manner. Team may be portrayed as effective work groups, whose effectiveness depends upon the degree of motivation, coordination and purpose and whose synergy produces as energy and creativity which is beyond them as an individual. This unitary and focussed energy can be harnessed by organizations to address increasingly complex problems and is a primary strategy for continuous improvement. Building teams is a rewarding task for management. It must be approached with knowledge and sensitivity. Effective grouping depends upon matching personality types and balancing levels of skills, knowledge and expertise so that potential conflict can be minimized.

Below are given the typical features of different role names in a group solution, which may be useful for planning team development:

1. Chairman: self-confident, calm, controlled
2. Resource Investigator: extrovert, enthusiastic, communicative
3. Monitor-Evaluator: sober, ceremonial, prudent
4. Shaper: strong, outgoing, dynamic
5. Sanitary Worker: conservative, dutiful, predictable
6. Team Worker: socially oriented, mild, sensitive
7. Completer-finisher: painstaking, orderly, conscientious
8. Planner: individualistic, serious minded, unorthodox

Team building is a desirable strategy yet little attention has been paid to introduce it in the hospitality industry. The main problem is the interdepartmental conflict common in hospitality organizations.

Interdepartmental conflict is a major characteristic of hotels because the framework in which activities take place gives rise to interdependence between departments. As work in hospitality operations is so group based, that knowledge of team processes is important to quality improvement. Rivalry between work teams within an organization can assist the internal unity because of those teams, but needs to be carefully managed.

People are indeed key assets of the business and management of people is a central strategic issue. Great emphasis should be placed upon the work group and teamwork as a means of benefiting both individuals and organization.

Measuring Performance

Performance measurement provides information through which organizations can set targets and measure progress towards achieving them. The question arises what criteria should be used to measure the performance in hotel companies. Productivity can be used to measure the relationship between the inputs and outputs of an operation. As regards to service outputs, it is not possible to quantify. Employee attitude could be the most important, critical success factor in hotel companies, but it is difficult to measure. Measure of productivity and performance in hospitality firms aim at short-term operational (financial) objectives rather than long-term strategic goals to the business. It is possible to measure outcomes i.e. growth and profitability, and the means of achieving those outcomes such as quality, flexibility, resource utilization. In measuring the outcome we utilize hard data. In measuring the means it is necessary to use soft, objective measures such as customer satisfaction. Customer satisfaction is quite difficult to measure. It may be appropriate to resort to the use of number of complaints as an indicator of customer satisfaction. In selecting appropriate aspects of performance for measurement, the organization's strategic objective must be considered.

In order to maintain a balance between financial and non-financial measures, it is necessary to select a range of measures. One technique is developed in France, known as the *tableau de bord* described by Chiapello and Lebas as similar to an instrument panel of a car or a complex machine. The principle on which the *tableau de bord* is based is that the manager needs information on a range of key areas, including information on external developments such as levels of competition, behaviour, etc.

A set of financial measures that report the results of actions already taken as well as operational measures that drive future performance are given in Figure 3.4.

The Figure 3.4 indicates the four perspectives:

1. Customer perspective: It is a key area of concern that seeks to measure customer satisfaction by formal and informal methods.

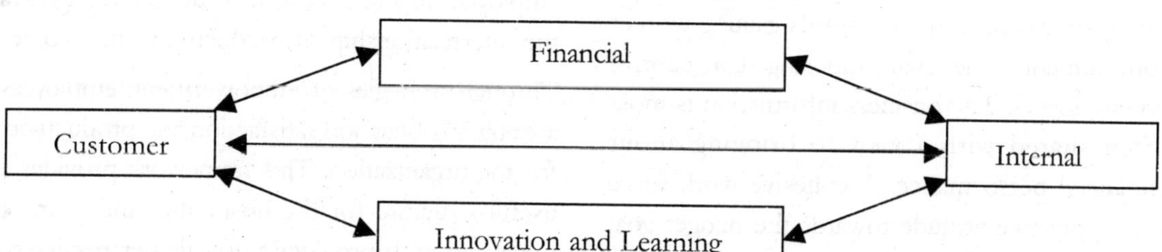

Figure 3.4: A set of financial measures–perspectives of the balanced score card

2. Financial perspective: It includes both on-line measures such as sales, profits and return on investment.

3. Innovation and learning perspective: Includes factors such as identification of new markets, staff development and improvements to facilities.

4. Internal perspective: These relate to those operations, processes and skills that have the greatest impact upon customer satisfaction, such as team work and employees development, as well as internal measures of efficiency such as gross profit percentage.

Measured performance becomes the means by which individuals and groups are controlled to bring about corporate objective. Control could be administrative, social or self-control. Administrative control attempts to pass on the organization's culture to individual members. Social controls arise spontaneously from day-to-day social contact among members. These constitute shared values and beliefs of members and represent an alternative culture. Both administrative and social cultures are enacted through the individual's behaviour and consequently their effectiveness may be constrained or enhanced by the individual's attitude, and actions, *i.e.*, by his/her self-control. These three types of controls should not be considered as independent of one another, as they clearly interact. There should be a move towards gaining worker commitment rather than imposing tight control on employees. The business information is most often shared with a view to bringing about enhanced performance. A cohesive work force with a positive attitude towards the budget goal will yield maximum motivation and efficiency. But a similar highly cohesive work group with a negative attitude to the proposed goal will result in a production slow down. Budgetary participation is not enough to motivate managers. They need sufficient communication, correct target levels, judicious performance appraisal and appropriate subordinate behaviour. The target level of the performance influences the effectiveness of the performance measurement system. In choosing a range of targets or measures, it is necessary to balance them to ensure that performance is not stressed to the detriment of others. Hotels should seek answers within their organization through internal analysis for relevant frameworks. The soft analysis approach is a good choice. It is important to pose the right questions to find the right answer to incorporate soft and hard data. Once a framework to measure performance has been developed, it is useful to compare that performance with others in a similar business. Companies could compare their products, services and work processes with those of others. It is best practice to benchmark active performance against best practices in order to monitor the effectiveness of their strategies.

The objectives of hospitality organization should aim at improving performance as measured by 'hard' or 'soft' measures by harnessing the latent creative energy of teams at every level in the organizations. This energy should be driven by top-level teams at lower levels, who are closest to the customers. Those organization who succeed will be those who harmonize the efforts of their employees in a unitary way. Figure 3.5 recognizes the interrelationship of productivity and people.

Through strategies of empowerment, employees are able to obtain job satisfaction and productivity for the organization. This framework provides a useful structure for the hospitality and tourism organization. It provides a holistic perspective of the key issues and their potential implications. Hospitality organizations can benefit from this

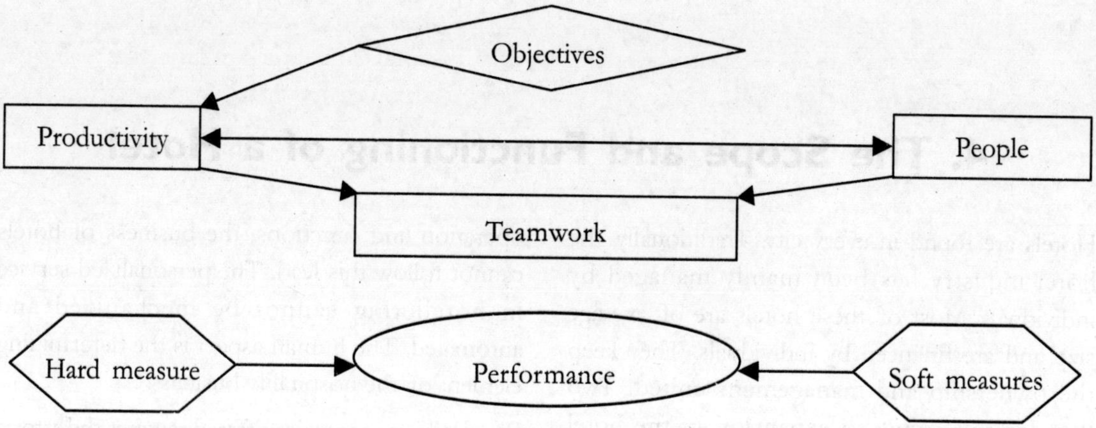

Figure 3.5: Performance through People

customer-driven and team-facilitated approach. The management vision should be a genuine and long-term one–taking full account of both intrinsic and extrinsic motivators. Due regard should be given to award systems, job security and working conditions. This can enable intrinsically motivating factors such as responsibility, a sense of achievement and personal growth to stimulate motivation and job satisfaction in employees. If the management vision is genuine and sensitive, it will elicit a genuine response from employees, which may result in mutually beneficial arrangement–improvement in the performance of both the organization and its people.

4. The Scope and Functioning of a Hotel

Hotels are found in every city. Traditionally, the hotel industry has been mainly managed by individuals. Most of these hotels are of average size and are financed by individuals. They keep the ownership and management united. Two decades ago owing to expansion in the hotel sector, joint stock companies have come into existence and a large number of the deluxe hotels are managed by them.

Hospitality is unique in many ways. There are different business operations simultaneously under one roof which guarantee jobs that are challenging and diversified. Presence of human elements promotes interest in a hotel job and provides a challenge. Each client who enters the hotel offers an opportunity to learn about human nature.

The industry offers the employees not only the responsibilities for its products but also the satisfaction of being instrumental in bringing about customer satisfaction and of personally receiving their approval. A hotel offers a clean, safe, pleasant environment as far as working conditions are concerned. Most of the hotel managers and departmental heads have worked their way up through the ranks. It is a variable trade, changes in national economy are quietly reflected in the hotel trade as well. The techniques, ideas and moods of operation of hoteliering undergo continuous alteration.

The principal factor that determines the guest's attitude towards a hotel is 'service' although other amenities such as – rooms, food and beverage are tangible ones. The nature of hoteliering places strong emphasis on people. There are industries who have introduced mechanization in their operation and functions, the business of hotels cannot follow this lead. The personalized service in hoteliering cannot be mechanized and automated. The human aspect is the determining element of the hospitality business.

Practically, every service offered requires the efforts of minimum two departments. In all the high level hotels, the employees who sell or serve a product have no control over its preparation, production or quality. This requires cooperation among the various departments of the hotel. For example, if you are an incoming guest in a hotel, you will approach the lobby manager to go to your room. It will involve the front office, the uniform department, and the housekeeping department. Cooperation of all of them is very essential for providing efficient service to the guest.

The majority of the jobs in this trade are of a semi-skilled nature. A person of average intelligence can easily learn the skills and regular routine. One must be able to adjust rapidly to a variety of unexpected and unpredictable situations. One has to have control over one's emotions even when under tremendous pressure. One has to display leadership and analytical abilities. One must have wholehearted interest and dedication to this profession.

The hotel job is a twenty four hours a day, seven days a week business. Employees have to work while the others are relaxing or enjoying a holiday. One must adjust to the busy cycle of work.

In our country, working in a hotel ranks from high to low on the social prestige scale, although a job in a hotel is considered quite prestigious nowadays. For those in this trade, sincere advice

Deluxe Room

is: once the hotel work really gets into your blood, the love for this business will come through experience and your motto must be *'Life is Service'*.

The ideal factors for hotel operations are dependent upon planning, staffing and capabilities of the individuals who establish the basic criteria. The plan for each particular hotel depends on the location, the type of service offered, the structural layout of the hotel, the background and training of the manager and the type of ownership.

The staffing requirements of a hotel depend upon a number of factors such as:

1. Size of the property
2. Type of the property
3. The degree of luxury as reflected in the extent of personal service
4. Rate of occupancy
5. The basic design of the hotel in facilitating operations and housekeeping
6. The extent to which laundry, maintenance and other functions are contracted out
7. The use of labour saving devices, machines and computers

Minimum Standards for Tourist Accommodation

There are some general guidelines for minimum standards of a tourist accommodation laid down as per international standards.

The Table 4.1 indicates the minimum standards for hotels and guest houses, including hotels and inns, drawn up by the British Tourist Authority, the English Tourist Board, The Scotish Tourist Board and the Wales Tourist Board. The BTA regards adherence to the minimum standards as a basic criterion for the inclusion of establishment in its publications.

The basic function of all the hotels is the same. An effort is made in the text to give an explanation of the functions performed by each department and the role played by each position within a department. This will give a good grasp of the variety of duties performed and of the importance of these duties to the hotel operation. The variation is mostly in case of specific methods, procedures and forms used.

Table 4.1: Minimum Standards for Accommodation in All Licensed Establishments and All Other Establishments with Four or More Letting Bedrooms

(Note: conversions are approximate)

A. Bedrooms

1. All bedrooms must conform to, or exceed, the following minimum dimensions for floor areas including private bath or shower areas:

a. Single Bedrooms	5.60 m^2	(60 sq ft)
b. Double Bedrooms	8.40 m^2	(90 sq ft)
c. Twin-Bedded Rooms	10.20 m^2	(110 sq ft)

   d. Family Rooms
   Minimum floor areas of 2.80 m^2 (30 sq ft)
   5.60 m^2 (60 sq ft) for each double bed and/or
   3.70 m^2 (40 sq ft) for each single adult bed and/or
   1.85 m^2 (20 sq ft) for cot

2. All bedrooms must have reasonable free space for movement and for easy access to doors, drawers and beds.
3. All beds, other than those for use by children, must conform to, or exceed, the following minimum dimensions:

a. Single beds	183 cm × 76 cm	(6 ft × 2 ft 6 in)
b. Double beds	183 cm × 122 cm	(6 ft × 4 ft)

4. All mattresses must be string interior, foam or of similar quality, and in sound condition. Bedding must be clean, and in sufficient quantity.
5. Beds must be made daily. Linen must be changed at least once per week and for every new resident guest.
6. All bedrooms must be equipped with a wash basin, having both hot and cold running water, either in the bedroom or in a private bathroom. A mirror must be above or adjacent to the wash basin.
7. All bedrooms (or bathrooms) must be equipped with an electric shaver point.
8. All bedrooms must be supplied, for every new resident guest, with fresh soap and a clean towel and these must be replenished or changed as required.
9. All bedrooms must be provided with:
   a. Dressing table or equivalent, and mirror
   b. Wardrobe, or clothes hanging space, equipped with at least four hangers per person
   c. Adequate drawer space
   d. Bedside table, or equivalent
   e. One chair, or equivalent, per person (minimum of two in family rooms)
   f. Wastepaper container
   g. Ashtray
   h. One drinking vessel per person (minimum of two in family rooms)
10. All bedrooms must be equipped with bedside rugs or mats, where no carpet is provided.

11. All bedrooms must have at least one window and be adequately ventilated.
12. All bedrooms must be equipped with opaque curtains or blinds on all windows.
13. All bedrooms must be adequately air-conditioned, according to season, at no extra charge.
14. All bedrooms must be adequately lit, to the following minimum levels, with a light controlled from the bed:
    a. Single bedrooms : 100 watts or equivalent
    b. Other bedrooms : 150 watts or equivalent
15. All bedrooms must be fitted with a lock that will ensure privacy for guests and security for their property. Guests must be provided with a key to their bedrooms, duplicate or master keys being kept by the management.
16. All resident guests must be allowed access to their bedrooms at all reasonable times.

B. Bathrooms

1. The establishment must have at least one bathroom, equipped with a bath or shower, for every fifteen resident guests (other than guests in bedrooms with private bathrooms).
2. Hot water must be available at all reasonable times, with no extra charge for baths or showers.
3. All private bathrooms must be equipped with a WC and either a bath or shower.
4. Running water.

C. WCs

1. The establishment must have at least one WC for every ten resident guests (other than guests in bedrooms with private bathrooms).
2. Where there is only one WC, it must not be in a bathroom.
3. All WCs, including those in private bathrooms, must be equipped with toilet paper and a disposal bin.

D. General

1. The establishment must provide a residents' lounge or lounge area, appropriate to the type of establishment.
2. All public areas must be adequately heated or cooled, according to season, at no extra charge.
3. All public areas must be adequately lit for comfort and safety.
4. A telephone must be available for residents' use at all reasonable times.
5. The establishment must be kept clean throughout, and all exterior and interior decorations, furnishings, floor coverings and fittings must be maintained in good condition.

E. Optional standard: Disabled Guests

The establishment may be or may not be able to accommodate severely disabled guests (e.g. those in wheelchairs). Those that welcome disabled guests, and wish to be so designated in publications, must conform to the following minimum requirements:

1. At least one entrance must either have no steps or be equipped with a ramp.
2. All doors (including those of WCs, private bathrooms, etc.) must have a clear opening width of at least 74 cm (29") with a head-on approach.
3. All essential accommodation, if not on the ground floor, must be served by an adequately sized lift.

4. Lift gates must be atleast 30 cm (12") wide; lifts must be at least 122 cm (48") deep and 91 cm (36") wide.
5. At least one bedroom and one public WC must be suitable for disabled guests.
6. In the bedrooms private or public bathrooms and WCs used by the disabled, the clearance around beds, and to reach wash basins, WCs, must be atleast 75 cm (29") and there must be turning space of 122 cm (48") by 122 cm (48").
7. The establishment must accept guide dogs, but may exclude them from dining or restaurant areas.

Although not required as minimum standards, it is strongly recommended that:

1. All beds, other than those for use by children conform to, or exceed, the following dimensions:
   Single beds: 190 cm or 6' 3" × 90 cm or 3'
   Double beds: 190 cm or 6' 3" × 135 cm or 4' 6"
2. There be at least one bathroom for every ten resident guests (other than those with private bathrooms).
3. There must be at least one WC for every eight resident guests (other than those with private bathrooms).

Code of conduct for establishments providing tourist accommodation and designed to ensure a fair deal for all guests.

In addition to fulfilling its statutory obligations, the management undertakes to observe the following code of conduct:

1. To ensure high standards of courtesy, cleanliness, catering and service appropriate to the type of establishment.
2. To describe fairly to all the visitors and prospective visitors the amenities, facilities and services provided by the establishment, whether by advertisement, brochure, word of mouth or any other means and to allow visitors to see accommodation, if requested, before booking.
3. To make clear to visitors exactly what is included in all prices quoted for accommodation, meals and refreshments, including service charges, taxes and other surcharges. Details of cancellation procedures and charges for additional services or facilities available should also be made clear. In the case of establishments with four bedrooms or more, to adhere to the Hotel Industry Voluntary Code of Booking Practice.
4. To adhere to, and not to exceed, prices current at time of occupation, for accommodation or other services.
5. To advise visitors at the time of booking, and subsequent to any change, if the accommodation offered is in an unconnected annexe, or similar, or by boarding out and to indicate the location of such accommodation and any difference in comfort and amenities from accommodation in the main establishment.
6. To give each visitor, on request, details of payments due, and a receipt, if required.
7. To deal promptly and courteously with all enquiries, requests, reservations, correspondence and complaints from visitors.

A knowledge of the various departments, their uses, functions and fields of responsibilities will enable a prospective employee to recognize the internal operations and communications of hotel facilities. The departmental break down requires that top management know at each phase of the operation and during each day of operation, what is happening, where it is happening and the cost of performing such duties.

In Table 4.2 are given some broad guidelines for manpower requirements for operating various services in a hotel.

Table 4.2: Manpower Requirement Guidelines for Hotels

Department	Requirement
I Front Office	
• Front Office Manager	
• Assistant Front Office Managers	
1. Information Assistant	1/Shift
2. Reception Assistant	1/Shift
3. Front Office Cashier	1/Shift
4. Front Office Supervisor	1/Shift
II Lobby/Bell-Desk	
1. Lobby Manager	1/Shift
2. Sr. Bell Captain	1
3. Bell Captain	1/Shift
4. Bell-Boys	1–50 Rooms/Shift
III Telephones	
1. Telephone Manager	1
2. Telephone Supervisor	1/Shift
3. Operators	1–50 Extensions
IV Housekeeping	
1. Executive Housekeepers	1
2. Assistant Housekeepers	1/Shift
3. Floor Supervisor	1–30 Rooms
4. Public Area Supervisor	1
5. Linen/Uniform Room Supervisor	1
6. Room Attendants	1–4 Rooms
7. Desk Control Attendants	1/Shift
8. Linen/Uniform Attendants	1–500 Employees
9. Housemen–Rooms	1–14 Rooms

Table cont. ...

Table cont. ...

Department	Requirement
10. Housemen–Public Area	1–2000 sq.ft.
V Laundry	
1. Laundry Manager	1
2. Laundry Supervisor	1/Shift
3. Washerman	1/Shift
4. Sorter/Marker/Packer	1/Shift
5. Steam Press	1/Machine
6. Shirt Press	1/Machine
7. Calender Operator	2 Feeders/Shift 2 Folders/Shift
8. Dry Cleaner	1/Shift
VI Security	
1. Security Officer	1
2. Assistant Security Officer	1
3. Car Park Attendants	1/Shift
4. Doorman	1/Shift
5. Security Guards	
a. Main Gate	1/Shift
b. Employee Gate	1/Shift
c. Floors	1/Shift
d. Public Areas	1/Shift
VII Engineering	
1. Chief Engineer	1
2. Assistant Chief Engineer	1
3. Engineering Supervisor	1/Shift
4. A/C Mechanic	1/Shift
5. Plumber	1/Shift
6. Electrician	1/Shift
7. Mason	1/Shift
8. Boiler Man	1/Shift

Table cont. ...

Table cont. ...

Department	Requirement
9. Carpenter	1/Shift
VIII Horticulture	
1. Horticulturist	1
2. Head Gardener	1
3. Gardener	1/1000 sq.yds.
IX Health Club	
1. Health Club Manager	1
2. Health Club Supervisor	1
3. Massuer	1/Shift
4. Massuese	1/Shift
X Food & Beverage Service	
1. Restaurant Manager	1/Outlet
2. Sr. Captain	1/Outlet
3. Captains	1/Station/Shift
4. Stewards	
a. Coffee Shop	1–14 Covers
b. Speciality	1–8 Covers
c. Room Service	1–50 Rooms/Shift
d. Banquets	1–50 Guests
e. Bar	1–40 Covers
5. Order Taker	1–100 Rooms
6. Bartender	1/Shift
XI Food & Beverage Production	
1. Executive Chef	1
2. Sous Chef	1/Shift/Kitchen
3. Chef-De-Partie	1/Section/Shift
4. Commis I	1/Section/Shift/Kitchen
5. Commis II	–do–
6. Commis III	–do–

The front office includes all the offices which are situated in or near the front hall or lobby of the hotel. It is the nerve centre of the hotel. This department is the first that is contacted by an arriving guest and is the information centre during his stay. It is the last point contacted when he leaves.

Requests for reservation are received by telephone, telegram, teletype, computers or across the desk. All inquiries relating to advance reservation and booking of accommodation and all the associated clerical work including correspondence is done in the advance reservation office. All particulars of booking are entered in the hotel diary. The advance-reservation chart is used for allocating rooms for specific periods. An arrival list is sent to the reception office together with the file containing a reservation card and correspondence relating to guest arrivals.

The work of the reception office is to receive, welcome and register the guests, and keep all other relevant departments in the hotel notified. All the guests arriving at the hotel must be registered. There is no legal obligation for the guest to write down, the required information, the receptionist may do so on his behalf. As soon as the guests approach the front desk, they are greeted by the receptionist. He/she inquires whether they have a reservation. Each guest is asked to give his full name and nationality. While the guest is filling out the registration card, the receptionist checks the reservation sheets, notes the arrival, and from the rack he/she picks out the room number that has been blocked. The room number and the rates are recorded in the registration card. A room slip is prepared in duplicate. The bellmen are handed over their keys and the slips. The reception office informs the front office cashier and all departments and the information is noted down in the room rack. Once the guest is roomed, his chief contact with the front office will be through the mail and information.

During his stay at the hotel, the guest is charged for several items. All these charges are sent by the individual departments concerned to the front office cashier, who posts it in the guest bill. At the time of checking out of the guest, the bill is presented and settled.

The food and beverage department is responsible for planning, coordinating and controlling all the food and drinks. This department alone can assure the success or failure of a hotel. The use of standard portion control and a general uniformity within the kitchen, from the purchasing to the kitchen, are the means by which a successful food and beverage (F&B) operation is achieved. This department controls three things–food, beverage and service. Food and beverages are tangibles and with a certain amount of skill and supervision, they can be instrumental in guest satisfaction. The service is intangible and it requires ability and versatility. Skill is highly essential in providing good service. A guest will not enjoy a meal when efficiency is lacking. Many people fail in the restaurant business, not only due to lack of knowledge about the industry, but also because they hold this misconception that the restaurant business is a simple business. There are people who are very successful in this business but only those who know that good food and good service are the prime requirements, which get the success they are looking for.

The person who initiates purchasing is called the purchase manager/purchase officer/purchase steward. He arrives in the morning and each day he follows a set routine. It is essential that all the food items he purchases is as close as possible to the time it will be consumed in order to assure freshness and top quality. The purchase assistant looks into the perishable products and ensures that they are consumed when they are fresh. He checks the banquet menu, daily menu, forecasts of the number of covers or guests to be served that day, and accordingly decides the amounts and kinds of foods to be purchased. Staple items are generally purchased two or three times a month. Meat is purchased daily. The methods of purchasing vary according to the location and availability of merchandise.

The responsibility of the person receiving the food is to ascertain quality and quantity based upon the quoted prices, orders and receiving of articles. Every item received is weighted or accounted and checked. Once the quantity, qualities and the price are checked, the bill is approved. Items like meat, fish and poultry are listed on the receiving sheet and a meat tag is attached.

After verification, the goods are entered into the respective registers. Food is kept in various types of storage: dry stores, vegetable, dairy, meat boxes and freezers. These are under the supervision of the storekeeper.

From the store, food is issued to the kitchen for preparation. At no time should any foodstuff be distributed, other than to those with the proper authority for the receipt of the merchandise. First, a requisition is written and signed by the chef or his assistant and accordingly the food is given out. The requisitions are priced by the storekeeper and sent to the food controller. At the end of each day, the storekeeper should review the requisition, categorize them and issue a statement to the management on the quantity consumed. Periodically, a physical inventory is taken and checked against the requisition for the month.

Great caution is required in the purchase, receiving, storage and inventory of beverages due to their very high cost. The basic aim is to receive the best quality at the lowest possible price. The purchase assistant (beverages) must maintain a continuing inventory, coordinated with the needs of the various bars and cocktail lounges. Like for storage of food, each beverage has its unique requirement. Bottles of beverages in store must remain vertical or horizontal or according to specified temperature. The beverage controller must have complete knowledge of all the products under his control.

The processing and production side of food is delegated to the executive chef/*chef de cuisine.* The next phase of food handling takes place in this section.

Staffing requirement and the size of the section will depend upon the type of meals to be provided and the number of guests for whom they are prepared.

The main kitchen is made of many small groups. Every section of the kitchen has a particular function in preparing food to be served. One section may prepare for the cooks, all meat, fish, poultry items etc., from the store room, the other may make salads and desserts and another may make appetizers and canapes. There may be groups making soups, sauces and gravies, roasting, frying, boiling, etc. There are also people who prepare vegetables for the cooks. Thus, there are several employees who contribute to the preparations of one dish in a hotel. The person in charge of each section of the kitchen is called *chef de parte* or section-head. He is specialized in that particular field. He is assisted by *commis chefs*. In small hotels the work of managing the different sections is combined.

The kitchen has a store. The storekeeper receives all the dry goods, and records the details on a card. Perishable goods such as meat, fish, etc. are received directly into the kitchen. On receipt of an indent or requisition from the chef, the storekeeper will issue the required stores for use that day in the kitchen. The kitchen clerk assists the chef in this work. He is also required to fill the job of a caller (*aboyeur*) during service time, *i.e.*, calling orders as they are received from the waiters, so that each section knows what has been ordered and prepares it accordingly.

The kitchen porter is responsible for cleaning of all the areas of the kitchen and its equipment.

Scullery is an area in the kitchen for the washing and storing of pots and pans.

Wash-up/Plate Room is a section where the waiters deposit dirty crockery and cutlery for washing, storing and reuse. The silver utensils are also washed here.

All beverages, bread and butter, sandwiches, toast, cereals, preserve, etc. are prepared and served from the still room/pantry.

In a large hotel, there may be a number of different areas like the restaurant, dining room, grill room, snack bars, coffee shop, room service, lounge service and banquet hall, offering a variety of meals and services. Similarly, there are several bars within the same complex like cocktail bar, public bar, hotel bar, dispense bar, etc.

The person in-charge of a restaurant is known as restaurant manager. The room is divided into stations, each one consisting of a number of 'covers' or places to set at a table. The in-charge of each station is called *chef de rang*/station waiter. He takes the customer's order and writes out the necessary checks. He is assisted by *commis* waiters/*commis de rang*. *Commis* waiter takes the checks to the kitchen and brings food and assists the *chef de rang* to serve. *Debarasseurs*/bus boys help to carry and fetch food from the kitchen.

The type of service of beverages varies from hotel to hotel. The bar manager is responsible to the F&B manager for the overall control of all bars–lounge bar, cocktail bar, public bar, dispense bar, etc. Each bar has a head barman with barmen/barmaids to assist him. The barmen/barmaids are responsible to the management for the stock held within the bar as well as for all cash taken. There is a great opportunity for pilferage in the bar. The management carries out spot checks of the stock in addition to regular stocktaking.

The beverage service within the restaurant is carried out by wine waiters (*sommeliers*). They take the orders from all the sections of the restaurant/bar and are assisted by *commis*/wine waiters (*commis de vin*). In a small restaurant the head waiter is in charge and is responsible for welcoming and seating all the guests and assists with the service of the food.

The head bartender is responsible for mixing all the drinks and maintains the beverage cost at the percentage decided upon by the management. At a briefing station before a meal, the special drinks for the day and the way it is to be served are discussed.

The restaurant cashier deals with the cash paid by the customers for the meals served. He prepares two or three copies of the bill under table numbers from the waiters/checks. The waiter presents the original bill to the customer and obtains the money in return. The money is paid to the restaurant cashier who stamps it as 'PAID'. The waiter returns the bill to the customer. In case the customer signs the bills, the procedure is almost the same except that the original bill signed by the customer is retained by the restaurant cashier. The latter practice is applied to resident guests, those having credit cards or those who have an arrangement with the hotel to sign the bills. Accounts of such bills are submitted at a later date. In large hotels, room service is a big business. Therefore, a separate section headed by the waiter floor (*chef de étage*) assisted by *commis* floor waiter (*commis de étage*) is made responsible for the service. The orders are placed over the phone. The room service order taker takes down the room number of the guest and confirms it by writing the guest's name from the room rack. The order is written in the same order as it is placed. The order taker makes three copies of the kitchen order ticket (KOT). The price of the food and drinks served in the room is generally higher than the equivalent served in the restaurants or bars.

Banqueting denotes a multitude of private functions, conferences, cocktail parties, weddings, receptions, private and official luncheons and dinner parties, and many more besides. The banqueting manager is responsible for booking functions, helping the organizers to choose menus, provide efficient service, booking the banquet and cabaret, ordering and arranging of flowers, costing of the functions for hiring rooms, food and alcohol, and ensuring that the junction is adequately staffed.

Housekeeping is the backbone of all the hotels. It is the busiest and most important department of the hotel. The head of the section is called as executive housekeeper. She is responsible for the cleanliness of most of the hotels rooms as well as neatness and orderliness of the guest rooms. She has an assistant and several supervisors to conduct her department. Duty rosters are compiled by the executive housekeeper or her assistants. Room-maids and chambermaids are informed which rooms are due to be vacated or relet so that linen can be changed and the room cleaned. All rooms are checked and bed occupancy lists, sleepers list and room station reports are prepared. In large hotels, there is a linen room in which the linen is stored, sorted, checked and repaired. It is under the control of the linen keeper who is responsible to the head housekeeper. The number of staff to be employed in this department depends on the size of the hotel and the amount of work to be done.

The uniform service comprises the doorman, bellman, elevator operators, lobby porters etc. It comprises all those members of the hotel staff who wear a levered uniform. The head of this section is called head porter. He keeps a log book in which he records all the happenings of the day. Other staff of this department are the hall porters, linen men, luggage porters, hotel valet, cloakroom attendants, lift attendants, inquiry clerk, page boy, night porters, etc. The bellman escorts the newly arrived guests to their rooms. The bell captain is in charge of the bellmen.

In every hotel there will be telephones. The larger the establishment the greater will be the need for more outgoing links and internal extensions. It is a department that the guests will never see but one with which he may have frequent contact. It handles all intra-hotel, local and long distance calls.

Hotels and their guests are vulnerable targets for thieves, prowlers and other undesirables. Therefore, the security officer and his staff must be vigilant every hour of the day. The security officer must have a law enforcement background. He must know in detail all local and state laws pertaining to hotels, and must actively cooperate with the police and authorities.

The chief engineer is responsible for effective control, repairs and maintenance. The work of the engineering department is divided into six main areas–electrical, plumbing, heating, ventilation, air-conditioning, refrigeration and building maintenance and repairs.

The personnel manager must know the local labour market and must design a programme that will attract qualified employees to the hotel. Hotels generally have a high turnover rate and this in turn magnifies the recruitment problem. Management looks to the personnel department for advice, suggestions and the latest development in the areas of wages, salaries, job evaluation study, service, etc. As regards training, the only way to develop a competent staff is to train it. The personnel department must supply the techniques of training to supervisors, departmental heads and executives.

Sales and marketing department deals with the activities associated with the identification of meets for the hotel facilities and services and the advertising, sales and promotion personnel. In a small hotel there is a manager while in a large hotel there is a marketing director who carries on these activities. In all sales rooms and public spaces, this department also promotes internal selling.

The work of finance, accounts, auditing, and control department is categorized as revenue, expenses, payrolls and statistical reports. The head of this section is called the finance controller/ accounts officer. Many of the accounts records are kept or originate outside the accounts office. The accounts of all guests are kept in the front office. The cashiers in dining rooms record the services, present cheques and collect the cash. The housekeeper lists the occupied rooms, the telephone and other minor revenue departments record their sales. The receiving clerks prepare the lists of all goods received and the time keeper records the arrival and departure of all employees. The general cashier receives cash from all cashiers and notes the deposit. He distributes payrolls, cheques and makes cash disbursements. The income auditor audits all the revenue and cash receipts of the hotel daily and checks the correctness of the guests accounts through the night auditor reports. There are clerks to look after the work of labour, accounts payable and payrolls.

Computers and Data Processing

All hotels have realized the importance of computers. Most medium and large sized hotels install computers for pure accounting functions. The two areas most in need of consideration are, firstly, the front office, including advance reservations, room status, arrivals and departures and guest billing. The second is the food and beverage control. Accurate record keeping is essential if a hotel is to make money and reduce expenses.

In a 100-room hotel, there is a choice you may install either the desk top computers such as the NCR 250 range or a full-blown 'on-line' real-time system with a VDU at the-front desk, two terminals in the food and beverage outlets. A hotel may require programme that will do:

1. Guest accounting
2. Advance reservation
3. Payroll
4. Sales ledger
5. Purchase ledger and
6. Nominal ledger

Choosing a suitable computer system is a complicated task. The following guidelines could be of help in this respect:

1. Functions you want computer to carry out with a view to future needs
2. Comparison of models and prices
3. Check the terms of conditions of sale
4. Check after sales support and training given

Before buying a computer you must take the help of an independent consultant to advise and evaluate the various systems available with reference to the hotel's needs.

Use of Computers and Information Technology

Now different software programmes are available which are invaluable to all–small, medium and large hotels. Rapid development over the last two decades has brought technology within the reach of every organisation at a price and size that every hotel that can afford and manage. The hotel industry needs to respond to the changing elements of its customers. The speed with which it can change will affect the cost of providing the service and the profitability of the venture. The hotel requires to acquire, collate, and manipulate information in order to make fast and accurate decisions within the establishment. A good hotel has to plan for the future and this requires managing information effectively. This is where computer system becomes a necessity. The computer could be used to collect information within reorganisation. It can provide any information, in any format, when and where it is needed and a systematic way for different managers e.g. chefs, executive housekeeper, food and beverage manager. Increasing use of information technology has made the changes from recording and communicating information on paper to digital recording using computers. The manpower of the hotel has to be trained in the use of computers and update each one's skills regularly for an organisation to be successful.

Front Office

Records of detailed information can be kept for all advance bookings, so that the hotel knows whom to expect, when the guest will arrive or depart and what kind of room is preferred. The computer can also assist by writing the information letters, keeping messages for guests and advising the management about regular guests, so improving the level of personalised service the hotel offers. When the guest arrives at the hotel the same information can be used to produce a range of information for other departments for instance–his preferences in hotels, his list of contacts, service required, etc.

Housekeeping

The professional housekeeper must know the names of regular guests and their individual preferences. These are the little details that make guests feel welcome and will ensure that they return on another occasion. Computer can help by keeping all this information up-to-date.

Food and Beverages

Calculation of costs

Wherever meals are provided in quantity, it is necessary to examine the costs which occur and to ensure that some control exists to monitor payments to suppliers and staff and to ensure that these costs are accounted for. At the end of the day, profit levels can be calculated. Cost could be compared against allowances, so that over spending does not occur. For example, in an industrial catering house, the additional expense of Rs. 1 per meal per person, becomes very significant, if the number of people being fed is 10,000 twice daily, five days a week. At the end of the year this represents the sum as follows:

10,000 people × 2 meals × 5 days × 52 weeks × Rs.1 = Rs. 52,00,000/-

In most of the hotels, food costs are calculated manually. The main element in calculating food cost is stocktaking. The simple formula for calculating the cost of each item is:

Opening Stock+Receipts of Purchases–Closing Stock = Consumption

Some stock items have to be calculated before the value of the closing stocks can be worked out. Many of these items are weighed and then valued at a cost per pound or kilogram. All these items are then counted and multiplied by their price. This needs to be done every week or every month for six hundred or a thousands of stock items. It means a lot of paper work. It is very time consuming finding the right price of each item and multiplying it by the quantity which was left. It is likely, therefore, that the opening stock, receipts and closing stock be worked out by measurement of weight, volume or numbers and only express the consumption in monetary value. It becomes difficult to get a precise result and calculation becomes far more complicated if you like to know the values of the receipt and closing stock. Other figures might also be added to these to make allowance for transfer from one kitchen to another, or to 'write off' food items which have been spoilt or wasted through over-productions.

Through computerisation all the prices are stored in the programme and every thing can be measured in terms of money and if necessary converted into weights and measures. Conversely, if given the weights and measures, the computer would express them in monetary value. It does not relieve you from counting every item at the end of the period, but it does reduce the amount of the work. The computer prepares the paper with all the information printed on them and then it only requires you to enter the amounts of the closing stock in figures, decimals or fractions.

Receipts, of course, are gathered on a daily basis as goods are received. The invoices are entered into the system against each item, so that at the end of each period, not only can the value of receipts be calculated but also you are in a position to make exact payments to each suppliers. The price of each ingredient is collected from each invoice so that the system can value all the items at the correct price.

As new technology has been developed now for collecting information for closing stock, small hand-held terminal with special light-sensitive pens can read the stock number of items and allow the stock taker to enter the quantities on a small keyboard just like a calculator. This information can be put straight into the system for processing, thus reducing even further the amount of work to be done by the operator. Stocks which were manually calculated required 10 to 15 days for completion, whereas with the help of the computer the entry process can be completed in an hour or two.

The procedure to arrive at the value of stocks consumed could be calculated by another method. Divide the quantities of the different ingredient by the number of portions each recipe provides, and then multiplying that quantity by the number of portions prepared or sold. This will give a 'notional' or theoretical stock consumption figure. To make projections, the computer must have not only the ingredients which have been used but also it must store details of the number of portions provided by each recipe.

Production Control: Recipe Report Sheets

The breaking down of menus and recipes into ingredients is known as menu expressions or recipe exposition. This need to be gauged more accurately to ensure a reasonable delivery system. These are usually performed manually. Now due to the use of computers, all ingredients are already in the system for stocking purposes. This record could not be used as a source of data from which recipe could be made. Of course, ingredients are rarely used in the same measures as they are purchased and it is therefore necessary to have a complete set of conversion tables so that an ingredient which is bought by the pound or kilos can be used in recipes by the gram.

The operator could built up a group of ingredients into recipes and express each recipe in cost per portion. See the cost of each recipe, should the price of any ingredient change, so too would the cost of all recipes using that ingredient. This application is generally referred to as 'production control' and presents major advantages, such as:

1. You can obtain from the computer comparisons of your actual consumption with your notional consumption and give the variance, or difference, in terms of money and quantity. This will give a clear picture of not only what was used but also of whether the recipes are being followed correctly. Explanation could be sought for large variables but the computer can indicate for the first time which ingredients should be investigated.

2. By planning a service of menus for some days ahead, the amount of ingredients required can also be calculated easily.
3. If a list of suppliers were maintained alongside the recipes and ingredients files, then the computer could easily produce a purchase order list exactly of the specification received by you.
4. In airline catering (in-flight), it may be necessary to write an invoice for meals supplied to passengers aboard particular flights. Some times it may be necessary to have more than one selling price for each item, so that a complex marketing policy could be followed.
5. In case of systems required for managing liquor stock in bars, it is quite common for the same beer to be more expensive in one than another although the purchase price costs the same.
6. Comparision of budget forecasts for the previous year and variations in past actual may be done with the help of computerisation.

Electronic Point of Sale (EPOS)

All sales are recorded and cash and credit card payments are recorded in a cash register. This helps in maintaining records and also provides some control in case mistakes are made. The new Electronic Point of Sale (EPOS) works in much the same way as the computer system. Both are electronics and could be linked together, interfaced to exchange information. There must be a number of registers in different areas such as restaurant, the bar or the room service, all reporting back to the main computer in order to provide important sale information or to change the cost of a meal to the bill of hotel guest. This equipment can also pass information rapidly to other departments. The orders taken in the restaurant can be transmitted electronically to the kitchen which receives instructions on a small printer. EPOS systems can record not only which soup was sold and by whom, but it can also provide the time at which it was sold, in order to enable better planning for the next day. To study the relationship between profit and popularity, it is important to know why certain dishes are popular or why the organisation makes a loss on same. How to make the recipes popular and profitable requires a great deal of information not only for one kitchen but also from customers.

Audit and Accounts

The computer is a valuable tool in finance, accounting and audit department. A great deal of accurate financial information is required for the smooth running of organisation. Accounting Department needs to know who owes money to the hotel and to whom it owes money. Detail of debtors and creditors play an important part in hotel management. The hotel relies on computers to ensure that there is sufficient money in the bank to pay suppliers or to provide wage packets at the end of each month. Computerized pay roll systems can be linked to computers at the bank and money wages or salaries can be translated electronically into employees' bank accounts.

Table 4.3 gives a classification of information required in a hotel.

Table 4.3: Classification of Information Required in a Hotel

Management Level	Types of Information	Uses
Top Management	Overall report of the Hotel: Planning oriented	Strategic planning for the future
Middle Management	Comprehensive report control and Planning oriented	Tactical planning for the present
Line Management and Supervisions	Detailed reports control oriented	Operational planning for the present Recordkeeping for the past

The systems used in the different areas of the hotel can be brought together to exchange information and to avoid having to re-enter the same information twice. On system could be interfaced with another and thereby, speeding up the task of information collection. Usually, a hotel may require varied information depending upon its use, and the management level, it has in operation.

5. The Guest in a Hotel

Hotel is an establishment which receives travellers and tourists who are willing to pay the price for the sort of accommodation provided. Everyone using the facilities of a hotel is not necessarily a guest. They can be both invitees and licencees. Invitees include:

1. Registered guests
2. Visiting guests and patrons of restaurants on the premises
3. Visiting guests and patrons of bars on the premises
4. Policemen and firemen
5. Others entitled by law to enter the hotel.

Licencees are those who may be allowed to enter the hotel but are not specifically invited or especially welcomed, such as:

1. News body
2. Solicitor for charity
3. Someone coming in off the street to a wash room.

Implicit permission to enter a portion of the hotel/ property is not without limits. Any person who may venture beyond the allowed area becomes a trespasser.

There are three basic conditions which must be fulfilled to establish a hotel-guest relationships:

1. Element of a 'transient': The person coming from or returning to his home, is a transient traveller.
2. Existence of a contract: A contract exists between the hotel and the person based on their consent, expressed or implied.
3. Agreement to pay: An agreement to pay is in effect.

A person does not become a guest of a hotel until he registers into the hotel. In actual fact the hotel-guest relationship can be and is established when each of the parties shows the intent to establish this relationship. One form of their intent could be by making a reservation. It is not necessary that a specific room be assigned to the person in order for the hotel-guest relationship to be established. Suppose, a person's luggage is stolen while he is waiting to register, the hotel would have the same liability as if the person had already registered and been assigned a room.

A person using a hotel for an illegal purpose, as well as someone sharing a guest's room without the knowledge or consent of the hotel, forgoes the right he might have been entitled.

Once the guest checks out and leaves the hotel, the hotel-guest relationship is automatically terminated. However, in many cases, the relationship may continue for a 'reasonable time' after the guest leaves and allows them to arrange for the removal of luggage, left at the hotel.

A guest may extend his stay beyond the period for which he made the reservation. This may result in the inability to accommodate incoming guests with reservations. Such situations may arise when hotels experience a spell of unpleasant weather like when there is a transporters' strike, the guest is forced to change his plans for departure under such circumstances. Most of the hotels seem to prefer to allow the guest to extend his stay beyond the reserved period. From a strictly legal point of view, the hotel is under no such obligation. At the end of the reserved period, there is an automatic expiry of hotel-guest relationship. If the guest attempts to remain without the consent of the hotel, he is termed a trespasser, and is subject to forcible removal if there is no more space available for incoming guests.

A hotel is obliged to receive travellers and their luggage, but not, if he does not wish, their vehicles or live animals, regardless of the hour at which they arrive. He is not required to serve hot food at a time when such foods are not normally served or to move out of his own bed or to improvise a bedroom when none is available. But, cases have occurred in which hotels have been successfully sued for damages when they refused to meet their obligations without sufficient cause.

A hotel may legally refuse accommodation to a person due to any of the following reasons:

1. When no accommodation is available in the hotel
2. When the hotel has reason to believe that the prospective guest might create disturbance, such as due to intoxication or irrational actions
3. If the prospective guest is a known criminal or his language is objectionable
4. If the prospective guest refuses to make advance payment or asks for lower rates, the hotel may turn away the guest

A hotel cannot refuse accommodation to a prospective guest on the basis of age, race, colour or creed. Similarly, it can evict guests or the visitors for the same reason they might be refused admittance. The right of eviction should be used with extreme caution to avoid damage suits and unfavourable publicity to the hotel. A hotel cannot legally evict a guest if in so doing it violates any of his rights or if the eviction exposes the guest to an unreasonable risk of harm.

A hotel has the following responsibilities:

1. Legal responsibility to accept a prospective guest unless it has a legal reason for refusing admission
2. Legal responsibility for protecting its guests
3. Legal responsibility to care for guests' property

An agreement made between two or more parties is a legally binding contract. Perhaps the most important element in a contract (though there are others) is consensus. This means that both parties are of the same thought, that there must be an offer on one side and an unconditional acceptance on the other and that the agreement must be entered into freely and voluntarily and without misrepresentation or fraud.

A conditional acceptance constitutes a counter offer which requires acceptance before it becomes a contract. When a counter offer is made, the original offer lapses and cannot afterwards be accepted.

To supply information, for example, in advertisements or in a brochure is not in itself an offer; it is merely an invitation to do business. In the same way, placing goods in a showcase or shop window, even with prices on them, is not an offer; the offer is made by the customer's tendering the price and it is accepted when the shopkeeper takes it. It has even been held that in a supermarket the contract is not completed by the customer's placing goods from the shelves in his wire basket; it is only deemed completed when the goods are taken to the cashier the customer offers to buy them and the cashier accepts the offer.

If an offer is conditional and the conditions are not fulfilled it has not been accepted. If an offer is made by telephone, subject to confirmation in writing, it cannot be accepted in any other way.

It is evident that when an offer (e.g. of accommodation) has been made and accepted there is a contract which cannot be rescinded by one party without the consent of the other. The law provides a number of remedies for a breach of contract, including, in some cases, specific performance (*i.e.*, the defaulting party is compelled to do what he undertook to do) but the normal remedy is the award of damages.

If an intending visitor has made a contract and wishes to cancel it, the hotel can claim damages. The contract may be to stay for more than one night, in which case staying for a lesser period than that agreed to would be a breach of contract. Similarly, if a banquet, or other service, has been offered and accepted, the customer cannot cancel without exposing himself to an enforceable demand for compensation.

The injured party (in this case the hotel) must minimize its loss as far as is reasonably possible. In the case of a room booked, for example, it must endeavour to relet it and in the case of a banquet it must endeavour to cancel the order for food and the engagement of casual labour. In an action for damages, it must be taken into account the time remaining between the cancellation and the date of the cancelled booking and any special circumstances, which might make it easy or difficult to reduce the loss. Even if it is not possible to relet the accommodation, or let it on the same terms, the hotel cannot claim the full price as quoted to the intending guest. A deduction must be made in respect of food included in the price but not supplied, linen not used, and any other expense which has been avoided by non-fulfillment of the contract.

If a deposit has been taken, the repayment of the deposit can be withheld if the booking is cancelled. It would still be open to the customer to sue for the return of the deposit but he would rarely do so, since the hotel would counterclaim for damages arising from the breach of contract.

A contract made by offer and acceptance is binding on the hotel also. If it has promised to provide accommodation or services and its offer has been accepted or if the customer has offered to take accommodation and the hotel has accepted his offer, it is liable for not fulfilling his promise. This could apply when a particular room, or type of room, has been promised and only another room or type of room is available. For this reason it is unwise to make specific promises without qualification. In the case of over-booking it will usually be sufficient to reserve accommodation of a similar or superior type elsewhere and to provide suitable transport. If the substitute accommodation is more expensive, the hotel at fault shall have to pay the difference to avoid the possibility of legal action in respect of his breach of contract. Even then there might be other damages, for example, if the guest had arranged to meet someone or to receive mail or telephone calls at the hotel, which could be the subject of a claim. Nevertheless, the court will always deal sympathetically with a defendant who has done his best to repair the injury he has caused.

Dominoes and cribbage may be played, but not for high stakes. This applies only to fully licensed houses and not to restaurants which are licensed. It is an offence for a person under the age of eighteen to take part in any gaming, even playing cribbage or dominoes, on licensed premises.

Other games of skill, or chance, or a combination of the two may be played and lotteries can be held for raising money for purposes other than private gain but there are restrictions contained in the betting, gaming and lotteries Act, which must be studiously observed. Those contemplating such activities would be well advised to consult local trade associations or a police officer before embarking on them.

Provided that permission has been obtained from the local justices, any equal chance game can be played under the conditions contained in the relevant Act. There is no fixed method of application and the concerned local authorities should be consulted as to the form and time of application.

It is not uncommon for a licensee to be asked for permission for a club or society, such as a darts club, to promote small lotteries. The society must first apply to the local authority and deposit the requisite fee.

A return has to be submitted to the local authority not more than three months after the end of the lottery showing the proceeds and how they were disposed of.

The name, nationality and date of arrival of every overnight guest over the age of sixteen must be recorded, but not necessarily in a book or bound register. It is not necessary that each guest should enter his name personally. A counter, for example, could furnish information in respect of his entire party. It is quite in order to make a collective entry when the names are the same, as 'Dr A and Mrs S and Miss Negi' provided it is quite clear what are the names of each member of the party *i.e.*, 'Dr A. Negi, Mrs S. Negi and Miss Negi and friend' would not be sufficient if the friend were over sixteen, since the name of the friend has not been recorded.

The hotel is not obliged to ascertain that the name entered is the true name of the guest and cannot demand proof. If he suspects that a guest has given a false name in order to obtain credit by fraud he can either report his suspicion to the police or obtain payment in advance. But if he knows positively the true identity of a guest giving a false name it is his responsibility to record it correctly.

Nor is the hotel obliged to ascertain whether a couple purporting to be man and wife are, in fact, married. If the same woman repeatedly came to a hotel with different men claiming that each was her husband, then, the hotel might expose himself to the risk of prosecution for keeping a disorderly house.

In addition to furnish information about name and nationality, aliens are required to state particulars of their passport or registration certificate and, on leaving, their date of departure, and next destination.

Hotels are sometimes requested to make their register available for inspection by private detectives. Only a police officer, or someone authorized by a court, can demand to see the register. If a request is refused the person seeking information can apply to the court for an order, or can subpoena the hotel to give evidence. The register of guests must be retained for at least twelve months.

Every business needs a policy for dealing with complaints which makes clear its desire to give the best possible service in every area of its operation, and that the staff must spare no pains to see that guests or customers are comfortable and satisfied. It must emphasize the fact that complaints which help to improve service, or organize a more efficient business are welcomed, and that properly handled, they can be the cheapest form of advertisement, improving goodwill and possibly turning an irate guest into a customer for life.

Notwithstanding the relaxation of the law relating to betting and the opening of betting shops, it is still an offence to allow betting or the passing of betting slips on licensed premises except where a room is licensed as a betting shop and has a separate entrance to the street. Few licensing justices would grant an application for such a licence though they are not prohibited from doing so. It is not an offence for betting to take place if all those concerned either reside or work on the premises, but a licensee who encouraged or permitted betting in such circumstances would need to be very careful that these conditions were complied with.

The playing of games of chance for money or money's worth is permitted on licensed passes within certain limits.

Games of skill, including billiards, skittles, shovehipenny and darts, are allowed and there is no limit to the stakes that can be played for.

A full on-licence includes permission for the playing of billiards between 1.00 and 8.00 a.m.. Holders of other licences must apply to a competent authority for a separate licence and must display a notice to the effect that they are licensed for billiards.

Applications for permit for an 'amusement with prizes machine' must be made to the licensing authority. Before a machine can be installed the permission of the owner of the premises, as well as the tenant, is necessary. The justices must afford a hearing to the application if they wish to refuse permission. There are certain conditions applied to the use of these machines. These include:

1. No player may pay more than a certain amount
2. The prize for anyone play must not exceed a fixed amount in cash, or goods or token for goods

Gaming machines with higher money prizes can be installed in rooms not open to the general public (e.g. in club rooms) but they must not exceed two in number and all stakes must be paid out either as winnings or for some purpose other than private gain (e.g. as a contribution to club funds).

Licensed premises are exempt from the need to hold a music licence for music and singing if the music is provided solely from reproduction of radio or television entertainment, by recorded sound or by not more than two performers. A television licence is, of course, required for each set on the premises.

In other cases, like dancing, a licence is required. This is not necessary for private parties to which the public is not admitted and for which tickets are not sold at the door.

The use of a television set or radio where it can be heard by the public is a 'performance' within the meaning of the Copyright Act which also prohibits the playing of certain music in any other way in public without the permission of the owner of the copyright. The playing of music as an accompaniment to a meal in a restaurant would be a public performance.

When music is habitually provided, the society may call for a return showing which items have been played. The band-leader can normally supply this information but the occupier of the premises is responsible for collecting and forwarding it to the society.

Apart from copyright in the music, the makers of gramophone records have a copyright in the recording. If it is intended to play records in such a way as to constitute a public performance it is necessary to obtain (and pay for) permission from the organization representing most of the owners of copyright in records.

Inclusive fees may be normally charged, based on the frequency of performances and/or the rateable value of the premises.

Infringement of copyright could lead to legal proceedings and to the award of damages and costs as well as an injunction to prevent further performance.

In the unfortunate event of death in a hotel, procedures should be known and dutifully observed by everyone who has to deal with such an emergency.

In the event of the death of a foreign national, once a check had been made on the country of origin, the consulate officer at that embassy should be informed. They, in turn, would report the death to their minister of foreign affairs who would wish to know:

1. Date, time and place of death
2. Cause of death
3. Belongings of the deceased
4. Details of police investigation
5. Home address of the deceased
6. Name and address of relatives
7. Any information available regarding traveller's insurance

Naturally, the wishes of the next of kin concerning the last rites of the deceased would be awaited, but the undertaker would be responsible for negotiating whilst the body rested in his care. Apart from the death certificate, he would be required to provide a certificate from the public health officer to the effect that the transportation of the body presented no risk to public health (*i.e.*, that death was due to causes other than such things as typhoid, cholera, smallpox, etc.).

Part-II
Departments In a Hotel

6. Departmental Structure

About twenty years back, a hotel used to have a large number of individuals and departments directly responsible to the manager. The hotel manager was the one who was directly responsible for the guests and was closely involved in all aspects of operations. The chef, the headwaiter, and the housekeeper exercised no authority of their own. The manager had most of the necessary technical skills and his approach was that of a technician rather than the manager of a business. Financial matters and control was in the hands of the owner/proprietor. Personnel management was limited to hiring of the staff according to the requirements of the hotel.

Gradually, the whole profile started changing due to growth in the travel market, increase in the number of hotels and the size of the ownership. New and scientific business techniques, management thought and commercial practices entered into the trade. Hotel education and training started flourishing. Higher quality of management found its place into the hotel world. The front office, uniformed services and housekeeping started acquiring individual responsibilities.

OPERATING DEPARTMENTS (Revenue Earning Departments)

A hotel is a business connected with several distant products, services and facilities, which are offered in various combinations. Most effective organization structures follow a classification and provide for clear profit and loss-centred responsibilities. The following is a common pattern of uniform and standard system of operating practice in a number of hotels:

1. Major (primary)
   a. Room
   b. Food
   c. Beverages
2. Minor (ancillary)
   a. Guest telephones
   b. Guest laundry and valeting
   c. Guest services
3. Support service departments (undistributed overhead)
   a. Administration and general
   b. Marketing
   c. Property operation, maintenance and energy

The organization of a number of hotels, large or small, deluxe or middle class show that most of them are organized on well defined principles of management. Traditionally, the hotel industry had been organized departmentally. In other words, individuals, who performed similar tasks, were grouped in a department, for example, housekeeping employees formed the housekeeping department, front-office employees formed the front office department. The organization chart of hotels vary. The larger the hotel, the greater the need for specialization. In small hotels employees are expected to perform a number of different tasks. However, in luxury and deluxe hotels, employees are more specialized. They have some knowledge about other tasks in the different departments but they have to know a lot about their own special jobs. Thus, in deluxe hotels there is a need for greater specialization than in middle level hotels.

The scope, complexity and pattern of a hotel organization will vary according to the aims, objectives and size of an individual unit. A hotel organizational structure, which would suit a large hotel, may be wasteful and ineffective for a smaller hotel. The purpose of a suitable organizational structure is to fulfil given objectives.

In many countries hotels have been graded in order to give the potential customer an indication of service and style of facilities he can expect. For example, luxury hotels are marked as 5-star and 4-star or grade-I, whilst modest hotels are marked as 3-star and 2-star or grade-II, and the low class hotels as 1-star or grade-III. Such grading is carried out by an official of an approved government body such as department of tourism or hotel division or a classification committee formed for this specific purpose. The facilities, the amenities, the comfort, the space, the number of rooms, the central heating and air-conditioning, etc. are taken note of while grading the hotel.

The success of the hotel business depends mainly upon the organizational and functional capacity of each of its departments. The goal of each department should be the overall goal of the hotel. The employees should be taught high standards of service and personal conduct, essential for the successful running of the hotel. The practices of hoteliering vary considerably throughout the world. The requirement of greater efficiency and a better return from hotel investments have necessitated a new approach to traditional hotel operations. Japan follows the American practice not only in the construction of building but also in the running of hotels. In India, hotel groups are trying to follow the latest and the most modern techniques of hoteliering. Personal supervision by the top management of the day-to-day hotel operations, is very common in the USA, with the result that the hotel industry in the USA has built some of the best hotel companies in the world.

The gradual development of the hotel industry has led to the expansion of its activities. Earlier hotels provided lodging, food and protection of luggage. A modern hotel, besides these, offers a number of luxuries under the same roof. These facilities and services are operated and provided by the hotel itself while outsiders contracted by the hotel provide some others. The various areas of activities of a hotel are:

1. Front of the House
   - Building Exterior
   - Lobby
   - Front Desk
   - Guest Rooms
   - Public Rooms
   - Functional Rooms
   - Housekeeping
   - Dining Room
   - Restaurants
   - Bars/Lounges
   - Retail Outlets
   - Valet Service
   - Swimming Pool
   - Health Club
   - Beauty Parlours and Saloons
   - Shopping Arcade
   - Business Centre
   - Entertainment
2. Back of the House
   - Finance, accounting, audit and control
   - Personnel
   - Food production (kitchen)
   - Engineering
   - Maintenance
   - Laundry
   - Store room
   - Security
   - Sanitation
   - Advertising
   - Data processing
   - Horticulture

A hotel may be defined as an establishment that provides goods and services to transit guests in search of overnight accommodation. The key business activities of a hotel are provision of accommodation, sale of food and beverages and provision of entertainment.

1. Accommodation

Room revenues are the most profitable source of revenue of a hotel. It yields the highest profit margins and as such constitutes the main source of hotel operating profit. Hotel accommodation has changed over the years with the rising standard of living. Former 'luxuries' like private bathrooms or bedrooms provided in the top class hotels, are now commonplace in modern simple hotels. In first class hotels, wealthy guests expect more than just a bed and bathroom. There are suites provided by the hotels, which include additional lounge, sitting room and private dining room facilities. For the modern set, single and double bedroom, 'studio' type accommodation is popular. Many hotel rooms come in a variety of sizes, shapes and decor.

As given in Table 6.1, a variety of rooms offered today are developed in response to customers' needs. As social and business needs change, the style of the hotel rooms must also change. Experienced hotels remain ahead of competition by developing and testing new concepts in rooms to meet needs of particular market segments. New room concepts may require design and engineering changes, deletion of furnishings and limited remodelling.

2. Food and Beverage

A hotel supplies food, beverages and drinks. These are tangible items and with a certain amount of skill and supervision, these can be provided to the guests' satisfaction. The traditional *table d'hote* and *a la carte* menus still form the basis of present-day eating. Each hotel has speciality restaurants and coffee shops.

3. Services

Service is an intangible item and requires ability and versatility. The hotel business is a highly personalized one. In addition to selling food, drinks and accommodation, it sells service to the public. Service depends on the staff. The employees who render the service should be pleasant and courteous as well as skillful. The cost of staff and their skilled labour is a vital item while computing hotel charges. Service is the only product, which cannot be purchased. It depends entirely upon its staff. Human behaviour in a free society cannot be standardized. It can only be guided and requires constant supervision, attention and training.

4. Entertainment and Business Facilities

A hotel is concerned not only with bedrooms and restaurant facilities; the guest may also seek entertainment. Therefore, orchestras, cabarets, dance, drama, music, etc. and other entertainment facilities are also interwoven into the fabric of hotel services.

Convention booking and selling is a highly competitive field. Conventions are held on local, national or international levels by large chains, companies, corporate, unions, educational institutions, etc.

In addition to activities described above a hotel may provide:

- Business centres
- Conference facilities
- Business displays
- Telex and teleprinter
- Teleconferencing
- Computer services
- Public stenographer and secretarial services
- Exhibition facilities
- Banking facilities
- Notary public
- Airline services
- Car rentals
- Travel agencies
- Reservation service
- Tourist cars and garage facilities
- Instant reservation
- Tourist guides
- Sight-seeing tours
- Excursions
- Tennis courts
- Squash courts
- Saddle horses
- Archery
- Croquet
- Boating
- Golf course
- Swimming pool
- Angling
- Health club
- Shopping arcade
- Book shops
- Handicrafts
- Jewellers
- Chemist shops

Table 6.1: Various Types of Rooms in a Modern Hotel

1. Adjoining Rooms	Two or more side by side without a connecting door between them. In other words, rooms can be adjoined without being connected.
2. Cabana	A room adjacent to the pool area, with or without sleeping facilities; usually separate from the hotel's main building, but still located in the hotel grounds.
3. Double	Room with a double or queen-sized bed for two persons. In many hotels single rooms could also serve as a double.
4. Double-Double	Room with two double beds
5. Duplex	A two-storey suite with parlour and bedrooms connected by the stairway
6. Efficiency	An accommodation containing some kitchen facility
7. Hospitality Suite	A parlour with connecting bedroom to be used by companies during conventions for entertaining, and trade shows. A hospitality room normally contains a bar and occasionally tables. It is essentially a parlour with a connecting bedroom.
8. Junior Suite	A large room with a portion separating the bedroom furnishings from the sitting area.
9. King	Largest bed available; may be 80" × 72"; may be formed by putting two twin mattresses crosswise on twin box springs.
10. Lanai	A room overlooking landscaped area, a scenic view, water or a garden with a balcony, patio or both (found in tropics and resort hotels).
11. Parlour	A living or sitting room not used as the bedroom. It is called a 'saloon' and is found in some parts of Europe.
12. Queen	Middle-sized bed larger than the normal bed, smaller than a king-size; dimension 60" × 80" or 60" × 72".
13. Rollway Bed	A portable, folding single bed that can be moved in and out of the guest room.
14. Model Room	A display room that is used for showing merchandise. It may or may not be provided with sleeping facilities.
15. Single	A room with one or more bedrooms. It is common to find queen or even king-sized beds in these rooms.
16. Studio/Extension Room	A one-room parlour set-up having one or two coaches that convert to a bed.
17. Suite	It is a combination of one or more bedrooms and a parlour. It may also contain a bar, more than one bathroom, a small kitchen, and other facilities.
18. Twin	A room with twin beds/two single beds.
19. Twin-Double/ Family Room	A room with two double beds for two, three or four persons. This room may be referred to as a 'family' room or double room.
20. Penthouse	This opens on to the roof and might be accompanied by a swimming pool, patio, a tennis court and other amenities.
21. Hotel within a Hotel	It is a club floor with special amenities for executive class travellers.

- Boutique
- Florists
- Confectionary
- News stands
- Tobacco and cigars
- Yoga and massage parlour
- Turkish bath and chiropodist
- Beauty parlour
- Discotheques
- Poolside barbecue
- House physicians
- Valet service
- Television
- Telephone
- Guest laundry
- Baby Sitting

The services and facilities found in majority of the deluxe hotels vary and change. However, all these facilities are not found in each and every hotel. Even the facilities offered by the same category of hotels differ. Every hotel decides what services should be provided based on public demands, the location, the size and character of the hotel and the class of patronage. In some of the hotels certain services are provided by renting space to other specialized agencies, e.g. retail trades like beauty parlours, barber shops, checkrooms, valet service, drug stores, etc. The departments leased by the hotel are referred to as privileges or concessions and these leases are known as concessionaires. These concessionaires operate independently so long as they conform to the policies of the hotel. Lodging and food is the principal business of each and every hotel and the extra services are merely necessary adjustments.

The hotel work is highly departmentalized and is truly a grouping of many types of business and professional services under one roof. Most luxurious hotels tend to demand a greater degree of departmentalization but every one from the manager downwards may need, at times, to be more of an all rounder.

Within a hotel there is a separation by the front of the house and the back of the house. The front areas are those portions of the hotel with which the guest is likely to come into direct contact during his stay. The back of the house has those sections with which the guest is indirectly related.

The departments of hotels are arranged in a manner so as to achieve the objectives laid down as per hotel policy. Whatever may be the division of hotel activities, all the functions carry equal importance in the successful management of the hotel. No department can function without the other and any breakdown in friendly cooperation between departments can cause catastrophic results. The departmentalization varies not only according to the category of the hotel but also according to the public or private ownership of the hotel. The following break-up illustrates the position of management in most of the large hotels:

1. Accommodation department:
    a. Administration
    b. Personnel
    c. Front office
    d. Housekeeping and laundry
    e. Uniformed staff
2. Food and beverage department:
    a. Food purchasing and stores
    b. Food preparation (kitchen)
    c. Food service (restaurant)
    d. Beverages (bar)
    e. Engineering department
    f. Sales department
    g. Security department (protection)
3. Finance, accounting, control and audit
4. Minor departments
    a. Telephone
    b. Cigar and check stand
    c. Hairdressers
    d. Checkroom

e. Porter

f. Guest laundry

g. Swimming pool

h. Others

The job breakdown by hierarchical division *i.e.*, levels of qualifications and responsibility in all these departments can be put as follows:

a. Manager
b. High level specialists
c. Medium level specialists
d. Basic level specialists
e. Miscellaneous labour apprentices

The hotel staff could also be grouped into four main categories:

a. The general manager and departmental heads
b. Sub-departmental heads
c. Assistant departmental heads
d. General staff and operating personnel

The small hotel has a relativity simple structure. The organization of a medium and large hotel is complex and varies considerably from one property to another. The organization of a hotel is mainly dependent on the staff requirement of the hotel, which in turn depends upon:

a. Size
b. Objectives
c. Services

In a small hotel having up to fifty rooms few persons may be employed. The various activities are put under the charge of one person only. In case of individually owned properties, the owner himself is the manager and performs much of the work himself. In these hotels, a simple system prevails and the number of activities is grouped under broad heads and minimum of staff is required. In case of medium and large sized hotels there is a lot of specialization and division of work, which necessitate specialists for each and every work. It results in the increase of staff and creation of more departments for the smooth and efficient running of the hotel.

The character of various departments of a hotel and its standard determines the pattern of organization. There is a close relationship between the price, the range and quality of service, and amenities provided.

In most of the luxurious and large-sized establishments, the following distinct level of authority can be ascertained:

a. The owners/shareholders
b. The board of directors/governors
c. Liaison between policy and operations
d. Supervision of operations
e. Operations

It is not possible to state the exact number of staff required to run a hotel of specified rooms, because so much will depend upon the interior layout of the building, multi-storied or spread out building, communication facilities and use of labour saving devices. In small hotels many functions can be combined and the duties can be performed by lesser number of people. Large hotels having 1,000 or more employees require more supervision, thus requiring more departments. Employees are assigned specific duties. The management of each hotel must determine the departments and the number of employees in each needed for its own operation. The departments advise and help the general manager in formulation of the operating policy and see to it that it is carried out. They supervise and share the responsibility for the daily function of the entire hotel staff.

The management structure of a hotel comprises all the positions of responsibility and authority.

The heads of management in any organizational structure are representatives of the company or shareholders *i.e.*, the board of governors or board of directors. Therefore, the hotel management team consists of the general manager, one or more deputy general managers/resident manager or assistant manager, and the heads of department. The chief executive of the hotel is designated in different styles such as managing director, executive director, president, general manager or hotel manager. He participates in the formulation of the hotel policies and strategies. He is invariably responsible for their implementation and for the performance of the hotel.

In large hotels, this level is bifurcated into two: managing director and general manager or resident manager. The managing director reports to the board and coordinates the work of the specialist departments and of the resident manager. The resident manager is responsible for the day-to-day management of the hotel activities. There are hotels where the positions of deputy managers exist, who have authority over the departmental managers. Whatever may be the title of the positions, an effective system of hotel management requires a clear definition of responsibility and authority. Each title must describe the specific role and responsibilities appropriate to the job associated with the position concerned.

The managers heading specific departments are known as heads of the departments. They have direct lines of responsibility and authority to their superiors and to subordinates of their respective departments. Heads of the department are specialists. They provide advice and service to line management plan. For example, the front office manager, head housekeepers, chef, and restaurant managers are treated as line management and purchase officers, accounts officers, personnel officers and other similar positions are treated as specialists.

The General Manager

There must be one person responsible for the overall operation of the hotel. He is known as the general manager. In the past the hotel manager was primarily a host, personally greeting the guests and seeing to it that they were properly cared for. Now the successful general manager is a highly trained person capable of directing a complex business enterprise.

The general manager has to be a versatile, specialist, businessman and administrator, accountant and controller, a salesman and diplomat, an astronomer and a competent man.

The general manager's duties can be multifarious but the main responsibility of planning, budget and control rests with him. Representing the ownership interests, he directs the activities of the departments and gets involved into the day-to-day operations of individual sections of the establishment. He follows the policies and procedures prescribed for him by the proprietor or management. He must know how to organize and supervise. He is in charge of personnel, the money for operating the hotel and publicity about the hotel. He is responsible for operating matters such as rates of the rooms, use of guests' credit and the assignment of personnel. He has overall responsibility for operating hotel profitably and providing the best possible services and comforts to guests. Accordingly, he must understand how each department operates and the duties of each employee. The general manager has many duties to perform, such as hiring personnel, overseeing the purchase of supplies, directing publicity, introducing improvements in service and determining rates and credit policies. In large hotels some of these duties are delegated to assistant managers. In small hotels, on the other hand, the general manager who is frequently the owner may also do the work relating to the front office.

A successful general manager should have cordial relations with the guests as well as the hotel employees in various departments. It is also important that the manager participates in the community affairs, since a good share of the hotel's business comes from local people. He should also come closely in contact with his fellow hoteliers for the improvement of the industry.

As an administrator he should have the ability to make quick decisions and adopt procedures which will help improve service. In large hotels, the ability to coordinate the operation of various departments with minimum of friction among staff members is a most important requirement. Under all circumstances he should be able to control his temper in settling problems with either guests or staff members. A considerable knowledge of all phases of hotel business gained by experience and training is necessary before a person can handle this. Long hours are often involved when civic or business groups are in convention. A great deal of physical endurance is also necessary.

The duties of a general manager are varied and difficult but every task should be carried out efficiently. The main duty of a manager is to pass on the orders and ensure that they are properly carried out. He must pay great attention to expenditure and should draw conclusion from his observations. It is the responsibility of the manager to see that proper discipline is maintained in the hotel and that all the staff regulations are observed and that there is proper coordination among the departments.

One of the biggest and more delicate jobs of a general manager is in the field of human relations, particularly relations with the staff. Everyone must be handled differently according to his personality, age, position, background and outlook. While dealing with the heads of departments, the manager should always remember their experience and professional skills. He must try to get himself accepted by them, which is possible by showing his hard work and intelligence in solving their problems. In certain circumstances he may be obliged to speak directly to a member of staff. In order to preserve the authority of the head of the department and respect his feelings, he should speak only to the person in charge of the department to which the concerned staff member belongs.

The manager must adopt a rigid code of conduct while dealing with suppliers and contractors. Quality and price are two important factors on which his decision must be based. Purchasing of goods and services should be carried out on a competitive basis. He should take these decisions on the basis of price, taking into account any guarantee or condition, the date of delivery, details of payment, and after-sale service.

The general manager not only assembles a team but moulds them into a coordinated, cooperating group of people capable of working together for the common goal, *i.e.*, making a guest satisfied. The general manager needs to devote adequate attention to policy making, financial control, staff management, market research and business promotion. He must be given the means and the authority to do his job and must enjoy the complete confidence of the management.

Control in the General Manager's Office

In the general run of hotels, the function of the general manager's office is all embracing, and its authority reaches into every department. The ultimate responsibility of the conduct of the establishment, and its success or failure has only one address, the general manager's office.

Persistent faults in the service of departments, inadequate exploitation of trading potential, and unplanned economy can only result from the 'mistiming' of the hotel's functioning mechanism by its chief operator, the general manager. The three weaknesses indicated cover a wide field in detail and form the general standard for measuring the case for an adverse balance in the profit and loss account.

The hotel in no way differs from the general aim of all business entities–to exist and to promote the security and prosperity of its future by extracting profit from its activities. A profound knowledge of the trade, coupled with sound business sense, is a must for progress along the road to success.

Case Study 602

A Day in the Life of Mr. Chander Prakash, a Hotel General Manager

As an owner-manager of a mountain lodge in Auli region of Uttranchal, Mr Chander Prakash can in real sense say that he is involved in every aspect of the hospitality business. That comes with running a small place. The mountain lodge has only 60 rooms, along with full service restaurant. You might be surprised at how much work goes into running even a small hotel, though. It is certainly not a nine to five job.

His staff and he have three basic tasks:

1. To satisfy the needs of guests
2. To keep the hotel operations running smoothly
3. To earn a profit.

Their one major task is to do all the above three at the same time.

Mr Prakash has to be well conversant with every aspect of the hotel:

1. Booking reservations
2. Food preparations
3. Cost control
4. Accounting, and
5. Maintenance procedures.

That is where his background comes in handy. His parents owned restaurant. Their house was always filled with conversation about menu planning, food storage and preparations, and customers' satisfaction. He did odd jobs for his parents all through his schooling years. At university, he took up a course in hotel management and spent his summers and the hours after college working in hotels and resorts. Every job he worked in (reservation, clerk, waiter, cook, kitchen steward, housekeeper, business manager) taught him something more about what goes in a hospitality business and how hotels could be run smoothly.

An important part of the Auli Mountain lodge's business is done in the front office where reservations are booked, rooms are assigned, guests are registered and payments are collected. For this purpose Mr Prakash has full time front office person, Mr Harish. He and Mr Harish usually hire part-time help at the height of the tourist season. Mr Harish and Chander get together weekly to go over the projected reservations. Only once, soon after he bought the mountain lodge, did Mr Prakash ever book two guests for the same room on the same night. They had no vacancies, so he landed up calling local lodging houses until he found one

Case Study cont. ...

Case Study cont. ...

with a room. He accompanied the guest himself and paid for the room. Believe it or not, the person is now a regular guest at Auli Mountain lodge.

When Mr Prakash took over the resort, he did extensive remodelling choosing fabrics and furniture that were attractive, durable and comfortable. It was up to the housekeeping staff to keep things clean and attractive. His executive housekeeper, Ms Devi, sees to that. In the Mountain Lodge, maintenance is an important part of guests' comfort. If hot water is not available, if the fire place chimney gets blocked, or if driveways and parking lots are snowed in, they have a problem. They do employ one full time maintenance person for such problems. Mr Prakash is known to do emergency repairs himself in the middle of the night.

The restaurant at the resort is open round the year and not just during high tourist season. Mr Prakash is proud of its good reputation in the area. Without its off season profits, the resort probably could not service.

In his staff, he has a steward, a master chef, and a group of kitchen and food and beverage helpers. Even though his staff is well trained, he keeps a close eye on the restaurant business too. He often talks to guests about food and beverage products and preparations and he even helps to prepare and serve meals on occasions.

As far as the business end of the resort goes, he leaves that mostly to Ms Sheetal, his business manager. Her weekly update keeps him aware of how things are going. He also has monthly meetings which help him to foresee any developing problems and future needs.

One most important thing he strives to do as owner-manager is to be a hospitable host. He tries to understand and fulfill each guest's needs by talking with guests. He generally makes himself available for comment or compliments when the transits come back from trekking. They are usually tired and hungry and eager to discuss their day. Mr Prakash greets them at the fire place with beverages and snacks before dinner. He considers some of the folks who return each year to be his good friends. He feels that it is one of the rewards of running a lodge in a small place, a feeling of closeness with his guests and a deep sense of enjoyment in meeting their needs.

The course through the industry of those who eventually arrive at the 'manager grade' is usually confined to study and practical experience in the mechanics of the business, and little or no opportunity is taken or presented, for developing a rational outlook and regard for the ultimate purpose of their efforts–profit extraction.

The make up of a successful general manager can be briefly noted as follows:

1. A comprehensive knowledge of the trade, acquired by training and practical experience
2. Administrative qualities
3. Organizing ability
4. A temperate disposition
5. Sound business judgment
6. Initiative and enterprise
7. Originality in outlook and a gift for translating from the mental blueprint and bringing new ideas to a functioning level
8. A capacity for moulding one's attitude and actions to conform to the tenets of what makes a true professional.

Organization

Organization of the general manager's office can vary a great deal in character, and is influenced by numerous circumstances. The size of the hotel, type of business, and the internal administration policy of the company etc., all have a bearing on the building of management schedules.

In hotels which form part of a group, and where the 'supreme management' is in the hands of a board of directors, the job of the resident manager is likely to be limited in scope and authority. Rules governing policy, both in respect of internal organization and trading is firmly laid down; not as a form of guidance but as a course that must be rigidly followed. In these circumstances, the board makes practically all executive appointments, and it very rarely happens that a manager can influence these even by personal recommendation.

The control of all departments (not making a reference in the clerical sense) is largely centralized and governed by the head office. The resident manager therefore, is provided with a range of highly specialized services, which have no claim on his time or personal attention. Where vast interests are involved, such a procedure is the only rational solution for assuring a high standard of efficiency.

The art of good management is knowing how to use to the fullest advantage the departmental services, which the directors have created for the conduct of their hotels.

The departments and their respective managers are, apart from established schedules, available for advice and cooperation in the performance of any task within reason at the request of the resident manager. The request, of course, may not be granted; in which event, should an issue arise in connection with a refusal, the head of a department will state a case and abide by the decision of the directors. There is sound reasoning in this.

Departmental Contacts

The departments most closely connected with the manager and the daily routine of his departments are:

Reception

The contact between the head of reception department and the manager's office is frequent. Current letting, advanced bookings, allocation of apartments, rates, etc., are under continuous review, and the closest cooperation is essential to assure the best results from the hotel's most important source of income.

The manager is advised daily of 'arrivals' and 'departures', number of residents, complaints, and vacant rooms. It is usual for Reception to report at once the arrival and departure of important guests to give the manager the opportunity, should he desire, of paying his personal respects.

Housekeeping

In this department's sphere are all matters regarding the comfort of guests, furnishing, repair and replacement of fittings; decoration of rooms; and thousand and one minor issues which fit into the province covered by the housekeeper. Through the housekeeper the manager is kept apprised of all such matters, which are important for him to know about.

The Chef

It is most important that the manager and the chef should consult daily on the drafting and planning of menus; on current and future buying; discuss the cause of complaints and their remedy; and generally review together the position as regards catering. It is not sound practice to leave the drafting of menus entirely to the chef, but his professional advice should be given due consideration. The manager is in a better position to assess the demands of customers, and to know what supplies, and the most favourable varieties in respect of price and season, is available. To leave the buying to the chef is not always the best policy for assuring advantage in price and quality. Where the influence of the chef prevails in the purchase of supplies, it is sometimes fairly safe to predict that prices will rise with a dip in quality.

Food and Beverage Manager

Food and Beverage department deals with food and beverage service. It may also include the headwaiter in the restaurant or grillroom; much depends on the size and organization of the business. Food and Beverage Manager's part in the scheme of things can vary extensively in importance and in some extreme cases reach beyond the direct authority of the resident manager. But to accept the general rule, he is under the control of the manager, and takes his cues from him. The daily contact and discussion usually revolves around details of service, trading and takings and the trend of demand in respect of food, wines, etc. Complaints are likewise dealt with; subject, cause and remedy. Plans for special parties, functions, etc., are submitted to the manager for approval.

Staff Manager

The daily report of the staff manager can cover a wide field.

1. Additions to personnel, termination of service, and transfers to other departments
2. Number of personnel employed, analysed under the respective departments and compared with the same period of the previous year
3. List of applicants
4. Vacancies
5. Requests for increase in pay
6. Requests for references
7. List of absentees and sickness report
8. Advice and details of accidents to staff
9. Complaints respecting conduct of individual members of the staff and course of action taken
10. Uniforms required and repairs, etc.
11. Summary of payments for overtime, and reasons for overtime

Even the above fairly extensive survey by no means takes into account all that the manager may require from the staff manager.

Secretary Accountant

Analysis of previous day's business with totals-to-date for the month; statement of cash banked; customers' accounts outstanding and paid; analysed cost statement of previous day's purchases, sundry vouchers, documents, schedules requiring manager's signature–these are routine details which the manager requires. The position of accounts on the 'tab' may be discussed, and all other matters to do with clerical administration. The relationship between the manager's office and secretary-accountant is out of necessity very close, and this contact usually covers the control and bill offices. The control office in the audit sense does not play any part in the routine of the manager's office, and its activities are confined to a set of definite schedules with respect to the financial operation of certain departments.

Daily Conference

Many managers make a rule of holding a daily conference each morning, which all the executives attend. It is not usual for the secretary-accountant to be present, as much of the information he has to impart is of a confidential nature.

This practice is very sound, for each department has a relation to the others, and any decisions made can be carried into effect by the full cooperation, provided that these meetings keep the care of the matter under discussion well within view.

7. Front Office Operations

Room division involves the letting and serving of guest rooms. It does not include public and banqueting areas. The departments and staff involved in room division are–the front office, including advance reservations, receptions, reception clerks, the doorman, hall porters and luggage porters; housekeeping including, room-maids, floor and bathroom cleaners, linen staff; and the assistant manager.

There are three main hotel activities engaged in the earning of room revenue:

1. Hotel front office
2. Uniformed services
3. Housekeeping

These are the main components of the accommodation function and are present in most of the hotels. Normally, these are organized in separate departments. The organization and staffing of these departments will depend upon the size, type and standard of the hotel. The main components of the accommodation functions (Refer Table 7.1) could be briefly outlined as:

1. Hotel front office:
   a. Room sales
   b. Guest accounts
   c. Mail and other guest services
2. Hotel housekeeping:

Receptionist delivers room key to the guest

Table 7.1: Activities at the Front Office

Guest Activities		Front Office Activities
1. Enquiry	:	Record enquiry details Describe product Sales opportunity Checking room availability
2. Reservation	:	Offer accommodation Record reservation details in room reservation form Check customer credit worthiness Update room availability chart
3. Confirmation	:	Confirm offer Record confirmation Record receipt of deposit Update room availability chart Check over-booking
	:	Prepare arrival and departure lists
4. Arrival		Car parking Luggage handling
5. Registration and check-in	:	Receive and welcome guest Check-in booking details register Allocate room Record room allocation Allocate keys Mail/messages Sales opportunity Book-out (if necessary) Notify other departments
6. Go to room	:	Direct or take luggage Sales opportunity
7. In-house	:	Open account Post charges from all sales outlets Monitor credit limit Mail/messages/calls Give information/communications security Monitor room status

Table cont. ...

Table cont. ...

8. Settle account	:	Finalize account (cash, credit, credit cards, etc.) Receive payment Sales opportunity
9. Departure	:	Notify departments

a. Servicing of guest rooms

b. Servicing of public rooms

c. Sundry housekeeping services

3. Uniformed services:

a. Servicing of arrivals

b. Guest information services

c. Arrangement for guests

d. Sundry uniform services

e. Servicing of departures

Most of the guests reserve their rooms in advance *i.e.*, a few hours to several days/weeks or months before they actually arrive at the hotel. The mode of reservation is in person, by telephone, telegram, telex, by mail, through travel agents or through central reservation system. The reservation of hotel services creates a contractual relationship between the hotel and its guest. This relationship starts at the time each reservation is made and continues until the departure of the guest or till the settlement of accounts after his stay. Advance reservation has two vital aspects: legal aspect and business aspect. It requires an efficient and clean system, which enables room reservations to be converted into room revenue.

On arrival, the guest is asked to register by providing the receptionist with certain particulars about himself. This register is maintained as per the requirement of the law and provides an internal record of guests for data analysis purpose. The allocation of accommodation could be done in advance or on arrival of the guest and immediately the guest account is opened. All the concerned departments such as housekeeping, uniform, telephone, and others are notified on arrival of guests.

The main records of the room sales in the front office are:

1. Reservation form/card
2. Reservation diary/daily arrival lists
3. Reservation chart
4. Hotel register
5. Reception room status board
6. Guest index

There are basically two systems of recording room sales:

1. **Selling by specific number:** In this method rooms are sold and recorded by individual numbers–allocate a specific room number, say 307, at the time the booking is made, even if it is a month or more in advance.

2. **Selling by quantity:** In this case rooms are sold from the density charge–delete a room from the list of total rooms available in the required category. Mark off a specific room from the total of say 50, left to sell.

The second system is most flexible and is practically used by most hotels.

Provision of accommodation facilities is one of the important activities of a hotel. The department looking after these facilities is commonly known as room department or accommodation department. In American-style hotels this consists of the front office, the housekeeping and laundry department, the uniform services, and the security office. The responsibility for the well-being of the guest is delegated to the resident manager/ house manager/room assistant manager, who is head of this department. From arrival to the departure of guests, some employee or the other of this department, is performing direct service for them. These employees need a thorough training as they come into personal contact with the guests.

Some hotels are experimenting with taking housekeeping out of the room division and making it a staff function, with the director of housekeeping reporting directly to the general manager. Some other hotels are combining housekeeping and other property management functions along with maintenance and engineering.

The room/director of room operations carries out the daily routine management task as directed and assigned by the general manager. He may be in charge of one department directly under his control. The sub-departmental heads, which come under his supervision, are executive housekeeper, the executive assistant manager, the front office manager, the telephone operator, garage manager, etc. They are responsible for reservation and registration of the guest, front desk, bell staff, PBX, transportation, concierge, maintenance and cleaning of rooms, providing information on the facilities of the hotel and local point of interest– cultural, recreational and amusement, etc. The resident manager is also responsible for handling guest complaints. He is also the one most in contact with the staff and guests as he moves around the operation and is available in case of queries, emergencies, complaints and special events.

The following forms are designed and printed to suit the requirements of this department:

1. Reservation density chart
2. Reservation and registration card
3. Rooming list
4. Arrival and departure list

General enquiry handled by a Receptionist

5. Writing slips and racks
6. Room cards and key cards
7. Hotel's services directory
8. Room charge advice pads

The jobs of pleasing people commences from the front office. The guests form their first substantial evaluation of the hotel and its property here. It is also a place where the guests come with their problems or complaints.

The main functions of this section are:

1. Process reservations and handling of communications with prospective guests
2. Register guests and assign rooms
3. Make credit arrangements
4. Give information about local shopping and places of tourist interest
5. Arrange miscellaneous guest services

In small hotels receiving guest payments is the function of the front office whereas in large hotels the cashier directly reports to the controller.

The front office is responsible for monitoring and coordinating the front of the house transactions and services. The front desk is the most visible segment of the front office and is located in the high traffic lobby area. The desk is the major source of guest information and is responsible for the maintenance of guest records. The front office is the logical connecting link between the guest and the hotel management.

It is not the building and the interior decor or delicacies served in a hotel alone which make an individual accept the hospitality and comfort, but also, the way in which he is received and the conduct of the staff play an integral part in the choice of a hotel. And this is where the front office staff comes in, because this is the first point of contact when a guest enters the hotel and the one last point of contact on his departure. It is, therefore, imperative on the part of the front staff to go all out to receive every guest with courtesy and induce in him a sense of belonging. His aim should be to make the guest feel at home, even though he is a thousand miles away from home. The front office staff must work like a team and make an all-out effort in achieving the standard of service and efficiency expected.

The front office is primarily responsible for the selling of the rooms. Besides room sales, the front office is also responsible for accepting reservation, registering arrivals, handling keys and mail, dealing with messages, maintaining statistical information and preparing for guests on their departures.

The front office also provides information on the services of the hotel, tourist attractions, travel conditions and also directs bellboys, porters and services to guest rooms. In addition, this office maintains guest accounts and prepares their bills. Many hotels maintain reliable guest history files. The plan and equipment for the smooth working and operations of a front office depend on the size of the hotel and the functions to be performed by this department. In all hotels, small, medium, or large, the equipment should be arranged near a counter or desk of convenient height to enable the incoming/outgoing guest to stand while performing the necessary formalities. The counter should be nicely arranged keeping in view the convenience of the staff and the guest.

The front office desk should be attractive and well designed for the guest to form a good impression. It is generally situated at or near the main entrance of the hotel. It must be spacious to accommodate a large number of guests checking in and should have a nicely furnished lounge close by for the guest to sit and wait while the formalities being dealt with are completed.

The main sources of reservations are:

1. Telephone

2. Mail
3. Telegram
4. Personal contact
5. Travel agencies
6. Hotel representatives
7. Airlines
8. Referrals from other hotels

1. **Manual Reservation:** Many hotels use the manual reservation system, which proves to be time consuming, inconvenient and error prone.
2. **Hotel Clearing Houses:** Under this system the data concerning space available in a city/area is gathered and consolidated. The prospective guests are provided with acceptable alternative accommodations if their first choice is sold out.
3. **Electronic System:** Under this system, in the lobby of each participating hotel there is a display board listing all member properties having vacancies in major cities. When a prospective guest calls a hotel for a room, and the hotel is full, the display board is referred to, for available hotel rooms and the information is passed on to the caller.
4. **Automatic Reservation:** This system is most suitable for hotels, operated by a chain. The customer's choice is limited to the properties comprising the chain. An independent reservation services organization may also offer limited customer service, provided it has data and makes reservations only in subscribing member properties.
5. **Integrated Reservation:** A total travel package could be available through an integrated reservation system. This enables the traveller to make reservations with one telephone call or at one place for hotel tourist accommodations, airline tickets, car rentals, tourist spots and other travel services. Many properties are making progress in evolving this system of reservations.

The internal reservation function is basically concerned with record keeping within the hotel properties to maintain room inventories and offer guest information.

Queuing up during check-in and check-out especially during convention and business meetings is a source of irritation for customers and of frustration to the hotel manager.

Hotels have been trying to eliminate registration and check-out problems by reducing clerical efforts and improving accuracy of information by the introduction of computers. The data input at the time of reservation is retrieved for use when registering the guest when he checks in. At this time an on-line computer guest ledger record is set up which can instantaneously record, room, food, laundry, valet and telephone charges. When the guest checks out, the complete and up-to-the-minute statement is retrieved from the computer.

There are some reputed chains which provide convention guests with a 'VIP check out' form. These guests fill in this form with billing information and leave, along with their room key at the end of their stay in the hotel.

Thus, the front office is primarily responsible to meet guests and to promote the sales of room and other services of the hotel. This includes operating a booking system, answering letter and telephone inquiries and keeping up a chart of rooms. The daily tab and visitors bills are kept up-to-date for settlement.

The vouchers are sent by different service centres of the hotel through pneumatic tubes or by sending staff members to the bill section.

On registration of a guest, a guest account is opened. It will record all charges and credits pertaining to the guest's use of the hotel facilities and services. They include room charges, restaurants, beverages, laundry, and valet, paid out and rebates. All cheques made by different departments to guests are collected and sent to the bill section by name of vouchers.

A guest's departure is the most critical phase of the guest cycle. On receiving the intimation of the guest's imminent check-out from the hotel from the lobby captain or the guest himself, the customer's bill is updated. The bill is presented to the guest for settlement.

Other Functions of the Front Office

Mail received is sent to the respective mail and key rack or in the appropriate box or index. For special mail special records are maintained. The mail is put in the respective pigeonholes of the key and mail rack or sent through the bellboy to the guest room. For the guest yet to arrive, the mail is kept in different sections marked alphabetically. The mail of the guest who has already left the hotel is directed as per the instructions of the mail-forwarding card. A complete record is kept regarding the registered and recorded mail, staff mail, and the mail of concessionaires is also handled by the front office.

All keys are at the key rack and handed over to the guest on arrival or when they are asked for. In certain hotels, a labelled box is maintained and guests are requested to insert the keys in the box when they leave the hotel for a short while.

The purpose of information is to make aware of the various services offered in the hotel such as historical and tourist spots in the city transport agencies and mode of entertainment, shopping centres, etc. The information section is always in a position to attend the various queries and problems from time to time.

In case of full reservation (house full) the prospective guests are given accommodation at other similar type of hotels in the city or in some other part of the region through instant reservation or central reservation system.

The house count, average daily rate, room occupancy report and bed occupancy report originate in the front office department.

Complaints are received from the guests and concerned departments and are informed accordingly. A patient hearing is given to the guests and adequate action taken to satisfy them. Complaints and suggestions of general nature are conveyed to the management and complaints regarding food service and bar service are conveyed to the management through the front office manager.

Services such as arranging and preparing group itinerary, arranging cars on rental basis, providing information about the city, arrangement of tickets for entertainment, booking of air and railway seats, arrangement of bouquet and flowers, helping in mail, changing of foreign currency–is the duty of the front office.

Collection of cash and credit for services rendered by the hotel is most important for the hotel's cash flow, its ability to pay its employees and creditors. The cashier must scrutinize personal cheques and deal with foreign currencies either in cash or in the form of traveller cheques. The settlement through credit cards had made the cashier's function more streamlined but it requires careful attention.

One of the important functions of the liaison department is to have close cooperation and liaison with the departments that provides guest services such as telephone, house-keeping, maintenance and engineering, food and beverage services, accounting, sales and marketing, manager's office and security.

The daily audit is done to ensure that all postings have been made correctly and that all guest accounts are updated. Different reports regarding the average rate, percentage occupancy, departmental revenue and their relationship to forecasts are prepared and sent to the management and departmental heads.

In large hotels, group business accounts for a large volume of sales. These groups may be organized by a member. The travel agent may arrange or initiate the trip. An airline may provide the impetus whereas a hotel may be the moving force. Group business may be classified under the following heads:

1. Conventions
2. Sales meetings, seminars, etc.
3. Incentive travel groups
4. Special interests

Conventions are a big business in itself. There are national, regional and intra-state conventions held annually. Conventions generate not only the direct sales but indirect sales as well compared to the vacation visitor, who spends 24 per cent of his expenditure on hotel rooms and about 4 per cent in hotel restaurants. The convention delegates spend 30 per cent for hotel rooms and 10 per cent in hotel restaurants, plus 5 per cent addition for beverages. It has also been estimated that the overall cost in time and money of attracting 100-200 individual guests is much greater than the cost of signing up one convention with the same number of delegates. Another advantage of convention delegates is that individual travellers are more likely to cancel reservations than convention delegates.

A large amount is spent for such meetings plus trade shows and exhibitions. These meetings may also be concerning training or management development seminars and may last for several days. The number of participants may vary from 10 to 200. Corporate meetings are prime sources of revenue for the hotel.

An increasingly important factor in the travel industry is the incentive travel, where the number of participants may vary from 15 to 6,000. The average duration of the trip may be five days. Holidays abroad are the most popular form of incentive travel.

The likely prospects for special interest groups are:

1. University seminars
2. University workshops
3. Technical meetings
4. Board of directors meetings
5. Sport, hobby groups, skiers, divers, golfers, amateur archaeologists, etc.

The hotel receives a large amount of business from such groups.

The group and convention sale requires long range planning. Handling of group reservation or block reservation, is one of the most important activities of the hotels. In large hotels, reservation for more than twenty-five rooms is confirmed with the knowledge of the front office manager. The reservation section sends the information about group reservation to the following departments:

1. Housekeeping department
2. Maintenance department
3. Food and beverages department
4. Accounts department
5. Bell captain

By analysing the need of the companies and associations whose need and patterns meet the hotel's facilities, and with intelligent staff training

A Lobby decorated for New Year

and a coordinated sales programme, group business could be effectively handled and successfully booked.

A guest may desire to change his room after he has checked into it, for various reasons such as location of the present room not being too sunny, etc. The reception office informs the house-keeping department. A proper procedure is followed for shifting of rooms.

In a small-sized hotel, the front office will usually be under the charge of one or more assistants dealing with all the office work, *i.e.*, correspondence, accommodation chart, guest billing, typing menus, and even deals with the staff wages of the hotel. In large and luxurious hotels, the work is generally divided into separate independent sections:

1. Reservation
2. Reservation of accommodation
3. Reception
4. Letting of accommodation
5. Guest account and cash transactions
6. Inquiry
7. Messages, keys, mails, etc.
8. Billing
9. Bills and departure of guests

In some of the hotels the counter clerk at the cashier's station, also serves as a bill clerk. In many of the hotels, the cashier's office is separated from the rest of the office. There is generally a pass window between the room clerk and the cashier's counter and another at a convenient point for delivery of account cards to the record clerk. In some of the hotels, pneumatic tubes are used for transmitting cheques and vouchers from the operating department to the bill section. The introduction of National Cash Register (NCR) and computerization by some hotels has increased the speed and improved the accuracy of bills, which are most beneficial from hotels as well as guests' point of view. Efforts are made in almost all the hotels to keep the guests' bills posted up to the last minute.

Case Study 703
Front Office

Situation

The front office of a hotel appeared to be over staffed and yet had difficulty in getting work done.

Results of Analysis

Analysis of the jobs of room clerk and cashier showed a large portion of time lost through poor work planning. It was found that too often the room clerk and cashier wished to occupy the same space at the same time. By rearranging the front office and moving the assistant manager and reservation clerk from second-floor office to a space in the lobby near the front office, Rs. 2500/- a week in salaries was eliminated. The reservation clerk or the assistant manager was available to cover relief and help in periods of usual activity. Moreover, the reservation clerk could perform additional duties such as typing of front office accounts and rack supplies.

The front office commands a view of both the main entrance and passengers' elevators. It provides sufficient space in front of the counter for arrival, luggage and counter office. The functioning of this office should not encroach upon comfort and convenience of the visitors. In the medium-sized hotels, front office must be planned in such a way so that the quick response to wide variation of service demanded is possible. The main purpose of the front office is the merchandising of accommodation. There is no other commodity more perishable than that of residential rooms of a hotel. A vacant room costs money. An occupied room makes money. Therefore, maximum revenue must be extracted from the lettable accommodation.

The Front Office Manager (FOM)

The front office manager must have organizing and administrative ability. He must have knowledge of manners, customs, tastes and ways of life of the main tourist generating countries and must have knowledge of the regulations governing foreign exchange transactions, organization of the hotel, hotel accounting, hygiene and safety regulations and relative labour legislation.

As front office management is subject to the requirements of individual hotels, a laid down standard cannot be maintained as regards the qualification of a front office manager. In general, the minimum requirements are to have a reasonable standard of basic education besides the hotel school education and knowledge of English and French, in addition to other foreign languages, is most essential.

Assistant Front Office Manager

In collaboration with and under the supervision of the front office manager, he is responsible for the smooth running of the department. He must have experience, good general education and knowledge of foreign languages. His responsibilities and duties are the same as that of the FOM and he assists him in all daily activities. He replaces the FOM in the latter's absence. He assists the front office manager in hiring, staffing, scheduling and training other front office personnel. He is responsible for monitoring the status of guest accounts and participates in the authorization of cheques, cashing and credit terms within the policy guidelines.

Reservation Manager

The reservation department of a hotel is headed by a reservation manager, who reports to the front office manager. In small and medium-sized hotels, these positions are combined like any other positions.

Reservation Assistants

The number of reservationists vary according to the size of the property. They are responsible for accepting reservations either by telephone or telegrams or telex or through mail. The reservation staff should have knowledge of total capacities of rooms and their break-up into singles, double twins and suites, special rates and discount applicable to groups, business houses, airlines, VIPs, forecasting of room sales, tracing of reservation charts, reservation codes, 'no show' problems, cancellations, deposits and refunds, guest complaints and redressal systems of reservation racks, etc.

Room Clerks/Desk Clerks

The chief clerk reviews the night clerk's report to get an idea of the preceding day's occupancy and the number of vacant rooms available for assignment to new arrivals. He checks the rooms and the total number of projected departures for the day, on the basis of the list submitted by the night clerk or one prepared from the rack slips showing a departure date. The list indicates the room numbers of guests who paid their room rent in advance. The accounts of these guests are already cleared; therefore, they leave the hotel without stopping at the cashier's desk to check-out. The responsibility for checking out these guests rests with the credit manager.

The room clerk must check the reservations of the day. He also notes the approximate date of arrivals, special requirements, deposits, etc. He blocks rooms for some of the expected arrivals by inserting a block out card in the rack on top of the rack card, with the guest's name and approximate time of arrival. The number of the room is noted on the reservation slip.

The room clerk also checks the supplies of registration cards, bills, pens, and other stationery. He checks the time stamp for the current date. The room rack is also checked against the housekeeper's morning report of the preceding night regarding occupied and vacant rooms. Discrepancies should be immediately investigated.

On departure of the guests, the room clerk clears the desk racks and gets the room made up so that they are available for new arrivals. The cashier informs the room clerk about guests' check out by giving the registration cards time stamped to show the actual departure time. The room clerk adjusts the room rack, informs the housekeeper and notifies the telephone operator and information desk. On receiving information from the housekeeper, the room clerk knows that the room is vacant. On room change, the room clerk changes the occupied room in the rack and notifies the housekeeper, cashier, and telephone operator and information clerk.

Another important function of the room clerk is the registration of guests, which varies according to categories he is handling–individual guest and small groups with reservations, walk-ins and group and convention guests.

The reception office is the 'show window' of the hotel. It needs to be well designed and well organized. It is the nerve centre of the hotel and is a contact point between the guest and the hotel.

The key to the reception is the room chart, which shows at a glance the state of the hotel. When a guest arrives and accommodation is allocated, the reception office issues, through a written voucher, all information to the bill office, housekeeper, head porter and the dining room, giving particulars of name, room numbers, rate and proposed period of stay. The bill office on receiving this information opens an account on the bill sheet. The other sections use this for adjustment of their record. The reception office enters all details on the 'arrivals' record and adjusts the housekeeping chart. Departures are notified to the various sections by a similar process.

A filing system giving the history of the visit of every guest is kept in the reception office. In every large establishment, the information is passed on to the record room. Most of the small-sized hotels operate with just two clerks, who perform the work done by reservation clerk, cashiers, bill clerks, telephone operators, mail clerks, record clerks, information clerks etc.

Reception Assistant/Receptionist

A receptionist must have good general education and thorough knowledge of the organization of the hotel, guest billing, posting machines, labour legislation and foreign languages.

While a pleasing personality is an asset, in a reception job, a good standard of education is equally important for a receptionist. There are certain attributes and qualities, which are essential for a good receptionist. An inherent sense of courtesy is the key to success in reception work. He/she should have a genuine desire to do everything possible to make the visitor happy and comfortable. He/she must be courteous with the guest as well as his/her colleagues.

The visitor and person making inquiries should be treated with courtesy and respect. There are many occasions when a receptionist has to refuse a request of the visitor due to hotel's rules. He should do it without offending the guest. It is the manner rather than the word, which welcomes the guest. The well-groomed receptionist who steps forward to greet the visitor in a cultured, well modulated voice with a gracious smile displaying simple courtesy and tact and having a charming personality is a valuable asset for the hotel.

A receptionist needs intelligence and a good knowledge about different hotels, tourist spots and other places of interest. He/she should have the ability and desire to solve other people's problems. In addition, a receptionist must be capable of acting independently and taking decisions.

A receptionist must have the gift of intuition and be able to understand the difference between the various people he/she meets and the most effective method of dealing with each of them.

He must develop a sense of responsibility. He often has to deal with unforeseen situations, which require immediate decisions. He must always remember that his words and actions reflect not only his own but also the attitude of the hotel management.

Information and Mail Clerk

The information and mail clerk is also responsible for the room keys. The guests drop their keys at the desk when they go out and ask for them on their return. This system ensures that they receive their mail since the clerk will give them the keys plus any mail in the box. In addition, the information clerk is also responsible to answer questions regarding the guest rooms and other facilities of the hotel.

Other employees of this department include night clerks, rack clerks, guest history/file clerks, key clerks, typists, telegram clerk, safe deposit clerks, etc.

8. Uniform and Guest Services

Guest service also includes the concierge, uniformed services, garages, attendants and specialized recreational and leisure activities. The bell staff, doormen, garage and parking attendants and other uniformed staff are in many deluxe hotels an integral part of the guest service and thereby the front hall functions.

Servicing arrivals and departures are the most common uniformed services. The meeting and greeting of arriving guests, taking care of their luggage and parking of their cars, and a departing guest's luggage and transportation are the primary responsibility of the uniformed staff.

The income of this department is derived from transfer of baggage and from messenger services in connection with the purchase of rail, road and aeroplane tickets. A record is maintained of the incoming and outgoing baggage, which serve as sales journals, so far as baggage transfer is concerned. The porters come in direct contact with guests and collect the cash. They receive considerable income from the gratuities; guests pay in addition to charges made for the service. Some hotels lease this department. The porters receive nominal salary and keep all service charges. Very few hotels get profit from this department.

The main services provided by uniformed services could be classified as:

1. Servicing arrivals:
   a. Meeting and greeting of arriving guests
   b. Luggage handling
   c. Parking of cars
2. Servicing the stay of guests:
   a. Information about hotel
   b. Locality

Guest registration procedure

   c. Arrangement for their tickets, tours, car hires

3. Other services:
   a. Newspapers
   b. Small articles as per guest's requirements
   c. To act as messengers, lift operator, men's cloakroom attendants
4. In case of night duty:
   a. To provide all services which are provided by other departments during daytime
   b. To receive and register late arrivals
   c. To serve light refreshments
   d. To operate the hotels switch board
   e. To arrange early morning calls
   f. To clean public rooms
   g. To ensure the security of the hotel
5. Servicing departures.

Depending upon the size, type and standard, the provision of uniformed services varies in hotels. The organization of this department is also influenced by the established practices of the hotel. There are hotels, where information services to guests may be provided by the reception office or uniformed services or both. Similarly, cleanliness of public rooms may be assigned to housekeeping, uniformed services or outside contractors.

In large sized hotels there are many aspects of work, which can be classed as 'general service'. This classification will include:

1. Pages
2. Doormen
3. Porters
4. Parcel clerks
5. Cloakroom attendant
6. Information clerks
7. Bellmen
8. Elevator operators
9. Night porters
10. Hall porters, etc.

The classification of employees of this section may be grouped as follows:

1. Service front:
   a. Lobby manager/superintendents of service
   b. Assistants
   c. Bell captain
   d. Bellmen
   e. Pages
2. Service elevators:
   a. Elevator attendants
   b. Escalator attendants
3. Service floors:
   a. Floor clerks
   b. Pages
   c. Employees taking control of lost and found
4. Service doormen:
   a. Doormen
   b. Service package room
   c. Package room clerks
   d. Package room messengers
   e. Baggage porters, etc.
5. Miscellaneous services:
   a. Librarian
   b. Shopping guides
   c. Lobby receptionists

All these jobs are grouped under the single term 'uniform staff' and their classification often differs since the system varies according to the size and type of hotel in question. Most of the employees associated with this department are usually persons not necessarily possessing any particular skill but have a pleasing personality and a sense of service. To perform most of these tasks the individual should be physically strong. A high educational qualification is not essential. However, this department comes into direct contact with guests, very often an active, alert and courteous department can contribute a lot towards the hotel's prestige and impression. Willingness, helpfulness, courtesy and smartness are some of the first and foremost qualities demanded of all uniformed staff from head hall porter to the most junior pages.

In most of the large-sized hotels the uniform staff comes directly under the hall porter. In smaller hotels the employees in this department are fewer in number as many of the details of these services are performed personally by the hall porter.

The lobby is an area located immediately upon entry into the hotel building. It is furnished with seating arrangements and is a meeting place common to all hotel guests. Being the first and the last area of contact of a guest with the hotel, the management makes the lobby attractive and convenient. The lobby desk, like the front desk, is situated in the lobby and is the point of all coordination between guest and hotel services.

The main functions of this department are:

1. To guide the guest to the reception area for registration
2. To carry the guests' luggage
3. To look after the guests' cars
4. To attend the guests' personal jobs

Lobby Manager

He is in charge of the entire lobby area and represents the management at all times. He supervises a team of senior and junior bell captains and bell boys. Knowledge of one foreign language is essential apart from English. The lobby manager coordinates the front offices with housekeeping, food and beverage, engineering, security, telephones, stores, etc. He might be required to meet the guests at the airport or at the railway station and escort them to the hotel. In the night the lobby manager is known as 'Night Manager' and is directly in charge of the whole hotel. He is a problem solver and has the authority to handle all guest grievances. His work in the night is to check the entry of unauthorized persons. He also deals with all the unusual events, which take place at night in the hotel. He is not a part of the front office staff, yet he must be included in reception area. He is stationed in the lobby area near the front office and he supervises the staff.

He should be well qualified, mature, experienced and diplomatic. Knowledge of hotel rules is very essential to be able to effectively deal with guest problems.

Senior Bell Captain/Head Hall Porter

In most of the medium-sized hotels, the head hall porter is responsible for the uniformed staff. As he has a very responsible job, he is one of the departmental managers in the hotel. He is constantly dealing with the hotel's patrons and must know the daily general movement and activities in the hotel. He must be well informed about the arrival and departures of all transport systems liable to effect guest movements and should have a good knowledge of local affairs and entertainment. In large-sized hotels he looks after the enquiry department and often acts as a medium through which guests avail of tourist trips, and obtain information about entertainment, shopping centres, names and localities of various medical services, secretarial and employment agencies, and other places of interest.

The head hall porter must have knowledge of foreign languages of customers of the main tourist generating centres. He should have good knowledge of the town and its surrounding area, topography, transport, excursions, entertainment, shops, etc. Knowledge of labour legislation, hygiene and safety standards is also essential. He should also be able to organize, conduct and supervise the training of the staff.

Bell Captain

He is directly responsible to the lobby manager. He organizes the duties of bell boys and other staff members under him and ensures that the standard service of the hotel is maintained efficiently. He keeps the records of the staff for the purpose of control and the preparation of bills. The primary goal of the bell captain is to obtain economy of operation and time, maximization of output with minimum of input and maintain the goodwill of the hotel. The left luggage room where all luggages left by the guests are kept also comes under the direct control of the bell captain.

He makes sure that new staff members in the department are well conversant with the room tariff, condition, services, etc. laid down by the management. Some bell captains supply newspapers and postage material to the guests, which calls for his full knowledge of the postal regulations of the country. He maintains a departure sheet/register and informs the housekeeping department about any departures, which have taken place.

A bell captain should have good manners and a good personality; he should be intelligent, honest and fully conversant with current affairs and must have full knowledge of the different hotel services and facilities. In addition, he should know at least one foreign language apart from English.

Hall Porter

He should have knowledge of the town and its surrounding areas. The porter must also know about basic principles of accounting, foreign exchange transactions, legislation and police regulations concerning tourists, hygiene and safety regulations and labour legislations. He must also have knowledge of the activities of the other departments and their relation to the uniformed department.

Night Porter

The night porter is required to have knowledge of all the departments of the hotel. He is the sole representative of the hotel on duty during his hours of work. He has to handle all eventualities. For example, if needed he will call a doctor, police or the fire brigade. He performs the duties of the head hall porter, receives orders from the porter and is responsible for early calls to guests. He provides drinks or snacks requested during his hours of work. He also carries out, if necessary, inspections and reports every morning on anything that might have happened during the night in the hotel.

He patrols the hotel building periodically during the night. Guests requiring early morning calls generally place orders with the night porter. The room number, time and order are recorded in a book/sheet. A copy of it is sent to the chambermaid/floor services. The duties and responsibilities of the night porter are increased in hotels, where there is no night manager. In large-sized hotels due to heavy work during night, additional night staff is employed which is headed by a head night porter.

Lobby Porter

These are found in very large convention hotels. In other hotels this function is performed by a porter of the housekeeping staff. The lobby porter is responsible for the general appearance of the lobby during the day. He/she picks up loose papers or other debris from the floor, cleans the ashtrays, mops up spills, etc. As the lobby is the area from which visitors and other guests gain their first and perhaps lasting impression of the hotel, the lobby porter's job of maintaining cleanliness of the lobby becomes all the more important.

Package Room Clerk

On receipt of packages, the clerk logs it in a book called 'logbook'. The logbook contains columns for the guest's name and room number, name of the sender, number of packages and a space for the bellman's signature. The guest is notified about the arrival of packages and these are delivered to him through the bellman. The clerk is also responsible to pack and mail anything the guest wishes to send.

Doorman

The first hotel employee who meets the guests at the hotel gate is the doorman. His place of duty is outside the main entrance of the hotel. He greets all guests who arrive by cars or taxis and ensures that their luggage is taken into the hotel. A smile and a pleasant greeting makes the guests feel welcome. During the stay of the guest, the doorman assists the guest in obtaining taxis, helps him in and out of the cars, gives directions to restaurants. When the guest checks out and leaves by car or cab, the doorman helps to load the baggage and thus becomes the last employee to see him off.

Case Study 804
Doorman

Situation

Management of hotel which has two entrances, stationed a doorman at the main entrance and believed it necessary to station a doorman at the other entrance (annex entrance) at least part-time.

Results of Analysis

An analysis showed that guest traffic was negligible at the annex entrance and that the entrance was used mainly for lucheon guests. The part-time service of a doorman at the annex entrance appeared to do more harm than good, since the guests find it was inconsistant. Doorman service at this entrance was discontinued with a saving of about Rs. 20,000/- per year.

The doorman is also responsible for cleanliness and order at the front door of the front entrance to the hotel. He wears a typical uniform, which varies, from hotel to hotel. He is responsible for calling the cars and taxis, for which purpose he uses a loud speaker and microphone. He is also responsible to see that only authorized members enter by the main entrance and other staff members use the staff entrance.

Luggage Porter

He unloads the luggage from the vehicle by which the guest arrives to the hotel and brings it to the lobby. Before taking it to the lobby, the luggage porter should take approval of the customer that all luggage has been taken out and is in proper order. It is his duty to see that it is delivered to the guest's room as promptly as possible. His responsibility increases, when the guest is ready to leave the hotel. It is the luggage porter who collects the cases from the room and brings them down to lobby or the porter lodge, and retains these with him until he receives a luggage pass. He calls the car/taxi and places the luggage inside. It is his duty to ensure that a record is kept of the entire luggage passing through the luggage room at the

Case Study 805
Bell Desk

Situation

With a problem of morning and evening rush hours, management of a medium sized hotel considered it necessary to schedule passenger elevators at practically all times except during the midnight shift.

Results of Analysis

By computing the relationship between passenger traffic demands and potential round trips per hour, it was determined that two elevators could handle the passenger traffic. However, it was necessary at times in the evening periods to detain "up" cars two to four seconds at the ground floor to avoid dispatching sparsely filled elevators. This delay was unimportant to passengers already loaded and saved considerable waiting time on the part of guests coming into the lobby. By eliminating one car, Rs. 25,000/- per year in operators salaries was saved without impairing guest service.

Case Study 806
Bell Desk

Situation

Service elevators in a hotel could not meet traffic demands at the relief and meal periods of the operators and it was found necessary to employ a relief operator.

Results of Analysis

Department heads were included in scheduling of their staff to eliminate unnecessary travel. The cars could then be shut down alternatively for short periods to provide for relief time for elevators during lull periods. Tremendous waste of time of the staff in waiting for elevators was substantially eliminated. The relief operator saving was Rs. 36,000/- per year.

Case Study 807
Bell Desk

Situation

It was believed necessary in a certain hotel to employ three bellboys during the morning watch. One spent 1½ hours of the morning in picking up the mail at the post office and doing duties other then bell hopping.

Results of Analysis

It was found that the man who relieved the elevator operator had a lull of almost two hours at approximately mail time. He was assigned the job of picking up the mail and doing the other extra tasks of the third bell boy. The third bell boy was not needed and Rs. 36,000/- was saved in payroll costs per year.

time of departure and the name of the member who handles it. In some hotels, he is responsible for the collection of keys at the time of departure from customers.

Linkman

He supervises the arrival and departure of vehicles. He keeps track of the guest with their luggage and summons cars and taxis when requested by guests. He also supervises the entire incoming and outgoing luggage. He opens doors of cars and taxis and escorts the arriving guest into the hotel.

Lift Operator

He operates the lift and helps the guests in and out of the lift. He is responsible for the cleanliness of the lift but not for the service and maintenance of machinery, which must be done frequently by the lift engineer. No unauthorized person should be allowed to operate the lift and the lift operator should never leave it unattended. He should make the lift unoperative before going away. No overloading should be allowed. He should be able to answer in a polite manner all the questions asked by the guests and should be able to guide the guest on each floor. Most of the modern hotels are equipped with self-service elevators. Elevator operators are found only in old hotels or in case of VIP guests the lift operator may be used.

Cloakroom Attendants

Gents cloakrooms come under the responsibility of the hall porter, whereas the ladies cloakroom is under the housekeeping department. Guest cloakroom attendants look after the hats, coats, overcoats, umbrella, briefcases, etc. of guests. The attendant should see that sufficient supply of hand towels, soaps and other toilet articles for the customer's use are available in the cloakroom always. He is also responsible for the cleanliness and upkeep of the place.

Courier

He is assigned the regular external duties, which involve going out of the hotel for delivering of messages, parcels, etc. Sometimes he is assigned the job of receiving guests at the airport.

Valet

His duties are to pack or unpack the suitcases when the guest is leaving or changing the room. He helps the guest in putting on dress, looks after the ironing of the clothes, and polishing the shoes.

Bellmen

After the registration procedure has been completed and the guest has been assigned the room, the bellmen carry the guest's baggage and take it to his room. On the way to the room, a well-trained and experienced bellman can sense the guest's mood and carry on a conversation explaining the facilities available in the hotel. On reaching the room, the bellman should show and check for the guest the different types of facilities like TV, thermostat, bathrooms, the ashtrays, waste paper baskets, closets and all e' ctrical equipment, etc. Any disorder or malfunctioning of equipment in the room should be immediately brought to the notice of the housekeeper.

During the stay of the guest in the hotel, the bellman provides service in various ways which mostly depend on the policy of the management–delivery of messages and packages, taking orders for cocktails, snacks and beverages from the bar and delivering them in the room, when room service is closed. Some hotels permit the bellman to buy food and beverages from outside for the guest when the hotel's outlets are closed. When the guests check out, the bellman carries down their luggage.

Pageboy

The pageboy is known as 'groom'. He is a young boy and is available near the reception counter. He is always at the disposal of the guest. In case the bellboy is not in the hotel, it is the duty of the pageboy to guide the visitors to their rooms and explain in short the different facilities provided by the hotel. In the corridors, he should walk along with the guest keeping to the right. In case he does not have the information, he should politely tell the guest to contact the reception office. Sometimes due to heavy rush, he may be required to do the job of the luggage porter and valet.

His main job is to deliver messages, letters, telegrams, etc., to guests or to run errands for them. To call a guest to the telephone or to meet a visitor, a pageboy goes through the public rooms, calling quietly the name of the guest. If the guest cannot be found in the lounges, he enters the restaurants and takes permission to page. Thus, he is responsible for paging.

Chauffeur

A driving licence is a must for a chauffeur. He should have mechanical ability to keep the vehicle in his care in good repair. His main duty is to drive the hotel's vehicle–car/bus. He should be a reliable person with a sense of responsibility. He comes under the control of the lobby manager.

Enquiry Clerk

He is required to answer the queries made by guests. His office is equipped with various reference books, which includes: street maps, road maps, telephone directories, post office guides, international hotel guides as well as guides to local theatre, cinema, and other entertainment guides. All mail delivered at the hotel is sorted. The business mail is sent to the manager's office and the guest's mail is sorted, room numbers are written on each. They are then placed in the 'pigeon holes' of the key racks, so that the guest receives his letter when he hands in or collects his keys. Any mail received for guests due to arrive is kept in a file in alphabetical order and necessary note is made in the hotel's diary. Guests who have already left, their mail is readdressed as per the forwarding address and details of redirections, are noted, in the mail-forwarding book.

In case a guest wishes to send a telegram, cable, parcel or letter, the enquiry clerk can deal with this for him. Amount of money is paid out by the enquiry clerk on behalf of guests and is charged to the guest's account on the Visitors' Tabular Ledger (VTL) by means of a Visitors' Paid Out (VPO) cheque. All payouts are reimbursed to the enquiry clerk. The enquiry clerk is also responsible for the safe custody and issue of room keys to the guests.

Control in Staff Manager's Office

The ramifications of the staff manager's office vary considerably in the hotel, and food and beverage trade. It is of course only the large hotels who have advanced the importance of the staff manager beyond that of a wages clerk and in some establishments the rank is merely equivalent to that of a superior basement porters' but where large number of personnel are involved the post calls for a high managerial sense and organizing ability.

Engagement of Staff

It rarely happens that the influence of the staff office covers more than the engagement of the ordinary rank and file and its function is usually limited to the recruitment of staff on requests from the various departments. When a department indicates staff requirements, the staff manager refers to the file of applications or contacts the local employment exchange and conducts the initial interview. Suitable applications are referred to the head of the appropriate department for final interview and engagement.

In most other industries, the qualifications of a 'tradesman' are defined by the trade union, but this practice has not advanced to any appreciable extent in the hotel and catering trade and is unlikely to do so. Promotion within this industry rests more with ability, opportunity and sometimes, self-assertion, than grading by a trade organization.

Hotel staff is a restless breed and the industry has a higher percentage of transients than any other. Tracing the history of the average employees can be very interesting and also bewildering. It can include employment as a cook, waiter, porter, barman, manager, secretary, and dishwasher and so on ad infinitum.

References are more often than not valueless as a guide. Usually, they play on one theme: the extreme grief of the former employer in having been deprived of the services of such an efficient, industrious, honest, sober and perfect paragon of an employee.

It is the duty of the staff manager to sift the chaff of oral and written verbiage in order to extract the grain of information needed before passing applicant to the ultimate level for engagement. It is reasonable to assume that the head of a department because of practice and experience in his particular sphere is in a better position to judge the suitability of an applicant.

Staff Records

These are compiled and filed in the staff manager's office. The normal form contains information in respect of date of engagement, period of service; rate of pay; position held; reason for termination and other information which the system requires. Copies of previous references are also filed.

On engagement of an applicant, a form giving the following particulars is filed in: name and address; health certificate; date of engagement; position; rate of pay; hours of service; previous employers. The head of the department signs this form, and a copy is sent to the staff office.

Each department makes up wage books or lists as follows: name of employee; gross amount due; deduction; net amount payable. This is signed by the department and sent to the staff office.

The account office extracts the following totals from each book: gross wage total; net wages payable. These are listed into a summary. Cheques are then drawn to staff manager for cashing and distribution to departments. Wage books and cash are collected from the staff office by each department for payment of wages within the departments.

The staff office usually pays porters, pageboys, cleaners, house staff, floor waiters, and sundry workers, etc., those who are not closely knit into self-contained units, directly. Wages for extra staff for odd duties of a few hours can be paid from the staff manager's float; or if this is not available from main cash by voucher signed by the head of the department. Some departments (where the incidence of extra staff is frequent and involves large numbers), are provided with a cash float for such wage paymen: . The foregoing is a review of a fairly common pattern in the industry. Details can vary to a great extent.

Accident Register

This is kept in the staff manager's office and records the history of all accidents to personnel. As it is compulsory by law to keep this posted to date, it is advisable for the control to add this to their schedules, to assure that it is being done.

Control

Auditing the work of the staff office and its connection with various departments could occupy a lot of time, and still have little meaning in the control sense.

The staff office is closely linked with the accounts office and as the latter section is audited by the company's auditors and its schedules are beyond the province of the controller, apart from the purpose of reference, the main concern of the control is to carry out specified checking as indicated by the company's secretary or auditors.

It is usual, where the main books of the company are concerned, for the secretary to point out the limits of control. Whether this is good practice or otherwise depends a lot on circumstances. Important defaults are often not exposed because of limitations imposed on the controller.

The normal schedules include:

1. **Checking Staff Office Float:** No specified times are, or should be, set for this audit. The float in the staff office of a large establishment, although reimbursed weekly by the accounts office, needs very careful checking because of the amount of 'play' on it *i.e.*, unpaid wages, payments to casual or extra staff, interim payments to employees who have terminated service, etc.

   Before checking the staff office float, it is always advisable to refer to the last records in the accounts office and to pick out and check all subsequent entries in the staff office records. The number of transient and interim payments are always weak points from an audit point of view when dealing with staff office floats in busy establishments. Unless records are posted to the minute in their schedule categories the feeling can persist that the balance finally determined is incorrect. It is the experience of those who undertake this form of audit, that quite often and after an intensive and well-planned check, items will come into focus which 'schedules of audit' have failed to reveal. To arrive at a total for 'unpaid wages' means extracting the entries in the wage books for which there is no signature.

2. **Checking Time Cards:** It is usual to compare the time cards with the staff office record. The check here takes the form of comparing number and name on the card with the corresponding entry in the wage book. Verify that 'time stampings' on cards are current.

9. Housekeeping

The housekeeping operation has the main task of keeping the hotel rooms and public areas clean and attractive. Scientific housekeeping demands employment of the most effective cleaning material and procedures, attention to purchasing of the most suitable items and cleaning supplies, decorating area of maintenance, and proper organization and supervision. Since the housekeeping budget accounts for nearly 20 per cent of total operating expenses, it is one of the most vital and interesting departments in many aspects.

The work of a housekeeping department in a hotel varies considerably according to the type and size of the hotel. This department in large hotels is headed by an Executive Housekeeper, who is one of the busiest and most important departmental heads. He is assisted by a Deputy Housekeeper who will probably have under him an assistant housekeeper, responsible for the work of chambermaids, cleaners, house-porters, linen maids, linen porters, office assistants, ladies cloakroom attendants, window washers, furniture polisher and seamstress. Also directly under the deputy housekeeper will come linen keeper, linen maids and a florist who have one or more assistants. Besides, there may be house porters or housemen, who work under the housekeeper and are usually responsible for the heavier work such as moving heavy furniture. This department is responsible for all the rooms and public areas of the hotel.

In small hotels the number of people working under the head housekeeper may be few and in

A Suite

Replenishment and amenities of bathroom supplies

some, there may be only one housekeeper, whilst in some other cases the job of housekeeper may even be combined with that of receptionist and even be integrated with both management and reception. The housekeeper not only handles all the supervisory duties but also helps in the actual work. He is responsible for maintaining the inventory of linens, bedding, furniture, furnishing, accessories and cleaning materials.

Today's Executive Housekeeper must have some knowledge of chemistry (cleaning agents and their uses), bacteriology (sanitation), interior decoration and textiles. A flair for colour selection and interior decoration is ideal.

The exact outline of the hotel housekeeping activities and function will decide the organizational approach to be adopted. In some hotels, a number of functions are integrated within this department, whereas in others, these works/functions are assigned to different departments, largely on the basis of physical areas. In addition, many hotels have a practice of buying from outside suppliers rather than operating them directly.

The Executive Housekeeper also investigates periodic storing, cleaning or redecoration, which is found to be necessary. He/she maintains exact records showing when any given area was last decorated and where it is next scheduled for decoration. Depending upon the seasonal fluctuations of the hotel, she sets aside certain areas for thorough cleaning at different times of the year.

The different areas which come under the direct supervision of the Executive Housekeeper are:

a. Guest rooms
b. Halls and corridors
c. Lobbies
d. Public areas
e. Offices
f. Stairways/cases
g. Windows
h. Stores and other leased areas

In large hotels, laundry, lost and found articles, repairs and other maintenance functions come under the jurisdiction of the executive housekeeper. The important functions of a housekeeping department are grouped as:

1. Cleaning and maintenance
2. Supplies and equipment
3. Training of personnel
4. Preparation of schedules and reports
5. Other functions:
   a. Flowers and floral decorations and arrangement
   b. Attending to complaints and requests of guests
   c. Attending to lost property
   d. First aid to guests and staff.

The housekeeping department ensures that the amenities and bedrooms used by guests are maintained at a high standard. It has to work most closely with the front office. The housekeeping department must be informed as soon as guests' check out and in-turn must notify the front office immediately when a vacated room is ready for occupancy. The housekeeping office notifies floor housekeepers of all vacated rooms and the floor housekeeper informs the executive housekeeping officer as soon as rooms are cleaned and inspected for re-letting.

The headquarters of the housekeeping department is the linen room. This office is under the charge of linen room supervisor/linen keeper. All orders and requests, pertaining to housekeeping, pass through the linen rooms. The cleaning of the corridors, halls and lounges, the making up of apartments are done according to a strict timetable. The executive housekeeper is in direct contact with the heads of other departments in the hotel, especially with the reception department, regarding the number of rooms required, arrivals and departures, rooms closed for cleaning and other matters of mutual interest. He has to cooperate with the maintenance and restaurant departments also.

Cleaning and maintenance of the areas under its supervision is the primary function of the housekeeping department. The guest rooms require cleaning, changing of the linen, and making up the beds which is done by the maids. The daymaids clean the guest rooms and the housemen thoroughly clean bathrooms, wash the tiles, and floor fixtures. The nightmaids service the room in case of late checkouts and if called for extra supplies or other requests by the guests. The maid gives the bathrooms a daily light cleaning, particularly the tubs, wall and fixtures, and a thorough cleaning is done periodically by the housemen.

Each maid is given a cart to carry her supplies. These carts are kept in front of the door of the room in which the maid is working with the maid's card on the door handle. Each morning these carts are cleaned before being equipped with linen and other supplies. These carts and supplies are kept under the charge of maids closet on every floor. The floor closet contains sheets, pillow cases, bath towels, wash cloths, bath mats, reserve mattress pads, bedspreads, blankets and shower curtains to replace what has been stained, soiled or damaged. Other items required for equipping the hotel are: glasses, toilet tissues, facial tissues, shoe shine cloth, soaps, ashtrays, matches, guest stationery, envelopes, post cards, pens, telephones, memo pads, laundry lists, guest laundry bags, room service memos, do not disturb card, and clothes hangers.

Room attendants are issued room trolleys and a basic set of work tools. Each trolley contains some basic items, which are required by the room attendants for setting the rooms before they are re-let.

The maid is required to inspect each room in her section for vacancies in the morning and afternoon, and prepare a room report. A good housekeeping procedure requires that a check-out be served first unless a guest requires early service.

Housemen give each room a general cleaning periodically *i.e.*, the period depends upon the hotel's policy. It involves a thorough cleaning of the room and everything in it. It includes high wall dusting, cleaning the tiles in the bathroom, washing pictures and vacuuming the drapes, blinds, sofas, cushions and mattresses as well as the carpets. Housemen also carry furniture to and from the storeroom and from one guest room to another. They also help in setting up a banquet room for dinners, dances, meetings, etc. and strip the room after the function in over.

The number of employees working in the housekeeping department varies from hotel to hotel. Numerically, this department has more unskilled workers (maids, porters, cleaners, housemen, wall washer, etc.) than any other department in the hotel. All of them are in direct contact with the guest, therefore, their arises a major need for training these employees in their duties and their relationship with each other, with staff members in other departments and with the guests.

Supplies and equipment includes the requisitioning, storage and control of the many operating supplies required for the daily routine of the department. The items in the guest rooms need replacement each day to maintain the standard set by the management. The maids and housemen need adequate supplies and proper equipment to clean and service the guest rooms, corridors and other public areas. Storeroom clerks should be instructed to record any item that falls below the needs of the operation. Effective control of the equipment should also be set up and maintained.

All guest supplies should be properly placed in each room. The items of guest supplies in each room are listed below:

1. Bedroom doors:
   a. Fire notice/room rate card
   b. Two breakfast order cards
   c. One 'Do Not Disturb' card
2. Dressing table top:
   a. One comment card
   b. One hotel service directory
   c. One room service menu
   d. One ashtray and match box
3. Dressing table drawer:
   a. The stationery kit containing 4 sheets of papers, 2 envelopes, 2 post cards
   b. Two shoe shine cloths
   c. One laundry list/dry-cleaning list
   d. One room service menu
   e. One mending kit
4. Wardrobe:
   a. Twelve coat hangers with bar
   b. Two laundry bags
5. Bedside unit:
   a. One ashtray
   b. Telephone
   c. Note pad and ball pen
   d. One restaurant card or other promotional material
6. Luggage racks: two
7. Wash basin counter:
   a. One box cleaning tissues
   b. Two toilet rolls (one in holder/one reserve)

c. One bath soap in bath soap holder.
d. Two bath soaps on the basin
e. Two glasses in cling wrap
f. Ashtray
g. Waste bin under basin
h. Two sanitary bags

8. For twin rooms:
   a. Two bath towels
   b. Two hand towels
   c. Face towels
   d. One bath mat
9. For single rooms:
   a. One bath towel
   b. One hand towel
   c. One face towel
   d. One bath mat

Record keeping for the control of payrolls is voluminous and important in this department. On the basis of monthly forecast of occupancy made by the front office, the housekeeping estimates the number of maids needed on any particular day and schedule them accordingly. The two departments constantly report the status of guest rooms to each other. The room clerk reports when a guest checks out and housekeeping reports back as soon as the room has been serviced and is in order and can be resold. Permanent assignment of rooms cannot be made as it depends upon the number of rooms to be serviced each day, out-of-order rooms, vacant rooms, and sleep-outs. It is advisable to assign all the rooms on the same floor to the maid, in order to save time.

The actual assignment of rooms is made by each floor housekeeper on the basis of the current status of room, which is obtained from the maids 'moving' report. Before the start of work, each maid checks the rooms assigned to her and reports the status to the housekeeper. The housekeeper's report is made on a simple preprinted sheet listing the room numbers by section or floor with a space for the code. The length of the housekeeper's report depends on the size of the hotel. It ranges from a single sheet, listing every room in the hotel to separate sheets for each floor. It is usually prepared in duplicate. The original of the morning report is also sent to the accounts department where it is used to check the preceding night's room income. A similar report is also prepared each noon, before the end of a daymaid's shift. In this case the original is sent to the front office where it is used to check the room rack. Copies of all such reports are retained by the housekeeper. In hotels where the housekeeper's report is prepared in triplicate or in quadruplicate, one copy each is sent to the front office, accounts department and the credit departments. A housekeeper's discrepancy report is also prepared which is signed by the reception and night auditor.

The maid's room report provides better control for the housekeeper. At the end of each shift the maid enters the required information and the housekeeper summarizes, signs and forwards the report to the housekeeping payroll clerk, who uses it in preparing the link sheet. This report is sometimes used as the source for preparation of the payroll.

The nightmaid report prepared by the nightmaids correspond directly to guest's requests. The report prepared by the nightmaids range from a simple entry in a logbook of every call received from a guest and the action taken to a very detailed and elaborate nightmaid's report. It is prepared with multiple copies; one copy is dropped off at the front desk so that the room clerk on duty can make a final check of the room rack.

A number of other forms are prepared by the housekeeping staff to meet the requirements of management or the desires of the housekeepers, like:

1. Signature sheets for pass keys issued daily to maids
2. Housemen's daily room assignment sheets for general cleaning and miscellaneous duties
3. Housemen's work order
4. Maids' assignment sheets
5. Overall schedules for the department
6. Time sheets
7. Weekly forecast of payrolls

In addition to purchasing carpets with due regard to quality and standard, carpeting requires a planned maintenance programme in hotels, such as:

1. Daily light vacuuming to remove loose surface dirt, prevent soil build and avoid permanent staining.
2. Carpets should be thoroughly cleaned every week with particular attention to high traffic areas and even those rooms that are infrequently used.
3. Seasonal cleaning with wet shampoo at least once a year. While this can be done with the carpets in place, if practicable, the carpets can be picked up and processed in a commercial cleaning plant.
4. Finally, periodic maintenance includes attention to permanently stained areas of carpets and such mechanical problems as loose ends, snags, etc.

Uncarpeted floor areas are in infinite variety in a hotel with many types of coverings and masonry. Each of these areas demand a different kind of maintenance. Special detailed instructions for maintaining them are required.

Whether to rent or buy–is a subject of continuous debate. Linen can be a major investment and the choice of this product is not easy. Small hotels generally decide to rent linen if the rental service is both reasonable and dependable. The increasing demand of particularly non-iron linens and uniforms goes in favour of owning linens in hotels.

Executive Housekeeper

The person in charge of housekeeping may have any of the titles such as executive housekeeper, housekeeper, housekeeping manager, director of services, director of internal service or director of housekeeping operations.

The Executive Housekeeper is in charge of the housekeeping department. He/she requires organizational and administrative talents and artistic sense, knowledge of laundry work, ironing and mending various fabrics; knowledge of their composition and how to maintain them are essential for an executive housekeeper. In addition, basic knowledge of child care and nursing, first aid, a good knowledge of hygiene, and safety standards relevant to the job, and some idea about labour legislation is also required. The Executive Housekeeper is also responsible for organizing and supervising the training programmes for housekeeping staff. He/she discusses complete direction-operational control, and supervision of the house-keeping, laundry and recreation departments.

Deputy Housekeeper/Housekeeping Manager

The responsibility of the Deputy Housekeeper involves the daily supervision of specific areas within the hotel. In the large hotels, his/her work is supervision and control of room, maintenance, operations of bedroom floors. In the absence of the Executive Housekeeper, he/she assumes the responsibility for the general administration of this department. He/she should have knowledge of laundry work, ironing and mending of fabrics, their composition and their maintenance. Like the

Case Study 908
Housekeeping

Situation

In one hotel each maid's daily quota of rooms to be cleaned was sixteen. A check on the maid's performance showed an average of about thirteen rooms cleaned per day. Extra payments had to be made for rooms cleaned above thirteen.

Results of Analysis

A study showed that 20 per cent of maids' working time was spent in getting linen from the linen room. This was caused by linen shortage which did not allow proper stocking of the floor linen closets. A stock system of stocking linen and other supplies was installed for floor closets. The maids were then able to report to their floors and to work uninterrupted. Maids were able to do their quota of 16 rooms and extra room payments were eliminated. Guests complaints subsided. Wear and tear on the service elevator was reduced and the hotel saved 10 per cent of housekeeping payroll.

Executive Housekeeper, an assistant housekeeper must have basic knowledge of child care and nursing, first aid, hygiene and safety standards and regulation, labour legislations and ability to train the housekeeping staff.

Floor Housekeepers/Floor Supervisors/ Inspectors

Floor housekeepers are finally responsible for the condition of the guest rooms. Each floor housekeeper is assigned three or more floors. She gives the maids their room assignment and floor master keys, which are returned at the end of each day. She supervises checks and approves the maid's work and makes periodical inspections of the physical conditions of all rooms on her floor. Any damage reported by maids or that is discovered is referred to the executive housekeeper for passing on to the chief engineer for appropriate action. For decorating and refurnishing of the rooms, requests are made to top management. The floor housekeeper supervises the redecorations, chooses the colour of the paints, upholstery, etc. Close cooperation and coordination between the engineer and the housekeeper is required to keep to a minimum the amount of time that the room is out of order.

Thus, the floor housekeeper must know the rooms to be handled, coordinate with the front office and housekeeping desk and laundry. He/ she must be familiar with fire prevention and security system of floors, maintenance order procedures, lost and found procedures.

Chambermaids/Room Maids/Housemen/ Room Attendant

He/she requires good knowledge of the methods of cleaning and care of rooms and furniture. Knowledge of hygiene and safety standards and labour legislation relevant to the work is also essential. The main jobs they undertake are the servicing of the rooms and private rooms. They are each allotted a number of rooms, called sections.

Daily Cleaners/Corridor Maids

They are responsible for the cleaning and maintenance of corridors, staircases, and cloakrooms, public rooms, corridors, halls, public bathrooms and the toilets and the various offices of the hotel. Her/his influence also extends to all areas of residential accommodation for staff.

Floor Porter/House Porter

The number of house porters depends on the size of the hotel and the amount of work to be done. All heavy work such as the moving of furniture or heavy linen baskets is done by the house porter. He is directly responsible to the head housekeeper.

Others

It includes head housemen, sanitors, furniture polishers, polishers, paint cleaners, shademen, wall washers, vacuum cleaners, elevator cleaners, lobby housemen or porters, street cleaners, yardmen, carpet cleaners, shampooers, floor polishers, drapery hangers, curtain hangers.

Double Room

Deluxe Room

Deluxe Suite

Monument Facing Room

Sitting Area of a Suite Room

Coffee Shop

Open Restaurant

Horticulture

Lawn

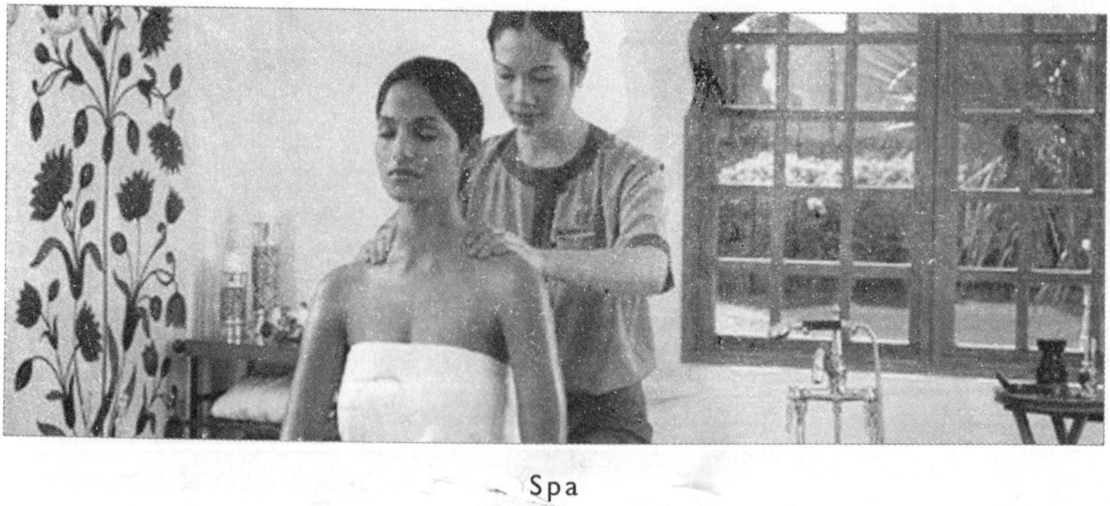

Spa

10. Linen and Uniforms

The linen and uniform room is the heart of the housekeeping department. Like storerooms for reserve linen, cleaning materials and other supplies, the linen and uniform room is adjacent to the executive housekeeper's office. All articles are received and issued by linen room uniform personnel. Each day the linen room person counts and sorts the soiled linen and prepares it for the laundry. The night person counts and distributes the clean linen and all supplies to the maid's storerooms on each floor. Overstocking and under-stocking both are deterimental to the hotel.

Linen inventory control and laundering is the responsibility of the housekeeper. All operating par stock must be maintained. It is ideally five times the daily amount in use as determined by the number of beds and bathrooms in the hotel. This makes sufficient arrangement for one set in the rooms and one each in the laundry, the maids' floor closet and the linen room and in transit.

Circulating par stock for restaurant linens is more difficult to set up and maintain. Compared to the dining room, the banquet poses the real problem. Control of the reserve linen is very important. The storeroom must be properly and securely locked with access given to only authorized personnel. No item must be removed without a requisition approved by the housekeeper and a perpetual inventory must be kept reflecting purchases, issues and balance on hand. Frequent stock checks, physical counting of every item in stock after every six months must be done.

Keeping track of the circulating linen is another problem. The linen is kept track of for normal wear and tear, improper use, carelessness in handling, losses in the laundry and theft.

The main functions of this department are:

1. Checking, inspecting, repairing and marking of linen
2. Issuing of linen to staff and departments and control of the return of soiled and unused items
3. Sorting of linen, preparation of records and dispatch of dirty linen to the laundry
4. Maintaining records of linen
5. Storage and control of hired linen
6. Handling personal laundry of guests and staff

The staff of this section includes:

1. Head linen keeper
2. Linen room employees
3. Seamstresses

Head Linen Keeper/Linen Room Supervisor

Head linen keeper should have practical knowledge of laundry work e.g., ironing and mending of various types of fabrics and their maintenance.

Linen Keeper/Assistants

All hotels have a linen room to store, sort, check and repair all the linen used. This room is under the control of a linen keeper. He/she is directly under the control of the housekeeper and is responsible for the sorting of all sheets, pillow covers, towels, table cloths, napkins, etc. The linen keeper issues clean linen and sends soiled and dirty linen to the laundry. Each item is checked and counted when sent to the laundry and again on its return.

Storekeeper

In large hotels a storekeeper may be appointed to a full-time position to control stock of equipment, cleaning materials, and so on.

Linen Room Attendant

He should identify the linen/uniforms by category/size even in fold. He must know the procedure of distribution of various types of sizes of linen/uniform, pest control, protection against dust, system of quantum of linen, exchange with laundry room, restaurants, etc. He should maintain proper records of discards and determine the percentage, follow the proper procedure of exchange of linen/uniform, observe the timings allotted to various departments, know how to segregate into washing and dry cleaning categories, and about par stock maintenance. He should have knowledge of darning and stitching of linen and uniforms.

Linen Control

The linen room is closely linked with the general application of linen control, but we will confine our present survey of this department to its primary purpose; viz. the issue of working stock and dispatch and return of linen from the laundry. The normal method is to issue 'clean' only in exchange for 'soiled'.

Soiled Linen

As each item is checked the linen keeper should note any damage and list it into a record, giving date, name of article, description of damage, and from which department it is received. A note giving advice of this should be sent to the head of that department. It is very rarely that a department will bring to notice any damage to linen whilst in its care, and almost the only check on this is the linen keeper.

There are often recurrent causes for damage to linen and unless these are dealt with immediately, and the cause traced and removed the linen stock will suffer. The linen keeper's record of damaged linen is therefore most necessary.

Discarded Linen

The housekeeper puts aside linen, which has become unserviceable for the use of clients, in the linen room for examination. Much of this linen may be still serviceable for staff use, and when discards are allocated for this purpose, the linen should be given a distinct marking to indicate the transfer from main working stock to staff stock. All discards should be recorded and the record signed by the housekeeper. A simple and effective method of marking is coloured stitching at the corners of the article, using always the same colour.

11. Kitchen and its Operations

One of the basic requirements of a hotel is to offer food and beverage to all visitors. Much of the reputation of today's hotels centres around its food and beverage service and much of the appeal of the hotel lies in its decor, atmosphere and service offered in the restaurants, bars and other sales outlets. Food and beverage has become a potential source of profit in many hotels. Cash-generation, profitability, image building and giving a new look to the hotel, are the main perspectives of the food and beverage management.

The food and beverage functions in a hotel are closely related, but at the same time, these have interdependence on other activities of the hotel operation. The same employees handle both products–food and beverages.

Most of the goods and services provided in the same outlet, may not be separately identifiable as either food or beverages. The revenue of each function can easily be separated, but it is impracticable to separate all costs of operation other than the cost of sales. Therefore, food and beverages though separate entities are treated as one group and analysed by the sales outlet and reflected in the organizational structure of the hotel.

Food and beverage control is an important activity and is an integral part of the total accounting function of the hotel. All restaurant cashiers, food and beverage control assistants, cost control clerks are part of the accounting department.

In hotels where the sales department is in existence, food and beverage sales are monitored by that department. In many hotels this department is headed by a food and beverage director. It represents a complex group in which there are many lines of authority and overlapping functions. No hotels are alike especially in the case of organization of the food and beverage department. They differ in regards to allotment of authority and duties of personnel.

The main activities related to the food and beverage are:

1. Purchase and storage of food and beverages
2. Food production and patisserie
3. Food selling and service
4. Beverage service

Food purchases are directed either by the food and beverage manager or the executive chef. There

Chef preparing Seekh Kebab

are many variations in purchasing methods depending on the location and availability of merchandise. In most cases, a clerk receives the stores and distributes the food supplied.

The next phase of food preparation takes place in the kitchen of the hotel. It is a place where artists and craftsmen work together under an executive chef (master chef) to achieve the most delicious combinations of food which must satisfy the appetite, the taste and the touch of the guests. A small kitchen might be divided into two areas: preparation and kitchen service. The preparation area is for preparation of vegetables, fish, meat and poultry as well as desserts such as cold starters, salads and decorative work. The kitchen service area is the cooking and plating or service area. A large hotel will split preparation areas into meat, fish and vegetable preparation and split the cooking area into sections or areas specializing in different methods of food cooking, preparation viz. soups, cooking, roasting, and grilling, vegetables and potato cooking, sweets and the larder area where raw and cold preparations take place. The executive chef is in charge and plans the menus and supervises cooks and pantry workers who prepare food in the various sections of the kitchen. The department is divided into butcher-shop, kitchen, pastry and bakery. In smaller hotels, the executive chef is responsible directly to the manager, but in larger hotels, he reports to the food and beverage manager.

The modern kitchens in good hotels are air-conditioned, well ventilated, spotless and a pleasant place to work in. The kitchen is the main production centre in a hotel. It has sub-divisions/sections/parts–roast, pastry, butcher, larder and so on, supplied by a production team known as kitchen brigade.

The planning of kitchen equipment and layout needed depends upon:

1. The advance planning of market segments to be sought after
2. General menu contents
3. Type of overall service planned

The guiding principle for restaurant planning and designing is 'minimum of effort with a maximum of efficiency'. The equipment should facilitate rapid economic delivery to the guests. The right equipment must be of the right amount and at the right place. The configuration of basic equipment and storage facilities varies according to the spectrum ranging from non-convenience food to a gourmet cuisine. A meticulous system approach must be used to ensure that all the pieces fit to form a unified whole. The system adopted be practical and must translate the menu into its constituent elements, purchasing units, storage requirements and processing steps. A given level of sales of a given menu will determine both the amount of individual items needed and the nature and volume of individual work steps. A limited menu can make do with limited equipment, but an elaborate menu calls for complex processing and storage equipment. Flexibility in the kitchen is required for adjustment in menu in the later stages.

Each menu item has its own logistical implications, from the receipt of food supplies, their storage and issuance, their production, to the delivery of the meals to the table. Analysing the menu in term of the work steps involved is the basis for determining the processing and storage equipment and its placement for minimizing labour costs.

Storage equipment must be designed with consideration of nearness and accessibility for movement into storage from the receiver and issuing out of storage to production.

Menu also determines the kind of equipment needed for the most economic preparation of meals. It determines how that equipment is used.

Young Chefs flambing a dish

The efficient use of equipment depends on how the various pieces are located in relation to each other.

The food preparation process is composed of a large number of individual work steps using variety of utensils, as well as major pieces of equipment; therefore, facilities layout is a critically important point. The labour cost includes a substantial amount of time used just for moving supplies from one location to another.

The basic principle of a well-designed kitchen in a specialized food and beverage unit is the establishment of individual work centres for specific food preparation functions.

In a normal type of restaurant the following work centres are generally required:

1. The pantry–to prepare salad, sandwiches and desserts
2. The broiler station
3. The fry/cook station

Each of these stations operate with separate equipment and supplies. Each is a self-contained unit, but not separated from others by walls or visual distraction, workers do not work in isolation. They are accessible to the necessary supervision and coordinations. Each work centre has its own crew of workers, each of whom is trained to perform all the functions of that particular work centre.

Equipment in each work centre needs to be installed with a view to workers' convenience. All work surfaces, controls and apparatus must be easily accessible and at right levels. The space allocated to individual work stations needs to be balanced between enough space and not too much. The greater the available space, the more workers have to move from one activity to another, and thus, the more time consumed. Equipment installation must also consider both workers' comforts and efficiency.

The relationship of each work centre must be carefully designed to flow from station to station and to the service area. The placement of facilities, the relationship to storage area and the dining area, and the sequence within the total meal need to be carefully planned. The kitchen should be able to operate as a production line. The food preparation should have smooth flow of work with successive stages of production accomplished as materials move along.

The layout of the kitchen relates direct to guest service. It determines the speed and efficiency with which guests' orders are received, processed and delivered. Thus, the kitchen layout flows direct into the layout of other facilities, such as:

1. Service areas, where servers deliver orders, price up foods, and assemble everything needed for delivering the complete meal to the guest
2. Supplies of linen, flatware, condiments, and other service related items

Various hotel delicacies

3. The dish washing and storage facilities

All these facilities are bridged between the kitchen and the service. All must be laid out for the convenience and access of both the kitchen and serving staff, depending upon the menu and the kind of service offered. For counter service, the supplies are outside the kitchen. In a table service restaurant the placement of these vary with the nature and complexity of service. In addition, the menu is a principal determinant of facilities and their placement. In some menus, some form of storage is needed in the serving area, whereas in some other menus, the service area must be specially designed to allow for final assembly or preparation activities by servers.

Self-service is increasingly common today. The fundamental principle is that it is labour saving. Guests not only come to the service area for food, but they also perform a number of other activities performed by servers in table service restaurants. They obtain their own dishes and flatware, and in institutional cafeterias, they even pour coffee and draw soft drinks from taps.

In addition to the introduction of such familiar practices as soft drink vending machines, restaurants have begun to introduce such innovations as salad centres in table service restaurants and the use of table services for desserts and beverage cafeterias.

The layout must allow for the most economic way of moving dishes and flatware from the dining area to washing equipment and for storing garbage before removal. Considerations range from prompt removal of dishes and flatware to provision for multiple garbage collection and transfer to the storage point. Effective control procedures and supervision for the handling and storing of food and for cleaning the premises is also needed. Kitchen work surfaces should be immediately cleaned when not in use. Extra perishables should be returned promptly to refrigeration. Rules on maintaining freshness should be communicated to all employees. These should be stringently enforced.

The kitchen manager or *chef d' cuisine*, controls the chefs and assistants dealing with different sections of the kitchen. In some hotels, the chef may report directly to the general manager whereas in some other hotels, he reports to the F & B manager, although he has direct communication with the general manager.

The chef, during the time of Napoleon in France, was seen wearing a long floppy cap, somewhat like a night cap as a symbol of his authority. Marie Antoiae *Careme,* who is the founder of *La Grande Cuisine Francaise,* the classic French style of cooking, is credited with the tall starched cap that identifies the chef or chief. The height of the *'toque blanc'* is supposed to correlate with his rank in the kitchen.

Great care is required in each stage of the kitchen operation–planning, production, financial and quality control. The staff requirements of a kitchen

Cakes, Pastries and Sweets

Case Study 1109
Kitchen

Situation

In a hotel formerly potatoes were peeled by machine. When the machine wore out, however, it was not replaced. Potatoes were again peeled by hand. Data from both the hand and machine operations were compared as to cost of peeling and eyeing 50 kgs of identical grade potatoes.

Results of Comparison and Analysis

	Cost when hand peeled	**Cost when machine peeled**
Number of workers used	3	1
Average daily wage rate per worker	Rs. 175.00	Rs. 175.00
Time of operation (minutes)	72.00	22.00
Total man-minutes	66.00	19.00
Waste in peeling per 50 kgs	26.00	28.00
Cost per 50 kgs	Rs. 24.08	Rs. 6.83

Since handpeeling cost more than three and one half times as much as mechanical peeling, no time was wasted in the purchase of another mechanical potato peeler.

Case Study 1110
Kitchen

Situation

A study of a vegetable preparation section of a hotel restaurant showed that 35 per cent of the time was spent in peeling potatoes. The potatoes were peeled rapidly but the eyeing operation could not keep pace with the peeling machine.

Results of Analysis

A special table was designed for the eyeing operation which permitted the women doing the work to be seated. The table was provided with pans, one in front of each worker to catch the trimmings and a hole made in the table through which eyed potatoes could be easily dropped into G.I. cans.

The workers were delighted. Seating the women saved 14 per cent energy expenditure. Production went upto 30 per cent with less resulting fatigue. When one vegetable woman resigned it was not necessary to replace her. Saving totalled Rs. 47,500 a year. The table cost Rs. 2,500 to build.

depend on the size and type of the hotel and the type of meals to be provided and the number of guests for whom they are prepared. In a large organization, the kitchen is divided into various sections (*parties*) and the number of *parties* depend upon the sizes of kitchen. In addition, the organization is contrasted for the traditional kitchen with its hierarchy of cooks and stewards and for the new institutional kitchen making great use of convenience products. In the convenience kitchen, minimum use is made of cooks and the butchers, bakers and most pantry workers are eliminated. Each section of the kitchen is led by a *chef d' partie,* who is responsible for preparing certain kind of dishes. The number of assistants required under each *partie* will/depend on the amount of work handled.

The basic concept of food production is the conversion of the raw material (purchased food) into dishes and meals. This process of conversion passes through four main aspects:

1. Volume forecasting
2. Yield test
3. Standard recipe
4. Portion control

Menu studies show that 75 per cent of all entree sales are luncheon and dinner menus limited to six or seven items. If you offer two or three times this number of entrees, the results are overproduction, waste and expensive preparation costs.

Inefficient purchasing, waste, overproduction, pilferage, underpricing, improper training and inadequate supervision all contribute to high food cost. Avoidance of waste can help a great deal in keeping food costs low.

From the organizational point of view the main sections of a kitchen are:

1. Main production centre
2. Ancillary food production
3. Administration
4. Pantry
5. Cleaning

Executive Chef/Head Chef

He is the commander of the kitchen. In large hotels he is more a department manager than a working craftsman. He is responsible for the organization, planning and supervision of the kitchen. He prepares the menu in accordance with the costing and catering policies laid down by the management. He has either full responsibility for staffing within the general kitchen, or has a major say in staff selection and dismissal in conjunction with the personnel department. A chef must have good health, a sense of hygiene, responsibility, organizational ability, special inclination towards the culinary arts. He must have extensive practical experience in all branches of cooking, knowledge of foodstuffs and their marketing. He must have a sound knowledge of phraseology and terminology used in kitchens and the names and composition of all dishes, characteristics of various countries. He must have ability to use kitchen equipments, knowledge of hygiene and safety standards and regulations and labour legislation relevant to the work of kitchen staff. The chef is a person with varied skills and normally commands a high salary.

In addition to the craft, skill and technical knowledge acquired as a result of apprenticeship, technical training and experience, the *chef d' cuisine* must acquire managerial qualities and administrative knowledge–particularly in regard to the organization of work, control of staff, efficient use of machinery, costing, and food control. He must be aware of modern developments in manufacturing and processing food and equipment for the kitchen. He must concern himself with the techniques of meal presentation. He must have good experience of controlling staff under his supervision.

The chef is in charge of the quality of food production, food preparation for banquets, catering and satellite centres such as coffee shops, speciality restaurants and room service. He has extensive dealings with other departments such as purchasing, stewarding, catering and with the *maître d'*.

Assistant Chef/Second Chef/Sous Chef/ Deputy Chef

Sous means 'under' in French and the *sous chef* is the second chef in command of the kitchen. He is the principal assistant of the *chef d' cuisine* in general administration, supervision of the work of preparing food and overseeing its service.

In large hotels, the assistant chef has a supporting role to the *chef d' cuisine.* He helps him in his varied duties. His position is, of course, regarded as an intermediate step between control of a part and the ultimate control of a kitchen. In small hotels, one of the principal *chef d' partie (chef saucier/ chef garde/ larder chef)* may act as a *sous chef.*

He acts as a *chef d' cuisine* in his absence. When the *chef d' cuisine* is engaged in menu planning, checking records, figures or in similar administrative routines, the *sous chef* directly supervises all the practical kitchen activities. He also supervises the meal service times and can make ad-hoc staff changes during the working day to relieve pressure. In large hotels there may be as many as four to six *sous chefs* particularly when separate kitchens are set up for grill room, restaurant, floors and banquet service.

Main Production Centre

Section Chef/Chef d' partie

'Partie' is a French word meaning 'part' (of a whole) or section. A *partie* system is one in which the kitchen space, equipment and jobs are divided into sections. The *partie* system operated by Escoffier remains an integral part of culinary craft's traditions and illustrates the enduring principle involved in determining task groupings. Each section has clearly defined tasks to be performed and coordinated by a supervisor.

Section chefs/*chef d' parties* work in close cooperation with the *chef d' cuisine.* They must have adequate kitchen training and a great deal of practical experience. *Chef d' partie* must have knowledge and almost all those qualities which are required for an assistant chef. He should have a good knowledge about the different frozen foodstuffs and their utilization. In the case of the pastry cook, he must have drawing ability and practical knowledge of designing. In the case of larder cook, perfect knowledge of the quality, cutting up and presentation of meat, poultry, game, fish, etc. is required. The duties of the *chef d' partie* can be divided into two categories:

1. General duties: It includes working with the *chef d' cuisine* and at his request work directly at the hot place. He is required to supervise the working of his staff and is responsible for the cleanliness of kitchen, utensils and premises. He also collects the necessary ingredients for the menu prepared by the *chef d' cuisine.* He also helps in the training of the juniors.
2. Specialist duties: The duties of the various specialists (cook/chefs) are explained under respective heads.

Larder Cook/Larder Chef/Chef Garde Manger

He is in charge of the larder, the place where the raw materials required for cooking are prepared and dressed. The larder chef prepares *hors d'oeuvres,* jellies, aspics, cold sauces, salad and all dishes for the cold buffet. In large hotels larder work may be broken into sections, and the subsections may

Basting of Tandoori Chicken

have an independent *chef garde manger i.e.*, Boucherie might be directly controlled by the *chef d' cuisine* or *sous chefs*.

The larder is normally adjoining the main kitchen and has its own cooking facilities. Depending upon the size of the kitchen, its subsections too will be separate to a greater or smaller extent. This also incorporates the *hors d'oeuvres* section and a salad room and a fruit room.

The larder manger keeps a complete record of all materials received and used. His own dishes include all those commonly found on a cold table and comprises not only cold joints but also galantine, ballotines and cold dishes and salads. Sandwiches are his responsibility with the exception of the hot or toasted sandwiches. Sauces and other dressings are made by the *garde manger*.

Fish Manger/Chef Poissionier

He must have the raw materials ready for the appropriate chef, either for *chef poissionier* or in some instances for cold dishes for *chef garde manger*. Products of sea, river and lake come to him for treatment, which includes skinning, filleting and portioning.

Butcher/Bouchier

His jobs is to dissect the quarters of beef and carcasses of lamb and sides of pork. It also includes the dressing of meat either for joints such as *contrefillet* or small cuts like noisette, cotelettes or tornadoes. He works under the supervision of the larder/chef.

Salad Maker/Saladier

He is responsible for the preparatory work and assembling of salads.

Hors d'oeuvire/Hors d'oeuvier

He prepares all hot and cold *hors d'oeuvre* or appetizers. This includes a wide range of dishes and involves the regular preparations of commodities e.g. preparation of various varieties of vegetables, salads, varieties of meat and fish dishes found on, *hors d'oeuvre vioture* trolley. He receives stocks from the *chef poissionier* for fish soups. This section involves a substantial amount of garnish preparation involving skilful use of the knife and other ordinary tools, particularly for preparing vegetables in a wide variety of shapes and sizes. He needs right judgement for a *potdge.* Personal judgement as well as technical skill is required. He works like a *saucier* in a section of the main kitchen.

Poulterer/Vollailleur

He is responsible for plucking, cleaning and dressing of poultry.

Sausage Maker/Pork Butcher/Charcutier

He is responsible for speciality pork butchery and preparation of pork products and sausages and also for the rending and classifying of dripping.

Roast Cook/Broiler Chef/Chef Rotisseur

This is one of the most important positions in the kitchen. The finest roast cooks are found in England, as roasting has always been renowned in England as a specialization. Roast is quite popular and entails complex work.

This *partie* is responsible for deep frying of foods of all kinds including fried potatoes and the *rotisseur* may have an assistant for this task who is known as frying cook/*friturier.*

The roast corner is situated in the main stores section and all necessary cooking apparatus for roasting, for deep frying, for frying of savouries in a salamander are grouped together and make this section. Some of the dishes require handling both by the *rotisseur* and by the *saucier.*

Foods like poultry, game and meat need roasting. The joints, poultry and game to be cooked by the *rotisseur* are given the basic preparatory treatment like plucking and preparation, for the oven in the larder by the butcher or *vollaileur.* Sometimes the *commis* from the roast corner may help the larder for cleaning and trussing of poultry or the dissection, trimming and tying of joints of the butcher's meat.

Grill Cook/Savoury Cook/Chef Savourier/ Chef Grillandin

His duties are grilling, using either the traditional methods like charcoal, electricity or gas. Where a separate grillandin is established, he might deal with the savouries and combine the function of *grillandin* with that of *savourier.*

Carver/Trallcheur

He is generally under the control of the *rotisseur.* He is skilled in both serving and cooking. He may operate behind the scene at the hot service counter.

Pastry Chef/Chef Paitissier

This chef has quite a different status but certainly not less than that of the *chef saucier* and the *chef garde manger.* The work of this department is normally separated from the main kitchen and is self-contained in the matter of cold storage, machinery and equipment. It has its own baking and cooking facilities. This *chef* is responsible for all hot and cold sweets for lunches, dinners and functions and for pastries served at teatime or other occasions. He is responsible for making short and puff pastry, fritter, batters, noodles and Italian pastas for supply to other areas of the kitchen, pies, cakes, special desserts, rolls, special breads, petits fours, souffle, biscuits, puddings, compotes, fruit salads, preserved fruits dough for noodles, macaroni, etc. In addition sorbets and water ice items are made in the pastry section. The service of ice and those sweets which are based upon ice cream are prepared and assembled in the *patisserie.* They include, sweet omelette and souffles, peach melba, *poire, helene,* sugar, ice cream with hot meringue exterior, and souffle, dipped fruits, etc.

The pastry chef must have knowledge of:

1. Storage of pastries–time and environment preparation and decoration of special cakes, supply of bakery products to the pastry shop.

2. Operation of special equipments of bakery and its utility.

The *chef patissier* requires great skill, imagination and experience.

In large hotels one or more cuisenaire will do no more than prepare pastry itself like short and puff pastry for making of pies, flans, etc. Semi-skilled assistants will prepare fresh fruit for fruit salad for service at lunch, dinners and breakfast. Thus, the *chef patissier* is like the *garde manger* or *chef d' cuisine* of a speciality kitchen. In addition to his own skill, he must coordinate and organize the work of a number of subordinates.

Baker/Boulanger

He is a baker working under the *chef patissier* and as such is responsible for all baking items like bread

Cake Pastries and Sweets

rolls, bread croissants, etc.

Ice-cream Chef/Glacier

He prepares all kinds of icecream, water ices, mousses, biscuits and glaces. He is one of the assistants of the *chef patissier.*

Fish Cook/Chef Poissonier

He is responsible for the cooking, garnishing and sauce making for fish courses, with the exemption of deep fried fish. The *chef poissonier* is also responsible for the cooking, garnishing, saucing and dishing of fish dishes featuring freshwater fish, other fish, shell fishes, etc.

He should have knowledge of various types of fishes (sea water, river fishes, etc.) and the cooking temperature for various types of fishes/dishes.

Sauce Cook/Chef Saucier

He is the person who supervises the kitchen in the absence of the *sous chef.* He makes note of the day's menu prepared by the *chef d' cuisine* and accordingly obtains the ingredients needed for the *'fonds d' cuisine'* and the various soups and prepares all fundamental sauces *i.e.*, bechamel, tomato sauce, veloute. He also prepares all sauces *saultees, saulted* meat, fish special soups. He prepares light and heavy *entrees*, for example, value vent (light *entrees*), heavy *entrees* (steaks) *i.e.*, meat, poultry and game dishes which are not roasted and grilled. He is considered to be the senior *chef d' partie* and takes over the responsibility of the *sous chef* when absent. He requires special knowledge because his work covers an extensive variety of dishes, especially sauces.

According to Escoffier, 'The sauce makes the dish. The garnish of a dish changes the whole appearance. A dish must taste good and look attractive to be appreciated. Application of sauce and garnish can make or mar a dish.'

The work of a sauce cook comprises cooking, garnishing of all meat and poultry and game dishes with the exception of those that are plainly grilled and roasted, which are cooked by the *rotisseur.* Thus, he is responsible for braises, entrees, *poeles*, bouillis, etc. The saucier is responsible for at least one of the *plats d' jour* or specialities of the day. He is assisted by one or more *commis* and apprentices. He prepares his own *mise-en-places* and receives prepared commodities from other sections.

Soup Cook/Chef Potager

He is responsible for the preparation and making of all the soups, and for the garnishes accompanying the soup. This chef may be assisted by the *commis* and apprentices according to the size of the establishment/hotel. The *chef potager* and his assistants sometimes begin their duty a little earlier than the other cooks. The work of the potager is important as soups give an impression of meals to follow.

His importance in the kitchen is supported by the fact that the repertoire of soups including consomme, cremes and veloutees, purees, broths, bisques and many speciality and nationality soups is extensive. Consomme alone can be composed with differing flavouring essences and garnished in hundreds of ways. Besides, all basic stocks are prepared by him.

Vegetable Egg and Noodle Cook/Chef Entremeteur

This corner employs the largest number of staff as the variety of vegetables to be prepared is quite large. The *chef entremeteur* is responsible for all vegetable dishes, all potato dishes, other than those that are deep fried, all egg dishes and all farinaceous dishes. He is responsible for preparing vegetable garnish for other *parties* for completion of a dish. Italian pastas but not noodles are also cooked by vegetable cooks. Items like cooked spaghetti and rice may be sent to another chef for garnishing. The cooking of eggs forms an integral part of the work at this section, particularly omelettes of various types–plain, garnished, stuffed and flat round omelette. The cooking of pancakes for service from the kitchen or cooking from the gueridon is prepared by this chef. Butter for these pancakes is supplied by *chef patissiere.* Vegetables prepared and cooked as accompaniments to the main meat, poultry and game dishes are also prepared by this section. The operations in this section are assembling, cooking, garnishing and flavouring, etc.

Ancillary Food Production

Relief Cook/Chef Tournant

His duty is to take over from any *chef d' partie* in his absence as demanded by the normal incidence of holidays and days off. This appointment generally goes to an older man of long experience as a prelude to appointment as *sous chef.*

Duty Cook/Chef d' Garde

During the break hours, when the bulk of the kitchen staff are off duty, this chef remains with appropriate commis and apprentices on duty. He attends to duties which cannot be delayed until the other employees return to duty. In large hotels separate *chefs* or *commis d' garde* remain in one patisserie and in the *garde manger* as well as in the more grey sections of the kitchen. Each may see the affairs of more than one of the kitchen *parties.*

Night Duty Chef/Chef d' Nuit

His main duty is to take over the responsibility when the main kitchen staff leaves. Night duty chef does not necessarily remain on duty through the night but until such time till the late meals have ceased. The duties of *chef d' nuit* are sometimes carried out by a *sous chef.* The *sous chef* doing the service of dinner only is responsible for all the work when the normal staff has gone off duty. The *sous chef* must make sure that he has all the necessary facilities and that the correct *mise-en place* is left by the *chef d' partie* before they go off duty.

Banquet Chef/Chef d' Briquettes

The chef given special duty responsibilities for special service of banquets is known as banquet

Hot Tandoori Chicken

chef. He is given the responsibility for the assembly and service of banquet and functional meals.

The work of this department is normally separated from the main kitchen and is self-contained in the matter of cold storage, machinery and equipment for making ice and with its own baking and cooking facilities.

Breakfast Cook/Chef d' Petite/Dejeuner

The cooking and service for breakfast in hotels is commonly entrusted to this speciality cook. He does not rank as a full *chef d' partie.* He works along with the *commis.* After finishing the breakfast, he prepares *mise-en place* and cooks, roast and grills for late service lunches when the *chef d' partie* and staff go off. The *mise-en place* for breakfast and boning and slicing of bacon and preparation of the various types of fish eaten at breakfast time, is done by a subordinate of the *garde manger* and similar skilled assistants. Preparation of fruit compotes and fruit salads is made by assistants in the *patisserie.* Thus, the breakfast cooks and helpers are concerned with simple assembling and cooking of eggs, grilling and frying of fish and bacon.

Staff Cook/Chef Communar

He is responsible for the preparation of staff meals which implies meals for the rank and file of uniformed staff, chamber maids, waiters and low grade clerical staff. He requires to have knowledge of the preparation of main dishes and the techniques of collective cooking. He must have the same qualification as that of the *chef d' partie.* He works as per instructions of the *chef d' cuisine,* obtains the necessary ingredients, and prepares the food for the two daily meals of the staff. He usually comes under the kitchen stewarding section which looks after the staff meals. However, in many hotels this job position has been clubbed with the kitchen brigade, because of the nature of his duties.

Short Order Cook

He requires same qualities as the staff cook and performs all those duties of the staff cook. He serves all light luncheon items and hot sandwiches.

Subordinate Personnel

There are various subordinate personnel of different types working under the various chefs.

Commis Cook/Assistant Cooks

They are the cooks who must have knowledge of the main dishes and know their names in various languages. They must have ability to use kitchen equipment and have a good sense of hygiene relevant to their work. They follow the instructions of their *chef d' partie* and help them in preparing and cooking dishes. They prepare simple dishes by themselves. The *commis* should have completed their apprenticeship or training but would still be gaining experience before taking on full *partie* responsibilities. The first *commis* should be capable of taking charge when his *chef d' partie* is off.

Case Study IIII
Pantry Work Schedule

Situation

A small dish pantry was staffed for four years on the basis of service for three meals a day. Later, when the morning meal was eliminated management neglected to change the work schedule.

Results of Analysis

A bar graph was drawn up which plotted the work schedule and rated the amount of work done by people throughout the day.

Chef demonstrating his Delicacies

Staff Mess Control

Attention to control of staff catering can have a beneficial affect on the hotel's economy. Where staff catering has been organized and rationally treated, vast savings have resulted. The ideal method to have good control is to have a staff kitchen completely divorced from the management of the main kitchen and treated as a separate entity as far as the purchase of supplies and its management is concerned.

A rational method of staff mess control is proposed as follows:

1. The appointment of a senior hotel executive, who will embody within his province the task of staff catering. The appointment need not be a full-time one for once organized very little is needed to keep things up to the standard set.
2. Appoint a steward in charge of the mess rooms, and give him sufficient authority to resist the influence of those who assume the right to interfere in his department. In every respect he must be the 'manager' of his section, responsible only to his senior executive.
3. Orders to suppliers for staff catering should be distinct and not included in those issued by the chef for the main kitchen.
4. All charges should be compiled into a monthly cost statement showing:
   a. Cost analysis of food consumed
   b. Analysis of meals served
   c. Wages cost of mess room staff
   d. Proportionate charge for fuel, lighting and water
   e. Cost of breakages and replacements (China, glass, cutlery, etc.)
   f. Cost per meal based on the points system *i.e.*, breakfast 2 points; lunch 6 points; tea 1 point; dinner or supper 6 points
   g. The total cost per meal can be sectioned to show: (i) food (ii) expenses (iii) total

The control operates all costings.

It may happen that the mess rooms will be graded for different classes of staff. Where this applies there should be a general menu for all sections, and not separate menus for each grade.

It is found that 90 per cent of the staff is not interested in a soup course with the main meal. They prefer the service to be focused on supplying them with a substantial main dish. Therefore, labour and material are often wasted in providing dishes which are unappreciated.

There is also a tendency in the over usage of sauces, pickles, etc., and this should be restrained and such sundries be only served on request.

Bakery and Confectionery Products

12. Restaurant Operations

The provision of restaurant and other food and beverage facilities should be based on detailed analysis of market considerations and economic feasibility. Entry to a restaurant should be through a reception lounge or foyer. This area may be little more than a widening of the entrance corridor to provide space as an assembly point before entering or on leaving the restaurant and as a lounge for cocktails and other drinks. The bar should be on the farther side of the lounge extension, so that the guests entering the restaurant do not need to cross directly along the front of the bar, and the guests can use the bar without having to pass through the lounge. Cloakrooms and toilets should be near the entrance lobby. All entrance and exits should be positioned to allow proper vision and control.

In a large establishment, there may be different areas offering variety of meals and service:

1. The restaurant–There may be a number of speciality restaurants–Continental, Chinese, Indian, executive club room service, roof top restaurants, barbeque, coffee shop, snack bars, lounge service and banqueting.

2. The bars–cocktail bars, public bars, hotel bars dispense bar, S/R bar, lounge bar.

Traditionally, it is said that 'you can't make money on food' and to some extent it is true even today because in many accommodation units food service is strictly provided as a convenience for guests. But in the hotel business, many of them have obtained a nice profit from their restaurants, coffee shops, food and beverage outlets and bars.

Guests in a Specialty Restaurant

A Japanese Restaurant

Nowadays, to be successful in hotel business, a hotel should conceive of and operate its food facilities and restaurants in competition with other food and beverage establishments rather than being merely an adjunct to their room business. A well-known hotel designer Jac Lessman asserts that each patron has four senses that must be satisfied if his dining experience is to be enjoyable. What he sees, what he smells, what he hears, as well as what he tastes, are all important psychology has a great deal to do with a diner's mood and response.

A hotel may prefer to lease out a restaurant or coffee shop rather than own them. This can prove to be a profitable arrangement for the hotel to provide needed food facilities for guests without the botheration of operating it. Great care should be taken in choosing the restaurateur to whom the space will be leased as the quality of food served, price and service standards will reflect on the hotel.

The layout of the restaurant should take into account the features of the room, external vistas and internal displays and entertainment, circulation patterns of customers and staff, method of food service, seat groupings and type of furniture to be used.

Restaurant areas require sophisticated environmental control. Depending on location and case, windows may be provided to take advantage of the view and/or to attract outside attention as a form of merchandising. For example, in resort areas the windows may be an important feature of the restaurant's attractions by opening on to swimming pools, gardens or vistas of the land or natural scenery. In case of the other type of restaurant intended for mainly evening dining, these may be completely enclosed within the interior of the building. Provision must be made for adequate ventilation and air-conditioning. Lighting is an important feature of design and atmosphere. Incandescent lamps should be used rather than fluorescent types, but the latter may be used as background lighting in coffee shops and fast food operations and to provide the colour balance for display purposes. Light with a greater emphasis towards red must be selected and infra-red-luminescent lamps may be maintained over hot counters. Within the restaurant a wide variety of light fittings are used. Indirect light should be frequently employed around the parameter to emphasize wall texture and other features.

A Bar cum Lounge

Background lighting may be provided within or immediately below the ceiling. Local lighting over tables, recesses and seating enclosures serve to create individuality. It is necessary to provide several lighting circuits with switches for control purposes.

Ceilings should normally be at least 2750 mm (9 ft) high and should provide sound absorption and sound damping of machinery vibrations and transmission noise. The ceiling construction may be based on panels, to allow access, or continuous surfaces, with relief provided by mouldings and architraves. Alternative wall surfaces include dry linings of laminated plastic, panels of glass, plastered surfaces, slabs of stones/marble and exposed brickwork.

Floors and floor coverings require special attention. Most restaurants are carpeted to reduce noise and to create a sense of comfort and warmth. Floor tiling is appropriate for tourist or economy class hotels. These may be used in coffee shops and bars, particularly in the heavily used areas in front and behind the counters. Stone slabs and mosaics may be introduced. Wood block or strip flooring provide an intermediary effect. Strip flooring is most suitable for dance areas. Wood construction is also advisable for a stage and entertainment areas.

The furniture must complement the theme and decor of the restaurant.

The table design must be considered in terms of its total effect. This must be reflected in the choice of table equipment, linen, cutlery, china and glassware and in the style of staff uniforms, menu holders and other specific features of restaurant operations. There is a need for rationalization in the range of equipment and tableware used in the hotels. For each item of china or glassware in use there are, on an average, one to two replacements in reserve, and perhaps more where designs are

Guest being presented with a Menu

manufactured to specific order. For table linen and uniforms the stocks are even greater to allow for delays in laundering, and a ratio of 1 in use, 5 or 6 in circulation and reserve must be maintained.

Table appointments and decorations, menu holders and certain tableware items associated with speciality dishes, should be specific to each restaurant. In many chain hotels and catering operations, tableware is used as a means of merchandising. In these hotels, insignia, emblem and other representations are standardized throughout the group.

Food Services

The service staff in the restaurant, coffee shop, room service, lounge service, grill room, bars and banquet rooms come into direct contact with the resident guest as well as with the general public who use the hotel facilities other than the guest room. Service is the prime objective of this department. Good food, well cooked and beautifully presented, can be easily spoiled by a careless waiter/waitress. Proper attention to the table set-up (silverware, china, glasses, etc.) and proper attention to the guests' needs are very important in hotel business.

Basically, food is served from the left, beverages from the right, with the simple reason that glasses and coffee cups are normally placed on the right side of the customer, and dirty dishes are removed from the right. These rules are applied when practicable otherwise concern for the guest's comfort is more important than any rule.

Most of the hotels lose repeat business due to poor service rather than poorly cooked food. Word-of-mouth advertising is the most powerful medium in this service industry. Repeat business in the hotel is the most important factor in the success or failure of the hotel as a profit making enterprise. There is a need for organizational training and supervision in this department.

The decisions on the style and standard of service must be efficiently communicated to the management and staff working in food service. These are usually covered in procedure manuals, instructions to staff and training sessions. The manager must ensure that everyone knows what to do, how to do it, when to do it and to what standard. He ensures that employees work consistently in some agreed manner.

One to two hours before the service commences, serving staff usually lay up the sideboards and tables and fill cruets, pepper mills, sauce bottles and sugar bowls. In small restaurants, the service staff is also responsible for cleaning the dining room and for simple food preparation such as preparing side salads, making dressings, preparing coffee and tea, setting up cold butter, sweet trolleys and cheese boards.

The staff must know exactly the type of service expected such as silver service, a plate service, combination of silver and plate service or family service.

On completion of service the restaurant must be ready for the next service.

Types of Food Services

Large hotels provide several types of food services. These include a restaurant offering an extensive *a la carte* and *table d' hote* menu, a specialist restaurant, a grillroom and a coffee shop. The surroundings of a restaurant will normally be luxurious and restful, as the customers would wish to take their time whilst enjoying the meal, the atmosphere, music, cabaret, etc. Restaurants in hotels are generally of the luxury type. They have elaborate decor, personal service and elegant cuisine. They attract people who want to be entertained as well as fed, who want a pleasant all-round experience in dining out.

French Service/Silver Service

French service means service at the table. All food is brought to the table on platters. It is individually serviced to the guests by the waiter or captain. In some instances, the actual preparation of food takes place at the tableside. Speciality dishes are prepared by the captain. This service is uncommon as it requires more space and more staff and is offered rarely by most of the first-class restaurants.

American Service

In this method the casual practice of service is as follows:

1. Portioned food is plated in the pantry by the kitchen staff.
2. The pre-plated food is then served to the guests from the right side.

Platter to plate service

3. The rule of this service is that all the beverages as well as food is served from the right and the cleaning is also done from the right side.

Russian Service or Plate Service

It involves directly plating of all food in the kitchen. Some of the hotels have adopted the combination of plate service and French service. They prepare certain speciality items like soups, bread rolls and salads at the table or service them from a service cart. Most of these items are relatively easy to handle on a table service basis.

Buffet Service

In this system the customers mostly serve themselves. Buffet service is adaptable to limited hot dishes where the cover count can easily be controlled like breakfast dishes. The composition of lunch buffet should be carefully planned to prevent cost of customer excesses and wastage from exceeding the payrolls. This type of service is getting very popular mainly because it speeds up turnover, which results in a greater number of covers and reduces the number of staff requirement.

English Service

The system followed in this system is as follows:

1. The butler brings the food on platters and sets in front of the host.
2. The host portions out the food and passes the plates to the hostess.
3. Then the butler places the plates in front of the guests.
4. In restaurants the dish is first presented to the host. The waiter then portions out the food on the sideboard and sets the pre-plated food in front of the guests, serving the host last.
5. The pre-plated food is served from the right and also cleared from the right.

Barbeque

This service is provided on an outdoor poolside or terrace. These are self-service operations with some staff behind the barbeque helping to service the guests with their choice of food. There is also staff employed for serving drinks and cleaning the tables.

Banquet Service

It covers conferences, cocktail parties, wedding receptions, dances, private and official luncheon and dinner parties. The banquet manager is responsible for booking functions, helping the organizers choose menus and the type of service required, dealing with order and arrangement of flowers, working out costs of the function of hire or rooms, as well as food/alcohol and staffing of the function. A full-time banqueting brigade of waiters is employed which is supplemented during the period when larger functions are held.

Gueridon and Flambé

It is one of the speciality services in deluxe restaurants. Gueridon service means side table service work. Food is carved out on a side table in front of the guest. For example:

1. Making a salad dressing
2. Salad carving
3. Preparing a grapefruit, etc.
4. Flambé work and flambé service

One of the main advantages of gueridon service is that it provides visual appeal to the customer. Guests are impressed by the skills shown in gueridon performances. Flambéing is a reliable means of attracting the attention of other tables in the restaurant, and has the effect of provoking repeat orders. The flickering lamp, the gleaming silver, the *mis-en place* on the gueridon adds substantially to restaurant atmosphere.

In addition to general equipment, a gueridon

service requires the following special equipment:

1. Gueridon trolley
2. Table cooking lamps or chafing lamp
3. Crepe suzette pan or chafing pans
4. Steak pans
5. Other tools--special carving knife, forks etc.
6. Shaslik swords

Room Service/Floor Service

It involves the service of both food and beverages operations to guest rooms. The peak period for room service is during the morning hours when the resident guests prefer breakfast in their room. Orders are taken on phones, which require an order-taker, a cashier, supervisory personnel, and service personnel. Removal of dirty dishes is a big problem in room service. Room service requires the maintenance of a number of service staff to handle this fluctuating service, therefore it results in unproductive payroll costs. It is the most unprofitable area of food and beverage operations. In many hotels, in order to plan efficiently, an advance breakfast order form is placed in each room, which indicates the order and the time at which the breakfast is to be served. The guest hangs it on the door before retiring and the service personnel collect it in the early hours of morning.

To be a first class hotel, room service must be available even though that room service may constitute a loss operation. Room service is a hallmark of a first class hotel. These hotels maintain floor pantries from which room service operates. Successful room service depends on getting the food to the room as quickly as possible.

In large hotels, the captain oversees each room service shift. In the small hotels the bellman, busboys or regular waiters make the room service delivery. A floor waiter (*chef d' etage*) assisted by *commis d' etage* is responsible for food and beverages served in the bedrooms or private suites. The number of staff required for room service depends on the size of the hotel and the demand for this service. In many hotels, floor waiters have their own service room or floor pantry connected directly to the kitchen by means of 'dummy waiters'.

Thus, room service is serving of food and beverage in guest rooms of the hotel. Small orders are taken on trays and larger ones in trolleys.

The Grill Room

In addition to a grill, a grillroom may carry a far more comprehensive menu, usually an *a la carte* menu. In hotels where the restaurant and grillroom operate side by side, it is usual to find that the latter offer simple dishes–mainly grills and perhaps snacks. The type of service determines the type of and number of staff.

The Coffee Shop

It is a place where guests (hotel and chance customers) can obtain beverages (tea, coffee, etc.) light snacks, cakes, pastries, etc., throughout the day and late evening, or sometimes throughout the night as well.

Cocktail Lounge

The lounge is intended as an intermediary area. The decor should be inviting and relaxing. Lighting should be intermediate in intensity except that the working space and display behind the bar requires a higher local intensity to attract attention and to facilitate efficient operation. General illumination should be adjustable, the higher level being necessary for cleaning. Lighting is also used as a design component to draw attention to features, create interest and personalization of different areas. A mixture of table and wall light fitting should be installed providing soft, warm incandescent light suitably screened and shaded to prevent glare.

Acoustic considerations include the need to reduce transmission of sound from associated working areas, such as the bar equipment. Waiter entrances from the server or kitchen must be effectively screened. Sound attenuation is normally provided by soft furnishings and carpeting and by ceiling absorption. It is an advantage to generate some sound of activity in order to provide a friendly relaxed atmosphere and attract attention from the lobby.

Furniture should be varied in type and layout. Around the walls and in alcove settings, fixed banquet sheets are appropriate. All furniture should be of high quality. Tabletops must be treated to prevent staining and absorption and upholstery work should be easily cleanable or removable for laundry or dry cleaning treatment. Carpets must be of good commercial grade able to resist marking and staining, damage caused by spillage and cigarette butts.

Dimensions must be related to the number of people likely to use the area and be suitably proportioned. Ceiling heights should be 2750 mm (9 ft.) or more over the general area. Lower ceiling in alcoves or under mezzanines help to provide better proportion and more interesting seating areas. Space requirements range from 1.1 to 1.7 sq.m. (12 to 18 sq.ft.) per seat.

A high standard of air-conditioning is essential. Variable heating and cooling control should be provided, regulated automatically to maintain correct temperature and humidity.

The Lounge

In the absence of a 24-hour coffee shop, a lounge service facility is offered to the guests to obtain snacks, beverages and other drinks outside the usual hours of service. In a lounge service area, it is usual to have two lounge waiters or waitresses who divide the day between them. When the lounge waiters go off duty at the end of the day, the night porter usually assumes the responsibility for this service.

Generally, a lounge is divided into two main areas– the table service area and the bar. Tables and chairs are arranged in the service area for consumers who do not wish to sit at the bar. For those who wish to be served at the bar, the chairs or stools are arranged in front of the bar counter. Service is provided by a table attendant or when the attendant is off duty, by the bartender. The cash register is also kept behind the bar accessible only to the bartender or bar attendant.

Cover

Cover is the space on a table for keeping all cutlery, crockery, glassware and linen required for a guest. Each cover requires 27" x 15" in space.

Hygiene

Apart from legal requirements, those who are engaged in the sale of foods have an obligation to the consumer to safeguard them against the dangers to their health and well being which might arise through carelessness or ignorance in the storage, preparation and service of food. In training staff, it may sometimes be necessary to confine oneself to teaching the basic rules of conduct but an understanding of the main causes of food poisoning and food contamination and the manner in which the dangers can be minimized is likely to lead to a more positive attitude towards hygiene than mere insistence on compliance with instructions and regulations.

In particular, it is important that all concerned with the handling of food should realize that food, which looks and smells perfectly wholesome, may nevertheless be a source of danger to health if it has been contaminated before or during preparation by harmful bacteria.

The food hygiene regulations relate mainly to:

1. The cleanliness of premises and shops used

for the purpose of food business and of the equipment used

2. The hygienic handling of food
3. The cleanliness of persons handling food and of their clothing
4. The construction of premises used for the purpose of food business
5. The provision of water supply and washing facilities
6. The proper disposal of waste material
7. The temperatures at which certain foods are to be kept on catering premises

From the point of view of caterers, the most important regulations are firstly those that require that no food business shall be carried on at any place the condition, situation or construction of which is such that food is exposed to the risk of contamination and secondly, those that relate to the handling of food.

A person who engages in handling food, shall, while so engaged, take all such steps as may be reasonable, and necessary to protect the food from risk of contamination, and in particular:

1. Shall not place the food as to involve any risk of contamination;
2. Shall before offering any food for sale, ensure that any food which is unfit for human consumption is kept apart from any other food;
3. Shall not in or about any forecourt or yard, place any food lower than eighteen inches from the ground unless it is adequately protected from risk of contamination;
4. Shall ensure where reasonably necessary that open food while exposed for sale or during sale or delivery is kept covered or is otherwise effectively screened from possible sources of contamination;
5. Shall not keep in any animal feed in the room where food is kept unless it is in a container of such material and so closed as to prevent the risk of contaminating the food.

A person who is handling the food shall:

1. Keep as clean as may be reasonably practicable all parts of his clothing or overclothing which are liable to come into contact with the food;
2. Keep any open cut or abrasion on any exposed part of his person covered with a suitable waterproof dressing;
3. Refrain from spitting;
4. Refrain from the use of tobacco or any other smoking mixture or snuff while he is handling any open food or is in any food room in which there is open food.

A person who handles open food, other than raw vegetables, intoxicating liquor or soft drinks, shall while so engaged wear sufficiently clean and washable overclothing, and every person who carries meat which is open food and which is liable to come into contact with his neck or head shall, while so engaged, also wear a clean and washable neck and head covering.

This regulation shall not apply:

1. To waiters in catering businesses;
2. To any person so long as he is engaged only in the carrying of unskinned rabbits or hares or unplucked game or poultry;
3. To transport of food:
   a. by railway undertakers; or
   b. in the course of the business of a carrier other than a railway undertaker in whom the vehicle used for the transport of food is not ordinarily so used;
   c. if in either case the person carrying the food takes all such other precautions as are reasonable and practicable to prevent

the food from coming into contact with any exposed part of his person or with any clothing other than over-clothing.

If anyone engaged in the handling of food becomes aware that he is suffering from, or is the carrier of, typhoid, paratyphoid, dysentery or any staphylococcal infection he shall inform the person carrying on the business immediately who in turn must notify the appropriate medical officer of health.

There are also regulations in the section relating to food premises, concerning soil drainage systems, water cisterns, sanitary conveniences, wash hand basins (which must have an adequate supply of hot and cold water as well as soap or detergent, nail brushes, clean towels or other drying facilities), first-aid materials, accommodation for clothing and facilities for washing food and equipment. Lighting and ventilation must be 'suitable and sufficient'. Food rooms must be kept clean throughout and kept in good order to prevent any risk of infection. The layout of the premises must permit waste and unfit food to be stored separately prior to disposal.

There are important regulations regarding the temperature at which food consisting of meat, fish, gravy, etc. is to be kept. When such food is brought into the premises of a catering business it shall, if it is not already at a temperature of 14°F (62.7°C) or above, on the one hand, or below 50°F (10°C) on the other hand, be brought to one or other of these temperatures without avoidable delay after arrival. Similar provisions apply to cooked food also.

Those who can be found guilty of offences under the regulations include food handlers, persons carrying on a food business and 'any person for the time being having the control or management of persons engaged in the handling of food'. Any person guilty of an offence is liable to a fine or imprisonment or both.

The regulation as applied to glass washing, simply requires glasses to be suitably constructed, kept clean and in good condition. It also requires sufficient sinks or 'other facilities' to be provided and properly maintained. Sinks must be supplied with hot and cold running water or hot water at a suitably controlled temperature or cold water only if a suitable bactericidal agent is used. Adequate supplies of detergent, clean clothes or other suitable cleaning and drying facilities must be on hand.

Clean glasses are to be provided during each serving. The following specify how it must be washed–that is, it must be either:

1. Washed in clean hot water and thereafter rinsed in water of 170°F minimum, or
2. Washed in clean hot water then washed in clean hot water with an efficient bactericidal agent in suitable quantity, and thereafter rinsed in clean water, or
3. Washed in clean hot water containing an efficient bactericidal agent in suitable quantity, and thereafter rinsed in clean water.

Case Study 1212
Food & Beverage--The Dubbingtons Case

Situation

Chrissie is a relatively new 17-year-old waitress at Dubbingtons, a large department store. One Saturday afternoon store security officers stop her as she is leaving, search her bags and find 11 lb of sliced ham and half-a-dozen eggs in them.

Chrissie admits that these came from the store restaurant's stocks, but claims that she was given them by Fred, the chef, in return for her helping out over her lunch break in the kitchen, which was short handed. Fred denies her story emphatically. 'She's lying...,' he says. 'You know I've no authority to make that sort of deal!'

Fred has been employed at Dubbingtons for the past twelve years. He is a big, genial man of 45, well liked by the other middle-rank departmental staff and undeniably possessed of excellent craft skills. However, the catering department (which comprises the customer restaurant, tea-room, coffee bar and staff canteen) has suffered for several years from higher than average food cost percentages and labour turnover.

The store has recently created the post of Catering Manager to control this side of its operations, and you have been appointed. You have been in the post for three weeks, and this is your second confrontation with Fred. The first was over the board's decision to close the senior staff dining-room and require staff to eat in the staff canteen: Fred apparently thinks you initiated this policy, and resents the fact that he will no longer be able to produce a limited number of high-quality meals and thus ingratiate himself with the senior staff.

There are few records, and those available throw little light on the reasons for the high food costs or the labour turnover in the catering sections. Fred's attitude of surly non-cooperativeness makes further investigations difficult. The other catering staff are non-committal, and it is very unlikely that they will be prepared to 'tell tales' against either Chrissie or Fred.

How would you deal with this situation?

Well, how should you? As it happens, this is one of those cases where you can use the classic problem-solving approach more or less as it stands.

The first thing to do is to re-read the case thoroughly until you are confident that you have assimilated all the facts (this isn't too difficult with a short case like this one, but is a bit harder with the longer ones). Some students find that it helps them to make a brief precise of the situation, though you shouldn't waste too much time in writing out points which you already have set down in front of you.

The second stage is to see what conclusions you can draw from the facts: in other words, to try to fit these into a pattern that makes sense. What has really been going on in this establishment? The facts–that Chrissie has been caught taking food home, the higher than average food costs, etc.–show that things haven't been going entirely according to plan, but what are the causes? Answering this kind of question will inevitably involve you in a certain amount of guesswork, because you can not know for certain what has been going on, but

Case Study cont. ...

Case Study cont. ...

some assumptions are more likely than others. For instance, there is a whole range of factors which could lead to high food costs, including bad purchasing, storage or portion control, but there isn't any supporting evidence in the case itself for most of these. On the other hand, there is some supporting evidence for an explanation based on pilferage. Ask yourself whether the other facts are consistent with this explanation, and see whether you can come up with a pattern of events which makes sense in terms of ordinary human nature.

The next stage is to identify the problems. As we have already said, make sure that you list them as well. Don't make the mistake of concentrating just on the immediate problem. This is a well-known pitfall in real life as well as in case studies. Keep in mind that your real objective is to get this unit running smoothly and efficiently.

Next, you have to consider the options open to you and their likely consequences. Remember that one of these options is to do nothing, though you may well feel that this is one of those cases where this course of action (or inaction) would simply make matters worse. Clearly, you have to make up your mind what to do about Chrissie, and you should also think hard about Fred, the chef. Be careful, though. It's no good writing something down as an option unless you actually have the power to do it. And be realistic. It isn't much good writing 'I would carry out a thorough investigation and gel to the bottom of this whole business. . .' The case has already given you Fred's answer, and what you are told about Fred suggests (deliberately) that he is a pretty tough, hard-bitten sort of character. How likely is it that he would change his story? The case has already told you that the records are incomplete. How likely is it that the other staff would volunteer information, especially about practices in which they themselves might have been involved?

Once you have established what your options are, your should go on to produce a specific recommendation or set of recommendations. Try to make these positive, and if possible try to manage with the resources already available to you. It is tempting to write 'If I had my way, I'd fire all the staff and start all over again', but top management doesn't usually look very kindly on this kind of approach. One of your problems in this case is Fred, the chef: no doubt you would like to see him replaced by someone else who is equally skilled but a lot easier to work with. However, you will get more credit if you can put forward a solution which allows you to operate effectively with the staff you already have. Try to make your recommendations practical. If you decide (as you might) that part of the answer lies in changing the system within which the staff are working, then you should outline what changes you propose to make and how you would introduce them to staff, both present and future.

Finally, a word about presentation. We have already indicated that this case can be answered along the classic problem-solving lines, which gives you a ready-made structure for your answer. How long should it be? Well, as a very rough approximation, you ought to be able to get 3-4 pages of answer out of every page of case study text. This probably sounds horrifying, but once you start, you'll find it very difficult to answer this one adequately in under 3-4 sides.

Case Study cont. ...

Case Study cont. ...

only that they committed the alleged act, but also that they knew it was wrong. Chrissie cannot deny that she took the items, but she might well argue that she thought Fred had the authority to let her have them, and unless we can show that she had been told otherwise our prosecution might well fail, especially since the law traditionally recognizes that 'perks' are a feature of the catering industry. As for Fred, we have to remember that it is Chrissie's word against his, and that he is entitled to the benefit of any doubt. So it is unlikely that we could successfully prosecute either of them, even if we were willing to accept the expense and loss of time involved.

The same arguments apply to termination. Fred is protected against unfair dismissal, and in the absence of any previous official (*i.e.*, provable) warnings he is likely to win in the event of an appeal. Chrissie is not protected to the same extent because she has not worked for long enough, and there may be grounds for dismissal.

Let us assume for a moment that we could indeed fire her: should we? We have to consider staff attitudes and morale. On the one hand, they may think it unfair if we dismiss Chrissie and retain Fred. On the other, a dismissal would show that we were in earnest about stopping pilferage. The arguments would appear to be evenly balanced, but we must also consider whether Chrissie and Fred are likely to work well together in the future after she has 'informed' on him.

In our view, this tips the scales against Chrissie, though we recognize that there is room for argument here.

c. Set up a proper control system. Neither prosecution nor dismissal really solves the underlying problems, and our emphasis must be on establishing control. This must include a proper system of recording orders, stocks, issues, consumption and wastage. It should also include issuing a statement of policy regarding 'perks', to form part of all present and future contracts of employment, together with an intensified programme of random checks to show that we really mean what we say. What this does is:

i. It helps to solve our problems with Chrissie and Fred by making it clear that we are doing something about the food costs.
ii. It should lead to a reduction in the food costs themselves.
iii. It may help to improve the labour turnover figures by improving morale, though this is not certain. We would recommend additional measures such as termination of employment interviews in order to establish the real reasons for the increase.
iv. It establishes our authority as catering managers, since we are shown to be not only in charge but doing 'something positive'.

5. Recommendations

Fairly obviously, it is alternative 4(c) which points the way forward. We would couple this with an investigation to discover the real cause or causes of the high labour turnover (which may turn out to have nothing to do with the immediate problem). We would also suggest an attempt to conciliate Fred by returning the responsibility for special functions to him. After

Case Study cont. ...

Case Study cont. ...

all, he is competent and well liked, and we should try to retain him if possible. If he accepts the new system, well and good. If he does not, then it is up to him to resign, which avoids any problems with unfair dismissal and allows us to recruit a new chef who will start with a clear idea of his position and responsibilities.

Notes

1. This uses the 'memo heading' format we mentioned earlier. There is no need to invent imaginary names: in fact, if you were doing this report as an assignment, you could put your tutor's name opposite the 'To'.
2. This kind of summary is possible with a relatively short case, but you will find that it becomes progressively more difficult with the longer ones. In fact, it doesn't earn many marks, if any, and you should reduce it to the minimum. We have included it here because it is required by the context (*i.e.*, a disciplinary report).
3. This gets round the case's failure to provide some important background facts. Most cases have this kind of 'hole' in them, and it is useful to be able to circumvent them smoothly.
4. A common-sense assumption, so obvious as not to need labelling as such. Practically all stores reserve the right to search employees and their baggage as a matter of course.
5. This is by far the most important conclusion you can come to in this section. The temptation is to concentrate on trying to find some way of proving Fred's guilt or innocence. In fact, the real point is to get this department functioning efficiently.
6. This is probably too introspective (*i.e.*, self-critical) to be included in a real-life report, but it is a genuine problem none the less, and you need to show that you have recognized it as such.
7. Again, this is a little too 'introspective' for inclusion in a real life report. At this stage, however, you are only practising decision-making, and it is useful to set out all the stages of your thinking. Common sense should tell you what is likely to strike an employer as unduly negative.
8. These two paragraphs provide a fairly bald summary of the legal position. They could be 'enriched' by references to the statutes involved and possible precedents. However, don't get carried away to the extent of seeing this as a purely legal problem. The real point is still control.
9. You will see that we have followed our own advice and climbed down off the fence here. As markers, we would be happy enough to see you argue either way as long as you recognize that there is indeed room for argument over this point.
10. These ought to be set out in much more detail in a complete answer. The necessary measures are obvious enough, and you should be familiar with them from your work on food and beverage control.
11. You might draft a specimen statement and show it as an appendix. This would certainly 'enrich' your answer. Remember that one of the things we are looking for is the ability to implement solutions.

The number of employees required will depend upon the size of the hotel. However, some of the positions found in a food and beverage service are described below:

Restaurant Manager

The restaurant manager is responsible for the overall operation of the establishments which serve food. He coordinates and directs the work of the employees. He is responsible for the food and equipment necessary for each restaurant. Periodically he inspects the restaurant to ensure the maintenance of health and sanitation regulations.

He performs many clerical and financial duties such as keeping records, directing payroll operations, handling large sums of money and taking inventories. His work usually involves a constant contact with the customers taking their suggestions, handling complaints and creating a friendly atmosphere. A number of hotels, employ specially trained assistants, often called food manager or assistant managers who supervise the kitchen staff and are responsible for the preparation of food served.

Guests in Coffee Shop

Servers primarily take the order for service of food and beverages, make out customer food checks/KOT and in some cases serve as a cashier in the smaller hotels. They have varied duties depending on the size and kind of hotel in which they are employed. They present menus to the customers after they are seated, assist in suggesting choices from the menu, inform the customer of special preparation and seasoning of food and sometimes suggest beverages that would be complementary to the meal. They check to see that correct silver is on the table and try to attend to any special requests by customers to make their dining more pleasurable. They follow the more formal and correct protocol procedures for serving food. Captain, waiters or headwaiters may greet and seat the guests and supervise the service. Busboys or girls may assist in cleaning table, refilling water glasses, pouring coffee, setting tables and removing dishes and soiled linen to the kitchen.

The restaurant manager is responsible for planning and organizing all the service activities of the restaurant such as staffing, scheduling, training, promotion of team spirit, motivation to achieve targets.

Food and Beverage Manager

The person responsible for this department is known as food and beverage manager. He heads the department that involves guest relations as well. He is concerned with the smooth flow of foods and service before they reach the guest. He must have organizational ability and foresight. He must have a thorough knowledge of hotel organization, supervisory techniques in the catering field and labour legislation. In addition, a food and beverage manager must have knowledge of commerce and accounting and a perfect and up-to-date knowledge of the preparation of dishes and prices of foodstuffs. He is directly responsible to the general manager for all service activities in bars and restaurants. In small properties he is responsible for the buying, receiving and storing of foodstuffs and beverages. He organizes banquets and puts forward proposals to the general manager regarding the marketing and pricing. He and the executive chef work together on menu designing, pricing, catering, banquet arrangements and staffing.

The duties and responsibilities of the food and beverage manager depend on the size and type of the establishment. He is either responsible for the implementation of agreed policies or for contributing to the setting of catering policies. The larger the organization the less likely the manager is to be involved in policy setting.

The food and beverage manager should concentrate on the short-term and long-term needs of the operation in the confines of the hotel's needs and objectives.

In order to give good service, a restaurant employee must have a thorough knowledge of the menu. Each day before going on duty, he should review the menu to determine those items specially prepared for the day including entrees, daily entree from kitchen, salads, soups and desserts. He should know the principal methods of cooking.

All food and beverage personnel, generally, fall under the jurisdiction of the F & B manager, who reports directly to the F & B director or general manager. He is responsible for the scheduling of service personnel, the reporting of hours worked, the control and distribution of all the administration function in the service area. The importance of this department will depend on the number and size of outlets available in a hotel. For example, in many hotels a variety of different types of restaurants, bars and banqueting facilities are aimed at the registered guests and outside customers, while in others, a restaurant and a bar may be exclusively for resident guests.

Senior Captain/Supervisor/Mâitre d' Hôtel

He must have the knowledge of foreign languages and knowledge of foreign and national specialities, wines and tastes of clients of different nationalities. He is also responsible for organization and administration of food and beverages, and conducting training for staff. He must have a sound knowledge of hygiene and safety standards and principles of organization.

Captain/Headwaiter/Mâitre d' Hôtel

He should have knowledge of foreign languages and thorough knowledge of various dishes. He assists the headwaiter in receiving the guests and taking orders.

He should have knowledge of different dishes and should be able to explain the dishes to the customers. In most of the deluxe restaurants, game birds are carved in front of the guests by the station waiter. Whenever the station headwaiter is busy receiving, the station waiter is responsible for all tables; he will do the gueridon service. He is in charge of a *rang* or group of about five tables to seat approximately twenty guests. In the absence of the station headwaiter he performs all his duties.

Station Headwaiter/Mâitre d' Hôtel d' Carre/Mâitre d' Hôtel d' Rang

In a large restaurant he is in charge of 125 covers. He is responsible for the cleanliness of tables, chairs, etc. He allocates stations, tables to the station waiters/waitresses. He also checks the layout of the covers, tables and sideboards. He receives the guests either directly or through the headwaiters and assists them to their seats. He takes the orders of the guests and passes it to the station waiters/waitresses for the service of food. He is responsible for smooth service and also attends to all the guest complaints. He also looks after the gueridon service, as it requires lot of skill.

Assistant Captain/Reception Headwaiter/ Senior Steward/Demi Chef d' rang

Knowledge of foreign language and national specialities are essential for the reception waiter. In a large restaurant the *maitre d' hotel* is busy, as he is responsible for a number of duties and cannot always welcome the patrons and lead them to their respective tables. To perform these duties a reception headwaiter is employed. He will have a plan of the room with the table number. He reserves the table and the place for the guests. He greets the guests upon arrival and will take them to the table and seat them, leaving them in the charge of the station headwaiter.

Senior Waiter/Steward/Commis d' rang

He/she should have sound knowledge of foreign and national cooking specialities and wines and of the tastes of clients of different nationalities, language, and of labour legislation. He should have knowledge of taking orders from the kitchen and service and cleaning.

Junior Station Waiter/Demi Chef

The duties of a junior station waiter are similar to that of a station waiter, the main difference being that in the beginning, he has a small station comprising 8-10 covers. He serves the food and also removes the soiled dishes himself.

Waiter/Servers/Garcon

He should have good knowledge of national and international dishes and should be able to handle restaurant equipment efficiently. Knowledge of hygiene and safety regulation is essential. His duty is to take the guest order directly or through *maitre d' hotel* or *chef d' rang*. The order is passed on to the kitchen. Thereafter he assembles the foods, carries it to the restaurant and serves it to the guests. If the waiter is busy, the *commis debarrasseur* helps him in all his work except that of service. On the allotment of station, the waiter should check and wipe the cutlery, crockery, glasses and the sideboard. In addition to this, the waiter lays the table cloth, folds the napkins, makes sure that the cruet set is filled, the ashtrays are clean, fills the sauce bottle, checks that oil and vinegar stands are ready for service and there is adequate stock of linen. Quite often, he polishes the cutlery and silver. He is also responsible for the presentation of the bill, when the guest departs, removes the dirt and cleanses the table.

Thus, the waiter is responsible for the service of all food and beverages to the guests seated within his station and also for the maintenance of that station.

Assistant Waiter/Commis Waiter

An assistant waiter must have knowledge of various dishes.

Assistant Trolley Waiter/Commis d' Wagon

He brings the trolley to the restaurant. Passes on the trolley to the station headwaiter or to the station waiter for the actual service. He is also responsible for arranging the *hors d' oeuveres*, pudding, desserts, etc. and also sets the gueridon service of *flambé* dishes.

Assistant Waiter (Cleaning)/Assistant Steward/Busboys/Bus Persons/*Commis d' Barrasseur*

This is the juniormost position in the restaurant. The main duties of the assistant cleaning waiter are to carry soiled dishes, dusting and sweeping of floor, cleaning of carpet, tables and chairs.

The busboy assists the waiter/waitress and serves bread rolls, coffee and other items and clears dirty dishes, sets the table, changes table cloths, picks up crumbs, fills water glasses and re-polishes silverware when necessary.

Carver/Tenchelier

Carver is usually under the kitchen department but included among the *maitre d' hotel* team. The duties of a carver are to lay the buffet tables for roast and cold meals, carve saddle or barn of beef, roast legs of mutton and roast turkey at the table as required. He tries to get the maximum number of positions, from each joint with as little wastage as possible.

Trainee Waiter/The Commis d' rang

He mainly fetches and carries and does a little service of vegetables, sauces, offering rolls and placing plates upon tables. He clears the table after each course and acts under the intimation of the *chef d' rang.*

Apprentices/Debarrasseur

Apprentice is the learner who has joined the hotel wishing to take up waiting as career. In continental brigades, young waiters and apprentices are known as *'piccolo'* which means little one in Italian. During pre-preparation periods he carries out the cleaning task and will keep the sideboard well filled with equipment. He also helps to fetch and carry items as required.

Room Service

Room service needs a designated area. In most of the hotels it is located next to the kitchen and elevator. In small hotels room service is handled from different kitchens during different shifts. In some of the units there is a designated room service, breakfast kitchen, which closes down after service.

The person in charge of dispatching, the manager or captain, should take the order and, in turn, give it to the next available server. The order should be dispatched as soon as received. There must be space for a desk and a light clipboard, one for each day of the week and one for the future. On these boards all special orders for each particular day, such as parties, receptions, cake orders and complementary orders, must be displayed. The room service manager's office could be used for administrative work. The servers, waiting area should be equipped with benches or chairs, a table, and a cloth rack. Room service requires a storage area for linen, fuel, heaters, silver and other equipment. There should be a refrigerator to keep flowers, butter and condiments. Space should also be provided to keep complementary fruit baskets and other gifts until delivered. For practical reasons the breakdown of tables and dish washing should be done adjacent to the room service department. Room service should have its own elevator. The 'flying kitchen' concept is also used by some hotels, which install in the elevator enough equipment to service a continental breakfast.

Room Service Manager/Head of the Room Service/Captain

He is known as room service captain. He is a very crucial employee for the smooth operation of room service. A successful captain must know a foreign language, have knowledge of national and foreign beverages, hygiene and safety standards, cleaning techniques. He should have a good idea about dishes and types of service in each restaurant.

Room Service Order Taker/Floor Waiter/Chef d' etage

He handles all calls from guests, takes their food and beverage order, and coordinates the service of these with the room service waiters and captains. In addition he also reserves table for the various restaurants. He is responsible to the restaurant manager.

Room Service Waiter/Assistant Floor Waiters/Commis d' etage

The room service waiter is basically a food and beverage waiter especially trained to service food and drinks into the room. He also writes bills and collects the money from guests. The room service waiter is responsible for the equipment he uses while executing his duties.

Lounge Waiter/Le Garçon d' (la) Salle

He serves light refreshments, afternoon tea and drinks in the lounge and other public areas of the hotel.

The Restaurant

The label 'restaurant' is in general use and is applied wherever food is served. It can refer to a wayside cabin catering for transport workers, factory canteen, fish-and-chip shop, and so on: the simplicity of their operation, only calls for the aid of control technique in a simple form.

But the restaurant in its highest developed expression of public catering service could not survive by its profits without the aid of control methods, and much depends on their office whether its potential is fully realized.

Case Study 1213 Restaurant

Situation

A restaurant maintained a staff of five bar boys. It appeared that only four were needed.

Results of Analysis

It was found true that four boys could handle all bus boys tasks. When one boy left the remaining crew readily absorbed his work. Management saved Rs. 45,000 per year.

Case Study 1214 Dining Room

Situation

In one dining room it was found that the average production per waiter fell three covers below that which reasonably could be expected.

Results of Analysis

Each waiter was given an additional day off per week. As a result, each waiter could do more cover per day and his average daily earnings were higher. The hotel saved Rs. 40,000 per year. The service did not suffer and the waiters earned approximately the same in four days as they formerly did in six.

Some types of popular restaurants are able to impose a 'system' on their clientele, which greatly facilitates the work of the control but in another class of restaurants all apparent system of a clerical nature is kept well out of sight and does not touch the customer.

Restaurant Control Clerk

Care should be taken in appointing the control clerk charge of this audit. It is not an easy audit to perform, especially where the volume of business is high. A flair for this task, coupled with a comprehensive knowledge of the working of the restaurant and its associated departments, are most essential.

The restaurant control clerk's work entails constant contact with the restaurant, bars, and kitchen personnel. These people are instant judges of whether the control clerk is skilled in the job, and are adapt at raising a smokescreen of diversion to confuse and mislead the novice. Once the word is passed around that the controller is 'easy' the flow of irregularities will rapidly develop from a trickle to a torrent. Another adverse feature of this audit is its temptations; and a weak or indifferent character can soon become involved to the point of compromise. The weakness in the operation of all protective systems is the human equation.

A method introduced to put a stop to the practice outlined above worked in the following way. All the service bills from the bar cellar are first dealt with by a controller before being passed to the restaurant controller. These checks are first entered into a record by the respective departments, and this record, together with the checks, is sent to the cellar controller for reconciliation.

The seller controller then analyses the sales under their appropriate groupings and gives the selling price value of the separate totals. These should, of a course, agree with the dissected totals on the restaurant business sheets compiled by the restaurant controller.

Tea Service and Its Control

The following survey does not apply to 'tea shops' but only where a hotel restaurant provides afternoon tea as a regular service.

This service, in many respects, is quite a simple one, and on the surface would not appear to give much scope for loss in revenue; but because of its apparent simplicity, it often happens that control is not applied with the same enthusiasm as to the other services. The tea service organizations can vary in their details in almost every hotel, but the major variation centres around and drawing of supplies and the billing system.

These two points are of primary interest to the controller when drafting the control schedules, and the wisest plan to adopt in the framing of these is to study the methods employed for drawing supplies; from the initial drawing of the service bill to the issue of supplies from the distributing points. The organization of the distributing sections is also of interest to the controller, for flaws in their operation can provide the main opening for 'play'.

It is advisable, wherever possible to bring the distribution service to one point, the still room. With 'set' teas, those that have an inclusive charge for a fixed menu, it should be quite easy to bring this into effect. But it does happen in some establishments that patrons are given a choice in pastries, in which case the distributing point is within the restaurant. Where this occurs the waiter in charge will issue an order for anticipated needs, and obtain the supply direct from the kitchen department. Control of the consumption of supplies, at both points, is checked by the schedules.

The system which gives 100 per cent protection against pilfering and other irregularities in this department has not yet been invented; and the most that can be hoped is to reduce the drain to a slow drip. It is possible to test the volume of this drain from time to time, and an alert controller will do so to assure that the trickle is not becoming a torrent.

Service Check Pad

This is the item, which sets the machine in motion, and follows the control throughout its entire course. It is used by:

1. Waiters for supplies from kitchen and still room
2. Wine butlers for supplies from bars and cellar. Also cigars and cigarettes
3. Cashiers for collecting bills
4. Control for checking charges on bills

In this form of the service supply, two distinct series are used, 'waiter's' and 'wine bullet's'. A pad has been devised which gives these bills in sets of three, the printing on each copy being in a different colour, and, producing two duplicates by the use of one carbon.

Waiter's Pad

1. 1st Copy – Black printing
   : main supply order
2. 2nd Copy – Transparent
   : For use of commies

and slotted metal box to await collection by the control office.

Control

At the conclusion of each service the control office:

1. Collects restaurant cashier's business record, duplicate bills, duplicates service bills.
2. Compares the cash receipt attached to business record with duplicate receipt in the cashier's office.
3. Removes the cash register total strip and verifies the amount on cash receipt.
4. Collects original service bills from the respective departments.
5. Duplicate bills arranged by the restaurant cashier in the numerical sequence of the bill numbers, are checked with the entries on the business record and with a total break-up under the respective headings. (The number of headings, which form this analysis, can be greatly exaggerated, and thus will waste a lot of time and effort and have no useful purpose. The normal headings are: Provisions; Coffee; Wines; Spirits and Liqueurs; Beers and Minerals; Cigars and Cigarettes; Sundries.)
6. Duplicate bills are sorted into the sequence of table numbers.
7. Service bills are sorted into the sequence of table numbers; food and bar bills are grouped separately.
8. The controller compares the service orders with the bill entries, and checks the charges with the hotel's tariffs.
9. All undercharges and omissions are recorded as follows: date; bill number; table number; service; details of query; amount.

These are dealt with immediately after the close of the audit. Under the 'credit' column of this record the details of settlement are shown.

Still Room

All supplies to this department, tea, coffee, sugar, milk, butter, jam, pastries, etc., are listed daily, by the control office, in quantity and not cash value, into a record under these headings. Credit to this account is given by service bills from all services: breakfast (tea or coffee), luncheon, afternoon tea, dinner and listed under the headings.

This statement covers the period of one month and is concluded by crediting the record with the supplies remaining in hand in the still room. The totals are then used to give the following information:

1. Tea (breakfast, where stated, and afternoon tea).
2. The number served per rupee: coffee: (breakfast, where stated, luncheon and dinner).
3. The number served per rupee, sugar (all services), milk (all services), number served per pint/rue.
4. Butter (all covers served in all services) quantity per 100 covers.
5. Jam (breakfast) (afternoon tea) quantity per 100 covers.
6. Pastry (afternoon tea) number consumed per head.

It is not necessary to await the end of the month before applying tests of consumption; nor is it necessary to carry out stocktaking to extract results. The still room rarely holds in stock more than its daily requirements, and it should be difficult matter to assess these.

Where the volume of business justifies, or reference to the record indicates heavy drawing from stores, the test should be made at frequent intervals. Unless the still room is brought under rational control, heavy leakage of supplies will develop.

Issues to Staff Hall

Where staff requirements are served from this point the following suggestions may be of use:

1. Endeavour, as far as possible, to limit the service to beverages. Unrestricted use by the general staff of still room service is a cause of confusion and is open to abuse. Such items as sugar, milk, butter, jam should be a direct supply from store to the staff hall and under the care of the staff steward.
2. Staff should not be entitled to draw supplies from the still room without a written order signed by responsible officials. Each order will be taken into the still room statement under the heading 'staff'.
3. The still room should be notified of staff entitlement in writing, with the signature of the manager.

Pastries drawn direct from the kitchen for service within the restaurant, as stated earlier, is supplied through an order by the waiter in charge. All pastry unconsumed should be returned to kitchen with a voucher stating the number, signed by both waiter and kitchen clerk. The total consumed will be compared with the number of teas served.

Where these control rules are disregarded the consumption per tea served, will rapidly rise owing to lack of governance.

Control

The elaboration of most systems is in writing and not in practice.

System No. 1

1. The control office issues the cashier with a stock of numbered bill pads. A record of these issues is listed in the control office, and the cashier gives a receipt for supplies.

   Note: The pads should be distinct from those used in other services and one giving three copies is preferable: bill, supply, waiter. Three copies, at one writing on the same numbered docket greatly simplifies the process of control when tallying the vouchers, returned by cashier, with those from the still room. 'Two-copy' pads entail the use of a service bill pad for supplies and comparing still room and 'charge' vouchers and this can be a lengthy and inconclusive process.
2. Prior to the commencement of the service, the cashier issues a pad to each member of the waiting staff. The cashier before the issue of pads prepares a 'waiter's card'. This card notes the following: date, waiter's name or number, sales. Unused folios are returned. The waiter signs for the receipt of the pad. It is vitally necessary to bring pads under a rational form of control.
3. Fresh pads required during the service will be issued only in exchange for the one used.
4. At the conclusion of the service the waiting staff will pay to the cashier according to the total of sales vouchers (No. 3 copy) and these will be noted, together with folios unused, on the 'waiter's card' by the cashier. Sales vouchers will be attached to the 'waiter's card' by a staple fastener.
5. The cashier will enter the business record from the 'waiter's card' summary. There is no need to detail the record of the 'waiter's card' on the business record, and each entry need only (1) 'waiter's card'. Number-cards should be numbered in numerical sequence and used in this order; (2) waiter's name or number; (3) folio number (*i.e.*, 0216/222); (4) sales total. This method spares the cashier a considerable amount of clerical work, and facilitates the control check.
6. The cashier after paying the amount to the

cashier's office and attaching the receipt to the business record, forwards all vouchers and records to the control office.

7. Control will apply the following audit:
   i. Check entries on 'waiter's card' with attached vouchers; agreeing cash totals and reconciling vouchers returned with those issued;
   ii. Compare entries on business record with 'waiter's cards' and cash receipt with sales total;
   iii. Check still room vouchers with those attached to 'waiter's cards' (No. 3 copy);
   iv. Destroy, or cancel, unused folios.

With reference to Schedule Number IV, it may be claimed that this is wasteful, but in practice it will be found that this is negligible. To bring them into re-use is confusing and may cause a break in the control system. Attempts to economise in this direction should start when orders are placed with the stationers by assessing the number of folios normally used by a waiter during this service. In cases where only one or two folios have been used from a pad the control may issue for re-use, but this rests with the discretion of the controller.

The foregoing system is simple to operate, does not impede the waiting service, and reduces clerical work to a minimum, and points all queries directly to its source.

System No. 2

This system is similar in principle to that applied for the lunch and dinner services. (Refer to notes on billing earlier in this chapter).

1. The waiter uses an ordinary service pad (1st copy supply, 2nd copy cashier, 3rd copy waiter) and quotes a table number.
2. The cash desk, for this service, is placed close to the service point, so that the waiter, when drawing supplies, can pass No. 2 copy to cashier.
3. On receipt of No. 2 copy the cashier opens a bill (loose, in duplicate form) and files it into a folder numbered according to the tables. As it is unusual for additional charges to follow for this service the cashier can enter the business record as each bill is brought into use.

The process then follows the same routine as indicated earlier.

Grill Room Control

The normal difference between the grill room and the restaurant is one of 'inclusive' and *a la carte* charges. In the grill room the charges are according to the items consumed; at least, this is the general policy. It is, however, customary to stipulate a minimum charge by way of covering the cost of service where sales to customer amount to only a small tariff charge, which would otherwise prove uneconomical.

A well-patronized grill room is often a more profitable undertaking to the hotel than the restaurant, primarily due to the absence of entertainment bands and cabaret–frequent features in the restaurant service. Admittedly, the cost of this is taken into account in the restaurant charges but many restaurateurs will agree it does happen that restaurant profits become absorbed in paying of entertainment.

From the control point of view, there is little or no difference between the grillroom and restaurant. Checking and billing are exactly similar, with the one exception that in the former items consumed are listed on the bill and not included in one charge, as in the other case. The control clerk compares all entries on the bills with the food and wine bills and continues the control process in exactly the same manner as with the restaurant. The fact of charges being 'per item' entails a close reference to the tariff and verification that all bills for food supplies have a corresponding entry on the bills.

It may happen that the grillroom manager will quote an inclusive charge to a regular patron, which will be slightly under the tariff charge for the items consumed, in which case the manager will sign the bill to this effect. Where this occurs frequently the control should make a record of the difference, quoting the date and bill number. Departures from standard tariff charges have a tendency to grow when such reductions fail to bring comment from an appropriate authority.

It is not the province of the controller to challenge the authority of a departmental manager to make price concessions, but where reductions are made it is normal routine to acquaint the general management. This, of course, applies to food only. To accept the right of a departmental manager to discount the charges for cellar supplies is not normal, and under no circumstances should these be passed by the control in the first instance without reference to and consent of the management.

The approach of the controller to these matters is very important. During the course of the daily working of the control department many matters arise which call for the exercise of tact and a sense of balance. The position of the controller can be a most invidious one unless perspective is correctly focused.

The management is interested in the smooth running of the establishment, and a controller is acting on a false premise if, in seeking credit for his efforts, he is continually referring matters for their decision which could be amicably settled at a lower level.

Such conduct will lose the respect and co-operation of those outside of the control office whose goodwill contributes a lot to control efficiency.

Incomes connected with F & B can easily be identified with either food or beverages. There are some incomes and expenses, which are applicable to both the heads. All such joint incomes and expenses may be segregated by using a equitable method of allocation. The basis of allocation may be based on estimated percentages applied to the total amount of joint income and expense accounts. Thus separate operating results can be calculated for both food and beverages.

The main incomes of this department can be classified as:

1. Sundry banquet incomes
2. Miscellaneous incomes

These incomes can also be divided on the basis of sales point:

1. Restaurant sales
2. Coffee shop sales
3. Grillroom sales
4. Room/floor service sales
5. Bar sales
6. Banquet sales

All beverage sales are credited to this account. The cost of beverage served on employee cheques, are deducted from cost of merchandise consumed and charged to the respective department as employees' meals, entertainment, etc. All beverage sales may be classified as:

1. Restaurant/dining room beverage sales
2. Room service beverage sales
3. Banquet beverage sales
4. Public bar sales

A detailed analysis could be made by further analysis such as:

1. Wine
2. Spirits and liqueurs
3. Beers
4. Mineral waters

13. Bar Operations

A Guest room

For purpose of beverages, a hotel may have different types of bars depending upon its requirement. Usually four types of bars are found:

1. Public bar
2. Service bar
3. Portable bar
4. In-room bar

Public Bar

It is also known as 'Front Bar'. In these bars the guest can interact with the bartender and other service personnel. There are provisions for guest seating at the bar itself and there may be separate room or area for the purpose.

Service Bar

This is also known as hidden bar. It is designed for the hotel's food and beverage service staff only and serves one or more food service areas and/or room service. Most of these bars are centrally located in the back of house spaces within and out of guest view.

Portable Bar

It is a bar that is easy to setup anywhere, for example, in a garden, by the poolside or a room, etc.

In-room Bar

It may also be called mini-bar. The beverage manager is deeply involved in the design of these bars and is responsible for their marketing and control. As regards the responsibility of inventory, it rests with the room service.

The staff should know exactly, which measures and glasses are to be used for different types of drinks. They must know the correct temperature at which to serve the various drinks, garnish, and presentation, and the prices.

For proper control of bars it is essential to set up systems to cover the following areas:

1. Billing and checking system for the bar
2. Cash handling and control
3. Cellar work
4. Handling complaints
5. Handling emergencies
6. Licensing laws

The bar must be properly equipped with corkscrews, crown cork opener, and sharp knife

Wine Bottles

Bottled Spirit presented

Table 13.1: Tips for Wine Service

Place all wineglasses on the table in the same order as the wine is served. All wineglasses should appear to the right of the water goblet–the only glass to the left of the water is the cordial glass and port wineglass. In a formal setting, the glasses would appear as follows, starting at the right:

1. Sherry glass
2. White wineglass
3. Champagne saucer or goblet
4. Water goblet
5. Port wineglass
6. Cordial glass

Always serve wine from the right and food from left. The wine stand should always be placed to the right of the host or person who orders the wine.

large bars is known as 'head barman'. He is assisted by barmen/barmaids, if the volume of business demands. In large hotels having several bars and a large volume of business there is a bar manager who looks after all bars and is directly responsible to the food and beverage manager.

In large hotels, the department in charge of food and services makes arrangement for banquets and is under the responsibility of a banquet manager, restaurant manager or *maître d' hôtel* to distinguish him from the head waiters of the different restaurants. In small hotels, the incharge of food service department is known as head waiter/head waitress. He/she is responsible for private dining rooms and banquet halls and the service of food and beverage in the guest rooms. In some typical hotels the headwaiter is assisted by a staff of captains who directs the service-waiters and waitresses, who take orders and serve. Once a function is booked and all 'selling' arrangements have been made, the banquet service group takes over. The headwaiter has a most important job and is responsible for a variety of duties. In addition to supervising the setting of the room, he must make sure that the banquet steward has the proper type and sufficient amount of glasses, china and silver available for the party. He must see the linen has been reserved and works very closely with the chef.

The wine steward handles the purchasing and receiving of the beverages. All liquor and wine is stored in the wine room or wine cellar and issued by a requisition. The requisition is made out and signed by the head bartender, who reports to the food and beverage manager.

The food and beverage department is responsible for planning, coordinating and controlling all departments in the hotel that are concerned with the purchasing, storage, issues, preparation and service of foods and beverages. The production side is delegated to the executive chef whilst the service side may be delegated to a food and beverage manager or to the various specialist managers and supervisors. It includes all staff engaged in the purchasing, preparation and serving of food. Roommaids, who serve breakfast in bedrooms, should be excluded from this department.

Excise Laws

The management and the members of staff who disperse and serve alcoholic drinks must know the relevant sections of the laws that immediately affect their work. The relevant sections of the law must be set down in writing and the staff should be trained accordingly. They should be given a copy of the relevant law; appropriate training should be imparted and should be told about the penalties for transgression..

These regulations are concerning:

1. Permitted hours for the service of alcoholic drinks
2. The difference between residents and non-residents in a hotel
3. Statutory measure to be used
4. Dilution and passing off
5. Underage drinking and the purchase of cigarettes
6. Drinking up times
7. Betting, gambling and lotteries
8. Prostitution
9. Price indication regulations
10. Drinking and smoking on duty
11. Gratuities
12. Over-rigging/under-rigging cash register

A wine/alcohol licence can be held by one person or by two or more together or, in the case of limited companies, by a director or secretary of the company as an individual. In the case of tenanted premises, it is the tenant, not the landlord, who holds the licence and whose name is, therefore, exhibited above the front door. Applications must be made to the concerned authority, with copies to the police, the rating authorities, and the fire authority.

An on-licence, permitting the sale of liquor for consumption on or off the premises may, at the request of the applicant or otherwise, impose conditions–making the licence a 'conditional licence'. Nowadays such conditions are normally limited to rendering a licence a six-day one (the establishment being closed on Sundays); early closing (closing the bar one hour earlier than the normal permitted hour in the evening); or seasonal (closing altogether for part of the year). When a renewal or transfer of a conditional licence is granted the competent authority must revoke the condition, if requested to do so. Such conditions can be applied to restaurant and residential licences also.

Residential licences permit the sale of liquor only to residents or their friends (the resident must pay for the drinks) on the premises but if a meal (e.g. a packed lunch) is supplied for consumption elsewhere it is permissible to sell liquor for consumption with it.

A restaurant licence permits the sale of liquor to persons taking table meals, provided the applicant is of full age and a fit and proper person, and the premises are suitable for residence or meals as the case may be. An application for such a licence, or for its renewal, cannot normally be refused. There are other grounds for refusal, such as where premises have previously been misused or where a large proportion of the customers are under eighteen; and the holder of any type of licence can be disqualified on conviction for certain offences, some of which are detailed below in the note on the responsibilities of the licensee.

A restaurant licence may be for six days, early closing or seasonal. When the premises are open for luncheon only there may be a condition restricting the permitted hours so as to exclude the evening and when dinners only are served, the earlier period of the day may be excluded.

For both residential and restaurant licences the court may make other conditions such as that there shall

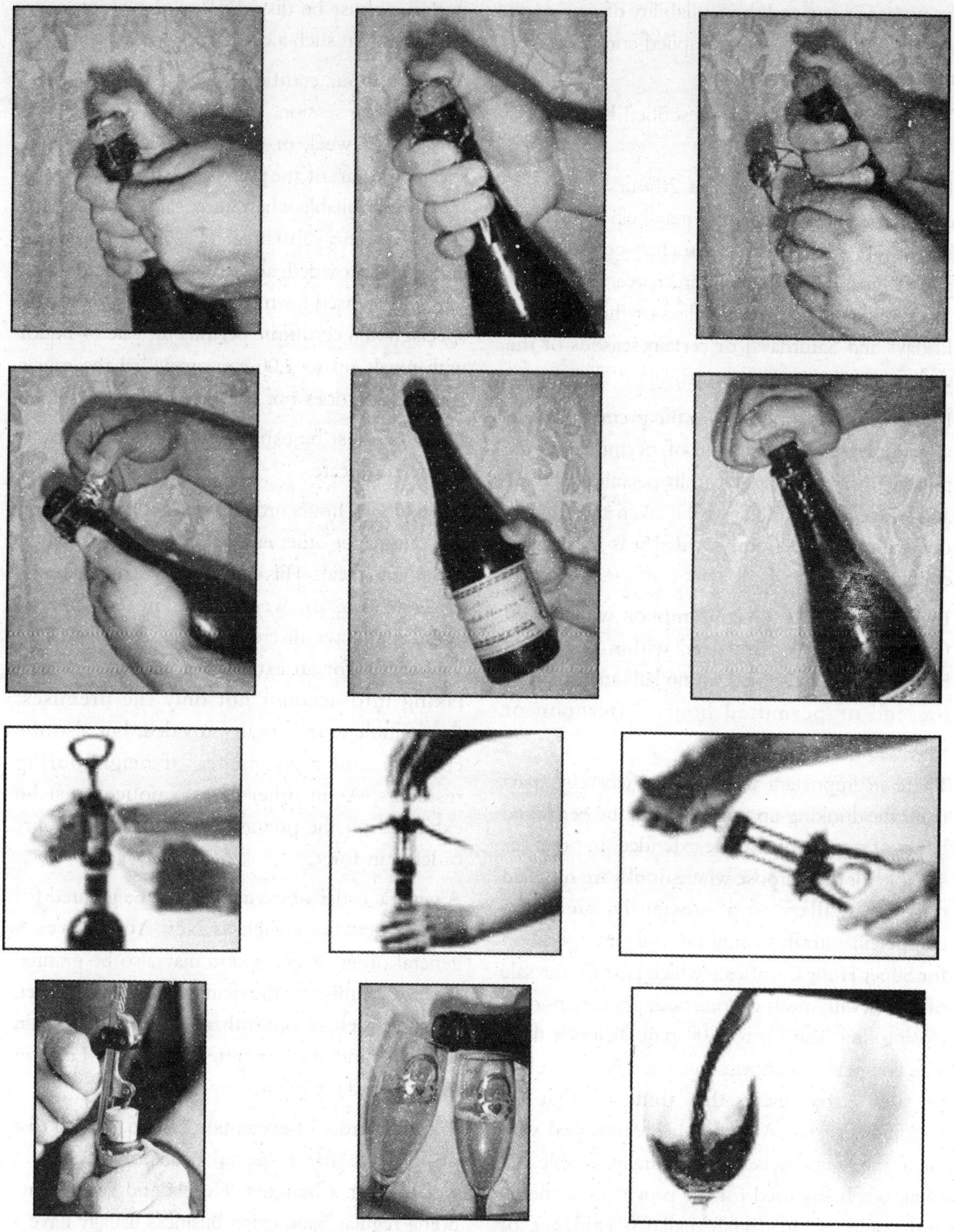

Wine Service

be no bar or tap, and the availability of water and non-alcoholic drinks is an implied condition of a restaurant licence.

The permitted hours are prescribed by the local authorities.

Provided there is a break of 2-hours after mid-day the competent authority may help to vary the local hours and can add an extra half-hour to 11.00 p.m. if justified by local circumstance. Sometimes this is done only for certain days of the week (e.g. Fridays and Saturdays) or certain seasons of the year (e.g. the summer months).

Liquor may be consumed on the premises for up to ten minutes after the end of permitted hours, provided it was bought within permitted hours, and liquor so purchased may be taken away during this ten-minute period provided it is in a sealed container.

Liquor purchased for consumption with a meal (provided it was purchased within permitted hours) can be consumed within half an hour after the end of permitted hours (afternoon or evening).

There are important arrangements whereby, apart from the drinking-up time allowed, the permitted hours of restaurants can be extended. In premises suitable for the purpose where drinks are supplied only as ancillary to a substantial meal, the competent authority cannot refuse the application for Super Hour Certificate which permits the sale of drinks with meals for one hour after the normal closing time and up to 3.00 p.m. at lunch time. The competent authority must satisfy themselves 'in such a manner as they think fit' that the conditions of the Act have been complied with (as to the premises being structurally suitable and bona-fide being used for the provision of meals) and could, if they wish, call for evidence or hear evidence to the contrary, but in practice they rarely do.

A notice must be displayed on the premises to the effect that such a certificate is in force.

A special hour certificate can be applied for at any licensing session. It may be granted for only part of the week or part of the year and may specify the part of the premises to which it applies. It is only available when intoxicants are supplied as ancillary to a substantial meal where music and dancing is provided, and, of course, the premises must be licensed for music and dancing also. The special hours certificate permits the sale of liquor with meals up to 2.00 a.m. provided the music and dancing does not end before then.

A notice must be exhibited outlining the details of the certificate.

An extended hours order can be applied for when live musical or other entertainment is provided in addition to meals. This extends the permitted hours to 1.00 a.m. on weekdays. The competent authorities have discretion whether to grant an application for an extended hour order or not, taking into account not only the premises, entertainment and meals provided, but also the comfort and convenience of neighbouring residents. As in other cases a notice must be exhibited on the premises if an extended hours order is in force.

A general order of exemption can be granted for special occasions such as New Year's Eve. A general order of exemption may also be granted to allow premises in the vicinity of a public market, or where there is some other local need, to remain open beyond the permitted hours. In London these orders are granted by the police.

A special order of exemption can be granted to a no-licensee for a special occasion such as a wedding or a banquet. Hotels and restaurants doing regular banqueting business usually have a well-established procedure for applying for SOEs (special order of exemptions) giving the required notice in advance. There may be difficulty in obtaining an exemption order for a Sunday in some special cases or for wedding receptions for actors or other workers who cannot hold the reception on a weekday.

Bar Manager

All matters concerning liquors, wines and beers are coordinated by a separate function within the food and beverage department called bar or beverage. The bar manager is responsible for all activities relating to liquor, wine and beer.

Barman/Garcon d' Comtoir

He is also known as head bartender. He handles the purchasing and receiving of beverages. He should have the ability to prepare alcoholic drinks, mixed drinks and cocktails and have some idea of the tastes of foreign visitors. Knowledge of hygiene and safety standards, labour legislation and price regulations is absolutely essential.

Bartender/Cocktail Barman

He makes cocktails according to hotel's prescribed formulae and procedures, serves cocktails to waiters and guests, maintains healthy sanitary conditions in the bar, accepts money and returns change to the guests. He must be a responsible person well versed in the skill of shaking and stirring cocktails and should have good knowledge of all alcoholic drinks, the ingredients, and of the licensing laws. He is responsible for *mise-en-place*, storage facilities, inside the bar, and decorative arrangements of liquor bottles.

Wine Butler/Wine Waiter/Sommelier

He must be a good salesman and sell as much liquor as possible as it is one of the main sources of income in a hotel. He is responsible for the service of all alcoholic drinks during the service of meals. Knowledge of foreign languages, beverage laws and laws relating to wines is a must for a wine butler. He requires complete knowledge of national and foreign wines, the good vintages and good years, the wine suitable for various dishes and handling and care of good wines. He must be proficient with wine lists. He must have knowledge of making and bottling of the wines. He should know how and when to serve the wines at room temperature or when chilled. In addition he should have the knowledge of stocktaking and also mixing of cocktails.

Assistant Wine Waiter/Commis d' vin

He should have good knowledge of wines and drinks and must know the correct methods of washing, drawing and handling of glasses. He should keep the wine tables, wineglasses, ice buckets ready for service. He takes the order of wines, spirits and beer either directly from the customers or from the wine butler. Thereafter, he collects the drinks from the barman and serves them.

Commis Barman/Barmaid/Commis Waiter/Waiter/Bar Waiter/Bus Boys

His job is to supply dining rooms with all items necessary for service, setting up of the dining room, assisting the waiter(s) in service and general maintenance of the dining area, relating to the preparation of client's order and organization of equipment and stocks. He obtains supplies from the still room and kitchen and replaces the barman during the latter's absence.

Assistant Barman/Barmaids

He needs a good knowledge of foreign beverages. He must be proficient in the use of bar equipment. Knowledge of hygiene, safety standards and regulation and labour legislations relevant to the job are also essential. He carries out the barman's order.

Bar Porters

Generally assists the bartender in all phases of preparation of drinks e.g. he cuts fruits, stocks ice and cleans the bar. This is a position for trainees who after a start as bar porter go on to become bartenders.

Bar Control

It is proposed to deal with these under three headings:

1. Service bars (dispense)
2. Public bars
3. Cocktail bars

Service Bars

These provide the service to the catering sections, such as restaurant, grill-room, floors, lounge, and public rooms. No cash sales should take place at these points, although there may be occasional exceptions when the system of the establishment demands that waiters in the lounge and public rooms pay for supplies as they are drawn. A controller much prefers that a service bill is used for all issues.

Standard Wine Stock

It is usual for the service bar, when part of a catering section, such as the restaurant, or grillroom, to hold a standard stock of all wines listed on the wine list. The 'standard' is only a loan debit against the bar and is included in the main cellar stock.

The cellar at the conclusion of each service replenishes it, by requisition listed from the sales bills.

Replenishment Requisition

This is a triplicate form:

1. Cellar office
2. Control office
3. Bar file: It is entered by the bar manager. The control compares these entries with the sales bills in the bar and in the presence of bar manager, and, before passing to the cellar office, checks the bills to assure that all is correct.

It can and does happen that a barman may issue a bottle in error (not in accordance with the number

Wine stored in a rack

stated on the service bill), which will not be noticed by the waiter, and necessitate adjustment in the stock.

The reason for a copy of the requisition being filed in the control office is to provide a check against any alterations in the bar and cellar copies after audit. The control office, when auditing entries in the cellar stock ledger, or collating records for these postings, will always use the control office copies, and not check by those filed in the cellar or bar. Nothing can be easier for the cellar than to balance irregular withdrawals from stocks by adding items to requisition documents.

The control certifies the replenishment requisition to protect the stock against the barman, and hold the duplicate to protect both the barman and stock against the cellar staff.

During the course of visits to the hotels, it has been asked more than once what protects the stock against the controller? The answer is quite simple the controller does not hold stocks, and neither has he direct access to them. There is a risk of collusion developing between the control clerk and the bar manager, and the protection against this will be fully detailed in the chapter titled 'Control Office', where the entire control machine will be amply explained.

Liqueurs Spirits Bar Wines

This stock is for dispensing by measure, and sales by the bottle is permitted only on the authority of the appropriate head of department (not the bar manager). He must have knowledge of the extensive range, variation in price and also in the number of measures contained in the bottle.

A common fault in many bars is the failure to acquaint the bar manager with the number of measures debited to the various bottles. This particularly applies to liqueurs and spirits contained in odd-sized bottles, also with ports and sherries. A list should be posted in each bar, for the guidance of the bar staff giving the measures in each bottle and the price per measure.

Another weakness, and one which can give a customer cause for complaint, apart from acting in an averse ratio and causing the bar to lose on its stock, is the casual attention given to the size and the type of glasses used. Some glasses are so shaped that, although the customer may be given the correct measure, there is an the appearance of under-serving. Also, barmen, becoming accustomed to the measure in some glasses, will continue the same basis of measuring for a new stock, which appears similar, and give in excess of standard.

It is surprising that this should happen when the bar staff are experienced and skilled in their work, but it does happen often.

Bar glasses before being used (or purchased) should be tested to ascertain that they conform to the particular requirements of the establishment. The system of 'lining' glasses, usually sherry, port and cocktails, according to the measure adopted by the establishment, is a good one. It aids the barman in speed of service, and assures the customer that the right measure is being given. Weakness in the control of bars has a diminishing effect on the profits.

14. Stewarding

The stewarding function of a hotel kitchen is essentially charged to maintain and preserve the cleanliness and condition of the china, silver, glassware, equipment and working area of the kitchen. In doing so the steward department maintains inventories and supplies of all equipment, china and silver and further, scrubs and cleans all the work surfaces and floors of the entire kitchen. Also the care of the employees' cafeteria is in charge of the steward department.

Executive Kitchen Steward

He is responsible for all silver, dish and glass washing and the maintenance of high standards of kitchen cleanliness. He reports directly to the executive chef. He should be familiar with all kitchen and service equipment, their usage, procurement, maintenance and storage, government laws enforced by health and sanitation department.

Assistant Manager (Stewarding)/Head Stewards/Senior Supervisor

He assists the executive kitchen stewards. He supervises utility personnel in the absence of the chief steward. He is a working supervisor and normally collects, bus carts, room service trays and cafeteria dishes. He scrapes and stacks dishes and racks up glasses. He also makes the coffee, fills up ice trucks and mops up spilled fluids. He distributes clean silverware in their proper storage areas.

Dishwashers

Their duty is to clear and feed the stacked dishes into the dishwasher; remove washed and dried dishes from the machine and stack them into carts, and run the glasses and silver utensils through the glass machines.

Potman/Potwasher

He cleans all the pots used in the kitchen.

Silverware Steward

He cleans, polishes and burnishes all silver flatware and hollowware.

Scullery Man (*Plongeur*)

He is responsible for the wash-up of metal kitchen vessels and implements. The kitchen scullery is known as the *plonge* and the scullery man as the *plongeur casserolier*.

Night Duty Steward

The peak workload occurs at different sections at different times during the work shift, therefore, the related steward in each section is required to pitch in and help each other out under the direction of the supervisor on duty.

Coordination is of great importance not only between the various service staff members but also between them and the kitchen. It requires proper layout of the kitchen, as would facilitate the systematic and easy pick-up of food by the waiters/waitresses. Pick-up areas should be clearly defined. Entrance and exits should be so placed to establish a standard format for traffic flow. In many hotels, a buffer zone is provided between the service and preparation staff by having a sideman, mostly the chef, who transmits all order to the cooks.

15. Sales and Marketing

Sales and marketing has become one of the most vital functions of the hotel business and an integral part of the modern hotel management. It includes packaging for selling, sales promotion, advertising, and public relations.

In small hotels, the manager looks after the sales but in large hotels this is not possible and hotels have vice-president (marketing) or director–marketing for the function of sales.

He looks after the banquet and convention promotion, food and beverage promotion, guest history, advertising, publicity, and other internal selling. It is the staff members' responsibility to continuously search for convention business and to encourage the use of hotel's facilities. The sales department attracts customers through well organized and coordinated advertising and sales efforts. The department is on a constant lookout for group or tour business.

The prime responsibility of the director of marketing is to generate new business for rooms, food and beverage departments of the hotel. This may involve direct sale calls to corporate head offices, travel agencies and other places. Advertisement, sales promotion, public relations and publicity activities are directly under the control of the director.

Other employees of this department include advertisement manager, publicity manager, press representatives, secretaries, stenographers, assistants, clerks, etc.

This department is responsible for administering and directing sales efforts within several areas into which the sales function is normally divided. Selling of hotel products/services may be done through a marketing group or directly through travel agencies.

In most of the countries accommodation facilities are mostly designed to cater for the domestic as well as the foreign market. Hotels and other tourist accommodation facilities predominate in countries with high volume of foreign visitors in relation to the volume of internal travel. For most of the users of tourist accommodation, hotel rooms and services are a means to an end and not an end itself. The supply of the hotel room is fixed in time and place. The number of rooms cannot be changed and location is part of the highly perishable product, which cannot be stored for future sale or follow the customer. The demand for hotel product fluctuates from day to day, week to week, month to month and from one part of the year to another. There are slack and peak seasons, which lead to waste and increase in volume of business, respectively.

The bulk of the hotel investment is in fixed assets, combined with the continuity of hotel activity, which give rise to high fixed costs. This is to be recovered irrespective of the volume of business. The key factors for a successful hotel operation are the right location, correct capacity and a high level of utilization. In the hotel operation, marketing can contribute through a continuous process of market research, product development promotion, selling, monitoring and review. All hotel services are not tangible and cannot be easily defined and described in terms of clearly measurable products and their qualities. All these services are bought individually or as part of the package.

It is the largest divisions of the sales department both in terms of time and effort and number of people employed. The hotel must evaluate the number of rooms it wishes to allot to group sales. After making an estimate of the transient business, the rest of the anticipated available rooms can be allocated to group sales. There must be continual communication with such organizations to learn of decisions made in respect of dates and geographical areas being considered for future conventions/conferences. The members of the group and convention sales department of the hotel must continually travel and visit the travel agents whose principal business is the handling of incentive groups and other groups and convention sales.

Travel agents are spread across the length and breadth of the country. It requires substantial travel by sales staff. Sales calls must be made even in small towns, which are potentially good sources of business. The representatives personally visit the retail and wholesale travel agencies. From retail agencies they can ascertain that brochures and rate sheets for their property/properties are displayed there. The staff of the retail travel agency must be familiarized with the characteristics of the property and motivated to sell the property or recommend it in preference to others. The wholesalers should be persuaded to incorporate the property into their packages, which requires negotiations on sales and room allotment. Some hotels use direct mailings of promotional literature to agents as a means of developing interest and business. The degree of discount and complimentary offer must be given to the travel agency personnel on the basis of the importance of the agency, its location and the amount of potential business that may be developed.

Many large hotels employ a group or convention coordinator for proper handling of business that is already booked. He works closely with the group leader or leaders to ensure that the entire event is handled properly from beginning to end. He resolves problems, soothes angered guests and meets all emergencies. He has the responsibility for handling of airport arrivals, baggage handling, proper running of all the functions and verifies with the group leader the daily changes into the group master account 'calls reports' and 'group booking sheets'. The call report is a record of results of a sales call on a prospective customer and the group booking sheet records the details of a prospective sale on an estimated, or tentative or final booking. These forms are prepared in several copies to permit follow-up or to advise those people who should be aware of the bookings or sales calls.

The staff must interact with travel agencies in various cities throughout the year. Presentations can be made in setting out the features the hotel has to make.

The banquet business consists of weddings, dinners, dance and social events, cocktail parties, meeting of business firms, companies, etc. Pre-established menus and prices should be used so that the potential customer could select an appropriate menu. The main source of business is the local community in which the hotel is located. Proper relationship and close contact with the community must be maintained with major companies in the area, fraternal and charitable organizations. Such organizations and associations have periodic meetings, dinners and other functions.

Other sources of business of the hotel trade also need to be tapped and the work could be assigned to the local sales manager. Important among them are airlines, travel agents and tour operators, secretaries, taxi drivers, professional people and embassies. Good relations and close contact with the following segments will help to promote business. Social packages should also be promoted to obtain weekend business.

Advertising

Advertising is one of the most common ways of promoting a hotel. Advertising must be effective and should be seen by the public the hotel wishes to attract. The theme of the hotel should be carried through; to give it individuality and make it easily recognizable. If budget permits, advertising agencies may be approached as they have a flow of ideas and are able to give advice on the layout of the advertisement, the timing and the placing in the newspapers and magazines.

Advertising and sales promotion includes all costs incurred in connection with the maintenance of the present goodwill of the hotel and the creation and promotion of new business. Many hotels enter into contracts for advertising for long periods. The cost thereof should be pro-rated over the term of the contract, and the unexpired portion carried as a deferred asset in the balance sheet.

Public Relation Officer

The public relation officer should have a good knowledge of how the various services in a hotel operate. He must have knowledge of foreign languages. He works under the direct responsibility of the management and assists in increasing the clientele and makes contact for the purpose. He reports and makes suggestions to the management. The important job of this department is to organize publicity, receptions and to represent the manager at outside receptions. Publicity and preparation of brochures and folders is also under the charge of this department.

Hotel companies have fierce competition to attract large groups, companies and organizations. As booking for convention is done in advance, hotels are called upon to guarantee minimum room rate/ tariffs and offer other inducements such as free meeting rooms and discount on banquets. In many hotels we find public relations directors or guest relation directors who are responsible for promoting the image of the hotel.

The entertainment of VIP visitors is one of the major duties as it results in pictures and publicity in newspapers and publications. The public relations department is also responsible for fashion shows, beauty contests and other activities. It also holds the hospitality desk in the hotel.

With increased operating costs and competitions, all the hotel companies try to ensure that each of the facilities they provide is fully utilized. This results in the appointment of more marketing and sales staff, who need to have efficient training and education in selling and public relation areas rather than a background in hotel management.

Guest Relations Executive

In most of the large sized hotels a guest relations executive is appointed to handle the public relations with guests. He/she is responsible for receiving VIPs and attending to any coordination aspect regarding them.

Press Relations

A press fact sheet/mimeographed sheet giving the essential data about the hotel property must be developed. This may be a very useful aid to ensure accuracy in the media whenever they have occasion to refer to the hotel.

Press Conference

As a hotel manager or head of an institution/ establishment, you may have to hold a press conference on many occasions.

Public relations consists of 'doing good and getting credit'. All states are much concerned about the environment and hotels have great responsibility in supporting efforts to preserve a quality environment in and around the property as well as in the community.

As a hotelier your success depends on a clean environment as well as on service and providing a quality product.

Whenever you plan new facilities, acknowledge responsibility to give approval and direction to architects and building contractors that will minimize contribution to pollution and visual blight. This is an obligation to your neighbours as well as to future progress.

The construction plans should specify that:

1. As many trees and shrubs or as much ground cover will remain untouched, as possible. Should trees have to be removed, healthy new trees will be planted in other areas of the site.
2. Attractive landscaping will be planned.
3. The contractor will be required to schedule his work so that as little raw earth as possible will be exposed to the elements for the shortest possible time. If the construction site is large, or the schedule prolonged, to minimize erosion, vegetation, and mulch will be placed on earth, and sediment basins will be built to keep neighbouring ravines, streams, rivers and the like free from silt pollution.
4. At all times, the contractor will be encouraged to keep the building site neat and clean. (This decreases visual blight as well as minimizes windblown trash that might degrade neighbouring property.)
5. There will be no trash burned at the site. In this way the project will not contribute to air pollution. Also, whenever possible, the contractor will be asked not to burn trees or timber.
6. When poisonous chemicals must be used for termite control, to avoid polluting the soil, application will be directed by qualified, bonded expert.
7. The least possible amount of ground will be paved to minimize water run off that causes erosion and kills plants, trees and grass. When a large area of pavement is required for functional areas, trees, and plant beds will be built into the area.

16. Engineering and Maintenance

The engineering department of a hotel provides on the day-to-day basis the utility services, electricity, hot water, steam, air-conditioning and other services and is responsible for repair and maintenance of the equipment, furniture and fixtures in the hotel. The former are grouped in the financial statement under the head 'energy cost' or 'heat, light and power' and the latter as 'repair and maintenance' under the profit and loss statement. Proper maintenance and provision of hotel services have a significant effect on the attitude of guests towards the hotel. The engineering department has an important role in satisfying guest demands and helping to maintain the profit level of the hotel.

The cleaning, upkeep, repair, replacement, installation and maintenance of property and its furnishing, machinery and equipment are the joint responsibilities of engineering/maintenance and the housekeeping department.

The maintenance plan should take into account capital planning so that improvement, renovations and expansions can be brought on line. The plan should detail the work likely to be carried out during the coming year together with a budget cost figure. The plan should be reassessed every six months. Simple day-to-day maintenance can be carried out by the management or employees. But more technical work should be carried out by professionally qualified technician. Maintenance of lifts and hoists, boilers, ovens, air-conditioning systems, refrigerators, washing machines, extractor fans, pumps, cooking towers, ventilation and water system, fire arms and electric protection equipment and sprinkler systems are all of technical nature.

The maintenance plan must concentrate on the following points:

1. The aspect of the property requiring regular maintenance
2. Standard of maintenance
3. Regularity of maintenance work
4. Requirement of skilled workers and unskilled workers
5. Availability of expertise within the operation
6. Full-time/part-time help required
7. Provision for a contract with an outside agency

Careful and prudent care of gas, electricity and water is the most simplest form of energy management. Selection of most efficient equipment and use of time clock must be made for proper energy management.

Safe storage and disposal of waste in hotel varies according to the size of the hotel. Small hotels may use strong plastic sacks, which are tied securely and stored until collection. Large hotels may use compactors of different sizes for waste apart from bottles.

Proper care must be taken of cleaning of waste storage area and waste bins. Transfer notes and description of waste must be prepared and kept for future reference.

Repair and maintenance cost can be a sizeable item for a hotel. Large hotels have higher repair and maintenance costs per available room due to higher rates charged, more services offered and greater preparation of public space. To keep the

Case Study 1615
Maintenance

Situation

In a particular hotel, outside contractors had previously been engaged to paint a block of rooms. Now painters in the hotel staff do the same job.

Results of Analysis

The hotel's staff required twice as many hours to paint in a given area as did the crew of outside contractor. Although the hotel painters received considerable less wages per hour, the total cost of painting was almost as great using hotel painters as it was to engage to outside contractor. Including the fact that the hotel painters took longer and consequently reduced revenue by keeping room unrentable, the outsider contractor may have been more economical. It was concluded that poor supervision and training accounted for the inefficiency of the hotel painters.

A simple form as given below was devised which could be used for aiding supervision of all maintenance employees.

Maintenance
ABC HOTEL

Date ....

Name of the Employee ....

Time No .... Location ....

Time job commenced .... Time job concluded ....

Description of job breifly:

....

....

....

....

....

property demand high and repair and maintenance costs down, preventive maintenance and periodic routine inspection and repair is essentially required.

Chief Engineer

Chief engineer or director of building operations or maintenance engineer is the title usually given to the head of this department. He is concerned with the appearance and physical condition of the building and is responsible for the maintenance and running of all machinery in the operation: steam plants, heating, refrigeration, air-conditioning, elevators, lighting and others. He directly supervises the staff of technicians.

The size of the maintenance crew will again depend upon the size and age of the hotel's building. Some hotels have the repair work done by outside contractors, which is more economical than having a complete department. Hotels employ plumbers, painters, polishers, carpenters, steam fitters, upholsterers, air-conditioners, electricians, cabinet makers, silver polishers and some time even masons.

The chief engineer purchases all supplies necessary for the operation of his department and supervises his own storeroom. All matters relating to refrigeration, internal communication, radio and television maintenance contracts come under the chief engineer. The laundry, garage and all the machinery are also under his charge. The work of the engineering department is divided into seven main areas.

1. Electric system
2. Air-conditioning plant
3. Plumbing
4. Refrigeration
5. Ventilation
6. Repair and maintenance
7. The elevator
8. Air circulation system

In addition to this, he is also in charge of the safety programmes and of protecting the building against fire. This includes ensuring that fire buckets, hoses and extinguishers are in the right place and in working order. The chief engineer's office receives daily maintenance complaints from the various hotel departments like food and beverage, executive housekeeper, executive chef and is responsible for carrying out speedy and efficient normal routine work.

This department is also responsible for the public address system, all kitchen equipment including walk-ins, the television as well as the in-house VCR equipment, the piped music, the standby power generating plant and looking into the guest complaints.

The salaries paid to the chief engineer, assistant engineer, office and storeroom employees, engineers, firemen, electrician refrigeration engineers are included under the head 'heat, light and power' and the salaries of others are included under 'repairs and maintenance'.

In addition, a chief engineer must also have the ability to plan the installation of equipment and to draw up estimates for extensive maintenance work and repairs.

Cold Storage Man

He should have technical skill and wide practical experience. He works under the guidance of a specialized engineer and his duties are installation, maintenance and repair of air-conditioning and refrigeration equipment.

Painter

The painter must have the technical skills of his trade and practical experience. His duties are to apply coats of paint, varnish, shellac and similar material to exterior and interior surfaces, trimmings and fixtures of hotel buildings for protection and decoration.

Upholsterer

Technical skills and practical experience are the basic requirements for an upholsterer. He makes mattresses, cushions and curtains. He is also responsible for making and installing textiles or leather covers, upholstery and interior decoration.

Carpenters

A carpenter must have technical skill in carpentry and sufficient practical experience. His main duties are to cut out, shape, fit and assemble wooden parts. He makes and repairs woodwork and wooden fixtures, doors, windows, staircases, panelling and simple furniture. He selects suitable wood and repairs wooden articles such as cabinets and other furniture.

Electrical Fitters

Technical skill and practical experience are prerequisites for an electrical fitter. His duties are to fit, adjust, assemble and repair in a workshop or place of use the various electrical machinery and apparatus needed in the hotel.

Maintenance Electrician

He requires same knowledge as the electric fitter. The job of a maintenance electrician is to repair and maintain the electrical equipment of the establishment, checking of the electrical wiring and equipments to see that the wiring in equipments are in conformity with safety standards and regulations.

Plant Maintenance Mechanic

He also requires technical skill and practical knowledge for his job. He repairs and maintains machinery, plumbing, and other mechanical apparatus of the establishment. In addition, he may also install simple electrical equipment and repair wooden structures and paint walls, floors and woodwork.

Boilerman

A boilerman must have thorough knowledge of the operation of boilers and safety regulations. He must also have the licence to practise this activity. He is responsible for the functioning of the boilers for heating. He maintains the boiler equipment and installations and checks the fuel supply, records consumption and reports any malfunctioning of equipment.

Maintenance Hand

A maintenance hand must have all-round knowledge of sanitary, plumbing, carpentry, painting, electricity, cabinet making and upholstery. He is to carry out the orders of the head of maintenance department. He carries out repairs in his workshop or on the spot, including the guest rooms. He is also required to be on all night duty to do emergency repairs.

Garage Watchmen

Knowledge of the various types of cars and their service is very essential for a garage watchman. He is responsible for the hotel's garage and looks after the guests' cars and official vehicles. He has to register car movements and services to guests such as washing cars and petrol or oil supplies. He has to write vouchers and send them to the administration.

Maintenance and Engineering Control

In hotels which do the bulk of their own repairs and maintenance, this department may be a major one, and it is very rarely that the control is involved in its functioning, beyond periodically listing its stock of materials for valuation purpose. The scope of the maintenance section varies according to the size of the establishment, ranging from the services of an odd-job man to a self-contained unit embracing carpenters, plumbers, electricians; painters, upholsterers, seamstresses, etc.

Although a vital part of the hotel pattern, the maintenance department is a completely separate set-up.

To provide a cover to deal with emergencies, so essential in this industry:

1. There should be a plan of the entire electric system, as detailed as possible, and this should aim at facilitating the correction of any trouble in the shortest possible time.
2. Similarly, a plan of the water system, both hot and cold, showing the position of pipes, mains, cisterns, etc.
3. Plan of gas pipes and mains, indicating the position of points where gas is used and the control sections.
4. A convenient setting of the workshop, and

its complete equipment. All tools and materials whose use could be reasonably anticipated should be assembled at this point.

The limit of control is the listing of goods for valuation. Where expensive materials carpets, etc., are stocked, it is necessary that these should be brought under a form of control as far as their usage, movement, and history is concerned.

1. List items, which have a semipermanent status and a value of certain consequence.
2. Endeavour to trace date of purchase, name of supplier, price and full description. Where materials are concerned give original length, and current stock on hand.
3. State present sitting such as main lounge, room number, floor landing, etc.
4. Add subsequent and selected purchases to the list; and quote against the entry the official order number.

Paint and electrical equipment also require control, and a monthly inventory of these items, giving quantities consumed, is necessary.

Costing

The costing of jobs undertaken by the maintenance department have, more often than not have an academic value; economy could sometimes be better served had some of these jobs been undertaken by outside contractors.

17. Administration and Human Resource Development

The administration in a hotel is usually supervised by a director (administration). He/she is responsible for all the work connected with administration, personnel, manpower, employees' welfare, medical, health and security of the hotel. In large hotels, the work is subdivided and separate departments are created to look after human resource development, administration and security.

The hotel industry offers relatively limited opportunities for the application of improved technology, therefore, improved productivity and performance on the part of the employees represent the best chance for realizing, operating, saving and improving profits for the hotel. The industry is becoming dominated by chain operators, convenience food and standardized operating techniques. This requires ability, training, dedication, involvement, interest and service orientation of employees.

The management of hotels has to depend totally on the employees for guest satisfaction, which is the most important ingredient for the success of a hotel. In addition, payroll and related expenses account for approximately one-third of the distribution of the rupee income. Thus, the money and effort expended in obtaining, training and retaining qualified and highly motivated personnel is one of the most rewarding investments in a hotel business.

In small and medium-sized hotels, the personnel function is still regarded as a minor function and delegated to an assistant manager connected with some other activity. In the large hotel, there may be a separate department under a director who will look after personnel and manpower planning, administration and security.

This department has the specialized duty of selecting, serving and improving the human team. It is observed that in most of the small, medium and large-sized hotels, only one person is assigned the duties of personnel department. He is known as personnel officer or personnel manager or personnel director. He deals with all aspects of employees' relations, which includes employees' training and development. This department is entrusted the task of attracting good people to various jobs of the hotel and is responsible for recruiting employees at different levels of skill. It is seen that compared to other industries, hotels have a high turnover rate which increases the problems of recruitment. The personnel department should try to reduce the rate of turnover. The head of this department must also conduct job evaluation studies and wage surveys and the various benefits and incentive system. In addition, there is a need for training of hotel employees. Therefore, he is to supply the technique of training to all the persons connecting with the training department of the hotel. Besides, he is the architect of company's morale and unites all the human elements by minimising the misconceptions and by discussing the problems of the hotel employees.

The person in charge of this department must have a thorough knowledge of all hotel work and must have competence in legal and trade union matters. His main duties are to cooperate with the management in establishing terms of appointment and to direct and supervise the conduct of personnel. He has to establish general instructions, duty shifts, days of rests, etc. He has to also receive and examine requests and complaints.

The personnel manager/director also handles many problems and minor disputes with and among the employees that occur in the daily operation of the hotel. The personnel manager meets the union delegates and resolves their differences. The general manager steps in only when a dispute is serious or cannot be settled at the hotel level and requires arbitration or court action.

Top management sets policy and the management team defines the duties of each category of employees. The personnel manager as a member of this team, assists by recommending and finally formalising these duties. It is then up to this department to administer, interpret and implement. The important duties or functions of the personnel department are:

1. Recruitment of staff
2. Interviewing and screening of applications
3. Verification of references
4. Referral to departmental heads
5. Processing of successful applicants
6. Training programmes which are an ongoing process that train employees in not only what to do and how to do it, but also what to say and how to say it
7. Safety programmes
8. Benefit programmes, hospitalization, and major medical group insurance and saving, pension plans, etc.
9. Union relations and agreements
10. Introduction and implementation of labour laws and regulations
11. To look after the health, recreation and entertainment of employees

In small hotels the various aspects of personnel functions are the responsibility of the hotel manager. Medium-sized hotels delegate these responsibilities to an assistant manager. Whereas in large hotels due to larger size of operation, the personnel function is the responsibility of a separate personnel department headed by a personnel manager. Some of the positions in this department are:

1. Personnel director
2. Personnel research & development officer
3. Recruitment officer
4. Training officer
5. Welfare officer
6. Director personnel/human resource development

Director Personnel

The director personnel is one of the several specialists reporting directly to the general manager. The day-to-day operation of the department is divided between several subordinates who are responsible to the personnel manager. His job takes in the recruitment and selection of staff, employment contracts, grievance procedures and trade union contact as well as the training, development and motivation of staff.

He is concerned with all the personnel functions such as:

1. Employment policies
2. Issues of employment
3. Management of his department
4. Cooperating with the personnel department in establishing and maintaining an inventory of management and supervisory personnel
5. Preparation, operation and training manuals and other publications, teaching aids and material for employee's training
6. Representing the hotel in all matters concerned within and outside the hotel and advising the general manager and top management.

Training Officer/Training Manager

He directs and coordinates all training and maintains close liaison with the concerned officer related to welfare, recruitment and personnel.

Operating Training Officer

He is responsible for supervision and coordination of all operative training below the level of assistant head of the department.

Supervisory Training Officer

He is responsible for supervision and coordination of all training above operative and below assistant manager level, *i.e.*, head and assistant head of departmental training.

Management Training Officer

He is responsible for supervision and coordination of all management training above head of the department level.

Training Instructors

These are specialist trainers in food production, food and beverage service, housekeeping, reception and clerical services, providing instructions at all levels under the supervision of and in cooperation with training officers.

Training Aids and Equipment Officer

He is responsible for production, maintenance and storage of all aids and equipment, including operational and training manuals.

Control In Timekeeper's Office

The timekeeper is the guardian of the staff entrance and controls the movement of staff 'in' and 'out' of the premises. There is a large percentage of transient workers among hotel personnel and staff changes are probably more frequent than in other industries.

The duties of the timekeeper are primarily:

1. Issuing and withdrawal and supervision of time records.
2. Recording daily or weekly as the system demands, the hours of service, time of arrival and departure of every employee.
3. Checking parcels, packages, etc. carried by staff on entering or leaving the premises.

The staff entrance can be a considerable source of pilferage unless the timekeeper is vigilant. The timekeeper works in close relationship with the staff manager's office, whence he is advised on the engagement and termination of service of staff. The control interest in this department is mainly concerned with any attempt that could develop at what is called 'padding the payroll'.

All charges for extra pay and overtime should be carefully checked and the control should have such complete access to records as to enable them to build a statistical statement showing the weekly percentage of overtime paid in each department.

18. Accounting and Finance Control

The accounting department of a hotel is of vital importance especially because of the peculiarities of this business. Most functions of this department are of a technical nature and they require a good deal of background and training for comprehension. Every manager should have a knowledge of and a sound background in accounting and control techniques and procedures. The head of this department is referred to as financial controller/vice president (finance)/chief controller/chief accounts officer/auditor.

He has dual responsibility to the general manager and to the vice-president (finance) in the home office. His job and duties depend upon the size of the establishment and volume of work to be done. In a small hotel, his duties may be to keep books of account and do a good part of the general office work. In a large hotel, he will, of course, have a number of assistants depending upon the need of the establishment. In still larger hotels the work of this department is subdivided into two parts–treasurers office and credit department.

The finance and accounting department is concerned with the guest's bills, paying wages to the hotel staff, paying bills rendered for the hotel purchases and maintaining books, recording all items of income and expenditure. Many of the accounting records are kept in original outside the accounts office. Accounts of resident guests are kept with the front office.

This department provides records and information of out-goings, which provide management at regular intervals with the necessary knowledge to gauge the efficiency and profitability of each department. Final accounts are prepared at the end of the year which depict the performance for that particular period. After the completion of all the financial statements, the next job is to complete the statistical reports. These reports are pertaining to a period regarding comparison of room, food and beverage and incomes and expenses, which are necessary for successful hotel operations.

Utilize up-to-date purchasing techniques and procedures to control cost. In making purchasing decisions, following main points must be considered:

1. Quality
2. Service, and
3. Price

Therefore, a sound-purchasing programme must insure that the hotel obtains the right product in the right quantity and quality at the right time and price.

Most hotels have introduced centralized purchasing to get good control over expenditures and resulting in substantial reduction in overall cost.

Actual results of the business should always be compared to plans to check progress and identify areas that need attention. Management control is the process of ensuring that resources are obtained and used effectively to achieve the objectives of the hotel business. The control cycle may be as follows:

1. Formulation of the plan
2. Recording of the plan
3. Carrying out the plan

4. Monitoring performance against the plan
5. Evaluation and control

Thus, there are three fundamental points to run a business well, first, making plans, second, reviewing actual results, and third, taking corrective actions. Management control means being aware of changes that adversely affect the earnings of the hotel and cash flows and counteracting them, and finally identifying opportunities for–greater profitability of the hotel.

Budgeting in business is very important. It is an estimate of the income and expenses for a given period in the future. The controller is responsible for the budgeting and directing his staff to make the forecasts. With these figures as guide, he prepares the budget and presents it to the top management for final approval. Once the budget is approved, each member of the management team is obligated to abide by the budget.

The work of this department can be divided into the following parts:

1. Revenue/incomes
2. Expenses/accounts payable
3. Payroll
4. Cash receipts and banking
5. Front office accounting and credit
6. Purchasing method
7. Stores
8. Budgeting
9. AQI-statistical reports: internal reports, audit reports, financial statements

In respect of revenues, the position involves the checking of accuracy of the amount reported, thus ensuring that the hotel receives 100 per cent of the money spent by guests. Checking the expenses requires verification of mathematical accuracy of the creditor bills. The legitimacy of the charges as to both quantity received and price charged must be checked. The controller has to cooperate with the general manager and provide all reports and statistics required and needed to evaluate and operate the property.

The management requires periodic monthly, quarterly and annual financial statements to indicate whether each department is operating effectively and which will help to predetermine budget normally agreed to by the departmental heads and senior management. Proper procedure to record sales and expenditure is required to maintain proper control. Most of the large hotels have introduced accounting machines and computers for economic and quick processing and analysis of information.

Case Study 1816
Financial Accounting

Situation

The accounting procedure of a large hotel requires that restaurant charges be totalled twice by the dinning room cashier and again by the night revenue controller.

Results of Analysis

Accounting procedure was changed so that the restaurant cashier totalled cheques once except in instances where a page of the restaurant control report failed to balance. The position of night revenue control was eliminated by incorporating it in day revenue control. Rs. 75,000/- in salaries were saved per year.

Director Finance/Financial Controller

He must have a thorough knowledge of general and analytical accountancy and of the organization of the hotel and its service. He has to organize and direct accounting operations of the hotel. He is also responsible for organising and carrying out inspections and verifications. He advises on accounting and financial matters and informs the manager regarding the result of the business.

Deputy Financial Controller

He should have good knowledge of the administrative procedures. A controller should have knowledge about the various services the hotel offers and their operation. He must know the process of price fixation. The main responsibilities of the controller are to supervise the administrative running of services to check the delivery orders and issue of the stores. He checks the suppliers and equipment and any loss, breakage etc., must be brought to the knowledge of the manager.

Controller (Finance and Accounts)

He is one of the major departmental heads in a large hotel. In a small hotel this position is held by the chief accounts officer or the accountant. In chain hotels, he is responsible to the corporate controller or vice president (finance). Thus, he has dual responsibility to the controller, corporate finance and to the general manager of the hotel. The title clearly suggests that he is the one who controls and not merely records the incomes and expenses of the hotel.

In respect of the hotel's incomes, he checks the accuracy of the amount reported, thus ensuring that the hotel receives 100 per cent of the money spent by guests. Checking of expenses requires more than the verification of the mathematical accuracy of creditors' bill. He is responsible for checking the legitimacy of the charges of both quantity received and proceeds charged.

The general manager or a designated representative approves all the hotel's purchases, thus the controller in effect checks the general manager. The controller fully cooperates with the general manager and provides all the reports and statistics required to properly evaluate and operate the hotel business activities.

Since the controller is an active member of the top management team, it adds new responsibilities to his position. The complexities and diversification of finance, accounts, budgeting, control and auditing department's responsibilities are best reflected through the organizational chart of this department. It differs from hotel to hotel and many hotels change it to satisfy their own priorities on the requirements of the hotel. However, in most large hotels, the chart reflects two different aspects of the department's responsibilities. The first, through the deputy controller and such departmental heads under them, is the accounting and audit function. The second, those reporting directly to the controller, a lesser-known area of responsibility, the direct participation of the accounting staff in guest relations. To the general public, cashiers, credit personnel and night auditors are restaurant cashiers, and checkers are a part of food and beverages.

The accounting, finance, control and auditing departments in a hotel require standardization. Each hotel is required to forward forecasts, reports, statistics and operating results to the head office. These are valuable tools to judge the operation of the hotel. These reports should be uniform in content and in the methods used to assemble the information and comparisons. The controller is called upon to draw up new formats to present the desired information and interpret the findings.

All hotels operate on budgets. The controller is responsible for the budget preparation and budgetary control. The budget is an estimate or forecast of revenues and expenses for a fiscal year in the future. All the primary departmental heads with the aid of their department and sub-departmental heads are best qualified to make these forecasts. The controller gets these forecasts based on past performance and current price levels and future bookings. Based on these he prepares the budget and presents it to the corporate controller and management for final approval. This is done few months before the start of the period concerned. On approval by the board of directors, each member of the management team is responsible for budget implementation. They have to control their departmental expenses to the allocated amount as per the budget. Any change requires frequent consultation with the departmental heads and meetings with the management both before and after approval. Thus, the function of the controller is an all-round full-time job.

The classification of employees connected with this department is given below:

Account Office

1. Chief accounts officer/chief accountant
2. Assistants
3. Chief/head cashier
4. General cashiers
5. Book-keepers
6. Income auditors
7. Controllers
8. Payroll clerks
9. Statisticians
10. File clerks
11. Stenographers
12. Typists
13. Clerks
14. Office boys, etc.

Data Processing

1. Supervisors
2. Analysts
3. System Personnel
4. Programmers
5. Operators
6. Data processing clerks
7. Key punchers
8. Code clerks

Credit Office

1. Credit manager
2. Assistants
3. Credit investigators
4. Stenographers
5. File clerks

Receiving Section

1. General receiving clerks
2. Food and beverage receiving clerks
3. Restaurant supplies receiving clerks

Night Audit

1. Chief night auditors
2. Night auditors
3. Transcript clerks

Accounts Officer

The accounts officer must acquaint himself with the following:

a. Trial balance of the sundry debtors ledger
b. Sundry creditors ledger
c. General ledger
d. Preparation of payrolls and relevant sheets
e. Preparation of statement pertaining to sales tax and other taxes
f. How the various monthly statutory returns to appropriate government authorities are

submitted e.g. provident funds, family pensions, off-days, etc.

g. Maintaining of fixed assets register as well as statistical records and registers.

The accounts officer is responsible for:

1. Writing of all books of accounts and preparation of vouchers/credit notes
2. Scrutiny of the supplier's bills and payment made against the vouchers
3. Preparation of the following statements:
   a. Profit and loss account
   b. Income and expenditure
   c. Balance sheet
   d. Monthly and annual accounts
4. Attending to auditors
5. Hotel insurance matters
6. Monthly stocktaking and spot checking of stock entries
7. Bills and catering records
8. Outstanding bills
9. Statement of travel agents regarding outstanding payments
10. Catering statements like food cost, staff food, complementaries as well as relevant reports to head office
11. Payment of wages and salaries and other dues to the staff members at the end of the each month
12. Drawing of money from the bank as and when required
13. Maintaining the register for the following:
    a. Cheque deposited in bank
    b. Unpaid wages and salaries
    c. Revenue stamps, etc.
14. Checking how accounts are recorded for cash, money, cheques, foreign currency, demand drafts and how the above are deposited daily in the bank
15. Various correspondence on all related matters

Cost Controller

Finance and cost control techniques are interrelated to the accounting cycle and a pre-requisite for any cost controller is a sound basic knowledge of the double entry accounting procedures. For purposes of effective directions and controls the establishment may be sub-divided into the major and minor revenue producing departments. The activities of each department may be controlled by organising and imposing a control system network. The head of the department should be responsible that the principles and procedures of finance and cost control system are adhered to by the members of staff in the department. They should ensure that all information data, charts, statements and statistical data required by the controller are forwarded to him at the correct appointed time. The information must be up-to-date so that corrective action may be taken immediately.

Food and Beverage Controller

The food and beverage controller keeps a check on all the food and beverage outlets of the hotel. The control is done on two broad spheres, namely:

1. Food
2. Beverage–alcoholic and non-alcoholic

For food items, all the food checks are collected daily from all the food and beverage outlets and arranged serialwise. These are tallied with the Kitchen Order Tickets. The price is checked and total sale is calculated to see whether the amount is justified or is in excess. If any discrepancy is discovered, the concerned employees are informed and necessary action is taken.

Income Accountant

He is responsible for ensuring daily that all cash and credit sales and services required by the hotel have been correctly charged and accounted for. At the close of each day, a complete summary of the type and business done by each department is prepared after checking the night auditor's report and other revenue data for the previous day. Copies of daily report are sent to the general manager and concerned departmental heads. At the end of the month, the departmental sales are posted to the ledger which are used for preparing monthly financial statements.

Accounts Clerk (Expenses)

His work involves handling of expenses. Purchases are initiated by individual departmental heads. All purchases must be certified, recorded and paid. On receipt of invoices, it must be certified by the departmental head that goods are received, they are in order, and the charge is correct. These invoices are returned to the accounts department for recording and passed to the manager for approval. All invoices for food and beverages are channeled through food and beverage controller for statistical and control analysis. The accounts clerk prepares a list for all outstanding creditors and a summary of all payment made over the period at the end of each accounting period.

Payroll

This work is looked after by a payroll clerk. He prepares the payroll and checks the individual time sheets to ensure its correctness. A summary sheet of the payroll for each department is prepared to draw the amount and make up the individual pay packets for payment.

Case Study 1817
Payroll

Situation

The management of a hotel was very payroll conscious. It kept the hotel staff at a minimum. However, an analysis of the kitchen payroll showed excessive overtime.

Results of Analysis

It was found that the present employees could not complete all the work required in the normal working hours. Two employees were hired to reduce the tremendous pressure on the staff. This eliminated most of the overtime payments with a reduction in aggregate salary expense.

Front Office Cashier

The chief front office cashier is responsible for all the transactions at the front office. He is responsible to the chief accounts officer or income accountant depending upon the size of the hotel. Close cooperation between the front office and the cashier's section is required to avoid financial loss and ensure prompt payment to guests' financial requirements.

The front office cashier is responsible for posting all guest charges received from the various departments. The department charges are posted by night auditors. He balances all guest bills and prepares a recapitulation of day business. The chief front office cashier is responsible for checking that all guest bills are at all times posted up-to-date and are ready for immediate check-outs. His section is the last contact between the guest and the hotel and as such is vitally important in forming a lasting impression in the guests' mind.

The front office cashier must be a knowledgeable person and should have a wide experience of accounts with a good general education.

Case Study 1818
Payroll Cost

Situation

A municipal regulation required that a fire watch be maintained at all public functions in hotels in a particular city. The regulation was sprung on the management of a particular hotel in the midst of a public function. Casting about for someone to fill the watch a plumber who had not gone home was pressed into service. The plumber continued the job of a fire watch whenever required and that too at half the wages. No one thought to hire less expensive labour.

Results of Analysis

Another employee was hired to do the job at a saving of Rs. 37,500 per year in payroll costs.

Case Study 1819
Payroll

Situation

A certain hotel served an average of 500 room service breakfasts from about 7:00 to 11:00 am. However, most of the soiled dishes did not reach the dishwashing station until about 11:00 clock. In the dining room, the bulk of the service took place from 8:30 to 9:30. The complete dishwashing crew reported for work at 7:00 am.

Results of Analysis

Employees were not needed on the morning shift until 9:00 am. On the night shift only one of the two personnel was required between 9:00 pm and 2:00 am. One-third of the employees were not needed. When these were eliminated Rs. 500,000 of payroll was saved per year.

Restaurant and Bar Cashier

These cashiers are attached to different restaurants of the hotel. They must have perfect knowledge of the menu of the establishment and its prices. They should be able to operate the cash register.

Cashiers are essential. No restaurant or food outlet can operate without them. In most of the hotels the cashiers report to the controller of the hotel but for all practical purposes, the cashiers work much closer with food and beverage department.

Cashier

Most of the luxury hotels have complete automation of the front office reservation and accounting functions. Automation is designed to improve guest relations. It provides fast and accurate information to speed up the registration and check out procedure, generate and forward up-to-the-minute reports and analysis to the management and thus reduces maintenance and operating costs. Introduction of computers eliminates the need for room racks, rack slips, stock card, guest bills and telephone and information rack. For guests with reservation, the rate, type of room, location, etc. is already in the computer and for those who walk in, the clerk only needs to input the information and the computer assigns the room to the guests. On registration of the guest, an electronic in-house folio is created and switchboard terminal is updated to include the guest name and room member, which helps the telephone operators in immediately accepting incoming calls or messages. The electronic folio remains in the computer until the guests check out. At the time of check out the computer produces completely itemized guest folios and transfers them to the proper city ledger if they are not paid in full.

Thus, an automated system eliminates most of the accounting functions of the night auditors. Room rents and taxes are automatically posted to guest bills each night.

Although cashier and night auditors are not members of the front office staff, they work closely with the room clerk and are directly involved in guest relations. They are in direct contact with the guest during their stay. They give the guest change, convert their foreign currency and cash their travellers' cheques.

The cashier's desk is situated at a place where the guests go to check out and settle their bills. The cashier is the last member to come into direct contact with the guest. Close co-operation between the front office cashier and front office is required in order to avoid financial loss to the hotel and to ensure prompt attention to guest's financial requirements.

Auditors

The main duties of the auditors are:

1. to post all charges not posted by bill clerks
2. to verify the accuracy and completeness of all guest accounts
3. to analyse the nature and value of all transactional documentation
4. to be responsible for guest folio entries and departmental record balancing.

The Control Office

The control office is a form of clerical administration designed to cover all the points relating to revenue, expenditure and material, and to afford protection against leakage and misuse. It is a specialized task calling for considerable experience within the industry, and must not be confused with normal book-keeping or accounting. Clerical schedules are the cogs by which this machine works, and in their assembly it is not sufficient that the cogs should just turn. Each part interlinks with the others, and failure to adjust the units to a common synchronising level will greatly reduce the efficiency of the machine.

This machine is the instrument used by the controller for adjusting potential, and to adjust the gearing from time to time to meet the current needs of the establishment. Control planning, instituting, and practice are not an accountant's task. The accountant deals with history; the controller forms it. In approach to control there are four points, which must be kept in view.

1. Make control schedules a servant. Do not become 'schedule bound'. It is a common fault to become so immersed in the operation of clerical schedules that no time is left for dealing with the essentials of control.
2. Once having established the system, keep it alive. Variations in trading and other circumstances may necessitate adjustment and revision from time to time. Collation of masses of figures and storing them into records is often mistaken for control.
3. Avoid over-elaboration of detail; simplicity is the essence of control. Aim at obtaining results quickly. Analysis of business is frequently dissected to a farcical degree, and devised to cover circumstances that may never arise.
4. When replacing old methods with new, care should be taken that all loose ends created by the change are tied to the new schedules.

Control Accounting is Not Normal Audit

What is the line dividing hotel control accounting and the process of normal audit?

Control accounting in a hotel, and orthodox accounting have little in common, and the average hotel controller would probably be as much at sea in an accountant's office as a qualified accountant would be in a hotel control office.

Control Staff

The permanent personnel of the control office frequently have trainees under their guidance. Normally these trainees are undergoing a general training and are not destined to become part of the control department. Thus, their interest is minimal. They just want to complete this phase of their training and move on to the more interesting fields. Therefore in the majority of cases, it is advisable to make the course as interesting and instructive as possible but have their activities confined to minor matters.

In some hotels, the use of trainees in the control office is an economy measure: the most costly form of economy. Swamping a control with this type of staff not only discourages the permanent and trained control clerks, but also creates havoc in the control organization. The number, which can be absorbed without causing disruption, should be left to the discretion of the controller. The directors and managers are only too prone when badgered by/friends and business associates to place a youngster in the industry, to use the control office as the general nursery or dumping ground.

The primary purpose for bringing a trainee into the control office is to give him an insight into the working of all departments, which the control is in a unique position to provide. Members of the control in the course of their duties have to visit almost every section of the building, undertaking orders and collecting vouchers, etc. and this routine soon conveys a knowledge of the functioning of a hotel. After leaving a control office and having acquired experience in other departments, a trainee is well advised to return for a period for a refresher course, when the pattern will be much clearer.

To assemble an efficient team to staff the control office is not simple. The policy which can be applied, follows along the lines of filling permanent replacements to the senior grades from a reserve composed of juniors with three or four years service in the control office. During this period they have been attached to the various sections and in the course of their training have revealed whether they have essential qualities to make good control clerks. Strength of character and a temperate disposition, rather than outstanding ability, govern the selection.

Control trainees are given individual treatment according to type and are carefully nursed through all the phases of the work. So far as possible an itinerary of training is adopted and at the conclusion of a fixed period in a certain section, the section-head gives a report on a trainee's progress. It is sometimes noted that a trainee who repeatedly fails to jump one particular hurdle, after being transferred to another section would return and acquit himself with honour.

To encourage an interest in the work, trainees are invited to submit suggestions for improving the schedules. Apart from evoking an interest, it is a good means of testing how far they understood the full implications of the schedules.

All suggestions are treated seriously no matter how elementary and in debating the ways and wherefore, an opportunity is given for them to trace the entire process of a particular schedule from its initial source to its following in the control office. Some small award is given when merited, and where a suggestion is adopted, the trainee is given the privilege of instituting it. A general weakness in the control build-up comes through employing a clerk permanently on a certain set of schedules, and not making the staff interchangeable, so as to give each experience of the entire work of the department. Furthermore, the almost casual attitude of introducing the newcomer to the duties assures a high degree of inefficiency.

Schedules

Each controller should have in his possession a set of lists outlining the fullest details of the schedules, which cover his department. The schedules should be numbered and divided into groups, each group representing the duties of the various sections.

It so often happens, unless specially defined to the staff, certain schedules may be over-looked and fall into abeyance when staff changes take place. Apart from this, the controller will have a complete pattern of his province and be in an improved position to deal at any point below the control office. Although this is rarely applied, it is the only rational way for the controller to check the functioning of his machine.

Grouping the schedules into sections is a coordinating factor, which assures continuity of audit, no matter how suddenly staff depletion and changes arise. Each section should be under a senior clerk, assisted as the circumstances warrant, by juniors and trainees. Heads of sections will alone be responsible to the controller for fulfilment of all schedules within their grouping.

Staff of all sections including senior clerks should be made interchangeable. When the senior clerks have covered all groupings and, they have become familiar with the entire operation of the department, there is little need to carry on with the process.

The principles underlying the foregoing suggestions, can apply in any circumstances no matter how numerous are the control personnel.

The control staff of two, or even one, can be governed by the 'control schedule chart', and a copy of this should always be filed in the manager's office for in such cases the manager is, in every respect the controller.

In dealing with control, staff planning, a large establishment is more revealing, rather than a small one. A large organization in its functioning is far more intricate and throws a number of sidelights, which may be missing when the subject is at the other end of the scale. To build upwards would not be so practical as refining down to all levels, where all that does not apply can be discarded. Control in theory and control in practice are poles apart. Each hotel has its own peculiar problems and in this outline of the wide field control covers, an answer to some of them will be found.

Grouping

Division of schedules can be arranged to suit the organization of the office. The best plan is that of segregating those involving personal contact with the other departments, and normal clerical routine.

Group No. A

1. Sorting of service cheques and bills
2. Analysis of business records (restaurant, grill room, etc.), posting the business and sundry ledgers
3. Compilation of statistics
4. Extracting debits and credits to bars and sundry sales points
5. Preparation of stocking booklets
6. Issue of control stationery
7. Departmental trading accounts
8. All work of a routine clerical nature which can be completed within the department

It is usual for this work to be given to the female clerks who are under the supervision of a senior male clerk.

After the service in the catering sections, this group concentrates on the sorting of cheques, bills and analysis of the business sheets, in preparation for the audit clerks.

Group No. B

Audit of the catering sections:

1. Restaurants
2. Grill room
3. Banqueting department
4. Kitchen
5. Cellar
6. Bars
7. Sundry sales points

Having all vouchers and documents prepared by Group No. 1 enables Group No. 2 to deal exclusively with the main task of audit; and being free from subsidiary tasks, such as sorting cheques and bills, gives the group a better opportunity for applying itself for the investigating of queries and omissions. Previous to the introduction of the grouping plan 60 per cent of the time of these trained audit clerks was spent on duties, which could be undertaken by juniors, and the effectiveness of the audit suffered accordingly.

Group No. C

Audit of:

1. Bill office
2. Cashier's office
3. All sections where charges to client's accounts arise

Group No. D

Stocktaking of:

1. Bars
2. Cellar
3. Provisions
4. Material (China, glass, cutlery, and plate, linen), and stocks held at sundry points

Official Order Books and Purchase of Supplies

Before dealing with the documentary side governing purchasing, a note on buying would not be amiss. Small units do not have a difficult problem here, for it is quite a simple matter to tie this up exclusively with the management.

With larger hotels, the problem is a very different one, and the system employed for bringing it under control will depend on many factors within the organization. Theoretically, the real solution would be to have a buying department, but the needs of a hotel are so diverse as to place such an idea beyond rational practice. It is customary in hotels managed by an active board of directors for much of the purchasing to pass through the director's office. These operations cover wines and spirits; contracts for beers and minerals; cigars and cigarettes; furnishings, cutlery, China and glassware, linen, bulk supplies of groceries and tinned goods; and also indicate the sources for purchasing sundry food items, stationery household and toiletries, etc.

These arrangements would appear to take everything into account and preclude any risk of things going wrong. To a large extent, the system does provide a form of protection, but it is far from being complete in this respect. Purchase director's office is chiefly related to the replenishment of the main reserve stocks, and has little bearing on the orders for day-to-day requirements. The catalogue of these is extensive, and there is little purpose in listing them here.

Official Order Form

The official order form is a very important document, and its uncontrolled use can lead to many abuses. Even in well-regulated establishments, it is not unusual to find several order books in use at one time, and their supply almost a 'free issue' by the stationery office. For orders to go directly from departments to suppliers is unsound and, apart from weakening the general control system, this practice will impede the clearance of accounts and delay the closing of the monthly records.

It is also opposed to economy and is a common cause for overbuying. Departments with similar needs ordering directly from different sources and at various prices, may result in an accumulation of stock. It can be quite easy to find a way through a loosely knit system and one disadvantage of an order book getting into the wrong hands is the drawing of supplies from tradesmen for personal use and filtering the account through the system for payment by the company. The first movement towards bringing the ordering of supplies under control is:

The official orders to pass through a central medium. There are two ways of achieving this; either through the 'triplicate' order book, or by an automatic recorder. These methods are as follows:

Order Books:

The usual standard type, with orders in sets of three:

a. 1st copy to supplier

b. 2nd copy to goods receiving office

c. 3rd copy to control office

The order form is printed in continuous stationery and gives three copies; first copy to supplier, and second copy to goods receiving office; third copy to the control office, where the voucher is automatically passed to the locked compartment in the machine. An objection to this method is that the signature of the management will not appear on the third copy; and does not assure that the general ruling (manager's signature on all orders) has been carried out. Also it entails the management having to sign both duplicate and original whereas with the book three signatures are obtained in one writing.

The control office is best fitted to deal with the drawing of orders, and for the following reasons:

1. It is organized in logical units, and independent of departmental interests and influence.
2. Its personnel have no direct access to stocks.
3. It has or should have up-to-date records of all the stocks in the hotel.
4. It has close contact with the goods receiving office

Order of Requisition

1. The management will indicate to the control office those departments, which have authority to requisition.
2. Dockets will be contained in book form (duplicate), and signed by the head of the department. The control office will issue these books, and collect those completed for reissuing.
3. Departments will only make requisition for current and general trading requirements.
4. Requisitions for furnishings, equipment reserve stocks, contract work, etc. will be signed by the manager before being passed to the control office.
5. Departments with authority to requisition will be given a number and this code will be quoted on the official order, together with the requisition number. The code is to acquaint the goods receiving office of the identity of the ordering department.
6. The control office will submit all official orders to the management for signature before dispatching to suppliers.

Quite frequently, orders for purchase of provisions is over the telephone. When this occurs, requisitions will be made as usual and 'telephoned' noted alongside it. The official order will quote 'confirmation of telephoned order'.

The foregoing schedule should be included in Group No. A and as far as possible the duty should be kept to an individual and not serviced by several from time to time. The control clerk should add his initials to each order, inconspicuously, for reference purposes. The requisition voucher should be given the official order number, and filed in its numerical sequence. Where an automatic recorder is used, the filing copies should be removed from the machine daily. When this system is first introduced, it will be found that the requisitions will be brought at odd times during the day with a demand for immediate attention. This must be discouraged, and a definite time set for this work. The easiest way of dealing with of those who persist in breaking the time rule is to refer them to general manager for his signature on the requisition.

Control of Trade Accounts

Although the accounts office is the clearing house for these accounts, it is strongly advocated that these are processed by the control office before posting to the bought ledger. For accounts to flow from various departments to the accounts office is not a rational procedure, or a safe one. Where authority is spread for the certification of invoices, it will be difficult to link the history of the supply to its original order, point of receipt and usage. To find invoices floating around seeking a home is quite a common occurrence when there are gaps in the system; and their ultimate fate is often decided with a greater sense for obliging than of responsibility.

Many accountants with hotel audits claim that tracing the history of charges previous to posting to ledger provides one of their major headaches. This arises from a sense of insecurity that all may not be well, and having no means for testing accounts back to their source without involving such a mass of research as to render the operation beyond the scope of normal schedules. In building a system, this should be taken into account, and an auditor should be able to check rapidly from point to point. It is easy to evolve a scheme to avoid this. Where the design is patchy and obscure, the usual troubles are:

1. Charges omitted from one trading period and carried into the following one. There are cases where these have been of sufficient importance to render the results shown on the trading accounts entirely misleading. When this has happened, design has been more frequent than oversight; and even carried to the extent of altering invoice dates.
2. Payment for goods, which have never entered the establishment. Slack methods invite dishonesty, and it is an unfortunate fact that there is usually someone to take advantage where such circumstances exist. Filtering accounts through for payments, which have been diverted elsewhere is not a rarity.
3. Delay in clearance and a payment of accounts. An accounts department is at a disadvantage when it has no means of testing whether all charges for the period have been cleared. Many suppliers are very dilatory in forwarding statements, and sometimes, this is the first intimation the accounts department will have that such charges exist. The position of the trading account will be subject to continuous amendments, and even then there can be no assurance that the final figures are correct.

The following suggestions, which link with the system ordering, will be found useful:

1. Goods receiving office: The copy of the official order will be the authority for the acceptance of goods. On receipt of the delivery, the departmental code, official order number (running numerical sequence according to the number of delivery) will be noted on the invoice or delivery note.

2. All invoices or delivery notes will be listed into a record, daily, by the goods receiving office. This record will quote: serial number, official order number, and name of supplier. It is not essential to give a description of the goods, or their value.
3. The record, together with all the vouchers, will be sent to the control office, who will check the entries and sign the record for receipt.

It is advisable for the record to be in duplicate form and for the control office to retain a copy. To keep the system uniform, all invoices for contract work, telephone, gas, electricity, etc., which do not touch the goods receiving office, should be added to the record by the control office on the day of their receipt. These of course, will be given a serial number, and the control office will advise the goods receiving office of the opening number for the following day's record. The serial number, which should be carried into the bought ledger by the accounts office is a guide to the auditors when tracing the history of any charge and it is, therefore, essential that reference should be confined to one source.

1. The record, together with all the vouchers, will be sent to the control office, who will cross check. The control office will give the following verification to all invoices: correct order number, goods received as charged, prices, correct additions and extensions. Where the charge is for contract work, gas, electricity, water, telephone, rent, rates, etc., the account will be checked with the internal records.
2. The control office will list all invoices sent to the accounts office and obtain signed receipts. At the end of the month, the control office should advise the accounts office of all invoices and charges outstanding.

Control of Working Equipment

The initial cost and replacement of stock of China, glass, cutlery, linen, etc., is a heavy item of capital expenditure, and ill usage, theft and breakage can cut deeply into profits. Except for a few of the larger groups of hotels, rarely, has sufficient attention been given to their care and protection, and in most cases it is difficult to discover any system for their governance.

The distribution of these stocks throughout a hotel needs careful planning, and frequent tests are necessary to assure that the rules covering movement and usage are actively applied. These floating stocks are handled by all and sundry of the staff, and easily escape from any regular channels laid down.

To those without experience in checking the inventory of working stocks, the range of what does happen to them will not be appreciated. It is the exception, rather than the rule for the staff to have any regard for their treatment and unless stocks are so organized as to trace the source of misuse, a tendency to mishandle will become unrestrained.

Jamming a knife blade under a table leg to steady it, is a costly and general practice. Using table napkins as table rubbers and shoe-wipers; forks for pricking off covers and sundry uses as a tool, sheets and tablecloths converted into wrappers, or used as aids to towing loads and so on–these are abuses to be looked for and checked.

Service linen used for cleaning metal rarely recovers from contact with acids, and we have no need to warn hoteliers that much of the discards results from this practice.

Before outlining a system, which will be based on division into standard units, a few preliminary hints may be useful.

Linen

1. New stock should be marked with a code by which the name of supplier, price and date delivered can be easily traced in the stock record. Where stocks go into the reserve before release to service, an additional mark should be given noting the date on which it was put into use. A small triangular mark enclosing a number is all that is needed, the number being the reference to the stock book record. The purpose of this is to establish a record for each article. Having the history of stock at easy command has a value in many ways.
2. The life of linen will be considerably shortened if it is continually put into service a few hours after laundering. The best results are obtained when linen is allowed to rest for two to four days after coming from the laundry, as the fabric needs time to restore itself. It may necessitate the purchase of extra stock to bring this system into effect, but adding to the life of the stock will compensate for the outlay.
3. Over-usage of linen in services (this applied to dining rooms more than elsewhere) will add to laundry costs, apart from increasing wear and tear. To test, whether this is happening, a check should be applied from time to time by extracting the number of soiled articles from the linen keeper's record and comparing this with the number of meals served, or, where the old linen is concerned, with the number of residents.

This is quite a simple schedule to maintain as part of the routine of equipment control and need only include tablecloths, table napkins, bed sheets and pillowcases. Once the record is established–daily entry will take only a minute or two–reference to ascertain the position will not take up much time.

China and Glass

When breakage is above normal, this level can only be ascertained by instituting methods of stock control–the whole course of usage should be followed to discover the cause. It will be found that the main breakage will occur at certain points, and the elimination of the trouble will greatly reduce loss. Causes for breakage are numerically wide. In one case the losses in coffee cups were very heavy through handles breaking off; the cause was traced to the washing solution containing an acid, which weakened the attachment of the handle to the cup. Altering the form of the solution stopped the trouble.

Faulty training of the staff in handling is another reason for continued replacement. Points in the service where stocks are accumulated should be given attention, for losses are often heavy here. Inadequate shelving and racking space is the usual trouble. With glassware the percentage of breakage will rise if, after cleaning, it is stored at a low temperature. Contraction and expansion takes a heavy toll. Glasses in service should be stored in the same temperature as in the pantry.

When bringing new glassware into service from the store, it is advisable to allow it to 'rest' for a day or so in the department, in which it will be used, in order to take on the temperature. Glass, which has been in storage for some considerable time, should have extra careful handling when first brought into use.

Standard Stocks

The assembling of working stocks into standard units is the only rational solution for bringing them under control. Without this form of system there can be no definite check on breakage, damage, theft, and in most cases shortages will only be revealed when stocks fall short of service requirements. It is claimed that this type of distribution involves the purchase of additional stock and entails a percentage remaining dormant.

This system, as in all cases, needs adapting to fit the circumstances and its detail will vary according to the business and organization of the establishment. A residential hotel with only a few rooms could cover the stock through two points, the linen room and the dining room. Others would need to cover with a separate stock in perhaps thirty to forty sections.

The essence of stock control is being in a position to know where the stock is, and being able to pinpoint any loss to a certain cause. Without knowledge where losses have occurred, or are occurring, there is little prospect of being able to deal with and put an end to them. Standard units render stocktaking effective–and this is the primary check–and does not disturb normal routine. It reduces this schedule to its simplest equation. Where stocks are on a floating basis throughout the hotel stocktaking is ineffectual and a correct inventory impossible.

It entails checking stock in linen room, restaurant, grill room, banqueting section, floors, pantries, kitchen, still room, mess rooms, staff quarters, bars, cellars, offices, and every nook and corner in the building.

With standard units, a general stocktaking is not necessary, but where it is required the stock takers have definite points to check. To select certain points and check these from time to time is a simple matter.

When drafting the plan for distributing into standard units the following suggestions will be of use:

1. Make provision so that the allocation is sufficient to cover all needs. The system will be defective should the stock be surplus, or deficient, in respect of requirements.
2. The head of each section holding stock will be responsible for the number and condition.
3. Discourage borrowing between sections.
4. Give a list of the persons responsible who will sign for its receipt to each section.
5. Keep the number of sections, within reasonable limits. Where it is possible to group two or more, under one authority, do so. Bringing under one authority does not necessarily mean merging the units.
6. To dispose of the need for requisitioning, make replacements only according to the needs revealed by stocktaking. Where many units are involved, the stocktaking should be so arranged, that the stock of each unit is checked once a month, and replacements made to bring up to standard as soon as possible after stocktaking.
7. In spite of supervisions and rules, it will be found that stock will drift from one unit to another. Where this occurs, use the stock, which is surplus to standard, to restore the deficiency in others. A note of this movement however, must be made in the stock records, and where it has a recurring tendency the management should be advised.
8. Assemble bed linen into standard units for each floor, according to the number of rooms in service, for which the housekeeper is responsible. Each floor should carry a reserve equivalent to the number of pieces in the rooms (sheets, pillowcases and towels) and a record should be made giving the number of pieces in each room. Owing to acceptance, the stock takers may not be able to check the stock in bedrooms, in which case the numbers on the 'room list' can be accepted.
9. Shortages will be debited against the sections in numbers and cast in a 'shortages' record.

Note: It is much better to advise the management monthly, when a total comparison can be given, than to report on components.

Where it is practical the control of working equipment should be included in the control office schedules. This department has information available in its records e.g., analysis of residents on each floor, and meals served in the hotel, which are used to establish the exact position in respect of losses. A report on numbers missing and broken is incomplete without the foregoing information. Figures, which may not appear to be heavy, may actually be very high in proportion to the amount of business done.

A controller, when sending reports to the management, should not be content with just a statement of figures, but should always carefully scrutinize them and keep them under constant review. To accept them without comment and without any obvious action is likely to be reflected in the rising percentage of loss. Failure to make this schedule constructive and productive of results is commonly due to lack of this necessary stimulus.

The departments or cogs, which will be indicated, are distinct in their operation and to a greater or lesser degree calls for special treatment. In other words, a person in charge of a particular section must have acquired knowledge of the task of the following departments through training and experience.

1. Timekeepers office
2. Goods receiving office
3. Provisions store
4. Kitchen, still room and subsidiary sections
5. Staff manager's office
6. Linen room
7. Staff mess rooms
8. Maintenance department and stores
9. Engineers' department
10. General stores, China, glass, cutlery, stationary, etc.
11. Cashier's office
12. Manager's office
13. Control office

Cash Control

To convey the ramifications of this department and present a complete picture of its operation, let us take, as a model, the cashier's office of a large 'international' hotel. Say a cash float of Rs. 5,000.

Action on Float

Customer's personal cheques; bills of exchange; traveller's cheques; foreign currencies; subsidiary, and temporary cash floats to ancillary trading sections; departmental IOUs (for emergency payments); loans to staff; staff bar tickets; (having a cash value and treated as part of the float); petty cash disbursements (covering a very wide range); visitors' paid-outs (paid on visitors' accounts to tradesmen, etc.), and other transactions-varied, trivial and numerous.

Daily Takings

The entire trading revenue of the hotel is paid into this office–house accounts, restaurant; grillroom, banqueting, bars and ancillary sales takings.

Visitors' Deposits

These are frequently very heavy and quite often in foreign currencies. To device a system for bringing all this activity under control did not present any major difficulties, but, as in the case of all protective methods, the test of effectiveness comes when attempts are made to defeat its purpose.

In checking the operation of a department with this amount of scope, its entire activity had to be merged; cash float, takings, and visitors' deposits. It would be beneficial to segregate them, for there is always interplay between the first two; and on some occasions the third was brought into use to cover a deficit.

The rules laid down for the cashiers are simple to follow:

Receipts

1. Receipt books are issued by the controller on indent from the head cashier. They run in numerical series and the receipt numbers in each book are listed in control records. All cash receipts issued by the controller have to be accounted for.
2. A receipt is issued for all cash received. Cheques arriving by post as payment of customer's ledger accounts are listed by the accounts office and sent to the cashier's office for issue of receipt and banking.

   Where there is not a lot of action in a cashier's office and the receipt book is not brought into frequent use, an advice to the auditor is that when checking the cash, he should refer to the receipt at the back of the receipt book. The possibilities are obvious. Cash could have been received and a receipt issued, but the transaction left unrecorded, and normal checks which would refer only to the receipts in the front of the book, would fail to bring this to light.
3. Receipts are then entered in numerical sequence, into an analysed record under the heads: customer's accounts; ledger accounts; restaurants; grillroom; banqueting, etc.

The summary is the total of the day's cash takings. They are banked daily.

The Control

The record is audited daily by comparing receipt duplicates with entries in the cash book. The summary in the cash book is compared with the amount paid into the bank.

Foreign Currency

In many hotels, the cashiers share the profit on the foreign currency exchange; and where there are considerable dealings in this the perquisite is a valuable one. It is the volume, which produces the profit, for the customer is usually paid the current rate. But arrangements with a bank for exclusive dealing can produce a slight balance in favour of the cashier.

In the particular department under survey, the profits on foreign exchange had always gone to the cashiers until the company discovered that this amount was over a certain fixed amount a year. The perquisite was stopped and the cashiers were compensated by a small rise in salary, which fell about 90 per cent short of making up their loss.

As a controller you can only be interested in carrying out the instructions of you employers; but it is felt that the move is unsound, in as much as the post called for considerable skill, experience and integrity and was only attractive because of its perquisites and not its salary; and suddenly to cut so deeply into the income of its incumbent was inviting trouble. Subsequent events may prove that you are right.

To assure that all currency went into the right channel the following system may be adopted:

1. Every transaction immediately on completion, is listed on a duplicate record as follows:
   i. Detail of exchange (example dollars 500, francs 10,000 etc.)
   ii. Paid by whom
   iii. Rate paid
   iv. Bank rate
   v. Balance
2. Dealings with the bank, and all control of foreign exchange were transferred to the head of another department.

3. The total shown on the foreign exchange record as cash paid out by the cashier for foreign currency was reimbursed daily to the cashier by the accounts office.

Cash Check

An auditor checking the cash of a department such as described above can be forgiven for a feeling that the balance he reaches is built on shifting sands. A balance five minutes old can be obsolete. The controller's approach to the problem may be as follows:

A member of the control office, who is conversant with every phase of cash office work, is given a float and handles all transactions during the period of audit. This leaves the cashiers free.

Float Report

Every entry is itemized in the fullest detail.

Debits

a. The main float.

b. Receipts; each is shown separately, giving number and payee's name.

Credits

a. *Cash:* This is not grouped into one amount, but given a denominational analysis.

b. *Cheques, etc.:* These are shown separately with details of: date on cheque; name of payee; name of bank.

c. *All disbursement vouchers:* These are shown separately and detailed as much as possible usually at the 'clearance' period following the audit float check for the accounts office to check entries on the float report with the reimbursement schedule from the cashier's office.

Cheques

Let us return to the matter of cheques in order to point out a weakness, which could be used as a cover to conceal irregular practice by the cashier. In a busy cashier's office the number of cheques handled daily can be considerable, and as most signature are indecipherable, a cashier, short in his accounts, could during an audit, present 'rogue' cheques to cover the deficit. In most cases when listing the cheques, it was necessary to refer to the cashier to decipher the name of the payee. It was quite impracticable to refer to the payee for confirmation.

To protect the company and the auditors against this possibility the following rules could be adopted:

1. All cheques taken by the cashier's office are immediately, following enactment, given a number following in numerical sequence to the previous cheque.
2. Details of each cheque–date; serial number, name of payee, bank account–are entered into a cheque register.
3. All cheques paid to a bank are detailed on a 'pay-in-slip'.
4. The control at regular intervals compares the cheques' register and the pay-in slips.

The auditors do not list a cheque in their float report unless it has passed through this process. Once the cheque is serialized, it has to be banked and as all 'returned' cheques are forwarded by the bank direct to the company's secretary, the loophole is definitely closed.

At the first introduction of this system, the cashiers may grumble a little at the extra work it involved, but a little practice reduces the task to a few minutes daily.

The adoption of this system is recommended, which is quite simple to operate all cash departments where cheques come into play.

Visitor's Pay-outs

These are recorded in a register, used exclusively for the purpose by the cashier's office. The bill office for debiting the accounts on bill sheets uses this register, and they also initial each entry on receipt of supporting voucher. The control checks all entries with supporting vouchers daily.

Visitor's Deposits

When dealing with this section, the protection rules are quite simple and effective when applied.

1. A receipt (usually in two-part form, perforated and used exclusively for this purpose) is given at the time of deposit.
2. This report states: date of deposit, name of depositor, details of deposit–and is signed by the recipient.
3. The deposit, is enclosed in an envelope designed for the purpose and is placed in the deposit safe.
4. Records of receipts are posted in the deposit register.

Withdrawals

1. The depositor, who also signs for the return in the deposit register, surrenders the receipt.
2. The surrendered receipt is perforated 'canceled' and re-attached to its former position in the deposit receipt book.
3. In the case of cash deposits, the depositor will often withdraw amounts from the total. When this happens, a fresh receipt will be given after surrender of the original receipt, for the amount remaining in the deposit.

The Control

1. Entries in the deposit register are compared with receipts.
2. Deposits on hand are indicated by absence of signatures for return in the deposit register, and cancelled receipts in the deposit receipt book. These are listed by the control.
3. The contents of the deposit safe are checked with the control list, and the contents of envelopes containing cash counted.

The system is watertight, provided the foregoing rules are carried into effect.

Main Cash Floats

One may be averse to the main cash float being used for a multitude of purposes other than its primary function, which is the receipt of cash and service to customers.

A dilatory accounts office, or one not adjusted to the needs of the establishment, is prone to use the cashier's office as a clearinghouse for an endless and varied assortment of cash transactions. It is quite common to find a float composed chiefly of odds and ends of paper, all several months overdue for clearance.

Cash floats, where there is any degree of activity, should be kept liquid and reimbursed daily.

Staff Bar Tickets

In some establishments where there is a staff bar, or where staffs are allowed, to use a service bar for their needs, 'staff bar tickets' are used instead of cash.

Where a service bar is used, it is essential that tickets should be the medium of exchange. Prices to the staff bar are usually lower than establishment charges and the only guide to bar credit for the difference in price is by the use of tickets. The sale of these tickets, is either undertaken by the staff office or cashier's office. In either case they have to buy from a central source–control office or accounts office.

When the sale of these tickets is through the cashier's office, the cashier debits his cash account by issuing a receipt (usually the credit of the cellar department) for the value of the tickets being drawn by his department.

Part-III
Minor Operating Departments

adjusted on a weekly basis. The control will audit laundry slips with the laundry register and laundry charges with term of contract and the laundry register.

Visitor's Laundry

A separate list should be made out for each parcel quoting the visitor's name and room number, and the laundry should be advised that all such parcels must be accompanied by a charge on return. The linen-keeper giving date, name, room number, serial number and charge should list this charge into the record. This book together with the charge voucher should be sent to the bill office, who should initial the book for the receipt of the voucher.

To reduce losses:

a. Maintain proper accounts so that the cost of the items of restaurants and banqueting departments could be calculated.

b. Let the restaurant manager know the laundry cost of each week.

c. Install a linen control system.

Palace Hotel

Lake View Hotel

Leisure Hotel

Sea Facing Room

Flotel

Speciality Restaurant

Conference Hall (Board Room)

20. Sub-rentals and Concessions

Rentals from stores and concessions are good source of revenue in many hotels. Hotel executives should consult real estate brokers and attorneys, regarding the type of tenants and consideration should be given to the kind of tenants or concessionaires, the fair rental value of the premises and the type of leases to offer. The kind of tenants depends on the location of the hotel, the facilities and shops available. Reliable tenants who can provide the goods and services required by the guests will contribute more in the long-run to the financial success of the hotel than the immediate increase in income realized by just renting to the highest bidders.

All stores should have an entrance providing direct access to and from the hotel. The hotel's reputation will be directly affected by the success or failure of the tenant's business. Hotel lease should clearly define the responsibilities of the tenants in the areas of cleanliness, hours of opening, signs, prices, control of personnel, etc.

The type of agreements will depend on the kind of tenants, the product they sell, the service they perform. The tenants and concessionaires should permit the guest to charge their purchases or fees for services to their hotel bills. The management must agree to accept the charges and reimburse the tenants in full for them. These charges are processed through the hotel's accounting and collection system at no extra cost to the tenants and concessionaires. Problems arise when the guest disputes the charges on checking out. The result is that the hotel has to pay collection charges, commission to credit card companies, collection agencies or attorneys and legal fees and court costs for law suits and in some cases it writes off the amount as bad debts. Solution of such problems can be reached only by the direct initial negotiation between the two parties.

The income from rental arises mostly from:

1. Flats and apartments let to tenants for residential purposes on a long-term basis
2. Offices let to business and other organizations for their purposes
3. Shops let to retailers
4. Clubrooms let for purposes of a member's or proprietary club
5. Display rooms let to others
6. Showcases let to others for display of their wares.

Services to guests may also be provided by concessionaires. The concessionaires are given right to operate on hotel premises with a view to undertaking services to guests. These may include services provided by newsagents, hairdressers, souvenir shop, cloakroom, etc.

The rental denotes greater independence for the tenant than the licence to use the premises on certain conditions, which is the essence of the concession. Rental and concessions are seen as alternative means of providing services to guests. This relieves the hotel from operating unfamiliar services and thus it concentrate on its primary activities. There is a recent trend in the hotel, under which even the primary activities such as restaurant facilities are entrusted and operated by an external organization.

21. Facilities

Telephone and Telex

Prompt, efficient and accurate telephone service is an important element in building and maintaining good guest relations. Courtesy, efficiency and helpfulness in handling guests' requirements and prompt and effective demands make a great contribution to the efficiency of hotel operation. Generally two basic types of telephone equipments are used:

1. Manual system
2. Dialling system

In a manual system all outgoing calls must be made by the hotel operator whereas in a dial system the guest can dial their own calls.

Chief operator, supervisors, operators, cashiers and messengers are some of the employees working in this department.

Chief Operator

He is the departmental head and is responsible for the quality of service, work schedule, supervision and recruitment and dismissal of the operators. In large hotels there are day and night supervisors, who assist the chief operator, as telephone service requires continuous 24-hours a day coverage.

Telephone Operators

The job of the telephone operator is mostly handled by females. She should have knowledge and good command of foreign languages and complete knowledge of telephone service regulations. Technical education and experience is essential. Promptness and responsibilities are among the attributes of a telephone operator.

Operators

The practical role of the operator is to service incoming calls and handle all incoming house calls. They answer the telephone calls and connect the callers with the desired parties. They must have access to an alphabetical rack, which contains rack slips that display the name and address of guests. It must be up-to-date at all times. This rack is placed near the switchboard.

Due to room changes, arrivals and departure, it is difficult for the operator to keep the rack in a large hotel. Therefore, an electronic system is installed which replaces the rack. On receipt of a call for a guest, the operator punches the surname of the guest on a vending machine installed at each station. The computer automatically flashes on a screen the room number, name and address of the guest and the operator completes the call.

Circuit Operators

For faster and more efficient handling of all rack changes, the circuit operators are located in the front office near the room racks. All incoming calls requiring room numbers are referred to these employees. They question the caller and obtain the room number and give it to telephone operator.

Message Operators

If the guest is not available and a message is to be conveyed, the caller is switched to message operators. They take verbal messages and note it down. All such messages are forwarded to the mail and information desk to be placed in the respective mail slot. The bellman delivers a copy to the guest room.

Console Operations

In some hotels consoles are installed. It is a device through which a light in each room can be activated. The light is a signal to a guest that there is a message left for him and if required, he can obtain it by dialling the console operator. Once the message is delivered the light is disconnected.

Telex Operator

The telex operator must have knowledge of various codes, framing of messages, system of accounting, proper debit and tallying of monthly bills. He should have liaison with overseas communication service.

Garage And Parking Lot

Many of the garages are operated either as concessions or on a management fee basis by car rentals or garage operating companies. Hotels with in-house garage offer parking to the general public at the prevailing rates of their locality. Controlling garage revenue is required in every hotel. A clear distinction is required to be made between the guest cars, which park free and those of the paying public. In case an outside firm operates the garage, it is the responsibility of the firm to thoroughly check the revenue as per its natural procedure. The verification of revenue and an actual inspection of the parked car are required to be made.

The manager, parking attendants, starters, drivers, mechanics, helpers, workers, cleaners, deskmen, clerks, etc. are the employees connected with this department.

Hotels without in-house garage make arrangements for parking cars. An agreement with the operators of a nearby garage or parking lot is made. The guests are required to pay for parking their cars and the hotel receives a percentage of the total charges as a commission. The guest leaves the car with the doorman, who calls the garage to send one of the employees to pick up the car and, when desired by the guest, to deliver it to the hotel. Parking fees are charged to the guest accounts. For daily postings, a garage attendant delivers each night, to the front office cashier or night auditor, a list of the guest cars in the garage. The list shows the room numbers, guest name and the amount due. Reimbursement for the parking charges can be made in full to the garage attendant delivering the charges and treating the charge as paid out and posted in the guest bill or these charges are accumulated for a specified period and the net amount after deducting the commission is sent to the garage operator. Some hotels offer free parking to their guests even though they have no in-house garage. The procedure for parking the car is the same except that the hotel assumes the responsibility for parking charges. Similar agreements are also negotiated with car rentals, firms, and photographers, telegraph companies, vending machines and leasing companies.

Swimming Pools, Cabanas And Baths

Swimming pools are built to attract guests. The hotel may have outdoor, indoor or on-premises swimming pool. Some of the hotels have a health club, which provides facilities like sauna and massage. The facilities of swimming pool are generally available to the public on payment of a

A Swimming Pool

daily admission fee. As regards the health club, it can be run by the hotel or given to concessionaires. The employees are paid salaries plus the commission of a percentage of their sales. In case, these services are given to concessionaires, they collect their fee directly from the guests and pay to the hotel a fixed rental or a percentage of the gross income.

The income from swimming pools, cabanas and bath include:

1. Rental receipts
2. Revenue from the operation of Turkish, Russian, Sun or other baths, swimming pool, solarium
3. Services of masseurs, rubbers, chiropodists, swimming pool instructors
4. Sale of merchandise
5. Income from cabanas and lockers.

Expenses

1. Employees' Remuneration and Benefits

It includes the salaries, wages and other benefits paid to managers, cashiers, clerks, masseurs, steam room boys, linen handlers working in this department.

2. Employees' Meals

The cost of the meals furnished to the employees of this department is debited to this account.

3. Cleaning Supplies

Same basis as in the room department.

4. Laundry

The cost of laundry chargeable to this department is debited to this account.

5. Linen

Same basis as in the room department.

6. Operating Supplies

The cost of supplies of the following items is debited to this account:

1. Alcohol
2. Lotions
3. Oils
4. Powders
5. Soaps
6. Tonics.

7. Printing and Stationery

Same basis as in the room department.

8. Uniforms

Same basis as in the room department.

9. Miscellaneous

All items which are not distributable under other captions.

Valet

The practice of employing valet is hardly seen in any hotel in modern times. The process is almost dead as the housekeeping staff arranges a quick dry cleaning and pressing services from outside the hotel. Guests who wish to undertake their own laundry and ironing, dry racks and irons are available in the room maid's pantry. The usual practice in all the hotels is to provide pack of needles, thread and buttons for guest's emergency repairs.

The income of the valet department is derived from the pressing, cleaning and rearranging of guests' clothes. In some hotels shoe shining is added to this, when a guest calls in for the service from his room. Valet also keep a small stock of collars, collar buttons, shirts or similar articles for the convenience of guests. The sale of such items is an income of the department. In small hotels there is only one employee in this department, who renders the service and records the sales. In many hotels, the bellmen answer all calls for the valet and delivers the garments after they have been pressed. In large hotels, the valet department is very active and a clerk is employed for keeping all records.

Head valet, tailors, pressers, dry cleaners, clerk runners, delivery boys etc. are the employees of this section.

Tobacconists, Cigars and News-stand

Guest may avail the services of cigars and news-stand from the respective sale points. These sale points are recorded separately. The sale of cigar or cigarettes is generally made at the stand direct to guests or other customers for cash. The cigar clerk keeps the record. This record is prepared in a form of report and forwarded each day to the income auditor, who compares it with the report prepared by the night auditor. The cigars and cigarettes are also sold in the restaurant from a tray carried to the tables. The cigar clerk controls such sales by recording the issues and returns and calculates the quantity sold and the amount of sales. These sales must be charged on the waiter's bills, so that the guest may have such purchases charged on his account, together with the charges for the meal. In some hotels, the waiter has to pay at the cigar stand when he obtains cigars or cigarettes, and collects from the guest separately without any record of such sales on his (waiter's) bill.

Cigars and cigarettes issued for banquets on requisitions of the banquet department are recorded in the same way as sales by waiter in the restaurant. Sales of packages of candy, chewing gum, smokers' supplies and other small merchandise are included in the total sales of cigar stand. The method of checking foods and beverages may also be used to check the sale of cigars and cigarettes.

If the cigar stand is operated by a lessee, only the sale charged to guests enter into the hotel's records. These charges are treated in the records in the same manner as sales, except that the total for the month is credited to the lessee instead of to a sales account. If the lessee pays a certain percentage of the sale as rent, the hotel should verify the cash sales.

The amount received from sale of various items is included under this head:

1. Sale of cigars
2. Sale of tobacco
3. Sale of smokers' accessories
4. Sale of newspapers
5. Sale of magazines
6. Sale of books
7. Sale of candy
8. Sale of novelties

Gift Shops and Souvenirs

Sales from gift shops are recorded separately. These may include the sale of candies, confectioneries, mineral waters, soda, icecream, sandwiches, food products, novelties, fancy goods, etc.

Revenue of gift shops includes the sales of various items such as:

1. Candies
2. Confectioneries
3. Soda/mineral waters
4. Ice cream
5. Sandwiches
6. Food products

Barber Shop/Hair Dressing Saloon

Hair dressing saloon or barber shop is one of the minor revenue producing departments of a hotel. In some hotels, this department does only cash business. The barber or cashier collects from the customers and records all sales in the cash register. The charges for manicure service and shoeshine are recorded on the same bill but shown separately so that the sales can be properly analysed.

The cashier enters all the bills on the analysis sheet.

In addition to a fixed salary, the barbers and and beautician are paid a certain part of their sale above a fixed amount. Each barber is credited only with the amounts earned for his services. Charges for shoeshine and occasional sale of tonics and other supplies are listed separately, as the barbers do not receive any part for such sales.

This section provides number of services to the guests. Revenue from this division includes services of barbers, chiropodists, boot and manicurists and other beauty parlour services.

Beauty Parlour

In most of the deluxe hotels the beauty parlour is one of the main sources of income. Income from hair dressing saloon, chiropodists, manicurists, and masseurs are recorded separately.

Revenue from this service includes the amount received from the various services and products used by guests:

1. Hair nets
2. Licences
3. Lotions
4. Powders
5. Razors
6. Tonics
7. Vibrators
8. Hair pins
9. Hones
10. Oils
11. Scissors
12. Soaps
13. Tweezers

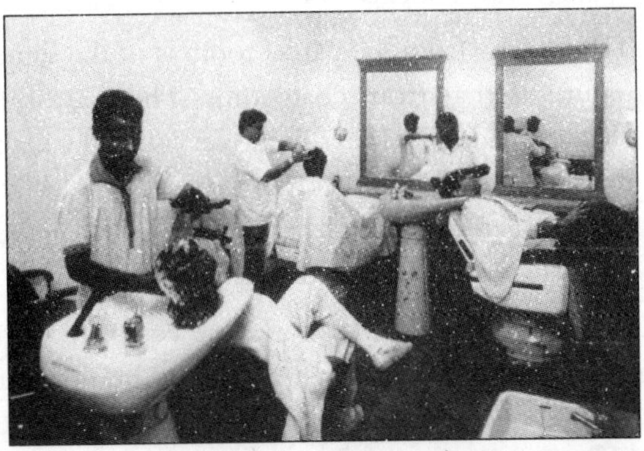

A male beauty parlour

A female beauty parlour

Concierge

The concept of concierge has been traditionally practised in Europe. Now it is being introduced in all the reputed hotels. These hotels usually have concierge in the main lobby, but also have a person designated as a 'concierge' specifically for the upper level. In some of the hotels the bell captain also holds the concierge title. A concierge is the orchestrator, who maintains control of the lobby, sets the tone of the hotel and monitors the mannerisms and habits of the individual employees. He sees that in every operation hotel standards are maintained. He makes certain that the guest is not lost from sight after checking in. The concierge calls the guest to make certain that all is well and to find out if the guest has any request.

The concierge provides directions to points of interest, recommends restaurants or nightclubs outside the hotel, arranges tickets to the theatre and tours and other similar type of services. Most of the guests turn to the concierge for any kind of service required.

Thus, he assists guests with most problems concerning their accommodation, takes charge of the keys when they leave the hotel and handle their mail. The concierge's log is more than a record of the converge actions, it is a summary of the activities in the hotel. Thus, the concierge is a part of the management structure of the hotel. With the growing sophistication of travellers and the increasing efforts of hotel to differentiate, in a competitive market the services of a concierge has become important to the hotel's position in its market.

In brief, a concierge provides the following services:

1. Directions to point of interest
2. A recommendation for restaurants or night clubs outside the hotel
3. Tickets to the theatre
4. A rundown of the tours offered and tickets for them
5. The purchase of airline tickets
6. Other related services

Thus, a concierge is the equivalent of the superintendent of service. He also works as an assistant manager, mail and information clerk, doorman and travel agent, so far as the functions of guest relations are concerned.

Florist/Horticulture

An outside firm may be contracted to supply floral arrangements in a hotel. The housekeeper should be made fully aware of the terms and conditions of such a contract. Large hotels have their own horticulture department managed by a horticulture manager with a number of supervisors, head gardeners, senior gardeners and gardeners.

Entertainment and Recreation Facilities

On the basis of location and type of clientele, a hotel provides different types of recreational facilities to its guests, such as:

1. Golf
2. Tennis
3. Squash courts
4. Horse riding
5. Game rooms
6. Billiards
7. Movies

These services are managed by a manager for entertainment and recreation. He is responsible for keeping the guests occupied in pleasurable activities. Proper procedure is required to control the revenue received from these activities and frequent on the spot checks and surprise audits are very essential in order to control the income.

Checkrooms and Washrooms

It covers revenue received by the hotel from sources such as:

1. Coatrooms
2. Parcel rooms
3. Coin locks
4. Shoe shining service
5. Weighing machine
6. Vending machines in public lavatories

In large hotels there is no fixed charge for checking coats but the revenue consists of gratuities from the guests. The coatroom attendants receive fixed salaries and all cash collected by them goes to the hotel. In many hotels the coatroom attendants are required to drop all receipts through a slot in the counter into a locked box.

The income from the parcel room is of the same nature as that from coatrooms. There are the charges made for shoe shining service and a cash register is used for recording the receipts. The attendants are required to account only for the fixed charges and retain the gratuities.

Coin locks in public lavatories are equipped with a counting device, which show the number of coins dropped in. The cash is collected from the locks by the head cashier accompanied by an assistant of the auditor who records the readings of the counting device.

The cash from weighing and vending machines is collected in the same manner as that from coin locks. The nature of these personalized services is such that they never involve any charges to the guests' account. A report for the sale is made at each point, which are verified by register readings wherever a cash register can be used.

Many hotels lease these personal services and thus receive a fixed income. In some hotels, the income from this source is insufficient to pay the salaries of the attendants; therefore, these attendants receive only a nominal fixed compensation and retain all gratuities.

The revenue derived from the following items:

1. Coatrooms
2. Coat racks
3. Parcel checkrooms and washrooms
4. The collections from lock machines in public lavatories
5. Receipts from shoe-shining service

In case the checkrooms and washrooms are operated by a concessionaire, the expenses in connection therewith are charged against the income received for the concession in the 'other income schedule'. Where there is no income, the expenses should be included in the room department expenses.

22. Banquet Functions Conferences and Catering Operations

Banqueting or functional catering may be defined as the service of special functions for a specific group of people at specific times, the food and beverage being predetermined. In a small hotel where there are fewer functions, the functions normally take place in a room set aside for the purpose.

The hotel manager or assistant manager is responsible for all such functions. He may employ the banqueting staff on a casual basis. In large hotels, banqueting or functions form the most important activities. All functions take place within the banqueting suite or banqueting halls. The banqueting manager has the administrative control of all such functions. In addition, there may be one or two assistant banqueting headwaiters, a dispensing barman and a secretary to the banqueting manager.

The functions may be categorized as follows:

1. Banquet (formal meals)
   a. Luncheon– companies, clubs, etc.
   b. Dinners
   c. Wedding breakfasts
2. Buffet Receptions
   a. Wedding receptions
   b. Cocktail parties
   c. Buffet teas
   d. Dances
   e. Anniversary parties

Sit-down Buffet at a Banquet Hall

f. Conference–national, international seminars, training courses

A detailed break-up of functions could be as follows:

1. Social Functions:
   a. Dinners
   b. Cocktail parties
   c. Luncheons
   d. Charity performance
   e. Receptions
   f. Fashion shows
   g. Rentals
   h. Balls
2. Conferences/Functions
   a. Political conferences
   b. Trade union conferences
   c. National sales conferences
   d. International conferences
3. Public Relation Functions:
   a. Press parties to launch a new product
   b. Fashion parades
   c. Dealers' meetings
   d. Seminars
   e. Exhibitions
4. State Banquets:
   a. Intra-governmental for heads of states
   b. Inter-governmental for heads of states
   c. National days

Income from banquets vary from hotel to hotel. The usual method of dealing with the sales in connection with banquets and selling parties is to record it in the respective selling departments. In case there are some banquet sales of goods and services not sold in the ordinary course of business by any selling department of the hotel, there are two alternatives to deal with such sales:

a. In case of occasional banquet sales being of negligible amount: The amount is credited to the various expenses account to which the cost should be charged. For example, revenue earned from sale of music should be credited to music and entertainment account. There may be some other expenses/cost of goods and services sold in connection with banquets, which are not applicable to any expensive item in the food schedule, these may be debited to banquet expenses account and the relative sales is also credited to the same account.
b. If the banquet sales are of large amount: A separate banquet income account is opened. The profit/loss is calculated and the same is carried over to the food schedule as 'sundry banquet income'.

A large part of hotel business is concerned with letting rooms for various types of functions. This is a direct source of revenue and intends to increase revenue from other hotel facilities such as guest rooms, bars and restaurants. It ensures greater utilization of kitchens, engineering plants and staff. Rooms intended for this purpose are usually designed to be multifunctional to ensure frequent use and justify the high cost of providing the space. A large room may be adapted as a ballroom, banquet hall, convention or exhibition hall. To provide even further flexibility the room may be divided by separate partitions into smaller areas providing accommodation for a number of meetings or functions held at the same time.

Case Study 2220
Customer Handling

You should not underestimate how difficult customers can be.

Every hotelier must have had one of those disastrous days when he believes that things cannot possibly become any worse and then they do. We had one such day last Saturday. Our problems began in the evening, at the commencement of our regulator Saturday night dinner dance. A party of 22 had booked wishing to eat early at 7:30 pm. We had agreed to this and the band were due to begin at 7:30 pm. However, at 7:45 pm, as the party were being served with the main course, the band had still not arrived. They eventually turned up at 8.00 pm and spent the next 40 minutes setting up the equipment and establishing that their amplifier was faulty–it was emitting a high pitched buzzing noise at regular intervals.

By this time, our other large party of 15 people had arrived and things began to heat up. We suggested this party that they might like to congregate in the bar and we would take their orders there. Their 'organiser' seemed to assume that we were delaying their dinner for some reason, and having seen the party of 22 already seated in the restaurant, complained that it was unfair that this party should be unable to sit down until other people had left. We assured him that this was not the case, and his table was already prepared.

He accepted this and returned to the bar, although, as we later discovered from our bar staff, he omitted to pass on the information to the other members of the party.

Having successfully served the first course to this group, our next big hitch came with the main course. The same gentleman waited until all the dishes had been silver-served and the vegetables passed round, and then called us over without even picking up his knife and fork to taste his food, he demanded that all the meals should be returned to the kitchen as they were stone cold (some of the party had already began to eat their dinner, and with obvious enjoyment).

Chaos reigned for the next few minutes as plates of food were hurtled back into the kitchen, the other large party clamoured for more coffee, the band's amplifier buzzed and other 'awkward' customers told everyone in the restaurant that their meal had obviously came straight from the freezer.

In order to make amends to those people who had had their meals whisked from under their very noses we provided the party with additional complimentary wine. The meal was reserved, and despite a number of sarcastic comments to the members of our staff, all 15 people ate it.

Comments continued throughout the service of the sweets, although at all stages in the meal no wasted food was returned to the kitchen.

The chain of events was completed by a disastrous mistake over the bill and the complimentary wine was charged for.

Despite our apologies, the atmosphere created by these few unpleasant people permeated the restaurant and the smaller parties were also affected. The 15 left declaring–they would not return–a sentiment of which we heartily approved.

Case Study cont. ...

Case Study cont. ...

We certainly never wish to relive that night. After a post-mortem of the evening's events, we agreed that we had all learnt some valuable lessons about human nature.

We feel sure that some of these 15 people would have behaved in a similar way in a bank, shop or in their own homes, but good manners are sometimes not preserved for hoteliers. To make matters worse, when we expressed our dissatisfaction to the band they refused to accept any responsibility for their faulty equipment and the resulting poor performance. We wish we could deal with the complaint in a similar fashion although we should soon be out of business.

We were delighted when one of the smaller parties present that night returned later in the week for dinner, and made a point of telling us how badly behaved they considered the party of 15 had been. We are hoping that others present on that fateful night also thought along those lines!

(Note: This is an extract from "Business at the Bear", a series of real life articles written by John and Amanda Willmott, then the proprietors of the Bear Hotel; Wantger, Oxfordshire from weekly Catering Industry and Newspaper)

Meeting Rooms

Requirements for meeting rooms usually depend on external demand and are influenced by the character and location of the hotel. These rooms are multifunctional, being used for business activities, lectures, private parties, meetings of societies and many other purposes. The need is for arrangement of furniture and facilities, including built-in audiovisual aids equipment, adjustable engineering services, large furniture storage areas and efficient food and beverage services. To provide flexibility, a large room may be divisible by sliding or folding partitions into separate areas, each self-contained and having a

A decorated meeting room with buffet set-up

separate entrance and independent service facilities. The division of rooms in this way is an expensive investment. Movable partitions must provide a high degree of sound insulation and this involves special attention to the design of panels, joints and supports. In addition, lighting, air-conditioning, sound systems and other engineering services must be capable of separate operation and control with provision for balancing when the room conditions change. The advantages of room division by movable partitions include wide range of room sizes made available common storage, kitchen service, and engineering facilities and easy control and management

One method of increasing space utilization is to combine daytime use of rooms for small business meetings, etc. Rooms for multiple purposes must be larger than normal guest rooms and provide facility for family use during vacation periods. The room must be easily converted with minimum of effort and disturbance with features such as sliding or swivelling bed recesses, convertible divans, closets for desks and furniture, etc.

Meeting rooms must be conveniently, and directly accessible from the hotel lobby without any need to pass through the guest reception area. Large function rooms are situated at or near the street and may be approached through stairs or escalators leading directly to the entrance foyer. Smaller rooms may be near the main elevator service and located on one or several floors. Separation from the guest rooms is important to facilitate management and reduce noise disturbance. Clear sign posting and direction control is essential and this should also apply at the main or secondary entrances and at the car park.

The requirement of cloakrooms, toilets and entrance areas will depend on the number involved on location and on the relative importance of the functional business. Meeting rooms may have individual cloakrooms and toilets or use the facilities provided elsewhere such as near the main lobby, restaurant approaches, etc.

An entrance foyer is usually necessary to provide a reception area. If required provision may be made for various services such as cocktails, coffee etc., to supplement functions.

These rooms should be designed for multipurpose use and a natural decor with minimum ornamentation is usually adopted. Walls are often panelled to allow access to service voids and suspended ceilings are necessary to accommodate the engineering services. Ceiling heights should be at least 2,750 mm (9 ft.). Depending on size and access, the ceiling construction may be plastered or acoustic tiled and panelled. Recessed light fittings, ventilation grills and deflectors, speaker panels and automatic fire detectors and sprinkler equipment will usually need to be built into the ceiling. Wall construction will involve a combination of different materials to provide a balanced decor, acoustic properties, noise insulation, and resistance to impact and scraping.

An important aspect of design involves sound control, which may have noise attenuation and noise insulation. Space allocations per person depend on the size and use of the room and furniture layout.

Tables will usually be rectangular with provision for linking together to meet banquet needs. In large rooms some circular tables may also be provided. Seat spacing is usually based on width of 600 mm (2 ft.) per diner.

Furniture requirement will also include serving trolleys and mobile sideboards and other meal sources equipment. There is also a need to install a temporary bar, either in the meeting room or at the entrance foyer. Carpet and furnishings should be movable.

The principles as applied to meeting rooms are also applicable to large halls, balls, banquets, conventions, exhibitions and other large-scale facilities. This provision may be made within the hotel and be of sufficient size to accommodate the delegates and visitors or as a part of a larger complex. Direct access for public users is essential and accesses requirements for food and beverage services and for exhibition or stage material must be determined. Stringent legal requirements will apply to places of assembly and multiple fire exits will normally be stipulated.

Public cloakroom, toilets and powder room facilities must be designed to meet the intensive peak periods of use before, after and during intervals of an event without creating congestion in the rooms or in adjacent circulation areas.

The entrance foyer serves many purposes such as a gathering and waiting area, for cocktail and bar service, for coffee and light refreshments and as a social annexe. An area between one-tenth (1/10th) and one-third (1/3rd) of the main hall is usually allocated for this purpose.

The entrance and exit doors must be suitably positioned, proportioned and protected. Special attention should be given to location and positioning of the main entrance door, exit doors and service doors.

Division by movable partitions is usually warranted to provide for flexibility in size and use. A ceiling height of at least 4600 mm (15 ft) is normally required. In addition to general engineering equipment and fittings, separate booths or cubicles for slide and cine projection must be provided and the separation must meet local fire and safety code requirements. This also applies to storage and operating areas. Other storage space will be required for audiovisual and equipment furniture and the tableware and utensils required for banquets or functions in the area. Electric installations, lighting, communications and mechanical services need special attention. For furniture, same considerations apply as for meeting rooms. For ballroom use, large spring floor is required.

The Conference Room

The organization of conference facilities means that the hotel has to consider the needs of a special sort of guest–a guest who is on the premises in the role of a student to study, listen and absorb information.

A good conference room will never by itself result in learning something more quickly. However, the physical surroundings do have a marked effect on the responses of students, whatever their age.

A conference room should ensure a comfortable, awake audience, not distracted by outside disturbances, undue extremes of temperature or inconvenient tables and uncomfortable chairs. The room should be pleasing to the eye, comfortable to be in and above all flexible.

The size of the room selected will depend on the maximum number of participants at the conference. A room which at first sight may appear to be too large should not be rejected out of hand for although small groups could feel uncomfortable in a very large room, as uncomfortable, in fact, as a group that is overcrowded in a small room, conditions can always be improved.

No hotel can exist without booking groups, conventions, meetings, trade shows and social business such as seminars. The selling of the entire hotel, with emphasis on guest room sales, is done by the sales department. The banquet and meeting space not sold in conjunction with room and group sale is sold by the catering department to the local market for social parties. Large hotels having convention facilities for handling meetings and trade shows require a separate convention service department to handle all meeting room demands not related to food service and social business.

The revenue generated by the catering department can be substantial and it is seen that in many hotels, the food and beverage department could not be profitable without the revenue from this department.

In a large hotel, this work is assigned to a separate department whereas in a small hotel it is an extension of the activities of the restaurant and bar.

Organization

Banquet Manager/Director of Banquet Service

Banquet manager must have a thorough knowledge of banqueting, banquet booking, banqueting facilities, scope, menu and price structure, type of banquet layouts and equipment, furniture and fixtures. He must have an idea of the number of service personnel required for varied functions and services.

Director of Catering/Catering Manager

He should be a good administrator and be able to sell. Many individuals start in the sales department and are later transferred to the catering department. Some others have general hotel management background but all should have a food and beverage background. In addition to administrative duties, this department is required to do revenue forecasting, preparation of sales reports and marketing plans. In order to sell food and beverages effectively, knowledge of food and beverages is needed. Hotels have to have printed suggested menus *i.e.*, canned menus, which offer many choices and possible combinations. The customers could be advised in the selection of choices, as per the capabilities of the kitchen, seasonal availability of items, the service limitations, the availability of equipment, etc.

Function/Banquet Sales Manager

He should have a hotel sales and food and beverages background. He assists the director of catering. In large hotels, the banquet sales manager requires to specialize in different areas such as:

1. Commercial business
2. Meetings
3. Trade shows
4. Seminars
5. Large social dinners.

The function sales manager is responsible for the sale of banqueting facilities of the hotel. He makes the initial approach and contact and refers the client to the banqueting manager. He must have an extensive knowledge of accommodation of space, locations, size, light switches, electric points, height of doorways, maximum floor load, etc. The client is usually given a well-presented booklet containing menus and price range plus all details about the facilities available in the hotel. He should have photograph of the various table layouts for different members.

Banquet/Conference Manager

He is the administrative head for all the banquet and functions such as:

1. The meeting of prospective clients
2. Discussing arrangements with the clients concerning menus, table plans, costs, wines, bands, toast master, etc.
3. Knowledge about:
   a. Type of function
   b. Name and method of service
   c. Date
   d. Wines inclusive on cash
   e. Time
   f. Type of organization
   g. Number of covers

h. Table plan (final number 24-72 hours before)

i. Price per head

4. To decide about

   a. Toast master

   b. Band, cabaret, dancing

   c. Plan card

   d. Seating plans

   - Type of menus and printing-format,
   - Special information: vegetarian, non-vegetarian, ethnics, etc.

Banquet Captain

He assists the director of banquet service. He supervises the service operation. In large functions, one captain and floor captain are put in charge of a specific function, who work closely with the client in all aspects of service, timings and other requests. Captains rely on the information received from the floor captain when coordinating the planning of the food with the banquet chef. Floor captain conducts an informal head count at the beginning of the meal in order to have the right amount of portions prepared.

Banquet Head Waiter/Supervisor

He is in charge of banqueting suites and the organization required to prepare for various form of functions.

Dispense, Bar Staff

Their duties and responsibilities are:

1. To allocate bar staff for stocking for various functions
2. The setting up of bars
3. The organization of bar staff
4. Control of stock and cash during service
5. Stock taking of stock and cash on completion of network
5. To do the restocking of the banquet dispense bar

Banqueting Head Wine Waiter

He works in conjunction with the dispense bar staff. If hotel has no permanent dispense bar staff, the responsibilities and duties of banquet headwaiter are same as that of dispense bar staff.

Permanent Waiting Staff/Chef de' Rang

These are experienced *chef de' rang*. They can handle any jobs concerning banqueting, most of the *mise en place* before the function (the laying of the table is done by the *chef de' rang*). Their main job during the service is the wine waiting. They may also help to clear after the wine servicing is completed.

Banquet Servers

They have a difficult job, which is hard and hectic. They are always on call. They perform individual jobs or functions.

Meeting Room Attendants

They handle smaller service functions such as coffee breaks, supply of materials, and ice water, etc.

Banquet Room Attendants/Housemen

The cardinal rule of the catering department is that the room must be cleaned and set up after every party, regardless of when the function ends. Therefore, the work of these attendants is physically very hard. They move carpets and furniture to change a function room from a meeting to a ballroom.

Technicians

The catering department requires audio equipment. Audio equipment service is crucial for the success of a meeting. Many hotels provide these services through an outside contractor. In case the hotel has equipment built in or owns the equipment, the audio equipment technician is a hotel employee.

Casual Staff

The number of casual staff to be employed will depend upon the size of the function. They report a few hours before the function commences. They are allocated stations and briefed with regard the procedure for serving at a particular function. As soon as the function is over they are paid off.

Porters

Hotels with banqueting facilities require two or three permanent porters in the banqueting staff. They are essential staff. A great deal of heavy work is required during banqueting/functions.

Banqueting Control

The term 'banquet' is used to cover all functions and special parties whose numbers cannot be accommodated by the regular restaurant service. It is a specialized form of catering, and in hotels where this type of business flourishes, the banqueting department is organized as a distinct unit having no connection with the other catering sections, apart from the probably exception of the kitchen.

A separate kitchen is not generally brought into use for 'banquets', although many hotels have made provision for this in case of emergency. There are several reasons for this. Banqueting business is, to a large extent spasmodic and varies greatly in its demand for kitchen service. To provide a kitchen organization for the exclusive use of the banqueting department, with its fluctuating requirements, would not be a sound practice.

1. The staff could be only a 'nucleus' basis, as on frequently recurring periods they would be redundant.
2. Augmentation of personnel (always a problem) and engagement for brief periods would result in a low standard of service through employment of 'casual' types, invariably unacceptable for regular employment.
3. Duplication of the purchase and usage of commodities would adversely effect economy, and tend to limit the variety of the menus.
4. The risk of developing a prolific source of wastage would be very potent.
5. It would be an additional overhead charge; cutting deeply into profits without bringing compensating advantages.

In every other respect the banqueting department is treated as a self-confined unit, having its own executive and key personnel, equipment, bars, still room, service points and stationery.

Staff

The permanent personnel generally consist of banqueting manager, assistant manager, secretary typist, general clerk, and three or four headwaiters. Supplementary staffs are recruited, as the occasion demands, through the medium of agencies, which specialize in the supply of this class of labour. As the 'banquets' are booked in advance, staff requirements can be anticipated, and many 'casual' help are listed for re-engagement by the banqueting section and become what may be termed 'regular casuals'.

There is a large element among waiters, which prefers casual to regular employment, and these nomads, during the summer season and when banqueting business is at its lowest ebb, gravitate to the resort hotels.

Leakage occurs when there is insufficient vigilance, because there will always be, in hotel work as in other trades, those who will be quick to take advantage of laxity. Certain departments present either greater opportunities and/or greater temptations and thus in such instances there is a greater need for the strictest governance by the control.

Table Planning

This responsibility usually falls on the assistant banqueting manager and is not a very simple task. Fitting together the component parts of an assembly to form a harmonious setting necessitates collaboration with the organizer and attention to a hundred and one details: placing of tables, number at each table, grouping of guests to satisfy personal wishes, arranging order of precedence, etc., and it is rarely that a plan is adopted without revision.

Poor planning delays the commencement of service, and this disturbs the entire timing and is reflected throughout the course.

Equipment

It is preferable that the equipment of this department should be complete for all services and emergency needs and not be a part of stocks in general use in the establishment.

Linen, cutlery, China, glass should carry a pattern which will identify it with this department. Storage of these items, when not in use, should be within the section.

Apart from the aspects of service requirements, which necessitate these rulings, it is essential that the cost of replacements to maintain the standard schedule should be charged against the cost of operating this department; and the only way to bring this into effect is by segregation.

The use of casual labour on the scale employed by the banqueting department can subject these stocks to a higher rate of depletion than elsewhere, and it is important that stocktaking should be undertaken at frequent intervals to gauge the degree of loss.

Where the stocks are large and in continual service, a good scheme is to appoint a *chef de material* who will be responsible for the condition and restoration after use. In some hotels a quarterly bonus is paid to the *chef de material* based on losses under a fixed percentage. This is a form of encouragement, which can pay good dividends.

In assessing the rate for this bonus, it is necessary to establish the average basic level of loss and the following procedure can be taken as a guide.

1. List the loss in cost and numbers over a period of twelve month separately for each item such as table napkins; cutlery–knives, forks, spoons, classified in their respective grade (*i.e.*, table, dessert, fruit, fish, soup, coffee, etc.); China and glass–classified in grades.
2. Divide the loss in each unit, both in respect of numbers and cost, by the total number of covers served during the period to arrive at the cost (which will be in fractions of a rupee) and the percentage in numbers (which will be in fractions of a rupee) per cover.
3. Multiply the cost and percentage in each case by 100 to bring the figures to a basis of 100 covers.

The scale of average loss indicated by this assessment should provide the standard gauge when reviewing subsequent results.

The information derived can act as a guide for deciding on reward points.

Assembling the first figures will entail a certain amount of extra work, dependent on the amount of information contained in the appropriate records, but once the format has been laid, a monthly check should present little difficulty.

A similar check should be applied to other departments where these stocks are used; for abnormal losses will occur and persist unless brought to light and checked from time to time. It is surprising how few establishments are in a position to analyse and pinpoint this wastage, and are only informed by the annual trading account figure of the cost of replacements.

Booking the Banquet

The initial booking of the business sets in motion the machinery used in covering every phase of the function throughout its course. Details in respect of requirements must be as comprehensive as possible and listed on five copies:

1. Banqueting office record
2. General manager's office
3. Kitchen: Where large numbers are involved, the chef will draft the general menu of the day to correspond as far as possible with the banqueting menus, to avoid undue pressure in the preparation of dishes.
4. Cellar office: Stocks must be checked to assure adequate reserves are on hand to meet the demand indicated by the 'advice', and to prepare them for service. Also, the normal cellar service may need adjusting to deal with additional pressure.
5. Control office: Apart from this 'advice' being an essential element in the control scheme, certain clerical schedules may have to be prepared for dealing with sales outside the 'inclusive' charge. The likelihood of such sales arising are indicated on the 'advice' the control office issues from a stock contained within that department. A set of 'check-bill' pads are assigned for the particular function and passed to the banqueting office for distribution.

Supplementary to this 'advice' it is usual to issue, at the beginning of each month, a summary of the month's bookings. Subsequent bookings for this period should be inserted in this diary.

Details needed for control purposes are:

1. Rate
2. Name of function and to whom the account will be rendered
3. Time (commencement of function)
4. Service (lunch, dinner, buffet, etc.)
5. Numbers expected (it is usual to insist on a guaranteed minimum)
6. Price
7. Menus
8. Wines, etc. (it must be stated whether the charge includes these)
9. Band and entertainment (although these are usually subject to a separate charge, it does happen on occasion that special arrangements will make them 'inclusive', and notification must be stated)
10. Flowers and sundry decorations (state whether inclusive)

Kitchen Service

Where the kitchen is accessible and its service points are used for direct service to the banqueting rooms, great care must be exercised not to allow confusion with service to the other catering sections. Unless a kitchen has been specially planned to deal with this direct service, and where 'banquets' are a regular feature in the hotel's activities, such an arrangement will have many disadvantages.

The service points, hot plates, etc., should be an integral part of the banqueting department. Personnel from the kitchen can work from this section and attend to the plating and distribution; and by bringing this into effect the interests of all will be best served. The essence of good catering is, of course, to bring as close as conveniently possible the service to the consumer.

The number of portions sent to the banqueting service point is based on:

1. The original advice of numbers, and
2. The final check of those seated at the tables. These are listed by the kitchen clerk for subsequent comparison and agreement with the banqueting manager's record at the conclusion of the service.

All items in excess of requirements are

immediately returned to the kitchen as the service of each course is concluded.

From the time the food leaves the kitchen until it is served, it is supervised and handled by members of the kitchen organization; or, at least, it should be. The primary cause for spoilage and waste comes through delegating this task to those lacking in practice or indifferent to its importance.

Cellar Service

The formula for this depends to a large extent on the main organization of this department and also whether the sale is 'inclusive' or cash. We will deal first with those inclusive in the charge.

Inclusive

It is preferable, where the volume of business justifies, for the banqueting department to have its own service bar holding a complete stock of spirits, liqueurs, bar wines, beers, minerals, etc. If possible this bar should be used for 'inclusive' issues only, and an effort should be made to avoid drawing supplies from its stock for cash sale.

There are reasons for this: Merging 'inclusive' and 'cash' issues at one point would give the widest opportunity for irregularities, and it would be quite simple to draw supplies for cash sale and note the withdrawal against the consumption on the 'inclusive' charge. The leakage might be on a considerable scale and remain unreflected in the bar results.

Aperitifs

Is not usual for the choice of these to extend beyond a variety of four. Popular cocktails subject to bulk preparation are set out in glasses ready for service to the guests. 'Bottle extraction' is usually very high at this service, and for purposes of control costing and bar credit the number of bottles consumed in its preparation are noted on the order for the particular function.

Table Wines

The average assessment of consumption is three to the bottle. The cellar department forwards sufficient stock of the wine ordered to cover the numbers on the above basis, or one stipulated by the organizer and, should these be consumed and additional supplies be required, the banqueting manager will need to sign a requisition to this effect. It is customary for a member of the cellar department to supervize the service of wines, and to assure that these are not misused.

When wines are sent from the cellar a record, in triplicate, is entered by the cellar office and remains attached to its binding until the service is concluded. The issues are then summarized–first issue, additions, and returned bottles–and is signed by both the cellar and banqueting managers. These are distributed as follows:

1. Cellar office
2. Banqueting office
3. Control office

All bottles, full, partially used, and empty, are returned to the cellar immediately after the service.

Dessert Wines, Brandies, Liqueurs, etc.

These are served, in bottles, by the service bar on a requisition signed by the banqueting clerk. Only full bottles are issued and credit is noted on the requisition for returns.

Cash Sales

These necessitate the following organization and records:

Aperitifs

A temporary bar is arranged at a convenient point and the supplies for stocking this can be drawn from the service bar, on a requisition signed by the banqueting manager.

This stock is entered into a duplicate record showing the items supplied, selling price, total debit, stock unconsumed, balance consumed, filing value, and cash taken. The record is completed immediately after the service, when the unconsumed stock is returned to the service bar and the record is signed by the bar manager for its receipt.

It is usual for the opening and closing of these bars to be supervized by the banqueting clerk, who will also collect the cash and issue a receipt to be attached to the original (or control copy) of the record. Where the volume of business justifies the course, it is well to have a cashier on duty at this point, and also to include a cash register.

Stock remaining unsold should be listed at the temporary bar–and not by the temporary barman–before dispatching to the service bar. The service bar manager should check the items returned from this record. Stock can be lost between the two points.

When it happens that several service bars are in simultaneous operation, the controller should plan to bring them under the supervision of the control office. These temporary bars offer considerable scope for sharp practice, especially when sales are heavy and a rush of business develops.

Sales of mixed drinks, cocktails, etc., should always give a surplus above selling rates, and where the results from these bars consistently show an even balance between consumption and cash receipts, the position should be closely watched.

Table Wines

The wine list used in the banqueting department for cash sales is rarely so comprehensive as the one used by the other catering sections. This does not, of course, apply where wines are ordered in advance. Conditions of service may render it difficult to offer the entire range of the hotels' stocks: this and other reasons may guide the policy in this respect. When the cellar is sited at a distance inconvenient for reasonable service, it is not practical from many points of view to duplicate its stock and function within the banqueting department.

The wines listed on the banqueting cash sales list will be held on a standard basis, with adequate reserves easily available, in the banqueting service bar. Issues from this stock will be replenished daily according to the record of sales. This stock must not be used under any circumstances for 'inclusive' sales.

Bill-Check System

The rules applying here must be rigidly obeyed. The links in the usage of these pads are:

1. Issued by control office to ....
2. Banqueting office to ....
3. Wine Butlers, and returned to ....
4. Banqueting office, and finally passed to ....
5. Control office

The system can operate through two separate pads, made up in sets of duplicate vouchers: one used for charging the customer and the other for the drawing of supplies. This method is used when the charge is made directly to the customer by the wine butler.

An alternative system is to use a cashier and bill the charges along the same lines as in the restaurant. The latter method would serve only on certain occasions and when large numbers are not involved.

At 'banquets' the guests take their seats at the tables at a given time, and the period of service may spread over two or three hours. It is always the conditions of service, which govern the system. Reverting to the first suggestion the pads used, both for service and billing, must be of a pattern distinct from those used in the other catering sections. They must be numbered and only issued by the control office in their consecutive order;

and the banqueting office should follow a similar procedure.

They must be issued only to wine butlers. Those appointed as wine butlers at functions are usually people well known to the banqueting management, and their place in the scheme of things is indicated by an elaborate insignia of office.

The supply voucher is used in the ordinary way: original copy to the bar the duplicate remaining with the wine butler. To protect this procedure, the banqueting office before distributing these pads should stamp each voucher with the number and name as obviously as possible of the wine butler to whom it is issued. The service bar manager before accepting the bill for service, should note that the number on the bill corresponds with the wine butler's badge. The vouchers on the bill pad should be treated in the same way. Also stamped on the vouchers of both pads will be the name of the function for which they have been issued.

The bill charge will be made out by the wine butler who will quote on the voucher the 'chair' number of the customer: this will also be noted on the supply bill. The banqueting clerk is usually responsible for collecting cash from the wine butlers, and comparing record of sales with the duplicate bill and supply vouchers.

Charging of Functions

In some cases where the price quoted only covers the menu, wines, cigars, etc., are also debited to the main account, according to what has been consumed. A fixed charge is made per head for the kitchen service, sandwiches, confectionery, etc., but the drinks are charged on the basis of what is consumed.

The customer may indicate, in the first instance, how much in the way of drinks should be distributed, and when the limit is reached the customer should give his consent before further supplies are brought into use. The original 'advice' contains all the necessary instructions in respect of charging, and should be sufficient for the controller for the purposes of audit.

Accounts are drafted in the banqueting office, but require verification by the control office before passing to the bill office for charging.

The statement is made in three copies one each for:

1. Banqueting office
2. Bill office
3. Control office

Control

Instead of awaiting a statement for each account from the banqueting office, a duplicate account is drafted in the control office from supporting kitchen, bar, and cellar documents, and this is compared with the statement prepared by the banqueting office. The advantages are:

1. An audited statement is ready before the banqueting office has drafted its account;
2. Differences can be investigated and adjusted immediately;
3. Drafting a duplicate account in the control office gives the extra assurance that the control clerk has correctly applied the control schedules.

Kitchen

The main orders from the banqueting department to the kitchen are collected from the chef's office by the control, and these are compared with the duplicate copies from the banqueting department. It is not unusual for the chef to amend, the numbers of covers shown on the main order, and nearly always in excess of the original figure quoted, and when this happens the banqueting manager will be advised and his initials given to the final figures.

When a minimum number of guests has been guaranteed and this figure is not reached by the number of covers served, the charge to the customer will not be affected, but the number of covers actually served will be used by the control in drafting the profit and loss account.

Cellar

1. Wines supplied direct from cellar to 'banquet' service. The entries, as previously mentioned are entered into a triplicate record by the cellar office:
   a. Banqueting office
   b. Control office
   c. Cellar office.
2. This shows the final consumption of supplies for each party. Each record is separate and does not merge issues to various parties. The control compares its copy with those held by the banqueting office and cellar office and adds the audit certification.
3. Replenishment to standard stock in service bar for cash sales: These are listed into a triplicate record by the bar manager:
   a. Cellar office
   b. Control office
   c. Service bar.

The control office certifies this before the cellar makes replacements. This record is checked by control, against bar orders issued by wine butlers.

4. Spirits, bar wines, etc., served by service bar on 'inclusive' charge: The service bar order is compared by control with the duplicate in the banqueting office, and is taken to the control office for recording credit to the bar and charging to the profit and loss account.
5. Cash sales (temporary bar): All relative documents are checked by control and cash taking is compared with receipts in the banqueting office. These documents are also used for crediting the stock of the main bar and including in the business figures of the profit and loss account.
6. The wine butler's duplicate supply bills are collected from the banqueting office by control and compared with the original orders taken from the service bar. These are listed into a record, by control, showing:
   a. Bill, or order number
   b. Wine butler's number
   c. Name of the function
   d. Amount of each bill
   e. Cash total: against this entry will be shown the banqueting office cash receipt number. The banqueting office pays the total cash takings into the central cashier's office daily; and this total is reconciled by the control with the summary of the cash business. Both original and duplicate receipts are compared.

Audit must follow close to the banqueting business for delay often leads to confusion in records and omissions. These losses become irrecoverable.

Trading Statement

A trading statement is made out for each function by the control manager's office, copies being sent to the director's office and general manager's office, and one remaining in the file in the control office.

Access to this statement by the banqueting manager is via the general manager's office, the reason being that, as costs come into play in this account, the entries are of a confidential nature, and the information should be limited to the highest executive.

It is not usual for these statements to include establishment charges, such as rent, heat, light, etc., and the entries are confined to credits (sales) and debits (cost of food, drinks, etc., and sundry expense items, such as special decorations extra labour, printing of menus, etc.).

They are useful for managerial guidance, and are merged into an accumulative record by the control office, which is summarized at the end of each month. This gives, apart from analysed totals, the average takings per head for food, wines, spirits, liqueurs, beers, minerals, cigars, cigarettes, etc., and also the average per head of the total takings.

On the cost side, the average cost per head is also shown for the charges listed, together with the average per head of the total cost. Comparing the month's results with those for previous years is an excellent barometer and signposts every detail of the banqueting position.

Kitchen

The credit figure for this department shown on the statement is the one charged on the customer's account under this heading with 'inclusive' charges. The credit is the figure remaining after deducting the selling price value of cellar and other supplies. As, however, the consumption of the latter has been anticipated in the original tender, there is not usually a marked difference between the 'suggested' kitchen credit and the final allowance.

In spite of this, disputes may arise between the chef and the banqueting manager over this particular issue, and a discreet controller can often pour oil on troubled waters by 'showing' the chef a figure he wants to see. On 'gala' nights when tickets are sold at a fixed price (exclusive of wins, etc.), the *chef* is often under the impression that his kitchen should be credited with the full amount of the ticket sales; and his views on the cost of extra entertainment, labour, decorations, favours, etc., which are charged against the total before the credit to his department emerges, have to be heard to be appreciated. To ask the chef to quote the cost per head for the kitchen is to invite a hypothecated figure.

Some controllers will try to sort this all out; but it is far more sensible to accept his figure without comment and leave it to the subsequent deployment of totals to stifle doubt. The usual procedure, in debiting the cost, is to reduce the credit figure by the current percentage to date shown on the food statement.

Cellar Supplies

The details are shown as on the customer's account. When these are 'inclusive' in the charge, as noted above, details of consumption and selling value are shown.

Cash Sales

These are listed under a separate heading on the statement and shown in their respective cash totals as: wines, spirits, liqueurs, beers, minerals, etc. Although the control office will have cost schedules, there is little point in costing out each item, and the general percentage of profit on this type of supply as fixed by the establishment can be used in arriving at a cost. To apply a basic percentage to the drink sales will not be misleading.

Sundry Charges

Costs extra labour: All these will be submitted to the control office by the banqueting department, and should be certified by the staff manager.

Flowers

It depends on who deals with these. In establishments, which have a florist section, the charge will come from this department. Regardless of where it comes from, the banqueting manager should certify the debit.

Band and Entertainment

When the customer does not pay this charge directly, the debit should only be accepted on a certified invoice.

Menus and Printing

Where this work is done outside the establishment, the printer or stationer should submit a special charge for each function.

The appropriate authority should certify all charges sent to the control office for debiting to these statements.

Service Bar

Standard stocks should be checked at frequent intervals to ascertain that they are complete. In fact, this could be done when checking the replenishment record.

Spirits, liqueurs, bar wines, etc.–the stock of these should be taken once a week.

Industrial Catering

Industrial catering is the provision of meals in establishments that come under the Factory Act and is under the supervision of the factory inspector. In India every factory having more than 200 employees must have a canteen. The canteen is under the supervision of the factory inspector's department who has attached to it a catering specialist.

The essential points necessary for the efficient working are:

1. That it should be so designed to provide a quick and efficient service.
2. As the canteen is open to view by the workers for whom it provides meals, special care should be taken in its cleanliness.
3. Its design should be as simple as possible to enable the type of labour normally found in a kitchen in an industrial canteen to do their work as easily as possible.

Meals

As the type of meals to be provided are to be as cheap as it is possible, plain wholesome food must be provided. Whether it is vegetarian or non-vegetarian great care must be taken in the preparation and service as it is not possible to offer any great variety of range of foodstuffs. At the same time the nutritive value of the food served must be carefully calculated. Care must also be taken that the portions served are adequate. One of the aims of the factory department is to try and induce employers to treat their canteen as part of welfare. Thus, many of the factories find themselves faced with a considerable deficit in this endeavour to provide a substantial wholesome meal at a low cost. The normal price for a midday meal varies from Rs. 5 to Rs. 20 in many of the subsidized canteens.

Control

There are many ways of ensuring an accurate cash return in addition to a speedy service:

1. The sale of tickets or vouchers or tokens prior to the time of the meal.
2. The normal cafeteria service with a cashier at the end of the counter after the food has been taken.
3. The system where each dish is served from a separate part of the counter and the cash paid for it over the counter. This is the least efficient of the three systems.

Management

The canteens are run in several ways:

1. Contractor
2. Cooperative
3. Direct management by the firm
4. By workers club.

1. Contractor

There are certain advantages of allowing a contractor to take complete charge of the feeding arrangement. He takes responsibility for variety, proper cooking, and conduct and also the provision of the necessary catering staff, thus no responsibility accrues on the firm. The disadvantage is that unless the firm heavily subsidies the canteen, the foodstuff in the canteen has to be charged at a higher price to enable the contractor to make a reasonable profit.

2. Cooperative

A cooperative credit society is composed of representatives of both the workers and the management who form a separate unit to run and manage their canteen. Normally the firm itself pays for general overheads and maintenance of equipment. The expenses of running the canteen have to be maintained out of the gross profit, which is made.

3. Direct Management by the Firm

The third method is for the firm itself to employ a catering manager who manages the canteen on its behalf and it is treated as a department of the firm. In this case the canteen is normally subsidized by the firm to enable them to obtain the maximum amount of goodwill from their workers. The disadvantage of this arrangement is that unless the canteen manager is experienced and efficient, this goodwill will not accrue to the firm.

4. Working Club

It is similar to the cooperative society. The committee of the workers themselves run the canteen with the assistance of the firm in regard to premises and the equipment. They conduct the canteen with a manager of their own choice. In such cases the cash taken in the canteen is treated separately and accounted for as a separate department. The welfare department or the personnel manager is the link between the canteen and the management of the firm.

Properly run industrial canteens can greatly effect increased production in many particular firm. A badly run canteen will have the reverse effect. The general term used for industrial catering is feeding on the job.

Railway Catering

Railway catering includes several types of establishments such as:

1. Snack bar
2. Restaurant catering
3. Hotel catering
4. Ship catering
5. Institutional and industrial catering.

1. Snack Bar Catering

The various refreshment stalls and snack bar trades in the train.

2. Restaurant

At the stations with *table d'hote* and *a la carte* services and in the trains also.

3. Hotel Type of Catering

It is very much of a transit type of catering. Its implications are that everything should be slick and quick. They are not a very high-class of hotels but are meant for the travelling public. These are owned by the state Railways or the Railway Board.

4. Ship Catering

The Railway Board can own ships also to carry passengers to short distances. They have got a snack bar and restaurant service.

5. Institutional Catering

They may run in schools for children of railway staff.

Ship Catering (*i.e.*, on long distances):

Here the catering must be on a different scale. There are three sections:

1. The crew
2. Junior officers
3. Passengers and senior officers.

The main luxury liners have a large variety on their menus compared with any other normal catering. There is plenty of room for refrigeration, which is run economically with the help of salt water, plenty of space to cook, ample cooking equipment and ample space to serve. So a greater variety of food can always be given.

Fuel

1. Oil fuel
2. Electricity

Galleys (kitchen) are spacious; hence, there is no necessity of stocking cooked food. Food can be prepared fresh. The junior officers have a good mess of their own. The food to the crew is better than the food given to the average industrial worker. Hospital ships or hospitals in ships have hospital catering. Both *a la carte* and *Table d' hote* menus are offered.

Organization

Now there are catering superintendents (trained people) to conduct the catering.

Air Catering

Air catering includes four kinds of catering:

1. Catering on ground, snack bars and restaurants
2. Catering in canteens for industrial workers
3. Catering in air–snacks and meals

Many airlines pick up food at different stations and keep it in hot plates or take food and then reheat it. It is a service, which is in the experimental stage. The latest method is to cook the food, plate it, deep freeze it and then serve to customers after subjecting it to crash heat.

Some of the big airports have hotels attached where people can stay during transit.

Cafeterias

Restaurants are the widest form of catering *i.e.*, from meanest to the finest:

1. A restaurant is a licensed place
2. A café is a non-licensed place

In a restaurant the food served is in the form of a meal *i.e.*, heavier. Cafés serve lighter food with *a la carte* service. The difference in price of food in restaurants and cafés is due to the amenities provided. Some cafeterias have self service.

School and Hospital Catering

The catering in hospitals has only recently in the West been put on a similar footing as that of a catering establishment. Previously the catering was done for the patients and the staff under the sole supervision of matrons and sisters and as a consequence the catering was done remarkably badly. This now has been changed by the appointment of catering officers with properly trained staff to take charge of the general catering both for staff and patients and a dietician to take charge of special diets to carry out the diet prescribed by the medical staff. As a consequence of this, the standard of catering and the quicker recovery of the patients has been very noticeable.

In India, we still have the system of lack of coordination between the cooking staff and any form of management and as a consequence wastage and inefficiency occur. General institutional catering is done on a low economic level and here again if no skill is used bad catering occurs.

The largest form of institutional catering is school feeding.

To give one example, in U.K. in a town of one million inhabitants 60 million school meals were served in one year. This multiplied by all the towns gives some conception of the colossal amount of meals served in one year. These are normally a 2-course meal with vegetables, served hot and is accompanied by ½ pint of milk, some orange juice and Halibut liver oil. School feeding in India has commenced on a small scale.

The municipality of Ahmedabad is providing 10,000 school meals at the present moment.

Although the meals are of a simple nature they should be cooked and served with skill and care. The effect of school meal is extremely noticeable in the physique of children taking them. Thus, the quantity rather than the number of courses is important.

In the West, school meals are now done entirely by the State through the Ministry of Education. They are subsidized for the very poor and a charge made to those who can afford.

At the moment there are two types of canteens, dealing in this type of catering:

1. Completely equipped kitchen
2. Meals cooked at a central kitchen

Hotel and Motel Catering

Hotel catering has recently become more important than ever before. The emphasis used to be on the comfort in the bedrooms and the lounges. But now a good hotel is rated by its excellence in its cuisines and many hotels have either gone down or increased in popularity due to the emphais having shifted to food. In addition to the normal restaurant type, a variety of other types of catering has to be carried out in a hotel. Invalid cooking, special diets, room service and depending on the size of the hotel many other forms. A brasserie, coffee bar, is not confined to visitors staying in the hotel but is also used by the general public who wish to patronize that particular hotel.

A motel is the form of catering similar to a dak bungalow. The characteristic of a motel is that it has a set of self contained units consisting of a garage, a lounge, a bedroom and a bathroom. While meals are taken in a common dining room they can be served in each of these units. They are obviously single storied and the normal size of a motel is 40 to 50 suites. They are growing in popularity for the public as they are much less formal than a normal hotel.

Transport Café

This facility is for transport drivers who make regular journeys and rely on these cafés both to sleep and eat in.

Snack Bar, Milk Bars and Coffee Bars

In recent years catering in snack bars, milk bars and coffee bars has increased enormously. People young and old from all walks of life patronize this form of catering. The normal snack bars serve a wide range of snacks and are patronized during the day by those people desiring a quick cheap lunch. These three forms of catering to be successful require a greater attention to hygiene than other forms of catering. In the west, more and more of this type of catering is developing due to shortage and cost of labour for waiting purposes.

23. Outdoor Catering or Mobile Catering

It is also known as off-premises catering. The hotel providing outdoor catering facilities should make it a continuing activity to ensure the full utilization of its equipment and staff. A full and comprehensive sales service such as, meals, drinks, confectionery, cigarettes, hot dog kiosks and so on should be provided.

The person in charge of outdoor catering needs to be decisive, quick to command and adaptable to various situations. He needs to have the respect of the staff, most of whom are taken on a casual basis.

Outdoor catering includes all those forms of catering not covered so far, a few examples being, catering for weddings, banquets in an outside hall, any form of light refreshment given in the hall or open, catering for every form of sports meeting, catering for any kind of gathering political or otherwise, etc.

There are three main categories of outdoor catering:

Weddings

To cater for a wedding, a caterer may need to provide food, the wedding cake, arrange a *pandal* or decorations, print invitations, provide flowers, drinks, tobacco, photographs.

Banquets/Dinners

The most difficult of outdoor catering is for banquets or dinners mainly because the places may not be equipped for cooking; so temporary arrangements have to he installed and care has to be taken to see that the necessary apparatus is available. There are various forms of fuel that can be used–bottle gas, coal, kerosene and in some cases electricity. The type of equipment used must be necessarily lighter in nature than normal catering equipment.

Catering for other types of outside functions is of the cafeteria or snack variety particularly at sports meetings and large gatherings of people where the amount of provision to be made is difficult to estimate. In recent years most of the food used at this sort of function is pre-packed and wrapped so that contamination in-transit is avoided. One essential feature of outdoor catering is that each separate function must be closeted and the overheads charges otherwise a true cost cannot be arrived at for future reference. The procedure for the fixing of sale prices in out-catering must be done by processing and then adding the necessary percentage required for overheads and profit. In costing for a function, the percentage of gross profit must always be higher than the gross profit of a similar function in a catering establishments as the overheads to carry out the same function in temporary premises will obviously be higher. Because outdoor catering is of a temporary nature and served in temporary premises this does not mean that the same care and attention in cooking and service should not be given. As an outdoor caterer's reputation depends on comparison with the same function in a regular catering establishment a standard form of enquiry must always be used in taking instructions for the carrying out of orders.

24. Exhibitions and Other Income Sources

Nowadays hotels are increasingly used for exhibition facilities. The main advantages–under one roof an air of luxury is provided with the added attraction of bars, dining rooms and sleeping accommodation. The hotel should, therefore, study and give thought to the available accommodation, recognising that exhibition facilities could be a source of additional income, particularly during its off peak periods.

Many of the precautions mentioned earlier in the Conference section apply to the planning of an exhibition. Some additional precautions are:

1. Stridently patterned carpets can instantly destroy the quality of a display.
2. Air-conditioning must not only be adequate, but constantly checked, as considerable heat is generated by the extra lighting needed and people.
3. If the hotel accommodation is small in exhibition terms and if well attended could result in very cramped conditions. Public rooms, usually adjacent to the area in use, should be made available for this purpose.

Thought should be given to storage space. Every exhibition, small or large, will carry with it crates, packing materials and articles. Because of this factor, extra portage can be useful.

Exhibitors bring bulky things with them and although they may have their own staff, but if space is to be cleared and set up in a short time, they need hotel staff standing by for help.

The role of the local fire officer must be given due importance in arrangements. His advice is of vital importance. The chances are that the exhibition organizers may try and force more stands into the area than in safe.

Light can be a grave problem if the hotel has not made adequate arrangements before hand. Lighting must be flexible, with points ideally in the middle of the room, either at floor or ceiling level. Extra points laid at the last minute can cost extra and the organizers are unlikely to look very favourably on the hotel who has asked the organizer to pay for extra points to be installed and then find wiring insufficient to carry the extra load.

Care should be taken over the sign-posting system. Information, which is well designed, prominent, flexible and clear can save a great deal of irritation to members of the staff and to all those involved in the exhibition.

Finally, the hotel should not use bedrooms for exhibition purposes. Apart from the particularly cramped conditions, visitors are likely to feel 'trapped'. Freedom of movement is essential to the creation of an overall sense of luxury.

Other Income Sources

There are many other sources of hotel income, which are connected directly with the operational activities. All these incomes are received in small amounts from different heads.

Rentals

There are many spaces, which are used for the operations of a hotel as a part of usual hotel service. Rental received from these is credited to rental account.

Some of these subheads of income are:

Office Rentals

It includes the rent income from space in the hotel building used as offices by tenants other than concessionaires.

Rent from Clubs

Rent received from rooms allotted to a club is included under this head and all expenses related to the clubroom are also charged to this account.

Others

It includes:

1. Rent from lobby space
2. Rent from showcases
3. Rent from other spaces

Commission paid to renting agents is charged against the gross income from rentals and after adjustment of expenses net rental income is calculated.

Concession

Concession is revenue received from outside for the privilege of operating departments which might be operated by the hotel itself as part of the usual hotel service. Expenses to the hotel in connection with the operation of a concession, should be charged as departmental expenses. If the departments are operated by the hotel, charges against the income received from the concessionaire are credited to this account. Some of the sources of revenue of concessions are:

1. Barber shop
2. Cigars and news-stand
3. Guest laundry
4. Restaurants
5. Transportation
6. Foreign exchange
7. Gaming machine revenue
8. Beauty shop
9. Gift shops
10. Public stenographers
11. Swimming pool, cabanas and baths
12. Valet
13. Showcase rent.

25. Purchase and Stores

This department should be completely independent of the other departments of the hotel. The department can be sub-divided into:

1. Purchasing
2. Receiving
3. Storing
4. Issuing

The creation of atmosphere by right choice of furnishings and equipment is a contributing factor to the success of food and beverage service area. Therefore, the choice of furniture and linen, tableware, small equipment and glassware is to be carefully determined by considering the following points:

1. The funds available
2. The site or location of the restaurant
3. The type of the restaurant
4. The type of service offered
5. The type of customers expected
6. The total layout of the food and service area

The following points need to be considered when purchasing equipment for the food and beverage service area:

1. Cost and funds available
2. Type of service being offered
3. Type of customers
4. Durability
5. Flexibility of use
6. Ease of maintenance
7. Design
8. Colour Scheme
9. Shape
10. Storage
11. Stockability
12. Rate of breakage
13. Replacement facilities
14. Delivery time
15. Psychological effect

The purchasing section centralizes all orders from the different departments and transcribes them on to official forms. These forms are submitted to the manager, who signs them if he is satisfied that they are neces ary and reasonable in quantity, quality and price. This section gathers and files all vouchers, quotations etc., for studying the market and comparing the prices. It checks all invoices and maintains a cardex both for 'goods cards' and 'suppliers cards'.

The control of deliveries by this section relates to the checking of quantity. The checking of quality is the responsibility of the heads of the various departments. The order is made out in quadruplicate. The top copy is put to the suppliers, the second to the account office, the third to the department receiving the goods and the fourth is retained in the purchasing section. The responsibility of this section falls on the purchase manager who is assisted by the purchase assistants.

The various commodities and items purchased for hotel may be grouped as follows:

1. Food and beverages
    a. Perishables
    b. Dry, canned and bottled provisions

c. Soft drinks

d. Liquor

2. Cooker, glassware and silverware
3. Kitchen's requisites
4. Linen, uniform and furnishing material
5. Household store
6. Stationery and printing
7. Maintenance department requirements and stores
8. Miscellaneous and sundry stores
9. Capital goods

The purchasing of these items can be done through following methods:

1. Annual rate contract
2. Period or term rate contract
3. Specific department requisition as when received specially in case of items such as linen, crockery, glassware, capital goods, etc.
4. Regular store item as and when necessary
5. Emergency and miscellaneous

Proper purchase policy requires the coordination between finance, production, food and beverage store and the receiving general manager, and the purchase manager as regards to qualities and quantities.

Although the purchase department is a non-revenue producing activity, it has to ensure continuity in supply of raw material and spares and at the same time reduce the ultimate cost of goods and service offered by the hotel.

The receiving section is mainly concerned with the receipts of goods and is managed by a receiving manager, who may be assisted by receiving assistants. All items which are purchased by the hotel have to go through the receiving department which ensures that the quantity and quality of the product meet the specification and standard required.

The manager (stores) is responsible for receiving the goods delivered to the hotel. He inevitably spends most of the time in his own department. The storekeepers are responsible for its maintenance and for controlling its issue, withdrawal and exchange. They inform the manager (store) when new equipment is required and keep record of all deliveries, issue, exchanges and withdrawals. These details are summarized periodically and entered in the stock books and bin card.

Food cost control begins with purchasing of food supplies on the basis of competitive bids to assure the lowest price and the required quality. Deliveries must also be closely monitored for both quantity and quality, otherwise food cost may get out of hand. Therefore, following steps should be taken to prevent questionable practices:

The food and beverages store could be divided into:

1. Dry stores/general stores
2. Perishable store
3. Cold rooms
4. Beverage stores or cellar
5. Linen, china, glass and silver stores

The storage arrangement of hotels may vary. A dry store may include items such as cleaning materials, stationery and guest supplies. Similarly, a cellar may be used for storing minerals, beers, wines and spirits, cigars, cigarettes, tobacco, etc. Restaurant linen may be stored in the housekeeping department or in the users' department with china, glass and silver.

The stores in a hotel may have different rooms for storing different items. There are walk-in refrigerators and walk-in deep freezers for storing perishables. Apart from these there are different storage areas for liquor, soft drinks, flour and oils, smokes, spices, canned food, crockery, cutlery, hollowware, stationery, etc.

Manager (Stores)

He is in charge of stores. He should have a thorough knowledge of the various commodities, foodstuffs and their prices. He must know what foods are perishable and their proper storage and preservation specially of fruits and vegetables.

Head Storekeeper

He is also in charge of the store and must be an honest man. A head storekeeper must have the knowledge of the various commodities and their prices. He must have the knowledge of perishable foodstuffs, fruits and vegetables and their preservation.

Store Controller

It is an administrative job. The store-controller must have good knowledge of the function and running of the various departments of the store. He should have adequate administrative experience and knowledge of the commodities and products and their market prices. He assists the head storekeeper in his various duties. He also replaces the head storekeeper in his absence.

Store Accounts Clerk

He requires the knowledge of various commodities and must be able to detect the defects of the product purchased. His duties are to supervise the delivery of goods and check weights, quantities, qualities and prices. He has the right to reject goods not supplied according to the order. He enters movement of goods in a register and notifies any irregularity to the head storekeeper.

Storekeeper

Knowledge of various commodities and their storage techniques is essential for a storekeeper. He takes order from the head storekeeper. Arranges goods in stores, issues stores against withdrawal vouchers and keeps the store checklist up-to-date. He is responsible for all the stored goods.

Cellarman

A cellarman must have the knowledge of the different categories of wines and their preservation. His duties are to take orders from the head cellarman and to be responsible for washing and rinsing all bottles and flasks and the cleanliness of the equipment and premises. He replaces head cellarman in his absence.

Assistant Store Controller

He must have the knowledge of functioning and running of the various departments of the hotel. He is also required to have the knowledge of the principal commodities and their prices. He assists the store-controller in supervising the deliveries and withdrawals of goods and the checking of stock.

Assistant Cellarman

He assists in handling the stores. He washes and rinses all goods and cleans the cellars.

At the end of accounting period, the accounts department prepares a financial statement, profit and loss account and a balance sheet. The account office provides the controlling figure as well as carries out accounting functions. The control stems from forecasting, which takes into account past performance as well as future plans on the basis of which the management draws up a budget.

There should be a close cooperation and coordination between all the departments. If the departmental manager commands the respect and loyalty from his staff and they in turn are respected by their assistants and juniors, the running of the hotel will be smooth. It is essential for a hotel that every aspect of its organization should function smoothly.

Control in Goods Receiving

Exact procedures for recording receipts may vary but the basic steps to follow during purchasing and receiving are:

A purchase order should be written or printed, serially numbered, and prepared in triplicate forms. The top copy is for the vendor. The second goes to the store-room clerk in order to verify receipt later. The third is usually sent to the business or accounting office for comparison with the suppliers' invoice (when that arrives) to ensure that payment is made only for goods actually ordered and received. For goods ordered by telephone, an order form should be sent later as a means of confirmation.

The following control can be fitted into any establishment:

1. The goods receiving office should be notified of all goods placed on order. This notification will also be the authority for the acceptance of the goods, and supplies arriving without this advice should be held until the appropriate department gives clearance.
2. Orders once completed should be placed on a 'cleared file'. The delivery note or invoice will quote order number.
3. The delivery note or invoice will give the following verification:
   a. All documents relating to the receipt of goods should be given a serial number in numerical sequence, as soon as dealt with.
   b. Date
   c. Order Number
   d. Checker's signatures
4. Incoming goods will be listed daily as follows:
   a. Date
   b. Department
   c. Name of the supplier
   d. Description of goods

The records will be audited by the control department daily, which will clear all vouchers and sign records for receipt.

Another duty of the goods receiving office is to attend to the return of empty containers (with the exception of those from the cellar department). These will be listed as:

1. Date
2. Consignee
3. Description
4. Value

The control will check this record with credit notes. One must emphasize the importance of keeping a rigid control over chargeable containers. Considerable losses can occur through neglect in this direction.

The goods receiving office is an important department and provides an independent check on all incoming goods.

Most people outside the industry have the impression that food and drink is about all that a hotel consumes. These are, of course its major trading items, but a hotel is a consumer of practically every class of article manufactured in the country. For example, every known type of furniture and furnishing, textiles, cutlery, China, glass, ironware, enamelware, tinware, electrical equipment, machinery, clothing, stationery, building materials, etc. –in fact, one would find it difficult to name an item, which is not, used somewhere in a hotel. Some hotels generate their electricity, have their own water supply, laundry, upholsterers, travel department, etc. and as self-contained unit are comparable to a small town.

Therefore, the check on incoming supplies is a major function. Usually, and for obvious reasons, it is not possible for the goods receiving office to cope with the entire flow, and their jurisdiction is limited to the current trading requirements, such as food, cellar supplies, China, glass, cutlery, stationery and sundry small items. In any event the cost of these amounts to large sums of money, and loosely knit methods in dealing with goods at this check can be very costly. The weakness in control at the goods entrance and check point can provide a fertile field for leakage.

There is an old saying in the industry: 'control starts at the back door', and it is very true.

In building a control system to govern in this department, the first thing to take into account is the location of the sections to which goods are distributed after passing the checkpoint. In many hotels, the goods receiving office is most inconveniently situated and this has a bearing on the control planning. The ideal setting is to be closely linked to the provision store, kitchen, cellar and general stores. When the receiving office is far away from these sections, goods can be go astray within the establishment and this inspite of following a system.

It is usual for the carrier to deliver the goods past the checking points to the various departments where he receives a signature on the delivery note for receipt, which he returns to the checking clerk. To assure that this is done, the receiving clerk retains the carrier delivery book and only releases it in return for the signed delivery note.

Dry Goods Store (Provisions Store)

In a large food and beverage establishment, this department carries a stock, which for variety and often quantity equals a large grocery store. Its operation is similar in many respects, the main difference being that requisitions take the place of cash. A good storekeeper is a considerable asset and one proficient in his duties can save his employers a lot of money.

The essentials, which go into making of a good storekeeper are, experience; a knowledge of how to handle, how to organize the stock in his charge; a tidy mind and a sense of detail; a quick grasp of figures; clear handwriting and a liking for his job and honesty.

Requisition Supplies

There are many departments which draw supplies from this store: kitchen, still room, mess-rooms, restaurant, grillroom, banqueting floors, service, etc. and in first planning control these should be listed. A copy of this list should be given to the storekeeper as indicating the departments he is authorized to serve; and to this should be added a copy of the signatures of the heads of the drawing departments.

Requisition Books

If possible, these should be distinct from other internal documents and in duplicate form. The stock of these should be held by control, which lists the voucher numbers in each book and to which department they have been issued. New books are exchanged for those used.

Listing of Issues

These should be listed daily into a record stating date; requisition number; department; description and quantity; price; etc. The control will audit this record daily and post the credits to stock into store stock ledger.

Store Stock Ledger

This is an important instrument and should be kept in the control office. Stock entries in the ledger should run in alphabetical order and this order should correspond with the positioning of stock in the store. A stranger to the store should by reference to the stock ledger be able to find any item in stock immediately.

Receipt of Goods

The storekeeper after checking additions to stock on arrival should distribute to the respective shelves as soon as possible. In listing the record of 'goods received', he should state date; order number; name of supplier; description and quantity; and the price. The control will carry out the process of daily audit by comparing delivery notes and invoices with entries and posting the entries in this record of store stock ledger. The control should extract from invoices all charges for containers and treat these items as stock, crediting the account from credit notes.

Stocktaking

This falls within the purview of the control. The stock balances in the store stock ledger should be checked with physical stock at frequent intervals. At least, once a month there should be a complete stocktaking and all differences between ledger balances and physical stock should be investigated and listed for the information of the management.

Ordering of Supplies

The storekeeper should list requirements in sufficient time to allow for delivery and not list until a particular item has run out of stock. A copy of this list should be submitted to control who will check with stock balance and rate of consumption as shown in the store ledger–mainly to avoid overstocking.

Food and Beverage

The path that the food products follow from procurement to service is referred to as 'food flow'. This path has to be considered in all plans made from the operation and service of the facility so that a smooth flow is assured. An outline of the facility is drawn on a drawing board so that food flow can be examined visually and required space could be allotted for all the different activities.

The Kitchen

It is important for the controller to know the entire organization of a complete kitchen.

Fuel Consumption

Fuel costs and fuel efficiency are both important items. Experience shows that very little heed is given to these at least on a rational basis. Most kitchens today have mixed plants. Using coal is four times cheaper than gas, and gas is twice as cheap as electricity.

Apart from keeping for purpose of comparison, a monthly record of the cost and consumption in the kitchen, helps in arriving at a figure for fuel costs per meal. A simple method for dealing with this is as follows:

Each class of meal is given a points-value (in terms of consumption of fuel):

Breakfast	2 points
Luncheon	6 points
Teas	1 point
Dinner	6 points

At the end of each month or period covered, add up all the above points and divide the the total cost of fuel, coal, gas, electricity, etc. for the same period by the total points. For example, say the cost per point is 1.23 of a rupee then the cost for producing a dinner is 7.38 or roughly seven rupees.

A copy of these figures should be sent to the chef and management, together with the comparison of previous periods. It is a useful guide and in most cases makes the chef 'fuel conscious' and watchful of wastage.

Normal Schedules: Charging Supplies

The system employed for charges is as follows:

1. Wet or perishable goods, such as meat, fish, poultry, game, fruit, vegetables, milk, etc., which go direct to the kitchen department,

are charged to the kitchen account on the date of receipt.

2. Dry goods drawn from store are charged on date of issue. These charges are collected into a daily analysed record, usually under the following headings: Grocery (tea, coffee coca, sugar, sauces, pickles, condiments, etc.), tinned meats and fish, ice and sundries.

Against the total costs are shown the receipts from meals served and percentage of gross profit. The position is also given for consumption of goods and receipts to date for the month.

Cold Buffet

Where a cold buffet is used, the chef must cooperate with the control department. There can be a lot of irregular play by waiters. To introduce a simple and effective control, a certain amount of experiment is necessary.

The system to apply is proposed as follows:

1. Before each service all supplies from the kitchen to cold buffet will be listed by control and given a 'portion' value. The basis for this assessment should be carefully worked out with the chef, and it will help if the *trancheur* (a person who does carving of fruits, vegetables, meat products for cold buffet) is consulted when the assessment is being drafted.
2. Service checks from the cold buffet will be credited against the respective items, together with the returns to the larder.

Once a basis for working is established, the application of the system is very simple and should not take more than half an hour of a control clerk's time daily.

Portion Control

It is said that 'portion' assessment can only have a hypothetical value. There is sufficient level of truth in this to encourage neglect; but applying a brake will have a slowing down effect on the volume of leakage, whereas lack of restraint will encourage the development of it.

Apart from the cold buffet, 'portion' control should be applied to special items such as oysters, caviare, smoked salmon, choice cheese, fruits etc. The check here is quite simple. Oysters being definite units are easy to account for, but a control check will probably reveal unexplained shortages. Apply the following methods of control:

1. List stock on hand at the commencement of the control period.
2. Add supplies subsequently received.
3. Credit account with oysters served as per service bills, also bills issued by chef for oysters used for kitchen purposes.
4. Compare balance with stock on hand at the close of the control period.

The same applies to other items mentioned; the difference being that these results will give the amount consumed per portion.

Larder Control

This is governed by a form termed as the 'Larder Chart' which gives the stock in hand in larder, cold room and other storage points within the kitchen. It shows daily the opening and closing stocks of the primary consumables, and is compiled by the kitchen clerk.

The chart is a valuable guide to the chef, not only as a means of protecting his stock, but also as a measure for determining his requirements. Unfortunately, the system is not in general use, and in 90 per cent of the kitchens it has been necessary to institute this control.

The general acceptance of the view that goods within the kitchen are beyond the scope of the control is not satisfactory. The stock held in the kitchen is often heavy and varied, and unless under some form of governance, the opportunity for pilfering can be more open here than elsewhere.

It is not always practical to have a member of the control actively carrying out schedules within the kitchen. But wherever possible endeavours should be made to bring part of the kitchen clerk's duties within the sphere of the control. The approach to the initial stage is:

1. Take stock and list the items you intend to control in the larder, cold room, and sundry storage points. Repeat this daily for a week. The object of this is to group and classify the stock determine the normal location and practice within the kitchen. It will guide in drafting the Larder Chart.
2. Do not bother to list such items as cheap vegetables or the varied assortment of inexpensive supplies, which are unlikely to attract pilferage. Confine the listing to poultry, fish, meat, ham, bacon, butter, fruit (not cheap varieties), cheese, etc. At first just select a few items and concentrate on these. In other words form the nucleus, and allow time, experience, and operation to build around it.
3. The daily stock position, to which will be added subsequent purchases, will enable the controller to gauge whether consumption is normal for the amount of business being done. The purpose here is to seek apparent overconsumption and bring it to the notice of the chef, as a preliminary to enlisting his cooperation in initiating control methods.
4. There is a point to make here. Always convey to the chef that any loss comes from activities outside his department and not within it. Emphasize that the particular interest of the controller is to prevent the chef's kitchen being robbed by the service staff. His response will be immediate; and further more you will have found a friend for life.
5. Once having settled the form of stock listing required and refined the working to its simplest equation, it should be an easy matter to pass it on to the kitchen office as a regular schedule. This entails:
    i. Taking stock of the items listed in the morning, and again at the conclusion of the last service. Much can happen during the night, or at any time when the kitchen is not in service.
    ii. Add daily purchases to the chart.
    iii. Refer to menus and service bills.

The above system, when intelligently applied and organized requires little time in keeping it up-to-date. Where it has been-introduced, it has been found that the chef usually increases its detail, and generally advances its development into an important instrument of control.

Still Room

The control of the still room is quite simple, but unless a system is put into effect, pilfering may develop. Tea, coffee and sugar can leak in considerable quantities, unless a tight check is kept on its use. The quantity produced per rupee in the preparation of beverages can vary considerably. Variations are dependent on many causes – quality of supply, type of service, condition of water, etc. It is, therefore, advisable to make a physical test of what can be reasonably anticipated before fixing a scale and formula that can be adhered to. The control form is based on the dual system of debit (supplies issued to still room) and credit (number of beverages served as per service checks). The record should be a daily one, so that at a glance it is possible to ascertain whether the still room is overdrawing supplies from store, and not wait for periodical stock checks to give the result. Milk, sugar, breads, butter are also used in this section and should be brought under the same form of control.

You could quote standards of consumption, but this might be a misleading guide, and it is better to investigate the standards of an establishment before formulating a scale.

In some hotels the still room is operated as an independent unit and does not come within the province of the chef. Some experts are not in favour of this; they much prefer the still room to be part of a kitchen organization. Charges to this section eventually become a charge to the kitchen account, and it is unfair to the chef when he has no authority in this direction. Separation has other disadvantages, an important one being the staffing on this section.

Service Checks

Careless handling of service checks within the kitchen can hinder the control and aid in covering collusion between kitchens and waiting staff. The most effective means of dealing with this is the use of locked slotted metal boxes, to which only the control and the chef have keys.

It is usual for the chef or his deputy, to keep the main checks under his control during the service and scrutinize them in his office at the conclusion. This is a normal practice but the chef should take care that the checks are placed in the box specially provided for their protection. The control should clear these boxes after each service. Where the control does not function after ordinary office hours, the boxes can be cleared first thing the following morning.

General Stores

Items included in general stores are China, glass, cutlery, linen, stationery, etc. The stocks held in the general stores constitute the unused reserves, and it does not always follow that the different categories are all contained at one storage point. This depends on the volume of stock held and the space available. It is preferable however where circumstances permit, to bring these together at one point. The reasons are numerous and some of these are as follows:

1. Concentration brings the receipt of incoming supplies and their examination, sorting into storage position, distribution to consuming points, stock records and general care, etc., under one control.
2. Where storage points are spread about the hotel, it is usual to find that the operation is being handled by several persons, which weakens the system for governance and check on movement.
3. Treatment at one point simplifies and strengthens the entire process of stock administrations.
4. It tends to eliminate casual handling.
5. It facilitates stocktaking and eases the task of the controller.

It is advisable to bring the governing of this section within the province of one of the larger departments and not allow it to function as a single or unattached unit. This class of stock is often of considerable value and heavy losses in it can be incurred where there is a failure to provide a rational cover.

The most suitable section to cover the general stores is the control office. This does not imply that members of the control staff should become involved in the receipt and distribution of stocks, but that the operation of this section should fall within the authority of the controller. The reasons for offering this suggestion can be summarized as follows:

1. The organization of the controller office has no departmental interest in the usage of these stocks.
2. It is an unrivalled position to enforce the rules of the establishment.

3. As all records and statistics relating to additions and issues of stock, stocktaking, stock balances, replenishments, and usage within the various departments, etc., are processed by the control, the entire procedure of governing is stabilized.

Suitable Storage Accommodation

1. Adequate space based on quantities normally held
2. Conveniently sited usually in the basement close to the goods receiving office. Also easily accessible to those drawing supplies
3. Ventilated
4. Well lighted. This is important – poor lighting is a frequent fault in this section, and a costly one
5. Moderate temperature – Excess of heat or cold will have an adverse effect on China, glass and linen
6. Plenty of shelf space – Avoid cupboards and the necessity for storing on the floor. Do not advocate shelves being partitioned into small compartments
7. Space for the unpacking of goods – This keeps the storage points clean and free from wrappings, etc.
8. Basic office equipment – Often nothing elaborate is needed here. Just space for desk and storage of records

Receipt of Goods

Incoming supplies should be unpacked, checked, and distributed to the appropriate storage points immediately on arrival. It is of equal importance to clear the work of this section daily as in the case of the dry goods stores and cellar department, a fact which is often, ignored.

Advice of Delivery

This is a daily record:

1. In duplicate or as the system demands
2. Compiled from delivery notes or invoices
3. With a separate form for each category of supply. This of course, may not always be necessary, but deliveries during the day should be grouped under their respective headers.
4. Delivery record will give date, serial number of voucher (delivery note or invoice); name of supplier, description of goods; order number.
5. The record will be signed by the person in charge of general stores, and the original copy together with the supporting vouchers, sent to control office.

Issues From Stock

The requisition book used for this purpose by the various departments should be distinct from those used in drawing other supplies; departmental requisitions should pass through a central medium. This would work as follows and come within the active province of the manager's office, or the controller's.

1. Requisitions, signed by head of department, should be sent to the scheduled office for drawing the official order from the stores.
2. The number of the official order will be noted for the departmental requisition, which will be filed for reference purposes.
3. The official order must contain the manager's signature, and issues from general stores will be made on the authority of this voucher only.

It may be claimed that this is a lengthy process where supplies are required in a hurry. But replacement of departmental stocks is only in the rarest occasions an emergency. Whatever system is applied there will always be exceptions, but these must not be made the norm for breaking down the rules.

Under no circumstances should issues be made direct from the general stores on departmental requisition. The main virtue of this system is its simplicity, and the bringing of all requisitions under the tightest possible form of control.

China and Glass

China and glass debits to stock should be recorded on the date of arrival. An ordinary full-scape book can be used for this purpose and, where the volume of incoming supplies justifies, used exclusively for the entry of China and glass this record will state: date of receipt; serial number of delivery note or invoice; order number; name of supplier, quantity and description of goods; and price.

Credits to stock will be entered into a similar record giving: date of issue; requisition number; department; quantity and description of goods.

The stock ledger will be entered from these records. It is not necessary that the stock ledger should carry the details of issues in respect of departments supplied. This information can be drawn from the original entries 'Issues' book. Entering too much detail into the stock ledger can be confusing, and where several departments are involved will necessitate multiple and special ruling. The stock ledger should be a simple instrument.

Stocktaking

Stock checks of the general stores should be undertaken once a month. This of course, need not include stationery. The control office can carry out this work. All differences between ledger balance and physical stock should be listed, investigated, and submitted to the management.

Cutlery and Silverware

The same requisitioning processes are employed as with China and glass. Issues from this stock are not very frequent, and the basis for replenishment is shortages in the departmental standard stock. This also applies to China and glass, but not with the rigidity, which governs the issue of replacements to cutlery and silverware standards.

This is not a departmental issue, and requisitions are based on deficiencies in the general working stock.

Although there can be a division of authority over 'bed' and 'table' linen, it is usual as the linen room comes within the province of the housekeeper, for this official to assume the responsibility over all matters pertaining to this stock. Therefore, all requisitions for linen should come through the housekeeper with the manager's signature.

Stationary Stocks

Although the use of stationery in hotels is considerable and expensive, it is not customary to apply a rigid, or rational, control of the stock and usage.

1. Issues will be made on the order of a requisition voucher signed by the head of department.
2. Requisitions should clearly state requirements.
3. A list should be given to the clerk in charge of stationery noting the particular types of stationery which departments are entitled to draw. Unless instructions are clearly stated, and strictly adhered to, abuses in the use and ordering of stationery will develop.
4. Such items termed as 'important', as cash receipt books, restaurant and sundry bill heads, waiter's bill pads, etc., should be issued only on the authority of the controller.
5. Stationery should be issued only at certain times on certain days. Unless this rule is enforced, exceptions to it will develop to the extent of rendering it valueless.

Stationery requirements should be standardized. The process of recording additions to, and issues from stock can entail considerable work in compiling information, which will never be used. It is not the type of stock, which invites pilfering and the main feature of its control rests with a monthly comparison of costs.

Incoming supplies should be noted as a record for the accounts office, but detailing of issues as a normal) schedule is more often than not a waste of time. In some establishments each department is advised monthly of its stationery charges, and this form of advice which occasions quite a lot of work, promptly finds a home in the waste paper basket.

It is customary to 'write off' stationery as a charge against trading and receipt of deliveries, and its issues from a central point is a means for governing its distribution. The controller can formulate a simple plan to enable the drawing of a mountable cost chart of stationery used in the various departments. This need not become a set schedule, and should be used as an occasional check for testing the rise and fall in consumption.

Part-IV
Security And Safety Systems

26. Security and Safety

It is estimated that lacs of rupees are lost annually by hotel businesses due to theft and dishonesty on the part of employees. Therefore, security is one of the most important responsibilities of the hotel management. The main points to be considered for hotel security are:

1. Preventing thefts and pilferages
2. Avoiding wilful waste by the employees
3. Development of emergency plan for the protection of guests in the event of civil disturbances.

Thus, the main functions of the security in a hotel are:

1. To safeguard guests and their property
2. To guard the hotel's property
3. To guard employees and their property.

The management has a duty towards his lawful visitors which is referred to as the 'common duty of care' and means a duty to take such care as in all the circumstances of the case is reasonable to see that the visitor will be reasonably safe is using the premises for the purpose for which he is invited or permitted by the management to be there. The management must be prepared for children to be less careful than adults, and is entitled to expect that a person in the exercise of his calling (e.g. an electrician) will appreciate and guard against any special risk, ordinarily incidental to it. These provisions are applicable to all guests and customers, postman, trade people, builders and decorators, window cleaners and others and the management should cover such risks to which they may be exposed by insurance.

The management's duty of care may not extend to parts of the premises not included to be used by guests, such as staff quarters, and such parts should be clearly identified, with the suitable lighting at night.

The principal ingredient in the security programme's effectiveness is the ability to respond promptly to security problems. Large hotels have security men both in uniform and plainclothes patrolling the hotel lobby and around the hotel. Now, a number of security systems are being introduced by modern hotels.

The most important aspect of property control is an adequate locking system with key control. Entrance, front, back and side doors' keys are normally held by the owner or general manager with spares held by a senior trusted employee. Internal keys are required to control storerooms, chillers, fridges and freezers, internal doors to public areas, different sections of the kitchen and preparation areas and storerooms. With internal keys it is good to work on master key, sub-master and single door key system. The master key is held by the general manager, the sub-master key by the middle manager or supervisors or head of the department and single door keys or grouping of single door keys by junior employees who are authorized to have access. Many deluxe hotels, instal electronic digital systems with available code numbers. Windows need to be considered from security point of view.

The wallet-sized plastic card substitutes the traditional metal room key. When a guest registers at the hotel, a special machine codes several cards at random. The 'control card', is inserted in a master console, while one or more cards are given to the guest. When he wishes to unlock the door to his room, the guest inserts the card into a slot near his door.

The card he inserts is electronically compared with the corresponding card in the slot matching his room number. If the code matches, the door opens with a click. It is virtually impossible to inadvertently duplicate a code. In the case of lost or stolen cards, an instantaneous change of lock sets can be arranged simply by coding a new set of cards.

Another system utilizes a keyboard to change key and lock combinations by remote control. The keyboard is wired to every lock in the hotel. When the guest registers, his key is 'validated' by the keyboard, in effect changing, in less than a second, the key and lock used by the previous occupant of the room.

If the valuables of a guest are stored in a hotel safe, the liability is generally limited. The guest must be informed of the limitation. In case the guest chooses to retain his valuables instead of depositing them in the hotel safe, it is not considered negligence and does not relieve the hotel of liability. You will find that in many hotels notices are put in guest rooms advising patrons of measures available for protection of their property and person.

One of the first laws affecting hotel-keeping was the establishment of the hotelier's responsibility for the protection of guests' personal safety and property. Nowadays, there are dual responsibilities of protecting both the guests and the hotel from harm, as both are vulnerable targets for thieves, prowlers and other undesirables. In small hotels this function is assigned to a watchman who records his regular rounds on a clock to prove his presence in every part of the building. During his rounds he is also responsible for noting and reporting anything which may seem unusual or undesirable. In large hotels this function is often assigned to a person known as chief security officer or chief house officer. The hotels for obvious reasons prefer not to have the methods and techniques of their security force publicized. In general, the security department must deal with:

1. The problem of doors being left unlocked or keys being left in the lock
2. Any potential hazard or indication of fire
3. The problem of inebriated persons
4. Illegal occupants in hotel rooms.

Hotels should display notices for guest and staff using the car park that cars are parked at owners' risk and that the hotel will not accept any responsibility for loss or damage to vehicles or contents. However, the management does have a duty to ensure that customer's property is safeguarded as much as reasonably possible.

Many hotels accept coats and bags from customers for safekeeping. A disclaimer notice covering loss or damage to property while in management care must be properly displayed. All receipts must be numbered and property returned on presentation of receipt, a disclaimer on the reverse of the ticket could also be printed.

There are many hotels, which have installed intruder or burglar alarms all over and closed circuit TV surveillance systems. These are very useful devices and include comprehensive recordings with date and time logging.

Some deluxe hotels have television cameras on each floor for observing the movements in corridors with a monitoring device located in the security office. Other hotels may have a computerized warning system. The guests at a time say one minute after they enter into their rooms have to insert a special card into a box on the television set. If they do not do so, a light flashes in the office, summoning the security officer. In addition to the precautions, the management should try to educate the guests to protect themselves through publicity, posters or any other available means. The guest should be requested to report any suspicious action observed by them, not to leave valuable items in the room, lock the room properly and observe the necessary precautions.

The main safe should be controlled by more than one key or combination lock. In a large hotel, two senior managers should he present to open the safe, each having one key or one knowing the combination and the other having the key. The safe room must also be controlled by two keys. Cashiers should be subjected to a detailed background enquiries before appointment. Fidelity insurance should be considered for management and those handling large amounts of cash or stock.

Security of property of customer and staff as well as food, drink and items of equipment need to be properly maintained.

The found register and lost register are maintained to manage lost and found property. Any property reported lost on the premises must be checked for against the found register and if it is not listed, it must be recorded in the lost register.

The finding of valuable property should be reported to the police. Efforts should be made to restore the found property to the rightful owner without delay. Property not claimed after a reasonable period of time can be disposed of by selling to raise money for staff fund or returning to the finder or giving to charity.

The hotel has a duty to have proper security and care of its personnel and customers. The management and staff must be prepared to deal with possible emergencies.

All allegations by customers of accidents involving injury, loss or damage to their property, and finding of foreign bodies in food must be fully recorded.

The hotel should set up procedures to protect the safety of their staff and customers. If there is a specific warning of terrorist activity, it should be established. Employees should be trained for emergency, fire prevention, fire fighting and evacuation drill.

Director Security/Chief Security Officer

He reports most often directly to general manager. In some hotels he is responsible to the resident manager. He handles the safety and security of the operation.

Security Officer

The security officer is responsible to protect the hotel and well being of guests and staff. The number of employees needed to properly staff this department depends to a great extent on the size and type of the hotel. Most of the hotels have in their security department retired defence or law-enforcement officers, who are thoroughly experienced in investigation and interrogation. The primary function of the security staff is to protect the guest against loss of their personal belongings. They have the responsibility to protect the building, personal property and reputation of the hotel without incurring any legal liability for themselves or the management of the hotel.

Besides this, security is basically incharge of fire fighting operations. Though during an emergency of this kind, all hotel employees lend a hand, the main responsibility of prevention of any such incident lies with security. Also in case some such emergency does occur, it is the security force who ensures the evacuation of the guests and the employees.

Security Precautions

A hotel, which is open to the public, guests, residents and staff over a 24-hour period, presents many problems of security. It would be almost an impossible task to safeguard property and premises completely, but common-sense precautions will help mitigate loss. Crime prevention officers of the local police will always help guide and advise establishments on security problems.

Residents' Property

The management has a duty to protect the property of his guests, all staff and in particular, the chambermaids should be instructed on safety precautions for the care of residents' property.

1. Any room maintenance required for broken locks, doorknobs and sockets should be reported immediately to the housekeeper.
2. If a guest leaves any valuables lying around the room, the chambermaid should report the matter to the housekeeper, who could advise the guest on their safer keeping.
3. It should be emphasized to cleaning staff that it is necessary to lock room doors after cleaning, and if rooms are on the ground floor, windows should be closed or locked if the rooms are empty.
4. All property found in rooms or elsewhere should be handed to the head housekeeper or some other person in authority who will see that it is entered in the lost-and-found book and placed in safe keeping.

Security of Premises

1. Staff must quickly familiarise themselves with guests, residents and other members of the staff, and be instructed to question anyone on the premises that they are not familiar with, and whom they consider may be acting in a suspicious manner.
2. Security, portering or housekeeping staff should make regular routine inspections of the buildings, carrying out checks on windows, doors and locks where necessary.
3. Keys and master keys must be under strict supervision at all times.
4. Money and valuables on the premises should be locked away, or under strict surveillance at all times if being handled during the course of business.
5. Staff must be instructed and made aware of the need of vigilance and security precautions at all times.

Doors

These should be solid and lockable and free from weather warping which can cause locks to become slack.

Windows and Skylights

All windows should be firmly closed and secured with a strong catch. Special locking devices are available and should at least be fitted to all ground floor windows. Local people can advise on high-risk windows requiring further protection.

Alarms

These can be fitted to doors, windows, refrigerators, cupboards and safes. Advice on costs and most suitable types can be obtained from insurance companies.

Locks

All locks must be carefully chosen to comply with the insurer's recommendations and regularly inspected and maintained. After a security breach, locks must be changed.

Refrigerator and other Stock Stores

All valuable stocks must be held in areas made secure by alarms or locks. The extent of security risk is determined by the value of stock items held.

Entry and Exit Security

Receipts and dispatch of all goods should be limited to those doors, which are controlled by a member of staff who will record all receipts and dispatches.

Bedrooms

These should be kept locked when they are not occupied. Chambermaids should be trained to ensure bedrooms are secure.

Fire Exits

All fire exits must always be accessible in case of emergencies but should be made secure against entry from outside.

Security of Staff and Guests

Engaging Staff

Care must be taken to see that stock and cash holders are vetted before engagement. References can be taken up and the extent of the security check is dependent on the values of goods or cash to which each member of staff will have access.

Routine Staff

Manager should make a point of spot checking shopping bags and parcels as staff leaves the premises. Staff cloakroom should also be checked.

Guest Security Checks

Suspicious characters may be refused entry into premises. Porters and receptionists should be alerted to spot unusual behaviours or movements and should report suspicions to the manager.

Security Training

All staff should be made security conscious by effective training. This should be designed to make staff aware of security risks and advise them on what action to take.

Security of Keys

Pass and Room Keys

These should be controlled by the receptionist or porters and the loss of key must be immediately reported.

Master Keys

These are the most important keys in any establishment and the loss of master key necessitates the immediate change of all locks.

Key Holders

A list of the staff entitled to draw and use all keys must be made. Unauthorized personnel should never be in possession of any key without the manager's permission. Local people must be given the name and addre 's of main key holders.

Signing of Keys

Both return and issuing of all vital keys should be against signature of the authorized personnel and a daily check made to make certain that keys, which are not in use, are back in safekeeping.

Key Boards

These must be located in a secure place and the key hooks well laid out to enable a missing key to be instantly obvious.

27. Security Measures for Cash and Credit

Security must be the concern of every manager in the hotel industry. Good security will have a beneficial effect in all areas. There are many aspects of security. The most important areas to which an efficient manager should give thought for security measures are:

1. Cash
2. Credit
3. Foreign exchange
4. Stock receipt
5. Paper control
6. Security of premises
7. Security of staff and guests, and
8. Security of keys.

Guidelines for Security of Cash

1. Banking and Night Sales

a. Changing the route and timings will greatly assist in maintaining security.

b. Transporting large amount of cash to or from the bank alone should be strictly avoided.

2. Safes

These should be kept locked at all times other than for withdrawal and deposit.

3. Cash Registers

a. Till (a cash handling instrument) readings should take place regularly throughout the day, and certainly whenever there is a change over in working shifts.

b. Errors and discrepancies between till readings and cash in drawer must be thoroughly investigated.

4. Fidelity Bonds

According to the amount of cash responsibility given to individual members of staff, fidelity bonds should be taken out.

5. Cash Records

A systematic checking procedure should be introduced and maintained for all cash receipts and records in order to highlight and bring to notice falsifications. In addition, spot checks should be employed.

6. Floats and Petty Cash

To guard against pilfering, floats and petty cash should be maintained at a predetermined figure and controlled through one person.

7. Payments

These should not be made in any instance other than on production of invoices, statements or signatures, from authorized persons within the organization.

8. Forgeries

Details of major current forgeries in local circulation should be supplied to cash handlers and kept in one place for easy reference.

9. Legal Tender

Exact details of legal tender should be made known to cash handlers.

10. Till Clearance

This should be regular to insure against an excessive build up of notes. Clearance should be by a responsible member of the organization, able to identify himself, if necessary by the production of an identity or authorising card.

11. Cash Disbursements

These can be used for petty cash purposes or for staff convenience.

Credit Losses

The popularity of various credit instruments has reduced the number of customers who pay in cash. Nowadays, every hotel has started accepting payment by cheques, credit cards and travellers cheques. A Negotiable Instruments Act governs these credit instruments.

Many countries have statutes that make it a criminal offense to defraud the proprietor of a hotel or motel by obtaining food or lodging without intending to pay for it or obtaining credit under false pretences.

Hotels need to pay particular attention to their cheque cashing practices and verification of credit card ownership and expiry date if they are to avoid credit losses.

1. Cheques

A cheque is an instrument drawn on a bank directing him to pay a stated amount of money to the person named therein or to the bearer of the instrument.

The bank honour cheques provided the following rules are honoured:

1. The cheque must be signed on the spot
2. The cheque's signature must match the signature with the bank
3. The account holder's name must be written on the back of the cheque
4. The cheque must be received in payment of goods or services.

Precautions

Experienced hotelmen pass following suggestions for tripping up.

1. Ask for positive identification. Even printed and government cheques can be forgeries. They also may have been stolen and then forged. Credentials such as driver's licenses, credit cards, etc., can be cancelled, lost, forged or stolen. Make sure that the endorsement on the cheque corresponds to the payee's name. Also note if passer resembles photo on driver's license or other identification card.
2. Insist that cheques be endorsed in your presence while holding the identification card. This prevents the passer from copying the signature from the card, which may have been lost, stolen or forged.
3. Start stalling if you become suspicious, call the bank if possible. When you stall, a suspect usually will leave in a hurry, often leaving the cheque behind.
4. Warn your employees that bad cheque passers are particularly active over weekends, on holidays and during the summer vacation months.
5. Look twice before cashing a rubber-stamped cheque.
6. Question alterations. Remember–the payee's name can be altered, amounts raised, and dates changed.
7. Record all identification data before cashing cheques. This can be noted on back or face of cheque.
8. Try to obtain multiple identification.
9. Try to get the licence plate number of cashier's car, this provides a better identification than an operator's license. In copying license data, be sure to include state and numbers, note whether owner's description matches that of passer and if signature is identical.
10. Be cautious if the cheque offered is more than the amount of the bill.
11. Don't allow yourself to be hurried. Bad cheque passers try to work fast; you should take your time.

12. Don't accept a Social Security Card as identification, it is valueless for this purpose.
13. Don't let a stranger bluff you, keep asking questions.
14. Don't accept a suspicious cheque simply because it's perforated 'insured'. This does not mean you are insured.

Danger Signals that often indicate bad cheques

1. Misspelling, particularly of the maker's name.
2. Omission of the maker's name.
3. Unusually high serial numbers (five or more digits).
4. Payroll cheques without paise amount. Remember, 99 times out of 100 payroll cheques end in paises.

2. Traveller's Cheques

Like a banker's cheque, a traveller's cheque is worth a stated sum of money, but the main difference is that it is bought for cash by the holder for a set amount whereas an ordinary cheque is made out by the drawer for any amount.

The advantage of a traveller's cheque is that it saves the holder from carrying large sums of money, and provided the issuing agent is one of good repute, it will be acceptable in most parts of the world.

Traveller's cheques are obtainable from most banks and from certain well-known travel agencies, in the currency of the country in which they are issued. When cashed in India, local currency cheques are exchanged for cash at their face value, and any foreign traveller's cheques at their current buying value. Rates of exchange are those fixed by the RBI and are published in newspapers.

A person purchasing travellers' cheques will be required to pay cash for all cheques bought. When buying a travellers' cheque, the purchaser is required to write his or her signature on it in ink, in the presence of the issuing cashier. When the purchaser wishes to cash this travellers' cheque, he or she must countersign in ink, again on the face of the travellers' cheque, in the presence of the paying cashier. It is the responsibility of the paying cashier to see that the second signature is identical with the previous one already on the cheque. If both signatures are not identical, or the second signature is not signed in front of the paying cashier, the customer must be requested to sign a third time, on the back of the travellers' cheque. If in any doubt, the cashier has the right to refuse payment or to demand proof of identity, such as a passport, etc.

When encashing travellers' cheque in India, a hotel cashier or receptionist must ensure the following:

1. That the travellers' cheque is cashable in India
2. That the presenter completes and signs it in front of the cashier
3. That the signature agrees with the one already on the travellers' cheque
4. That the correct rate of exchange is used so that the equivalent amount of rupees is given
5. That the travellers' cheque is listed on the appropriate list of encashment

3. Credit Cards

Credit cards are yet another method of payment. An establishment can enter into an agreement with a credit card company whereby accounts may be settled by charging it to credit card. The credit card company will honour all charges provided:

1. The credit card must be properly signed and not mutilated in any way.
2. The expiry date on the credit card must not have been passed.

3. The card must not be included on a lost or cancelled card listing which most of the companies distribute to the establishments on a regular basis.
4. The details on the sale voucher must be complete, legible and dated. It is best to utilize an imprint available from the credit card company.
5. The signature in the sales voucher must match the signature on the card.
6. The value of the sales voucher must be within the limits stipulated or authorization to exceed the limits must be obtained.
7. Claims for payment should be made regularly and without delay. A duplicate copy of all sales vouchers should be kept.

The credit card company deducts an agreed discount from their payment to the establishment (usually between 3 and 6 per cent). Although all the major credit card companies are liable to pay promptly this is one point to be clearly determined when entering into an agreement. It may also be possible for the establishment to benefit from the advertising done by the credit card company on their behalf.

4. Handling of Foreign Exchange

The handling of foreign exchange is an aspect of hotel accounting that is becoming increasingly popular and prominent. A policy decision has to be made by the management to determine the way in which it should be handled, especially at a time when rates are fluctuating.

Many hotels calculate the rate of exchange at a level, which will cover all bank charges and provide a small return to the establishment for providing the service. This profit margin should be carefully set and controlled. If it is too great, there will be a considerable loss of goodwill. If it is too small, the slightest fluctuation in exchange rates may cause the establishment to actually lose money on foreign currency regulation. A reasonable return may be considered to be in the region of 2 per cent of the bank value of the currency.

It is considered by more enlightened companies a mistake to allow cashiers to retain the foreign exchange earnings. As a source of income it is liable to fluctuations and difficult to control. With the growth of international travel it is difficult to predict the increase in foreign exchange earnings and at the same time produce salary and wage forecasts for the future. It is therefore, more logical to credit foreign exchange earnings to the miscellaneous income section of the account and pay a fair, guaranteed wage to the staff in question.

In order to simplify transaction, it is a good policy to forbid cashiers to give any change to a guest in foreign currency. This will remove the risk of breaking the law on this point and will prevent confusion over the calculation of the amount of change.

A system of handling foreign currency and cheques should be clearly presented to the cashier with a simple explanation of the procedure to be followed. A list of currencies and cheques that are allowed to be accepted should be prepared. For this purpose, the assistance of the bank should be sought and the bank should keep the management informed of all the relevant changing currency control regulations etc. Guidelines laid down for calculating the rates of exchange should be followed and these rates should be clearly displayed for the guests. The rates the bank is giving must be monitored on a daily basis.

There are few basic methods to choose from when actually calculating values in foreign currency. Firstly, when the number of transactions is high and foreign exchange considerable, it is worth considering the utilization of electronic/

mechanical calculator or computer. By this method one is able to calculate actual equivalents. It is easy to alter the rate of exchange very slightly and therefore, regulate the margin in a very accurate manner. The alternative method is by utilising ready-reckoner tables; either those available commercially or specifically, prepared by the management. It is normal when utilising these tables to calculate a manageable limit of foreign currency.

The cashier should remit together with the other cash and cheques the foreign currency valued at the rate which was accepted by the chief cashier, or manager.

Accounting wise the easiest method of recording foreign exchange earnings (*i.e.*, the surplus of the bank value of the currency over the amount originally calculated by the hotel) is to add a column in the cashbook. At the end of the accounting period, the cashbook is closed off and foreign exchange earnings transferred to miscellaneous income.

If the trade is such that it is necessary to accept foreign cheques, the bank, and accountants should be consulted for the most effective way of organising the banking of these foreign cheques. If a good number of cheques are being accepted it may be worth considering the creation of a separate foreign collection bank account. This will simplify the reconciliation of the main bank account, and will aid the control of the foreign cheques. An accounting work paper can be devised for efficient control of the collection of foreign cheques which is necessary due to the length of time involved for the banking of foreign exchange cheques to be completed.

If there is uncertainty of whether or not to accept a particular currency, it is advisable to instruct the guests to visit the nearest bank. This is preferable to doing the banking on behalf of the guest as this can often lead to misunderstanding and disbelief.

However, if the situation is such that the foreign currency or cheque has to be accepted, and the banks are not available, then there is a 'rule of thumb' which can be utilized in order to arrive at an acceptable rate of exchange.

The business page of the important daily newspapers give the buying and selling prices of the major currencies on the international money markets. Take the higher of the two figures quoted of the particular currency and increase it by 2 per cent. This will provide a rate of exchange, which should cover all bank charges. It must be remembered that this is not an accurate way to calculate rates of exchange and should only be used as a last resort.

Example:

Pound Sterling (£) in July 2006	Rs 75.00–80.00
High Figure	Rs 80.00
Plus 2 per cent	Rs. 1.60
Rate of Exchange £	Rs 81.60

In order to calculate the value of one thousand rupees, divide Rs. 1,000 by 81.60 = 1000/81.60 = £ 12.26

Precautions Against 'Skippers'

'Skippers' present another problem. A modicum of protection against these can be gained by taking these precautions:

a. Be sure that complete and legible registrations are obtained.

b. Ask payment in advance, if you have reason to be suspicions, particularly if the guest is without baggage or checks in late.

c. Some hotels make a person to person telephone call to the registered guest at the address he gives; if the guest is bonafide the call will cost nothing.

d. Limit the amount of the bill you run up setting an appropriate limit of three days.

5. Stock Receipt

Quality and quantity

Quality and quantity of goods should be systematically checked at delivery points before signing delivery points.

Checking the order

The goods delivered should be checked against the original order placed.

Prices charged

All goods received should be thoroughly checked to ensure against correct charges.

Documents

Delivery notes or other documents should never be signed unless all details are accurate and agree with goods received.

Containers

All containers, which carry a deposit, should be treated as securely as goods and not released without credit.

Spot check

In addition to above, frequent spot checks on deliveries should be carried out by management.

6. Stock Control

Storeroom issues

These must only be made on receipt of a check with authorising signature-giving details of department to be charged.

Stock checks

These should frequently be carried out to determine whether quantity of both issue and consumption match the amount stated in stock records.

Stock levels

The volume of stocks held should not be allowed to exceed the establishment's specified level.

Stocktaking

This should be frequent and regular. The accuracy of stock value should be verified against goods received invoices. Spot checks should be carried out by management.

7. Paper Control

Cross-checking

A comprehensive system of cross-checking all documents should be introduced and maintained.

Reconciliation

Bank statements must be reconciled with establishment's cash records to reveal discrepancies and to safeguard against embezzlement.

Invoices

Before passing for payment, invoices should undergo a control system which will prevent double payment and guarantees that invoices relate to goods received.

Luncheon voucher

Voucher should be treated as cash. Cancelled vouchers should be kept in secure places until redemption.

Cheques and travellers cheques

Staff responsible for accepting cheques should be kept aware of foreign exchange rates, forgeries, acceptable currencies and upper limits.

Credit cards

Staff must be trained to recognize forgeries, credit limits and validity.

28. Pilferage and Theft

It has been said that 'security is probably the most underestimated responsibility that a hotel has.' One expert estimates that at least $ 10 billion is lost annually by American business due to theft, and that 30 per cent of all business failures each year are the result of employee dishonesty and that 7 per cent of all bankruptcies in the country are due to pilferage. 'Trusted employees,' he declares, 'ousteal the shoplifter by 15 to 1.'

If the management of an establishment has reason to believe that pilfering is taking place, it must be borne in mind that no private person has the right to search another without their consent, to do so would constitute an assault on that person. In order that an employer may have some rights of search, a clause is often incorporated in the contract of employment which states that the employer reserves the right to stop and search employees and the contents of their bags and packages on entering or leaving the premises. If the necessity to conduct a search does arise, the following points should be borne in mind:

1. The utmost tact and discretion should be applied. It is far better that such an operation is carried out with the co-operation of all employees and people concerned, remembering that unwillingness to be searched may only be because of embarrassment and need not necessarily indicate guilt.
2. Only persons in authority should have the right to search; there should be always a witness present, and for obvious reasons male employees should be searched by a male and female employees by a female.
3. If any member of staff has been found with stolen property, whether a prosecution is undertaken or not would depend on the circumstances and the policy of the management in such cases, but in any event, it should lead to dismissal of the employee, and serve as a deterrent to others who may be tempted to pilfer.

Handling Cases of Arrest and Search

The manager of a hotel, restaurant, or any other place of public entertainment, in the course of his business life, is likely to be faced with problems related to acts which constitute criminal offences by both staff and guests. One crime which will occur most often will be theft. It is therefore, important that the management is familiar with the laws and rules which govern the apprehending of suspected persons.

However, before a citizen including any employer makes an arrest, he must have the knowledge beyond any shadow of doubt that a crime has been committed. The police on the other hand, in pursuance of their public duty to prevent crime, may arrest on the grounds that they have 'reasonable suspicion' that a crime has been committed. It is obvious therefore, that for the private citizen to exercise his right of arrest does carry certain dangers, and it is not right to believe that there are reasonable grounds, or to understand or think that all the facts are available and true and therefore, arrest is justified.

Facts must be sifted and investigated, checked and double-checked to make certain that the truth has been presented and is accurate and backed by sufficient substantial evidence to present a charge and proved to be right in a court of law.

Examples

Suppose a man with a stocking mask over his face is seen by the hotel manager to rush into the foyer of a hotel, puts a gun to the head of the cashier, grabs a bag of money with his other hand and runs out of the main entrance, and if the hotel manager is quick enough and strong enough to halt him, then the manager's actions in using a reasonable amount of force to detain that person could be fully justified.

Let us take another case. Supposing the cashier excitedly reports to the manager that the guest just hurrying through the main doors has taken a handful of notes from her, and the manager accepts her statement and goes after the guest. There is nothing wrong with stopping the man by putting a restraining hand on his arm and asking him to 'step into my office' and then making it clear that the man may not leave – if it is proved that the guest has taken the money with the intention of stealing it. The danger is if the manager is proved wrong, then he might face charges of:

1. Slander, when he was overheard by other people in the apprehension of the man for an offence.
2. Assault when he took the man's arm
3. Imprisonment

Any member of the public has got to be right before he makes an arrest, which means that it would be unwise of him to take such a step unless it was based on the evidence of his own eyes (and preferably with a witness), certainly not on information which was passed to him and which he has not had an opportunity to check.

The manager of any hotel or similar establishment has of course common law rights as the landlord of his property to investigate any matter which gives him cause for concern, and there is no reason why he should not ask 'what are you doing?' without going so far as an arrest.

The power of arrest which a private individual has in common with the police, does not also give the right to search. Only the police have a right to do this. If a private individual attempts to do so without the consent of the suspected person, then this would constitute a civil wrong ('tort') from which a law suit could follow.

The freedom of the individual is zealously guarded, even when there is every reason to believe that the person has committed a criminal act.

A person is guilty of theft if he dishonestly appropriates property belonging to another with the intention of permanently depriving the other of it.

Such an act is labelled a criminal act. A person's appropriation of property belonging to another is not to be regarded as dishonest under the following circumstances:

1. If he appropriates the property in the belief that he has by law the right to deprive the other of it, on behalf of himself or of a third person, or
2. If he appropriates the property in the belief that he could have the other's consent if the other knew of the appropriation and the circumstances of it, or

3. If he appropriates the property in the belief that the person to whom the property belongs cannot be traced by taking reasonable steps (except where the property came to him as trustee or personal representative).

As a private individual cannot justify having made an arrest unless an offence has actually been committed, it is important to note that 'theft' involves more than just 'taking' goods. Guests, for instance, may pick up articles with quite innocent motives or because they thought that they were there to be taken – perhaps as 'mementos' but 'thieving' involves taking and carrying away goods without the owner's consent and with the intention to permanently depriving him of them. So, even if goods have been taken, the manager or detective or other responsible person should not make an arrest unless he is sure that the suspect intended to steal them. For this reason, it is wiser to wait until the suspect has left the immediate vicinity (*i.e.*, restaurant, bar, lounge, etc.) before accosting him, as then it would appear to be established that he had intended to takeaway the article or articles.

Case Study 2821
Theft by a Guest

Procedure

When a guest is caught in the act of picking up a bottle of whisky from the bar and putting it into his brief case, or slipping the silver pepper mill into his pocket and leaving the restaurant, or when a member of a staff is found leaving the premises with a piece of chicken under his overcoat, it is a reasonable assumption that there has been the intention to steal. In such cases, an arrest could be made. The following procedure might be adopted.

The suspect is asked to step into the manager's office to be questioned. Then, if guilt has been established, either on the admission of the suspect or based on the evidence of the person who saw the act, and a witness, a statement should be made to the effect that 'As manager of this hotel, I intend to report this matter to the police.' It is wiser not to state the precise charge with which the man is being accused as a layman, not knowing the legal terms, may make inaccurate charges, which could lead to further complications. Suspects may sometimes seek an opportunity to be alone and to dispose of any goods they may have to them by, for instance, asking to use the toilet. It is wise to refuse such requests where possible, but if this cannot be avoided, then it is imperative that the suspect is accompanied and kept in view all the time.

In making an arrest, no force should be used, which does not appear to be reasonably necessary in the circumstances. If, for example, the suspected person is willing to go with the person arresting him, and there appears to be no likelihood of his running away, he should not be taken by the arm or even touched, since such action is not necessary. This action will depend on the circumstances and the common sense of the person making the arrest. The use of force beyond what is reasonably necessary could expose an establishment to claim for damages for assault, even though the arrest itself was justified.

To exercise the right to arrest by the private individual means that, by law, the suspect may only be detained for a 'reasonable time' before he is handed over to the police, or allowed to

Case Study cont. ...

Case Study cont. ...

go free. A 'reasonable time' is not easy to define but it might be considered that to take a suspect to an office for questioning and give that person the opportunity of offering an explanation, and then make a decision as to whether a prosecution should follow, would not be regarded as unreasonable delay. There might also be justification in a certain time lapse whilst the manager on whom any final decision should rest was being located.

It will, however, be unreasonable to detain a suspect whilst investigations are going on to confirm suspicions or obtain further evidence. This sort of detention could possibly lead to a claim for damages.

If there is any doubt as to the proof of crime, it will be wiser to take the suspect's name and address, and let him go pending further investigations.

If there is a reason to believe that the suspect has stolen goods on him, the question of search arises. It is strongly recommended that this action is left to the police, but should the suspect request that he be searched, the only precaution should be that another responsible person is present.

If possible, it is a wise precaution to give the police prior notice of the anticipating questioning of a suspect so that an officer is at hand, but if this cannot be done (e.g. in an unexpected emergency case), then a phone call in front of the suspect to the police station should quickly conclude matters.

It might happen that the suspect (if a guest) demands that he is allowed to contact his solicitor before he allows matter to proceed. Naturally, this may not be refused unless the manager is quite certain that a crime has taken place, when he may then refuse the suspect the right to use his telephone. In such a case, the manager has to be prepared to prosecute and the suspect could call his solicitor from the police station once the charge has been made against him.

It is worth mentioning that as the final decision on the action to be taken rests with the manager, he is entitled to 'make a bargain' with the accused. In other words, he may accept the value of the stolen goods in cash – but only the value of the stolen goods and not more. In such an event, it would be wisest not to give a receipt to the accused, just in case the latter decides to sue for one of the reasons mentioned earlier and then the time element may affect things. For instance, he could say that he was accused of taking a bottle of whisky, but was able to produce a receipt for it; omitting the fact that the receipt had been given after the theft had occurred.

One other word of warning in the event of a mistake having been made and the suspect proven innocent, the manager should 'regret' what has happened to him, and not 'apologize' for what has happened. He may be regretful for the occurrence, but not apologetic that he was pursuing a line of enquiry to investigate further.

Responsibility

The detection and apprehending of suspected persons should be the responsibility of a few employees who can be relied upon to act with the necessary discretion. Where a house

Case Study cont. ...

Case Study cont. ...

detective such as an ex-police or security officer is employed, it would be obvious that the responsibility for investigations into losses and the subsequent charging of suspected culprits should be channeled through that office. Where such an officer is not employed, the responsibility for making arrests must be confined to selected employees who have been specially instructed in such matters.

In the latter event, obviously, the greatest care and discretion is needed, particularly when guests are involved. If, for instance, a dishonest act is seen by a member of staff, that person should merely keep the suspect under observation until the person authorized to make an arrest, or take matters further, is on hand. The authorized person may then have an opportunity of confirming the original suspicion himself (*i.e.*, that the bottle of whisky the barman saw, the guest puts into his pocket without offering to pay, is obviously still in the guest's pocket). The authorized person must then make the decision himself whether to take the matter further on the evidence of the first employees and this he would do if in the light of his experience and his knowledge of the employee concerned, he felt it reasonably safe to do so. In that case, the first employee should accompany the authorized person to the suspect and make the accusation himself in front of the authorized person. In no circumstances should a suspect be arrested or even approached on the evidence of a third party – for instance, another guest. It may well be incorrect information or even deliberately false.

If however, a police officer, is readily available and willing to act, the alternative procedure that might be adopted in to ask him to investigate on the basis of the hotel employee's evidence. This suspect could be kept under close observation until contact is made with the police officer, or if he has any suspicion that he is being watched he may try to get rid of the stolen goods, and then there is no case.

Model Guidelines

Instructions to Staff

On witnessing an act of suspected pilferage, report the matter immediately to a house detective. Keep the suspect under observation until the house detective takes over responsibility. On no account make an arrest yourself.

Instructions to House Detectives

When notified by a member of a staff of an act of pilferage, keep the suspect under observation but do not make an arrest unless you are confirmed in your belief that a criminal act has been perpetrated. You should quietly ask the suspect to step outside the lounge/bar/restaurant and then state, 'I am the house detective and believe you to have (e.g.) a bottle of whiskey in your pocket for which you have not paid.' The suspect should then be taken to the manager's office.

No force must be used which does not appear to be reasonably necessary in the circumstances.

On arrival at the manager's office, you should, in the presence and hearing of the suspect, report to the manager what has happened. Up to this point, you must not discuss the matter with the suspect.

Instruction to Manager

If, having heard the house detective's report you are not satisfied that the accusation of theft is justified, you should release the suspect, giving an opportunity for that person to say anything he wished to say, and using the tact and understanding which the situation demands.

If, on the other hand, you are satisfied that the accusation of theft is justified, you should thereupon give the suspect an opportunity of offering any explanation or making any representation by saying for example, *'You have been accused of stealing from the lounge/ bar/ restaurant, a bottle of whisky for which you have not paid. Do you wish to offer any explanation or say anything to me about this matter?'*

While the suspect is being detained, on no account should you conduct an investigation to determine whether or not the accusation is justified, or to seek evidence in its support.

If having considered the house detective's report and any statement volunteered by the suspect, you remain of the opinion that a charge should be pressed, you should arrange for the suspect to be handed over to the police without delay; otherwise the suspect must be released.

In Case of Theft by Staff

There is an important point to be borne in mind, and that is, that many employees in this industry feel that they have certain 'rights' to things as part of the 'perks' of their jobs. For instance, the kitchen worker may honestly believe that he is entitled to leftovers or off cuts of food and unless it is made clear from the beginning of employment (by including statements to the contrary in contract of employment), it might be very difficult to charge that person with theft.

The decision whether to apprehend a member of staff who is believed to be, or has been stealing, should be taken after consideration of quantity of the goods lost, their cost, and the possible need to make an example of his misconduct to other members of the staff.

In such cases, to dismiss without the usual notice would be an extreme step, and should be undertaken only where a clear-cut case of dishonesty has been proved, as where the culprit has admitted his guilt. Again an employer should safeguard his interest first by including a statement in the contract of employment to the effect that 'refused to consent to search could mean instant dismissal'.

As mentioned earlier, it is advisable to restrict any search to handbags or other such items. Body search should always be avoided and left to the police.

It might sometimes be convenient to suspend an employee from duty whilst further investigations are being carried out, but again the possibility must be made clear in the contract of employment.

Where lockers are provided for employees' personal belongings, it is not unusual (and good business practice) for regular security checks to be made. It would be unwise to undertake such checks in the employees' absence as this could lead to an accusation of theft against the employer. However, where it is impossible for the employee to be present, a manager should undertake to do such checking in the company of another responsible person *i.e.*, security officer.

The language in which these conditions are phrased is important and it should not arouse feelings of antagonism and fear. The following wording is offered as a guideline only:

'The Company reserves the right to search any employee at any time to inspect any parcels, packages, bags, etc. taken into or out of the hotel's premises. The Company also reserves the right to inspect the contents of personal lockers from time to time.

'All such inspection would be carried out as discreetly and courteously as possible.

'Selection for search does not imply suspicion and it is hoped that employees will appreciate the unfortunate necessity for such action when it occurs as refusal to submit could result in instant dismissal or suspension from duty.'

Responsibility for Acts of Employees

A hotel is responsible for the acts of his employees. In general terms, this is true but only for acts done by the employees in the premises and in course of his employment. It would be neither practicable nor fair for the hotel to be responsible for acts committed elsewhere.

When an employee is performing his duties for which he has been engaged, the hotel will be liable for all his actions. If a waiter carrying a bowl of soup drops it and scalded a customer (or another employee), the employer would be liable even if the waiter has been negligent. If a receptionist, acting without authority, did the same thing, the employer might not be liable unless it could be shown that it was the normal practice of receptionists to assist in serving meals.

Liability can exist when employees are performing acts, which have been expressly forbidden. In London, a transport driver caused an accident by driving across the road to obstruct a rival bus, something which he had been told not to do, the company was held liable because driving the bus was within the scope of his duties. In another leading case of the same period, a conductor attempted to drive the bus in the absence of the driver, the company was not liable because driving the bus was outside the scope of his employment. If a page boy, in the course of his duties, negligently caused injury to a guest's dog while he was exercising it, the employer would be liable, but if, on his own initiative, he took the dog home and gave it a bath, thereby causing some injury, this might be what a judge in another case described as 'frolic of his own'.

As a general rule, however, it is safest to assume that an employer is normally responsible for the acts of his employees while they are on duty.

Prevention of Robbery

Big city police departments suggest these tips to prevent financial loss or physical injury to employees as a result of attempted robberies:

1. Keep an eye open for suspicious persons loitering on the premises.
2. Maintain a record and description of all valuable property – serial numbers of big bills, identification of each register and other office equipment, serial numbers of TV sets, etc.
3. When large amounts of cash are sent to the bank, the route taken should be varied from time to time and the trip should be made at different times of the day.
4. Never allow the safe to be opened in the presence of strangers.
5. Don't keep too much cash in the register. Use the safe for large amounts of money and sent surplus cash to the bank as often as convenient.
6. Install an alarm – electronic beam or other non-obvious type – which can be tripped unobtrusively by the cashier or clerk in the event of a robbery attempt. The best burglary alarm system is the silent central station type, which does not warn the thief, as does a local alarm such as a siren or bell. In large cities, central alarm systems may be rented from private firms; in small towns, they are often connected directly to police headquarters. Often a part of the cost of installing a silent alarm system will be absorbed by a reduction in burglary insurance premium.
7. Keep all areas of the property – particularly where money is kept – well lighted.
8. Have the number of the local police department right at the front desk telephone so it is handy when needed.

9. Keep a little 'bait money' in the safe and cash register. This is money from which the serial numbers have been copied, 'marked money', which will make good evidence if found on a suspect.
10. Use closed circuit television to monitor areas such as parking lots and supply rooms where robberies are most likely to occur but which are not under constant direct observation.

Guard against Dishonest Employees

Internal controls can be very effective in limiting thefts or embezzlement by employees. The Fireman's Fund American Insurance Companies suggest these do's and don'ts:

1. Do keep important job functions separate. Don't let the same person make up invoices, bank deposits, cheque payments and reconcile bank statements. Purchasing should also be separate from receiving responsibilities.
2. Do make frequent surprise spot checks. Accounts receivable, inventory, accounts payable, sales and advertising departments should all be subject to examination without warning, as should every other department where cash transactions or valuable goods may be handled.
3. Do establish printed controls on forms. Invoices should be numbered serially at the printer. Delivery tickets should also be prenumbered, and duplicate copies of all forms should be sent to the accounting department for sales and inventory records. Cheques should be printed on safety paper that will not erase.
4. Do establish personnel controls. Check the job references of prospective employees for the past 10 years. If the staff is adequate, rotate employees between jobs. Require passes for after-hours entry to certain areas and check excessive overtime claims. Without being excessively negative or harmful to morale, let all employees know dishonesty will be prosecuted to the full extent of the law.
5. Don't let customers' unpaid balances accumulate. To prevent embezzlement of incoming payments, regular notices with return postage should be sent to customers with consistent unpaid balances. These can be worded so as not to offend the customer, and they should be returned to someone other than the person who ordinarily receives payments.
6. Don't let audits be routine. If an audit is only perfunctory, or if audits are held on regular and 'nvarying schedules, the embezzler can plan around it, kiting funds to cover lower bank balances or juggling records to hide inventory losses.
7. Don't ignore large balances that are as dues to your suppliers. Bills you have paid that still show as dues are suspect. Payments from you may be siphoned off in your paymaster's office or in the supplier's accounts receivable department.
8. Don't economize on loss prevention. Use a reputable CA/CPA firm for an extensive audit, preferably at least annually. Consult with layout experts and security architects about protective measures for inventory, equipment and important records. Ask insurance company's loss prevention engineers for assistance in developing an overall programme to prevent theft. And make certain you have enough insurance to cover your potential for loss.

29. Maintenance of Buildings, Machinery and Equipment

A full programme schedule of maintenance work should be prepared for the hotel. Maintenance not only helps equipment to retain its value but also prevents the development of potentially hazardous situations, which could injure or otherwise affect hotel users. For example, banisters and handrails which are loose on a stairway are a potential hazard to stairway users, whilst inadequately maintained electrical equipment in the kitchen may similarly contribute towards staff accidents.

Inspection

A periodic and regular inspection of all plants and equipment is vital and should include:

1. Fire fighting equipment
2. All building and structural elements
3. Electric equipment such as vacuum cleaners, cooking equipment, telephone, convectors, heaters, electric wiring
4. Heavy equipment such as boilers, service hoists, heating and ventilation equipment
5. Light fitments, both inside and outside the hotel
6. Furniture and loose fixtures, including carpeting, other floor coverings, chairs, etc.

A system should be devised to ensure the speedy reporting of failure or breakdown of a facility. Repair work should be undertaken without delay, not only to minimize inconvenience but also to ensure the safety of people in the building. A loose thread in a carpet, or an insecure stair carpet offers a considerable hazard if not attended to at once. The scheduling of maintenance work should be set out.

Maintenance Procedure

Maintenance schedules are generally prepared by the head of the department. For example, for the cooking area of a kitchen, the following schedule could be taken:

Daily Maintenance Schedule

Time	Maintenance work
2.00 pm and 9.00 pm	Stoves, cooking equipment, hot plates and sinks to be cleaned twice each day after use.
2.45 pm and 9.45 pm	All ledges and work surfaces to be cleaned and serviced when appropriate
3.15 pm and 10.15 pm	All floor areas to be swept and washed down twice each day.

Weekly Maintenance Schedule

Monday	2.00 pm to 4.30 pm : Defrost, clean and repack refrigerators
Tuesday	3.45 pm : Wash down stove canopies
Wednesday	3.45 pm : Remove, clean and refit the grills in stove canopies
Thursday	3.45 pm : Wash wall tiles and all paint work, dust light fittings
Friday	3.45 pm : Wash windows, clean out drainage, grilles, and area behind equipment.

Periodic Maintenance Schedule

These may be dealt with by each head of

department, but in most hotels, this is normally coordinated by management. A month by month schedule should be prepared. A layout could be prepared in the form of a checklist as given in Table 29.1.

Table 29.1: Monthly Maintenance Schedule

Month	Area				
	Heating and *Ventilation* Equipment	Catering *Department* Equipment	Fire-Fighting *Equipment and* Safety Measures	Housekeeping *Equipment*	General
	1	2	3	4	5
January	Routine inspection	Clean main drain	Staff safety drill		Window cleaning
February		Knife grinding	Check on safety precautions in handling		Office equipment maintenance
March		Inspection of ventilation equipment Inspection of mechanical food preparation equipment	Test fire alarm	Maintenance of mechanical and electric equipment	Window cleaning
April	Routine inspection	Clean main drain		Check service room equipment	Clean roof guttering & outside drains Window cleaning
May		Overhaul of steamer	Check safety precautions in building		Telephone maintenance Window cleaning
June	Annual boiler overhaul	Inspection of ventilation equipment	Test fire alarm		Window cleaning

Table cont. ...

Table cont. ...

July	Routine inspection	Clean main drain Overhaul of stoves Inspection of mechanical food preparation equipment	Fire safety drill		Office equipment maintenance Window cleaning
August		Knife grinding Review of restaurant furnishings	Check safety precautions in building	Inspection of painting work and general décor. Review of furnishings	Inspection of external paint work Window cleaning
September		Inspection of paint work and general décor	Check fire fighting equipment	Maintenance of mechanical and electrical equipment	Telephone maintenance
October	Routine inspection	Clean main drain Inspection of ventilation equipment	Test fire alarms	Check on service room equipment	Window cleaning
November		Inspection of steamer, and of mechanical food preparation equipment	Check safety procedure in building		Check roof guttering & outside drain
December			Test fire alarm		Window cleaning

Display of Notices

Guest, staff and other hotel users must be given adequate warning or direction on many matters in the hotel.

Those parts of the premises not open to them should be marked clearly with notices as appropriate:

'Private',

'No Admission',

'Fire Exit', and so on.

Other warning signs as well as warning of other hazards should be prepared, such as:

'Please Mind The Step',

'No Smoking',

'This Corridor Must Be Cleaned At All Times', etc.

As a contribution factor towards accident reduction, the display of each notice can be most beneficial.

30. Accident Prevention

Accidents may occur in a hotel in any situation involving men and women, whether guests, outside contractors or staff. The factors that may contribute towards an accident or some other unforeseen contingency are so numerous that it would be unlikely that accidents would not occur in hotels. Even when accidents happen for no apparent reason, a major and thorough probe would generally reveal a cause which, had it been anticipated, might have prevented the accident from happening in the first place. It is reasonable to construct a building to withstand adverse conditions such as freak hurricanes or uncharacteristically wet weather. Reasonable safety margins need to be considered and by identifying all other potential accident hazards for a hotel building, precautionary measures need to be taken.

In a hotel, the proprietor has certain statutory obligations towards his guests and other persons using hotel premises. Common law liability charges the hotel to accept responsibility for the safety of his guests and their luggage. Other legislation which also has application in this sphere of work includes: building regulation, fire precautions, health and safety, Factory Act food and hygiene regulation, Shops and Establishment Act, local bye-law and regulations, etc.

Accidents take place as a result of some kind of human failure. We can plan a safer environment for all people associated with the hotel and catering enterprises to examine all the relevant reasons, which might affect breakdown due to the human component.

Safety and Security Measures

Safety and security in the work situation is of vital importance in the hotel and catering industry. People and property are potentially the most important and valuable assets of any business operation. They are both sources which are capable of adding substantial value to the business and because of the accidents and losses in the work situation are possibly among the greatest costs which business has to face. They are costs in terms of lost production and service, damage to property, injury to employees and customers, lost business and a needless drain on profits.

1. Material
2. Machine
3. People

Continuous attempts are made to ensure:

1. Selection and assignment of proper people for the proper job
2. Effective job instruction
3. Development of effective work methods
4. Supervision of employees for effective production

Unless adequate precautions are taken, by their nature, operation in the hotel and catering industry can be full of risks. High risk areas involve machinery and tools, volatile and caustic chemicals, lifting and carrying, steam, gas and electricity, property, valuables and cash.

Most of the modern food production areas (kitchen) can be highly mechanized with slicers, mixers, mincers, lifts and hoists, potato peelers, dishwashers, boilers, high pressure steam ovens and knives all creating hazards for those who work there.

Housekeeping can involve use of harmful, volatile and toxic chemicals and cleaning solutions, lifts, chutes, incinerators, and lifting and carrying.

Whenever you look in any sector or job category within the industry potential hazards can be found in abundance. The greatest single cause of accident being slips and falls due mainly to bad housekeeping such as inadequate maintenance of staircases, defective floor coverings, trailing leads from electrical appliances and inadequate lighting.

Front office and reception, handling large amounts of cash and cheques, and holding for safekeeping guests' valuables, is also an area with a high loss potential.

Although safety and security is the ultimate responsibility of management, safety involves the cooperation of both employees and management. Together there should be conscious effort to:

1. **Plan :** draw up, organize and implement a safety plan
2. **Promote :** prevent accidents and losses

Safety Plan

A joint safety planning exercise should cover an identification, evaluation and elimination of the hazards by an examination of:

a. Organization
b. Fact finding
c. Analysis
d. Remedy selection
e. Remedy application

The Organization

This should involve a study of the organization to cover:

a. Management support
b. The assignment of safety responsibilities
c. The creation and maintenance of interest

Fact Finding

Before a realistic programme can be drawn up to meet the safety needs of the organization, management must know the exact nature of the problems. The fact finding may involve the use of:

a. Surveys
b. Inspections
c. Observations
d. Investigations
e. Inquiries
f. Record keeping

Analysis

This is essential to establish the causes and plan for practical corrective action. The analysis should explore:

a. Frequency
b. Location
c. Severity
d. Occupation
e. Causes
f. Effects

The analysis should also attempt to define:

a. Accident types
b. Operations
c. Tools and equipment
d. Hazards

Remedy Selection

Once the analysis has been completed it is essential that a practical and effective remedy is selected. This should involve the exploration of:

a. Personnel selection, placement, training
b. Job design
c. Discipline
d. Supervision

Remedy Application

Having selected a suitable remedy this should be applied and regular follow up should be undertaken to ensure its continued application to eliminate the problem.

Prevention of Losses

Once a planning exercise has been completed by management and representatives of the staff or union, consideration should be given to training personnel, supervising safe practices, inspecting the operation, installing sound maintenance and security procedures, recording accidents, evolving good housekeeping practices and practising first aid.

Training

Training is to be important to both:

a. Management, and

b. Staff

Management

Safety training needs and facilities must include the following:

a. Board of Directors and senior managers should give some attention to accident prevention as to other management functions.

b. Management should accept that it is important for them to learn about accident prevention as it is for employees.

c. The supervisor should be the key individual in the development of safety elimination in his department.

Hazardous conditions and bad work methods frequently result from a lack of knowledge as to hazard potential. Training for managers and supervisors in aspects of safety and security should be directed to the anticipation of accidents and control of safety, the setting of safety objectives and the measurement of results. The training programme should cover:

a. Fundamentals of accident and loss prevention

b. Cause and effects of accidents and thefts

c. The supervisor's responsibility in safety

d. Causes of accidents/methods of prevention

e. Safeguarding machinery and valuables

f. Safe working practices and procedures

g. Elementary first aid

h. Good housekeeping

i. Job instruction and personal factors in safety

Where no formal training personnel exist in hotels, professional bodies will often be able to assist in training.

Training for Staff

Staff should receive instructions so that they can make a significant contribution to accident prevention and security promotion. Most accidents or losses can be directly related to an unsafe act by the individual and it is extremely important that safety consciousness and knowledge should be built into every employee. It is the individual employee who can prevent practically all accidents if he knows the hazards and has the motivation to work safely.

Safety training should be built into all training. Safety is not a 'subject' but is best integrated into all job training with the prime aim of changing attitudes and creating an alertness to safety and security at all times. Induction training should incorporate:

a. The hotel's views on safety

b. Rules and regulation of the hotel

All subsequent job instruction should then be geared to pointing out how the employee should do his job with the emphasis placed on doing it safely and without loss. Objectives of such safety training should ensure that the employee:

a. Is familiar with the common accident hazards found in the hotel and in his particular job.

b. Knows the appropriate accident prevention control measures and safety procedures for common hazards.

c. Is able to recognize and correct hazardous conditions found in his department.

Every opportunity should be taken to maintain safety. For this purpose, visual aids and posters are ideal.

One of the most effective methods to reduce accidents is the practice of good house-keeping:

a. In kitchens, knives should never be left lying around or medicine left unguarded.

b. Electric sockets should never be overloaded and wiring should never be allowed to trail to the extent that it can trip someone upon staff or customers.

c. Valuation should always be safeguarded.

d. Equipment should always be returned to its place of storage after use and never for people to fall over.

This list is far from exhaustive that every member of staff should continually be acutely aware to the need for good housekeeping practices in the prevention of accidents and losses.

Maintenance of Safe Working Conditions

Supervisors should regularly make inspections and security checks to ensure that their staff are operating machinery, using tools such as knives or cutters and knowing security procedures in compliance with the hotel's standards of performance. A close examination should be made to see that staff are not using defective tools or equipment or using equipment in unsafe ways. Staff should also be inspected to establish whether or not there is any failure to use safety devices or protective clothing such as caps or hats in the preparation of food.

Wherever failings on the part of the employer or the system are established, supervisors should take steps to ensure that the employees receive corrective training or coaching to rectify fault or recommend a change in the practice or procedure to help improve safety or security of job.

Modern aids of prevention should be put into use. In the food production areas, protective footwear with reinforced toe caps not only supports the feet but protects the wearer from severe damage from falling objects, knives, equipment, falls on greasy or slippery surfaces. Rubber gloves help prevent dermatitis in those using cleaning fluids, hot water or washing detergents. Oven gloves are also useful in preventing burns when lifting trays or dishes from a hot oven.

Losses can also be prevented by the use of many of the modern alarm systems often designed to form an integrated communication system for burglary, theft and fire warning facility. Installing such a system or installing adequate anti-burst locks on all doors and cupboards will usually result in reduced insurance premiums so that initial capital outlay can be offset against lower cost of insurance.

Proper Maintenance of Accident Records

A system of recording accidents and losses enables management to measure results and determine whether or not action needs to be taken to prevent their recurrence. The method of recording should be kept simple, noting down the following:

1. Date
2. Place
3. Nature and time of every injury or loss

4. Circumstances
5. Causes

These details will also be found helpful in the event of any claim being made at a later date to aid the company in determining if the injury or loss was actually sustained. Record-keeping also encourages the supervisors to investigate and take preventive action in each case to prevent recurrence.

First-aid Facilities

Whatever precautions are taken, accidents do happen. The manager must ensure that there are adequate emergency and dispensary facilities. There should be reasonable first aid advice for employees suffering from non-industrial injuries and illness whilst on duty. Regular checks should be made to ensure that first aid boxes are properly stocked.

Handling of Bomb Threats

The number of bomb threats is increasing in all public buildings. Since bombs are often planned with political motives, they are usually accompanied by a warning, nearly always by a telephone. A call may come at any time and a telephonist or receptionist may suddenly discover that there is a terrorist at the end of the line. Upon the reaction to such a call may depend on the preservation of life and property. It is important to obtain as much information as possible from the caller; to contact the police, to appraise the threat and search the premises – all within a short time. If the threat is known or believed to be genuine, the premises must be evacuated regardless of the inconvenience caused to those inside.

Without training, even the most experienced telephonist may loose his/her sang-froid when the word 'bomb' is mentioned, but the telephone call will be the only contact with the terrorist and the only chance of obtaining vital information.

Even though it is virtually impossible to trace a telephone call made through STD, it is highly desirable to keep the caller talking. Those who plant bombs are often vain enough to enjoy talking about themselves and answering questions and it may be possible to find out where the device has been placed, what it looks like and when it is timed to go off.

It may even be possible to get the caller to identify himself or his organization or his motive. Apart from political ends, the caller may have a personal grudge; he might even be a disgruntled customer or an employee with a grievance.

Seemingly unimportant details – the sex of the caller, regional accent, a speech impediment, grammatical solecisms, even background noise such as the sound of a jukebox or a street or a factory – could be of immense value to the police but not everyone answering a threat call can maintain the calm and sympathetic manner needed to elicit the maximum information.

Dozens of calls are made every year. Most are hoaxes, often by children. Sometimes the caller may reveal ignorance of the location or layout of the premises, which make the threat less credible, but every call must be appraised and one person – the coordinator – must take charge of the situation. The task will be normally upon the duty manager who should have been instructed beforehand exactly what to do.

Many bomb threats are made merely for the fun of seeing the routine of the hotel disturbed, hearing the police and fire sirens, observing the discomfort and fear of those compelled to leave the premises hurriedly.

The coordinator's decision is a tough one, balancing the disruption of business and possibility of panic against the danger of personal injury or fatality. A genuine threat written off as hoax could hang forever on his conscience. The police can advise, but the decision to act one way or the other, rests with the coordinator.

Modern bombs are not the crude, easily identified, loudly ticking devices of earlier times. Searching is best done by volunteers who know the building well. Anything out of place – a suitcase, a parcel, a thermos flask, a torch, even carrier bag – should be suspect. The search is for something that should not be there. If the trained telephonist has elicited how and when the bomb was planted, the time taken will be greatly reduced.

When a suspicious object is discovered, it should on no account be touched, except by an explosive expert. Bravery is no match for booby traps.

The fire alarm will serve as a warning to evacuate the premises, but on no account should a 'bomb' be mentioned. But whereas with fire, it is easy to determine when the danger is over, no one can say after a bomb threat that it is safe beyond all doubts to go back.

31. Precautions against Fire

Hotels and restaurants inevitably contain areas of high fire risks and involve the increasing uses every year of more sophisticated equipment relying on electrical and/or mechanical services. In addition these establishments have the additional problem of the 'sleeping risk' where customers and staff may be unaware of the development of the fire until it is well advanced. This carries additional risk from the smoke and toxic gases which precede the effect of the fire–when apparently normal people will react in a completely irrational manner partially due to the poisonous effect of these gases on semi-conscious minds.

Causes of Fires

Fires fall into different categories and it is essential that the correct type of extinguishers are used to deal with them.

1. **Class 'A' risk:** Fires ignited in paper, wood, cloth or other types of combustible materials are most effectively controlled by the use of CO_2-water type extinguishers.
2. **Class 'B' risk:** Fires caused by flammable liquids such as petrol, fat or oils should be smothered by dry powder foam or carbon dioxide or asbestos or glass fibre blankets. Water on this type of fire has the effect of spreading the flames.
3. **Class 'C' risk:** Fires caused by faulty electrical equipment or wiring must be smothered by using an agent which is a non-conductor of electricity such as the vapourising liquids known as BCF (Bromochlorodifluoromethane) or tetrachloride extinguishers. Water or foam will spread this type of fire and increase the danger of electrocution.

The risk of a fire occurring in your hotel can be considerably reduced by constant awareness on the part of the management and repeated reminders to staff by fire drills, maintenance checks and routine training procedures. The procedures must also be demonstrated by notices and information to the public so that in the event of an outbreak, an efficient operation can be mounted to protect life, material goods and the structure of the building. In the event of a fire the smooth efficiency of the organization for evacuation and the obvious demonstration of control by responsible staff are the best means of ensuring that members of the public do not panic under these conditions.

The study of fire precautions could be studied under basic headings which are inter-related:

1. The designing of routes as means of escape in the event of fire, for the safety of life and systematic evacuation.
2. The structural containment of areas of high fire risk and the limitation of the spread of fire and smoke. Similarly, there is a need for the containment of the routes of means of escape.
3. The provision and installation of systems of fire detection
4. The provision of systems of alarm and communication
5. The provision of systems of extinguishing fire related to the various areas of hazards and types of risk

6. The implementation of good housekeeping standards and the maintenance of checklists etc., as well as regular inspection of all the items concerned with the safety
7. The regular implementations of staff training procedures, fire drills, etc.

Fire rules and instructions must be incorporated within the general safety regulations and these should explain the procedures to be followed in the event of fire. Certain precautionary measures are also necessary in order to minimize the outbreak of fire.

Structural fire precautions are prescribed in building regulations. Additional provision must be made for smoke proof, fire resisting escape routes, sufficient to permit all building users to pass quickly and without risk to a place of safety in the event of an emergency. Inspection of escape routes and emergency exits is essential to verify free access at all times.

Certain other features should be planned into new building projects, and existing establishments also should examine the need to make the following provisions with the hotel:

1. Smoke Stop Doors

These are required in order to hinder the spread of smoke throughout the building. These are especially valuable when placed adjacent to flight of stairs as they can greatly delay the spread of fire from floor to floor.

2. Alarm System

Provision should be made in different parts of the building for alarm points. Automatic fire alarms are also available. These are adjusted in order to respond to abnormal or predetermined temperature rise within the building. The alarm signals should be quite distinctive and unmistakably different from any other noise heard within the hotel. Bells, Klaxon horn or siren systems can be used. The alarm should be audible in every part of the building. For further protection, the hotels may have a direct link with the local fire service. This automatically gives warning when the fire alarm sounds.

3. Storage of Inflammable Materials

Special storage arrangements must be made for the storage of inflammables. Oil storage tanks should be located away from the main building if possible, and safety trip switches provided in the event of boiler breaking down or a fire outbreak in the boiler room.

4. Display of Notices and Signs

Signs must be displaced to show unmistakably the escape route from any part of the building. Signs should be illuminated, and designed so that they can be understood easily. Their size should be related to the area in which they are to be displayed. For example, the lettering on a 'FIRE EXIT' sign placed at the end of a long corridor must be sufficiently large to be read from a distance. In a more confined space, the size of the sign may be correspondingly reduced. Other signs may be used as identification of special hazards, and any symbols used should be in accordance with international standards. Notices concerning procedures in the event of fire should be placed in all hotel guest rooms and in other parts of the hotel.

Design of Equipment

The designing of individual items of equipment has much greater significance on accident rates. Equipment design should take account of antropometric and other ergonomic factors. Service doors hung the opposite way round or with too strong self-closing mechanism may cause waiters to become frustrated and hence more accident-prone.

Cooking utensils must be easy and natural to hold and use. Cooker control must be designed with natural movements or reflexes in mind. In an emergency, an operator wishes to switch off the power, he expects the switch to flick 'up' or the dial to turn in an anti clockwise manner. Responsibility for identifying these features rests with the design engineers, but hotel should be aware that safe working conditions are encouraged by natural and habit-forming body movements. Quicker and more effective learning of how to operate a machine or a piece of equipment is possible when controls are compatible.

Factors relating to body size and capabilities of body movements must be given special consideration. The design of a cooking range which forces the chef to lift heavy cooking vessels with his arms outstretched will make work very tiring as well as hazardous. Furthermore, body sizes vary widely. This affects the detailed design of almost every facility within the hotel – the height of the work surfaces, leg room for office employees, head clearance in stairways, and so on.

Surface Finishes of Walls and Ceilings

In the early stages of a fire in a building, the personal hazard to occupants can be severely affected by the internal linings and finishes of walls and ceilings. Material likely to be found in situ in existing buildings is often difficult to assess in terms of surface spread of flame and fire preparation. Some examples of these materials have therefore been broadly classified into eight groups with an indication as to where each group may be acceptable, with the normal travel distance recommendation in the guide, for particular circumstances.

1. Inorganic Group

Brickwork, blockwork, concrete, plaster board, ceramic tiles, plaster finishes (including rendering on wood or metal lathes), asbestos boards acceptable in all locations.

2. Cellulosic Group (non-flame-retardant)

Timber, hardboard, particle board (chip board), blackboard, acceptable in small areas of other rooms of floor area not exceeding 40 sq.ft. (3.7 sq.m.). They are acceptable in small areas of other rooms, areas not exceeding half the floor area of the room or 200 sq.ft. (18 sq.m.) but not acceptable on escape routes *i.e.*, staircases, corridors, entrance halls.

3. Cellulosic Group (flame-retardant)

Acceptable in all rooms, provided evidence of suitable treatment is available. Not acceptable on escape routes *i.e.*, staircases, corridors, entrance halls.

4. Woodwool Slab

Acceptable in all locations.

5. Plastic-thermosetting (decorative laminates)

Acceptable as for group 2 unless shown to be flame-retardant grade (evidence to be provided) in which case acceptability will be as for group 3.

6. Plastic Thermoplastics (expanded polystyrene wall and ceiling linings)

Acceptable on inorganic surfaces in thickness not exceeding 3/16 in. (5 mm.) on walls, ½ in. (12 mm.) on ceilings, provided not finished with glass paint, in same situation as group 2 (Expanded polystyrene tiles or surfaces which has been painted with glass paint should be removed.

7. The Vinyl and Paper Coverings (other than heavy flock wallpapers)

Acceptable in all locations, provided it is on an inorganic surface.

8. Heavy Flock Wallpapers

Acceptable as for group 2, unless shown to be of flame-retardant grade (evidence to be provided) in which case acceptability will be as for group 3.

Emergency Lighting

Emergency lighting should be provided in all hotel

areas. Such lighting circuits should be wired independently of the main system, and self-powered light fittings are recommended in this system so that in the event of a cut in power supply, main circulation routes can remain illuminated during the evacuation of the building.

Close liaison with the local authority is required as these and other precautionary measures, that is – provisions for mechanical ventilation, cut-off systems, licensing public rooms etc. Special fire and safety measures are expected to be more tightly enforced on hotels and other recreational establishments.

Legislation and Fire Precautions

There are various rules and regulations, bye laws and many local acts which require a strict control on fire safety in hotels and catering establishments. The provisions of these acts can be broken down to two parts:

1. Legislation affecting re-building, alteration, adaptation, and/or extending building.
2. Legislation affecting re-occupation and continuation in the case of buildings designed as hotels, boarding houses, etc.

Legislative controlling building is under the respective municipal/regional authorities. Means of escape are at present under the Fire Precaution Act. The local municipal laws require all applicants to include means of escape from building in case of fire, and for ensuring that the means of escape can be safely and effectively used at all times.

There is a provision in all the bye-laws that all applicants making material changes or alteration affecting a siting of licensed premises to submit drawings to the local authority defining what changes are proposed, what are the uses of the space concerned, and what are the means of escape in case of fire for both the public and the staff. Copies of these drawings are also to be submitted to the fire authority who will also render the advice.

The provisions made in the rules and regulations and acts regarding fire precautions are of importance to all since it requires them to make means of escape and related fire precautions in places of public entertainment and resorts, and certain residential establishments. These act entitle the authorities to issue designing orders to cover its application in any of the following classes of use:

1. As a sleeping accommodation
2. As an institution providing treatment or care
3. For entertainment, recreation for purposes of any club, society or association
4. For teaching, training or research
5. For any purpose involving access to the premises by the public whether on payment or otherwise.

Everyone owning or occupying hotel or boarding house accommodation, which would be subject to designing order, is required to fill in a form supplied by the Fire Authority registered under their premises. So long as the premises have been registered, the occupant can continue to trade there until such time as the Fire Authority makes an inspection and either issues a fire certificate or marks recommendation for alternatives to be made to the premises to conform to the provisions of the Act in which case the Fire Authority will issue a certificate.

When a fire breaks out in a building in which people are present, the primary need is for these people to be able to escape safely and quickly even before the fire brigade arrives. The fire authorities have a special experience and knowledge and ability to plan in advance what the escape route should be and how they should be protected and equipped so that they will remain effective in an emergency for as long as necessary. This is why enforcement of the Fire Act, which is designated to ensure the provisions of adequate means of escape and related fire precautions in the premises within its scope, has been given to the fire authority. The main instrument of enforcement is the Fire Certificate which is issued for particular premises only after the fire authority for the area is satisfied that the means of escape and other precautions are such that may be reasonably required in the circumstances of the case. The act is concerned only with the protection of life in the event of fire. It cannot be applied to the protection of buildings and their contents although it is likely that measures to protect life in the event of fire will also contribute to the protection of the building in which measures are enforced.

The Act requires the competent authority to issue a designating order in the premises, which involve members of the public being present there in any number or in any circumstances, in which they would be especially at risk in the event of a fire. After a competent authority has issued the designating order, the fire authority would be required to make inspections and to provide fire certificate for all such premises designated in the order.

The designating orders cover the use to which premises are put regardless of their description. This covers a building or part of a building by its category rather than any form of description.

When the competent authority issues a designating order, publicity will be given to this definition and owners or occupiers of property in this classification will be given a certain time limit to make the suitabie registration of their premises under the set. The form will be obtained from the Fire Authority requiring registration for fire certificate, and as long as the form has been submitted, the owner or occupier can continue to trade in these premises, until such time as an inspection is made. Failures to complete a suitable registration form by the required time can constitute infringement of the Act and render the occupier liable for a closure notice. After the application has been made, the fire authority has the right to ask for further information in the form of drawings or plans of the building or specified parts of the building and again a time limit may be specified.

Fire Certificate

In due course, an inspector from the Fire Authority will make an inspection by appointment of the premises and the inspector will carry a proof of his identity. Following the inspection, if the fire authority is satisfied that all the requirements of the Act are met by the premises, they will issue a certificate.

The fire certificate should specify:

1. The particular use or uses of the premises covered by the certificate
2. The means of escape in case of fire, and a plan will often be used for this purpose
3. The means for ensuring that the means of escape can be safely and effectively used at all times. This would cover such matters as emergency lighting, direction signs and smoke stopping, etc.
4. The means for fighting fire for use by persons in the building, and
5. The means for giving a warning in case of fire.

The fire certificate may also impose requirements relating to:

1. The maintenance of the 'means of escape' and keeping them free from obstruction
2. The maintenance of the fire precautions specified in the certificate

3. The training of members of the staff and the keeping of appropriate records
4. Limitation of the number of persons who may be in the premises at any one time
5. Any other relevant fire precautions.

Requirements of the certificate may relate either to the premises as a whole or to any part of it; if they relate to only part of a building, the certificate may be extended to other parts.

The certificate must be kept in the premises to which it related for so long as it is in force.

If the fire authorities are not satisfied following the inspection of the premises, they may serve a notice to the applicant informing him of their requirements prior to the issue of a fire certificate. They may also impose a time limit failing which they would refuse to issue a fire certificate. There are statutory time limits to appeal in this instance but if they are refuted, it can be unlawful to continue to use the premises for the designated purposes.

The applicant is responsible for doing or carrying out the required alterations and works specified in the notice and also for dealing with any other parties in the matter.

All the physical conditions specified in the fire certificate must be kept and observed by the occupants and the fire authority has the right to make inspections to ensure constant maintenance of these items.

If any changes or alterations are proposed in the building, the fire authority must be informed in advance. Such changes can be:

1. Material extensions or structural alterations to the premises, or
2. Making material alterations to the internal arrangements of the premises either in furniture or equipment with which the premises are provided.

The fire authority must also be informed if you intend to keep in the premises explosive or highly inflammable materials which might endanger the means of escape and the conditions of the fire certificate.

If the fire authority considers that the proposed changes or the alterations make the previous requirements of the fire certificate inadequate, they will serve a notice on the occupier informing him on their revised requirements prior to their issuing a revised fire certificate.

Appeal

An occupier of the premises has the right to appeal against any decision by a fire authority concerning a fire certificate within 21 days from the date of the authority's decision. The appeal will be to the magistrate court. The appeal can be on the grounds of:

1. The fire authority's requirements to be taken prior to the issue of a fire certificate
2. Any directions given by them in connection with the proposed alterations
3. Any requirements required by them to be taken due to the change in conditions
4. If the period allowed for 1, 2 and 3 cannot be met
5. The refusal to issue a fire certificate
6. The refusal to cancel or amend a fire certificate
7. The inclusion of anything or the omission of anything from a fire certificate
8. The amendment or cancellation of a fire certificate due to changes or circumstances

Pending the determination of this appeal, it will not be unlawful to continue to trade in these premises. Similarly, it will not be unlawful not to observe the requirements of the certificate pending such an appeal. The magistrate will determine as it thinks fit and if the occupant is still dissatisfied, there is further right to appeal to the higher court.

Enforcement

The enforcement authority and the Fire Act is the fire authority. These authorities are empowered to appoint inspectors for the purpose of enforcement. These inspectors may take such action as is necessary to give effect to the Act or regulations made under it. They are entitled to enter the premises at any reasonable time to which the Act applied or seems to apply, as well as the reminder of the buildings containing such premises. Inspectors may also make such inquiries as may be necessary to find out if the Act or regulations are being complied with and may require facilities and assistance to be given to them in the exercise of his power. The Act prohibits an inspector from disclosing any such information obtained in the course of his duties.

Penalties

If offences are proved under the Act *i.e.*, that premises within a designated use were occupied without a fire certificate or contravening a requirement of the fire certificate or carrying out changes or alterations to the premises without the permission of the fire authority or contravening any notices issued by the fire authority in connection with proposed alterations, there is a provision of penalty.

A fine could be imposed for failing to keep a fire certificate or a copy thereof. The fine could also be imposed for causing obstruction to an inspector in the course of his duties and for knowingly giving false information, forging a fire certificate or giving false information to receive a fire certificate.

Fire Precaution Requirement Guidance for Hotels and Tourist Accommodation

These guidelines are intended partly for the guidance of the fire authorities and partly for the information of those responsible for the management of hotels and tourist accommodation. The guide has no statutory force and is issued without prejudice to the statutory responsibility of the fire authorities for enforcing the Act and satisfying themselves that the means of escape in case of fire and other related fire precautions are such as may reasonably be required in the circumstances of each case.

A certificate will be required relating to the building in occupation and it is assumed that the requirements of building regulations and other relevant enactments will already have been met. It is recognized that there will be many individual variations in premises and the guidance, therefore, is intended as an indication of the general standard to be aimed at rather than as a set of requirements to be rigidly applied in detail in each and every circumstance.

For Travel within Rooms

1. In rooms with only one exit, no point should be more than 30 ft (9 m) from the exit. In rooms of high fire risk such as kitchen and boiler rooms, the distance should not exceed 20 ft (6 m)
2. Where a room has an inner room, the distance from any point in the inner room, through the communicating door, to the exit of the outer room should not exceed 30 ft (9 m) or 20 ft (6 m) in room of high fire risk. A clear vision panel should be provided in a suitable position between the inner and outer rooms except where consideration of privacy outweigh those of hazard to the occupants.

3. Where a room has more than one exit, both or all of which lead into an escape route which leads to safety in one direction only, the distance from any point in the room to the exit should not exceed 30 ft (9 m) or 20 ft (6 m) in rooms of high fire risk.
4. In large rooms such as drawing rooms, ball rooms and reception rooms, there should be not less than two exits, each leading by a separate route to a place of safety.
5. The distance from a point in a large room to an exit should not exceed 60 ft (18 m). However, this distance may be increased to 100 ft (30 m) in the case of exit which is a final exit provided that:
   a. there are atleast three exits
   b. the aggregate width of the exit complies with item 10 below, and
   c. the exit to which increased distance is permitted is adequate for the notional occupancy of the part of the room it serves.
6. Where a large room contains a high fire hazard, or the use of such a room, for example, as an exhibition or sales room would create a high fire hazard, the suggested travel distances may need to be reduced.
7. The contents of any room should be so disposed that the distance to be travelled from any point in the room to an exit from the room should not be more than one and a half times the distance recommended in item 1, 2 or 5 as appropriate.
8. Alternative exits should be distributed so as to provide means of escape in at least two separate directions from any point in a room. For this purpose, the position of exits will normally be satisfactory if in a room of regular shape, the angle between the lines drawn from any point in the room to alternative exits is less than 45° or if from any point from which this cannot be achieved, the distance to the nearest exit does not exceed 30 ft (9 m).
9. The width of an exit of a room should normally not be less than 2 ft 6 in (760 mm) unless the room will be occupied by fewer than five people. The width of an exit of a room occupied by more than 100 people should normally not be less than 3 ft 4 in (1 m).
10. In a room where more than one exit is necessary for escape purposes, then with any one exit excluded the aggregate width of the remaining exits should be:
    a. 2 ft 6 in (760 mm) for up to 100 persons
    b. 3 ft 6 in (1060 mm) for up to 200 persons and an additional 3 in (75 mm) for each additional 15 or part of 15 persons.
11. Exit doors, other than those in ordinary use by guests, should be distinctly and conspicuously marked by permanent exit notices.
12. The surface finish of walls and ceilings in any room should conform with the standards.

    Note: If surface finishes do not conform with these standards and there are compensating factors such as unusually high ceilings or automatic fire detection, the travel distance recommended above may have to be reduced.

For Travel from Rooms to a Stairway and Final Exit

1. The maximum distance from an exit from a room to the point of access into a

protected route, to an external route, or to a final exit should be in accordance with the following table:

Type of Room and exits	Maximum distance
i. Room with only one exit and with alternative rcutes	: 60 ft (18 m)
ii. Ground floor room with an exit giving immediate access to a place of safety	: no limit to any internal route
iii. Room with more than one exit and with alternative routes	: 60 ft (18 m) from any exit
iv. Room where only one route is available (dead land)	: 25 ft (7.6 m)

2. Bedroom doors opening on to escape corridors should have the same fire resistant material as the walls containing them, up to a modified half-hour's fire resistance. Such doors need not be made self-closing. All types of lights in the corridors should have a similar fire resistance and be fixed closed in the ceiling.
3. In corridors where escape is in one direction only (dead ends), the walls and partitions forming one corridor should be of fire-resisting construction and room doors (other than lavatory doors) giving into the corridor should be fire-resisting and self-closing. Doors to cupboards should be fire resisting and should be marked 'The door to be kept shut and locked'. Where the escape route consists initially of a dead end and then has alternative routes, the dead end portion of the route should not exceed 25 ft (7.6 m), the total travel distance should be separated from each other by fire-resisting, self-closing doors at the junction of the dead end.
4. A route is an alternative to another route only when it leads in a different direction to a separate enclosed stairway, external route, roof exit, final exit or a combination of these.
5. When it is necessary to pass a stairway to reach an alternative escape route, then that stairway should be enclosed by fire-resisting construction in such a way that a person need not pass through the enclosure to reach the alternative route. If this is impossible, then the stairway should still be enclosed and a by-pass arranged by means of pass doors between rooms or by means of linking balconies.
6. In a building having more than one staircase, doors from rooms, other than lavatories, should not open directly into a stairway. Where this is not practicable, a limited number of such doors may be permitted if:
   i. The doors are fire-resistant and self-closing
   ii. The doors do not enter the stairway above the third floor
   iii. Where the stairway serves any floor above the third floor, a fire-resisting screen incorporating a fire-resisting, self-closing door is provided at every level served
   iv. The distance from any such door to the door separating the stairway from the alternative route is not more than 15 ft (4.6 m) unless pass doors or a linking balcony are available to give access to the alternative route
7. Normally main corridors should not be less than 4 ft (1.2 m) wide and dead end

corridors should not be less than 3 ft 6 in (1.06 m) wide. Apart from small areas for decorative purposes, the surface finish of walls and ceilings of all corridors should be of a standard corresponding to class 'O' or should conform with the standards recommended in appendix.

Note: Where the above conditions cannot be achieved for any corridor or some other factor creates a higher fire risk than normal, the distance may be reduced. Where a corridor is a protected corridor or there are compensating factors such as automatic fire detection, the distances can be increased.

8. Where corridors exceed 60 ft (18 m) in length, fire resisting, self-closing doors should be provided at such intervals that no length of corridor between such doors exceeds 60 ft (18 m).
9. In basement, there should be alternative stairways to ground level, unless there is a final exit at basement level. This need not apply to small basements used for storage purposes only. The basement should be separated from the ground floor by two half-hour fire resisting self-closing doors, one at the basement level and one at ground floor level or by a one-hour fire-resisting self-closing door at basement level.
10. To give protection from smoke and heat issuing from below, link balconies should have solid floors. Alternatively, any windows below should have fire-resisting glazing in frames and be of permanently fixed sheet. Doors to the balconies should be capable of being opened either from both sides or from one side as appropriate.
11. Where inter-communication is required between rooms for escape purposes, there should be by pass doors not less than 5 ft high and 1 ft 9 in wide (1.5 m and 530 mm). Wall hatches, kick out panels, floor hatches and similar devices are not suitable and should be used only in exceptional circumstances.

For Travel within Stairways and to Final Exit

1. A single stairway may be accepted in a building having not more than three floors above the ground floor if:
   i. the stairway is enclosed with fire-resisting construction.
   ii. access to the stairway from any room (other than lavatory) is through two sets of fire-resisting, self-closing doors; and
   iii. at ground level, the stairway discharges directly to, or via, a protected route to a safe place in the open air or to alternative routes from the enclosure to separate final exits.
2. In buildings having only one floor above ground floor where it is not possible to satisfy item 1, a single stairway may be acceptable under either of the following conditions:
   i. If a floor exit or other external escape route is provided and the single stairway is screened at the upper floor with fire-resisting construction in such a way that the occupants of the upper floor can reach the alternative exit without having to enter the stairway enclosure; or
   ii. If the distance from the farthest room door on the upper floor to the final exit does not exceed 60 ft (18 m) and the escape route is a protected one throughout its length.
3. Two stairways which appear to provide alternative routes do not constitute alternatives for escape purposes unless they both descend into one common space at ground level so that the common space is an area of negligible fire risk and access

between the stairways is via two sets of fire resisting self-closing doors.

4. Accommodation stairways need not be enclosed at all other levels. (Accommodation stairway means a stairway provided for the convenience of occupants which is additional to any required for escape purposes.)
5. Where an alternative route is required, this may be:
   i. an extreme staircase; or
   ii. a special staircase, if it is for not more than 50 persons, the maximum height is 30 ft (9 m) and the diameter is not less than 5 ft (1.5 m); or
   iii. a route to a safe place by way of a roof exit where no other arrangement is possible.
6. Apart from small areas for decoration purposes, the surface finish of walls and ceilings of all staircases should be a standard corresponding to class 'O' or should conform with the standard recommended in the appendix.
   i. Wherein buildings having only one escape staircase, the surface finishes of the staircase do not conform with the recommendation at item 6 above, an alternative routeway may have to be provided.
   ii. In buildings where more than one staircase is necessary for escape purposes and the surface finishes of one or more staircase do not conform with the recommendations of item 6 above, this may nevertheless be acceptable if there are compensating factors e.g. automatic fire detection, lobby approach to the staircase(s) in question.
7. Where it is considered that rooms of high fire risk such as kitchen, boiler room or exhibition rooms might constitute a particular threat to an escape route, it will be necessary to separate them from the escape routes by construction and by doors affording one hour's fire resistance.
8. Lifts are not acceptable as means of escape. Vertical ladders, ropes, throw out ladders, chutes and other form of manipulative emergency doors are not suitable for escape purposes, except that in extreme circumstances, vertical ladders may be accepted for limited number of staff.

General Requirements

1. Where ventilation systems might assist the spread of fire or of the smoke and hot gases from a fire, it will be necessary to take steps to safeguard the means of escape against the hazard.
2. All fire resisting doors which are required to be self-closing should be fitted with a positive self-closing device; rising butt hinges are not suitable. The doors (other than doors to bedrooms and cupboards) should be permanently marked on both sides, at about eye level, with a red diamond with the words 'FIRE DOOR – KEEP SHUT' in white lettering of appropriate size.
3. Fire resisting doors which will close automatically on the operation of an automatic fire detection system may be permitted. If an electric fire warning system is installed, the door release device may be incorporated in its circuit. Unless the doors close automatically on the operation of a smoke detection system, they should be kept closed at night as an additional precaution.
4. All exits should be constructed when there are occupants on the premises and whenever

possible exit doors should open outwards. Exit doors may be fastened for security reasons provided that they remain easily operable from within.

5. If it is necessary to keep fastened the final exit doors from ball rooms or other rooms holding large number of occupants, they should be secured by panic bolts only and should be marked 'PUSH BAR TO OPEN'.
6. Exit doors on escape routes which are not the normal route of travel from a building should be indicated by notices bearing the words 'FIRE EXIT' and these should be illuminated where necessary. If such an exit door is not visible from any point on the escape route, a notice should be provided at such points reading 'TO FIRE EXIT'. Illumination of exit and directional signs should be provided by an emergency service independent of the main supply.
7. All floors should have a fire resistance of at least half an hour. Appropriate measures should be taken to ensure that the spread of fire or of the products of combustion from floor to floor by way of openings for hoists, shafts, ducts, etc. is prevented.

For Emergency Lighting

1. Some form of emergency lighting should be provided in all premises and whatever is provided for this purpose must be capable of illuminating all stairways, routes of exit, exit and direction signs sufficiently to enable persons to make their way out of the premises.
2. Emergency lighting should preferably be by electricity. Where a gas system is installed already, this may be accepted but there must be a requirement for the system to be kept on at all times when natural light is insufficient for escape.
3. In small buildings, *i.e.*, having not more than one floor above ground level and not more than 10 bedrooms, electric hand lamps may be accepted.

   Electric lamps should preferably be of a type which is connected and secured to an electric circuit and which is released and illuminated automatically on failure of power to the circuit. In small premises where escape routes are uncomplicated and relatively easy to traverse and there is normally indirect lighting from outside the premises, then ordinary electric hand lamps may be used. Where electric hand lamps are accepted, there should be a requirement that one such lamp should be issued to each member of the resident staff in addition to any provided for use by guests.
4. In premises other than small premises, the system should be a permanent installation supplied with electricity from a source independent of the main supply and as arranged that:
   i. it comes into operation automatically on the failure of the main supply; or
   ii. can be maintained to operate at all times when natural light is insufficient for escape purpose.

   Such a system should be capable of maintaining the necessary level of illumination for a period of three hours from the time of failure or disconnection of normal supply. However, a system which is capable of maintaining the required level of illumination for two hours may be accepted provided that the fire authority is satisfied that the system will be kept without condition.

5. Either self-contained battery-powered lighting units incorporating their own charger or lighting powered from a central source within the premises will be acceptable.
6. In ballrooms, conference rooms and other rooms where large number of person assemble and in all associated escape routes, the emergency lighting must be kept on at all times when the room is in use and when there is insufficient natural light for escape purposes.
7. The power supply equipment for an emergency lighting system shall not be used to satisfy any other equipment.

In Case of Fire

Means of Warning

1. In all premises, means of giving warning in case of fire should be installed which is:
   i. Readily available at all times
   ii. Capable of being operated without exposing any person to undue risk
   iii. Perceptible throughout the premises and capable of waking staff and residents
   iv. Distinctive in that it will not be confused with any other signal in the premises.
2. In building of one or two floors, manually operated sounders may be used provided that:
   i. any one sounder is audible throughout the premises, and
   ii. at least two sounders are provided in such positions that a fire arising anywhere in the premises will not render all the sounders inaccessible due to heat or smoke.

   Alternatively, self-contained electric or mechanical sounders, which once actuated will continue to operate for a sufficient length of time may be used. At least two such sounders should be provided.
3. Premises of more than two floors should have an electric fire warning system, except as provided for in Item 4 below. An electrical system should have break glass release button call points. In most premises, the operation of any one call point should cause the alarm signal to operate throughout the premises. However, in large premises with adequate degree of compartmentation and fire resistance, a two-stage alarm system may be used.
4. Where premises have an internal automatic telephone system and a continuous staffed switchboard, then the telephone system may be used as a means of initiating an alarm of fire, but a warning system will need to be provided for alerting the occupants. This type of system needs careful consideration to ensure that it will always be operated in the circumstances appertaining in the premises.

   The following are some of the points to be considered:
   a. Sufficient telephones must be available in public areas as well as bedrooms.
   b. The wiring of the internal telephone system should be protected against damage by fire as far as possible.
   c. A fire call should be given priority over calls already in progress.
   d. An automatic switch should be provided so that the dialling of a predetermined number will sound the warning if the switchboard is unattended for that period.
   e. Adequate instructions will be required for the staff operating the switchboard.

Instructions for action in case of fire should be prominently displayed in all rooms. Exits must be clearly marked and access to them kept clear and unblocked. All staff must be instructed on the location of fire fighting equipment and what action must be taken in case of fire or any other such emergency.

Procedure When Fire Occurs

If fire breaks out, the staffs have a definite responsibility for the safety of the guests and, along with the telephone operators, they are charged with notifying all guests in the danger areas to vacate. The basic rules in an emergency are as follows:

1. Report the fire immediately to the switchboard, who will notify the fire brigade. Use fire alarm system if necessary.
2. Switch off lifts and power appliances and close doors and windows.
3. Staff must only undertake fire fighting if they have been trained.
4. Hotel employees will assist all elderly, sick or infirm persons to the exits.
5. If possible, search all rooms and make sure no one is left behind.
6. The reception staff should remove the register of guests and lists of residents and staff from the building in order that all persons can be accounted for.
7. When the building has been cleared, staff and residents should assemble away from the area and be checked.

Detailed instruction should be incorporated into

ABC Hotel

In the event of a fire

Room No. ____

1. Any person discovering a fire must raise the alarm either at the nearest alarm point or by telephoning the hotel office.
2. Only if it is safe to do so, fight the fire, using the nearest available appliance. Do not expose yourself to a dangerous situation, individual heroics are not for amateurs.
3. On hearing the alarm, close all windows and doors and leave the building quietly and in an orderly manner by the nearest safe route.
4. Assemble in the car park at the side of the hotel and wait for the instructions from the hotel management.
5. The nearest telephone alarm point is located in the corridor to the left of the room door.
6. The nearest escape route may be reached by turning left into the corridor outside the room. Follow the direction arrows and 'Fire Exit' signs.

Note: 1 and 2: In the event of a small fire, circumstances may indicate that it is best to attack before raising the alarm.

3: This will hinder the spread of fire by eliminating the draughts.

4, 5 and 6: Describe the use, terms, the place of assembly and any other instructions.

Figure 31.1: Specimen of a 'Notice' in the Event of a Fire

Table 31.1: Portable Fire Extinguishers

<table>
<tr><th></th><th>Water Extinguishers</th><th>Foam</th><th>Carbondioxide</th><th>Dry Powder</th><th>Vaporising Liquids</th></tr>
<tr><td>Fire where electricity is present</td><td>No</td><td>No</td><td>Yes – Excellent. CO_2 is a non-conductor</td><td>Yes – Excellent. Powder is a non-conductor or gas are non-conductors</td><td>Yes – Liquid</td></tr>
<tr><td colspan="6">There are no electric fires as such but electricity can be present at any one of the following four classes.
Where 'yes' boxes agree under either appliances it can be used. Professional advise must be sought where there are two 'No's or a 'Yes' and a 'No'.</td></tr>
<tr><td>Solid materials paper, wood etc. prevents re-ignition</td><td>Yes – Excellent. Water cools and saturates and has smothering and wetting action</td><td>Yes – Excellent. Foam bubbles</td><td>Yes – Excellent. CO_2 replaces oxygen shielding cloud</td><td>Yes – Powder. smothers fire, produces heat</td><td>Yes – Smothering gas too is formed.</td></tr>
<tr><td>Gases and gas containers</td><td>Yes – Water will cool container.</td><td>No</td><td>No</td><td>No</td><td>No</td></tr>
<tr><td colspan="6">First aid action is to shut off gas supply and remove container from heat. If this is not possible wait for professional fireman.</td></tr>
<tr><td>Metal fires</td><td>No</td><td>No Limited applications</td><td>Yes – Special powder is used</td><td>Yes</td><td>No</td></tr>
</table>

general safety code for the hotel. Notices explaining the fire procedures should be displayed throughout the hotel as given in Figure 31.1:

The Management

The hotel management should make the following provisions for application in the event of fire:

1. Where possible, the hotel register or other suitable records should be removed, so that assessment can be made of those not present after the evacuation of the building.
2. Provisions should be made for members of staff (so far as the fire will permit without danger) to check that those parts of the building designated to them are fully evacuated.

3. On hearing the alarm or following a verbal report of a fire, the fire service must be summoned. All members of staff must be fully familiar with the procedure.
4. After evaluation of the building, persons must not be permitted to re-enter, except with the permission of the person or officer in charge of the fire fighting.

Fire Drills

Fire drills should be featured regularly so that staff members are familiar with all procedures.

Fire Fighting Equipment

Fire fighting equipment must be provided in all hotels, and by sensible siting appliances for free access and handling, a potentially serious fire outbreak can often be extinguished with ease if tackled in its early stages.

Before any fire can start and continue to burn, three conditions must be fulfilled:

1. A combustible material is required (such as fuel, oil, wood, furnishings, etc.)
2. A supply of air or oxygen must be available in order to support combustion.
3. Heat is required at a sufficient temperature in order to promote the combustion of the material.

Successful fire control involves the removal of one or more of these factors. Whilst it is not always practicable to remove or cut off the supply of fuel, elimination of the other two factors is generally more realistic. Water is generally the most readily available fire extinguishing medium, and as it will normally absorb heat with safety from most burning materials, temperature can be reduced until combustion ceases.

Fire Fighting Equipment in Hotels

1. All premises should be provided with means for fighting fire for use by persons in the building.
2. In other than small premises, hose reels should be provided and should be sufficient in number so that with 100 ft (300 m) of hose, the nozzle can reach every point on the floor area. The tubing should not exceed ¾ in (19 mm) bore and should be in accordance with the type of tubing. The water supply should be such that a minimum of 5 gal per min (22.7 litres) is discharged, which in the case of a 3/6 in (5 mm) nozzle requires a pressure of approximately 35 lb per sq I (2.4 bars) at the nozzle, and in the case of a ¼ in (6 mm) nozzle a pressure of approximately 11 lb per sq in (0.77 bars) at the nozzle. Hose reels should be placed on escape routes and normally adjacent to staircase enclosures.
3. If hose reels are not installed, hand fire extinguishers should be provided in sufficient numbers to give adequate cover to the premises. Every effort should be made to provide extinguishers of one pattern as this makes for a uniform method of operation and also for ease of maintenance. The number of extinguishers necessary will depend upon the size, layout, and fire separation provided within the building. One water type extinguisher of 2 gal (9 litres) capacity is normally sufficient for every 250 sq yd (209 sq m) or part thereof, with not less than two such extinguishers on each floor except in small premises. Double this number of 1 gal (4.5 litres) capacity may be used. Fire extinguishers should conform to the appropriate specification where no such specification exists. Approval of the Fire Authority may be taken as a guide. Special risks will require extinguishers of a type suitable for that risk.

Pressure Extinguishers

Pressure extinguishers of two-gallon capacity are available. The three types include – soda/acid type, gas pressure type, and stored pressure type. Care should be taken to ensure that clear instructions for the operation of each type are printed on the appliances, that staff receives instructions in the handling of this equipment and that regular inspection of all fire fighting equipment is carried out by an expert.

Hose Reels

These are permanently linked to the main water supply through a fire hydrant point. Hose reels should be located on each floor of the hotel and the hosing must be capable of reaching to within twenty feet of any part of the floor. Many hose reels are filled so that the nozzle attachment is freed only when water supply valve is turned on. However, staff should be made familiar with individual systems of hose reel operation.

Hydrant Systems and Dry Risers

These may be incorporated into buildings, and their installation facilitates the fire-fighting role of the local fire service. This apparatus enables a supply of water to be provided on each floor where most needed in an emergency.

Sprinkler System

It automatically comes into operation in the event of a fire or dangerous temperature rise. It may be used in certain areas within the hotel. Some combustible materials are best extinguished by eliminating air or oxygen from the burning zone. The use of water on burning oil or fat, for example, would encourage the spread of flames, thus methods have been devised to cater for this form of fire hazard:

Foam Extinguishers

Chemically produced and resembling thick soap seeds, this substance forms a floating seal over the material, thus cutting off oxygen supply.

Carbon Dioxide

It is stored in pressure cylinders and has a similar effect as of foam extinguishers. This is particularly suitable for fire hazards in kitchen areas and where electric apparatus is involved.

Powder and Vapourising Liquid Material Systems of Extinguishment

Adequate means of immediate action by staff on the source of the fire should be provided throughout the premises. The type of extinguisher adopted may vary from buckets of water, sand, stirrup pumps and portable extinguishers to asbestos blankets and hose reels.

Classification of Fire

Fires may be classified as follows:

Class A	:	Fires in ordinary combustibles (wood, textiles and paper)
Class B	:	Fires in flammable liquids
Class C	:	Fires involving gases
Class D	:	Fires in special risks (metals).

Suitability of Appliances

Some appliances are more suitable for treating certain fires than others. Table 44.1 relates classes of fire and appliances. Specific types of appliance may be required for particular risks and appliances finally chosen should have fire officer's and insurer's approval.

Type of Appliances

1. Fire Buckets

Fire buckets are usually of 9 litres capacity and may be sand or water filled. Covers should be provided to keep contents clean and reduce water evaporation. Round bottom buckets discourage use for other purposes but cannot be set down, either as a reserve or for use with a pump. Sand for fire fighting should be perfectly dry and free running. They should be fitted with a lid to prevent their misuse (*i.e.*, receptacles for latter). Buckets for fire are available either single or grouped. They should be fixed not more than 1 m from floor.

Fire prevention officers and insurers usually have requirements as to the quantity of buckets. Not all buildings need fire buckets; for those that do, a minimum of six buckets per floor or three buckets per 210 m may be used as a guide.

2. Manual Fire Pumps

These consist of a hand pump mounted in 9/14 litre container or a stirrup pump used with buckets. A length of hose from the pump terminates in an adjustable (fine spray to jet) nozzle. The pump should be able to produce a jet of at least 10 m. A team of three, one directing the hose, one pumping and one replenishing the water in container is desirable to operate a pump, but operation by one person is possible.

3. Fire Blankets/Asbestos Blanketing

Asbestos fire blankets are useful appliances for smothering small fires. Sizes range from 90 mm x 90 mm to 1800 mm x 1800 mm. Suitable applications are cinema projection rooms, kitchens – particularly frying ranges, and for wrapping people whose clothes are on fire. Woollen fire blankets are also available. Flames can be smothered by cutting-off the air supply.

4. Proprietory Portable Extinguishers

Portable extinguishers are of five types:

1. Water
   a. Water (Soda/acid)
   b. Water (gas/pressure)
   c. Water (air/pressure)
2. Foam (water with foaming agent)
   a. Foam (chemical)
   b. Foam (mechanical or gas pressure)
3. Dry powder extinguishers
4. Carbon dioxide extinguishers
5. Vapourising liquid extinguishers
   a. Carbon tetrachloride (CTC)
   b. Methyl bromide (MB)
   c. Chlorobromomethane (CBM)
   d. Bromochlorodifluoromethane (BCF)
   e. Bromotrifluoromethane (BTM).

Because portable fire appliances have a life of twenty years or more, example of all types are in service, especially in old buildings, but some are obsolete or obsolescent. Water (soda/acid) and foam (chemical) are obsolete and CTC and MB are obsolescent. Sales of CTC and MB appliances has already ended.

Clear indication of extinguisher contained in appliances is important; the name, *i.e.*, foam should dominate other lettering to assist identification in an emergency.

There is no standard colour for appliances at present; red, blue, cream and metallic colours are commonly used. Some manufacturers are beginning to use yellow to make appliances clearly visible, particularly in artificial light.

Not all buildings use fire extinguishers; where they do, fire prevention offers and insurers will have requirements as to number and type of appliances. As a guide two 4.5 litre or one 9 litre water-filled extinguishers will be required per 210 m^2 of floor area, with a minimum of 2 per floor. Other types (usually carbondioxide) will be needed for lift, motor room, fan rooms etc.

Most appliances discharge with considerable force and occupants of buildings should be trained in their use. Space may be required for training personnel in use of all types of portable appliances.

Housekeeping Standards

Management should accept full responsibility for ensuring that they and their staff are constantly aware of the potential risks of the outbreak of fire on their premises. It must be appreciated that the primary causes of fire are due to electrical and mechanical faults, smoking and careless risks by people generally.

The best way of reducing these risks is to provide regular maintenance check lists which should be completed at intervals by responsible staff.

A daily and nightly visual check should be carried out in all normally unoccupied areas *i.e.*, storerooms etc. and a more detailed checklist should be developed for the regular weekly, monthly or quarterly inspection of the electrical and mechanical equipment provided in the building. It may be advantageous for management to consider service contracts with the suppliers or installers of such equipment, who will provide certificates of inspection. This is especially necessary with all electrical equipment, which should be periodically inspected and tested in accordance with regulations by a qualified electrician. Similarly, all fire fighting equipment, extinguishers etc. should be regularly checked and periodically re-charged to ensure full working efficiency.

It is obvious that all escape routes should be kept free of all obstacles at all times.

All rooms containing heating equipment, or storing combustible materials, should be kept closed, and positions where waste material is being collected for disposal should be regularly inspected. If ash is being removed from solid fuel boilers, it should be dampened or contained in sealed metal receptacles. All workshop areas should be regularly checked to ensure that combustible material is properly stored and any combustible waste material is regularly collected and kept in sealed metal containers.

If any alteration work is proposed, by maintenance staff or outside contractors, the management should ensure that such areas are provided with the required extinguishers, and that the local hazards involving the use of blow-lamps, welding and cutting equipment, or the use of flammable liquids should be restricted to as small a working area as possible.

Potential Fire Risks

Smoking

Where smoking is allowed, ample ashtrays and ash cans should be available and placed at all strategic points. In public rooms, bedrooms, corridors and staff quarters there must be adequate ashtray, coverage. Ashtrays should never be emptied into water paper baskets or bins in case there are still smoldering butts present. Everybody should be cautioned to stub out cigarette or cigar butts in an ashtray and to make quite certain there is no danger of ignition. These points cannot be over emphasized because statistics prove that smoking is a major cause of fire.

In frequently visited parts of the building such as storerooms, or in any place where fire risk is high, smoking must be prohibited and the rule strictly enforced.

Chimneys

Defective chimneys and fireplaces are dangerous fire hazards. Likewise all chimneys which are not swept regularly. In the event of a chimney fire, the fire brigade should be summoned immediately. Unfortunately, chimney fires are usually only discovered once the blaze has taken a toll.

Electricity

Old overworked or overloaded electric installations are another potential fire risks. As with chimneys, so with electrical fittings, regular inspection and maintenance is the responsibility of the management.

Heating Equipment

Gas and electric heaters should be fitted with guards and, if possible, be sited in fixed position where they will not come into contact with combustible materials. Portable oil heaters, because of the possibility of being knocked over, present a dangerous fire risk.

Restaurants

It may not always be appreciated that the naked

flame for service lamps in a restaurant could be dangerous. Similarly, the flaming of foods in the rooms, unless undertaken by a properly trained member of staff, could go out of control and cause a fire. The obvious safeguard to be taken there is the initial instruction of all flaming work. Proper safety precautions must be taken. For example, never allow the neck of bottle containing spirits or liquids to come into proximity with the flames to prevent explosion.

Bars and Wine Cellars

These can be real damage zones in the event of a fire. Spirits and liquor are highly volatile and bottles exploding in the heat of a fire are akin to shrapnel and incendiary bombs, liable to cause grevious injuries and a rapid spreading of the blaze.

Boiler Rooms

No combustible materials other than boiler fuel should be kept in these rooms. Where solid fuel is used, ash should be dampened and placed in metal receptacles.

Waste

All forms of rubbish and waste can help a fire to take a hold. Waste or packing materials should not be allowed to accumulate in the service areas of a building. Rubbish bins should be kept covered with a well-fitted lid.

Storerooms

Places where combustible goods such as bedding, linen and stationery are stored will require particular attention. The store should be kept locked and entry should be allowed to only responsible persons, and the 'No smoking' rule strictly enforced.

Lighting and heating appliances should be examined regularly and care is necessary to ensure that the stored goods do come into close contact with them.

Linen Rooms

Electric irons and similar apparatus may accidentally be left switched on and thus start a fire. Pilot lamps on apparatus of this type, to show when current is on, help to avert the danger.

Hairdressing Saloons

Where there is a hairdressing saloon on the premises, the fire dangers of hair lacquers and similar flammable substances should be appreciated and guarded against.

Workshops

When a hotel has its own workshop, this is likely to contain easily combustible materials such as wood and paints. There may also be several sources of ignition which will need watching, and care should be taken that all waste materials are regularly gathered and disposed of.

Building Operations

Building or decorative work may introduce few dangers in the form of blow lamps, welding equipment and similar apparatus, and paint and varnish removers may add to the amount of combustible material on the premises. Management should ensure that the necessary precautions are taken and that outside contractors are made familiar with the establishment's own fire safety arrangements. One obvious precaution is to place fire extinguishing appliances at hand.

Kitchen

The flash points in the kitchen are deep frying equipment and dirty overhead extraction ducts. Chefs learn to treat deep fat with respect. Overheating frying oil is liable to burst into flames and if deep fat is allowed to boil over, a vast sheet of flame can ensue. A fire extinguisher should always be placed in the vicinity of the deep fryers for ready use in the event of emergency.

32. Staff Training: Fire Drills and Procedures in Emergency Situations

Whenever new staff is engaged, they should be taken on a complete inspection of the building and made familiar with all the routes of escape and the general procedure to be adopted in the event of the fire for evacuation and arrival at an essential point outside the building for a roll call. In buildings such as hotels, which involve multiple use areas, it may only be necessary to familiarize the staff with the means of escape etc., in their own area of responsibility.

In addition to making the staff familiar with procedures for evacuation, regular fire drills should be held to ensure that not only the staff carry out the correct procedures, but the procedures themselves are correct, and that any changes in the planning of the building or disposition of accommodation has not altered the adopted fire drill procedures.

In small hotels, it may be necessary to call for complete evacuation of the premises in the event of fire warning being given. But in large establishments such as hotels, where areas of different use are completely separate from one another, *i.e.*, restaurants, conference halls, bedroom accommodation, offices or garages, etc., a two stage alarm system may be considered. In the area at risk the alarm is sounded and the area evacuated, but all other areas are only warned that a fire signal has been given. It will then be the staff management's responsibility to decide on total evacuation in the event of fire spreading outside its original area.

The following outline proposals for training staff are therefore based on the single warning and evacuation system, and the two stage system.

When management is working out a pattern for routes of escape from all points a pattern will develop for seting fire points containing the warning and extinguisher devices adopted, and seting of these fire points can be related to staff throughout the building. The senior member of the staff in each area should therefore be appointed fire warden, responsible for giving warning and attacking the fire, and ensuring that the proper evacuation procedures are adopted. The fire warden should also be the last man out, having checked that his area has been cleared of all personnel. It is obvious that when a fire warden is on leave, or away from his position, a deputy warden should be appointed.

A decision should be made on the most suitable area in which evacuees should congregate upon evacuation. This area should be included in all evacuations procedures with a diagram showing where it is and the quickest route. At this assembly area, one person should be assigned to receive evacuees, and where possible, with the help of occupancy lists, checked on those present and missing heads of the department should be asked to draw up a list of the members of their staff who are absent, and be on hand (but out of danger) to advise fire brigade officials or responsible officials of those suspected missing.

Guidelines for Instructions to Internal Staff

What you should do?

Act quickly ! Seconds count!

1. If you discover a fire and it is obvious that you can't put it out without personal risk.
   a. CLOSE THE DOOR(S) to the room(s) concerned.

b. RAISE THE ALARM BY:

- Picking of the nearest telephone and dialing switch board or 101, then
- tell the operator the exact location of the fire, or
- Break the glass of the nearest fire alarm point.

2. On hearing Evacuation Alarm
   a. Residents of the rooms in the immediate area of the fire should be awakened and urgently directed to the nearest fire escape route.
      - Do not use lifts.
      - Do not stop to pick up personal belongings.
      - Do not endanger your own life and leave the building quickly and calmly by the nearest escape route to the street, collecting any guests en route.
   b. When clear of the building, report to your head of the department or other responsible person at the assembly area so that a roll call can be made.

      Your Assembly Area is: Location

Guidelines for Instructions to Fire Warden(s)

If you discover a fire in your area which cannot be instantly extinguished without personal risk:

1. Advise the telephone operator or the Fire Brigade.
2. Make your own arrangements for attacking the source of the fire with the approved appliances.
3. Clear all occupants from the area (other than those engaged in fighting the fire) in a firm but reassuring manner.
4. Close all doors of the rooms affected.
5. Check that all fire and smoke stop doors, hoists and windows are closed to prevent spread of the fire.
6. Check that all lifts are empty and immobilised at your floor level.
7. Wait for the arrival of the Fire Brigade.

The instruction to sound the general evacuation alarm will be given by a senior member of management or an official of the Fire Brigade only.

On hearing the general evacuation alarm:

1. Delegate the member of the fire party to be available to receive instructions from the Fire Brigade officials.
2. Delegate one member to report to the person made responsible at the assembly area to assist him in his duties, collecting the occupant's book from reception.
3. Ensure that fire alarm can be heard as far as your area of responsibility extends.
4. Direct all occupants from the area to the nearest fire exit.
5. Close all doors to the area affected/having checked that rooms are empty.
6. Check that all fire and smoke, stop doors, hoists and windows are closed.
7. Check that all lifts are empty and immobilised at your floor level.
8. Leave the area yourself. Be on hand (but out of danger) to advise Fire Brigade officials about the occupancy of the hotel.

   Your Assembly Area is: Location

Guidelines/Instructions to Telephone Operators

1. Act Quickly !
2. Seconds Count !
3. Speak Distinctly !

4. Give Accurate Information !

Immediately on receipt of the message 'Fire' and its location:

1. Sound the appropriate alarm signal (either single or two stage technique)
2. Inform the Fire Brigade either by telephone, direct line or 101
3. Clearly announce

   FIRE AT (your exact address)

   Come to Main/side entrance
4. Listen for acknowledgement by the Fire Brigade
5. Contact by most immediate means available (telephone, messenger, beep) the following persons:
   a. The duty manager
   b. The duty engineer
   c. The duty electrician
   d. The reception desk
   e. The maintenance engineer/manager, or
   f. The members of the hotel and restaurants
   g. Fire Party, if they are different from the above.
6. Tell them:
   a. The exact location of the fire
   b. Confirm arrival of Fire Brigade
7. Stand by to receive instructions from the manager or a Fire Brigade officer.

   The instruction to sound a general evacuation alarm will be given by a senior member of management or an official of the Fire Brigade only.
8. On the sounding of the general evacuation alarm:
   a. Telephone the person responsible for receiving evacuees at the assembly area and tell him to act in accordance with his instructions.
   b. Leave the building by the nearest available fire exit and proceed to the assembly point.

Your Assembly Area is: Location

Guidelines for Assembly Area Checker

On being advised by the hotel telephone operator that evacuation of the hotel is in progress, the following action should be taken:

1. Obtain the assistance of the first available person in order to advise any nearby persons or resident that evacuation of the hotel is in progress.
2. Stand by to await the evacuees.
3. Using a portable tannoy, advise all members of the staff to congregate in departmental groups.
4. With the help of the Fire Warden, check on the occupancy of the hotel (or restaurant) against the evacuees present.

Guests

In every guest room, a notice should be prominently displayed which sets out the procedure to be adopted:

a. If a fire breaks out in that room, and
b. When the fire alarm sounds.

This notice should also incorporate a diagram showing where the bed is situated in relation to at least two alternative routes of escape, and the designated assembly area.

An example of such a route is given in Table 32.1:

Table 32.1: Guidelines for Guests

Fire Instructions

On hearing the Fire Alarm Bell/Siren

1. Leave your room immediately, closing the door behind you.
2. Make your way quickly and to the Assembly Area shown below, using one of the routes indicated.
3. On arrival at the Assembly Area, make contact with a responsible person there to confirm evacuation.
4. Do not stop to collect personal belongings.
5. Do not use the lifts.

If fire breaks out in this room, and you cannot put it out without personal risk:

1. Pick up your telephone and tell the Switchboard Operator, giving your room number.
2. Confirm that you are leaving the room, and where you are to be found if not at the Assembly Area.
3. Do not stop to collect personal belongings.
4. Do not use the lifts.
5. Do not return to your room.

Table 32.2: Manager's Checklists: The key questions

1. Have you accepted full responsibility for the safety from fire of your guests, staff, property?	
2. Have you nominated some one immediately below you to take responsibility in your absence?	
3. Do you observe a programme of fire prevention checks, daily and periodically?	: Daily Checks
4. Are your staff trained to prevent fire?	: Staff Training Checks
5. Are you satisfied that, in the event of fire, the spread of fire and smoke will be controlled e.g. by means of smoke-stop doors?	: Fire Authority, Architect
6. Are there means of sounding an alarm which can be heard by all occupants?	: Fire Authority
7. Has every occupant a choice of alternative means of escape in case one should be obstructed by fire or smoke?	: Fire Authority, Architect
8. Are all fire exits and escape routes clearly signposted and lighted?	: Fire Authority

Table cont. ...

Table cont. ...

9.	Is there an emergency lighting system in case of mains failure?	: Fire Authority
10.	Are the staff trained as to the action they should take to ensure the safe escape of guests?	: Staff Training Checks
11.	Are notices pasted in guests' bedrooms and public rooms giving information on how to report an outbreak of fire, what to do if the fire alarm is sounded, what to do if escape is cut off?	: Fire Authority
12.	Is suitable fire extinguishing appliances provided and placed in the best position and is it maintained ready for use?	: Fire Authority
13.	Have staff been trained in the use of the fire extinguishing apparatus?	: Staff Training Checks
14.	Do you have a plan for fire safety while building or maintenance work is in progress?	: Maintenance and Building Checks

Fire Procedure Checks

1. Has someone preferably the switchboard operator been instructed to call Fire Brigade immediately on a fire has been reported, and to alert the manager, all guests and staff?
2. Has the night staff been instructed to carry out the above procedure during the night?
3. Has someone been nominated to call the roll at the agreed assembly points outside the hotel?

Staff Training Checks

General Points for All Staff:

1. Have all your staff read and understood the fire instructions?
2. Do the staff know what action to take when a fire breaks out?
3. Are they familiar with the means of escape and able to direct guests to the escape routes?
4. Have they tried out all the escape routes?
5. Do they know how to operate the fire alarm and fire fighting equipment provided?
6. Do they understand the importance of closing doors to check spread of fire and smoke?
7. Do they know where to assemble after evacuating the building?
8. Have they been instructed to report any potential fire hazards such as faulty wiring or heaters?

Front Office Staff

1. Do all office staff know how to operate telephone switchboard and how to call the Fire Brigade immediately in case of a fire?
2. Have they been instructed to alert you or your deputy, all guests and staff, in the event of fire?
3. Have the front office night staff been instructed to carry out the above procedure at night?

Housekeeping Staff

1. Have the housekeeping personnel been instructed to keep bedroom, corridors, and other rooms free of waste and rubbish and

to ensure that such material is placed in the receptacles provided?

2. Have they been made aware of the dangers of smoking and been instructed to take particular care in places where combustible goods such as bedding and linen are stored?
3. Have they been instructed to report any potential fire hazards in bedrooms or other working areas e.g. faulty heaters?
4. When working in the pressing room, have they been made aware that electric irons or similar apparatus if left on can start fire?

Food Preparation and Cookery Staff

1. Do the kitchen staff know how they must keep the kitchen free of waste and rubbish and ensure that such material is placed in the receptacles provided?
2. Have they been instructed to keep ovens, cooker hoods, and other places where deposits of fat are likely to form clean?
3. Do they know that frying operation needs to be kept under constant surveillance?
4. Do they know how to extinguish a 'fat' fire with the equipment provided?
5. Do they know how to use a fire blanket in the event of clothes catching fire?
6. Have they been instructed to report any potential fire hazards in the kitchen e.g. faulty wiring or cooking equipment?

Food Server Staff

1. Do food server staff know that they must keep the service areas free of waste and rubbish and ensure that such material is placed in the receptacles provided?
2. Do they know where the fire extinguishing apparatus is in the food service areas?
3. Do they know how to operate the equipment which has been provided?
4. Are they aware of the dangers of smoking and, after service areas have been vacated, do they check to ensure that no cigarettes are still smouldering?
5. Have they been instructed to report any potential fire hazards in the service areas e.g. faulty electrical wiring and heating equipment?
6. Are they familiar with the fire hazards of flamed dishes?

Maintenance and Building Checks

1. Is wiring periodically inspected and tested in accordance with regulations by a qualified electrician?
2. Are outside contractors made familiar with the hotel's fire safety arrangements?
3. Are persons carrying out maintenance and repair work kept under surveillance and in the case of blow lamps, cutting and welding equipment, and flammable liquids are they taking manager's permission before using these?
4. If the hotel has its own workshop, are combustible materials properly stored and is all waste material regularly gathered up and placed in the receptacles provided?
5. If there has been re-arrangement of the premises, or new equipment been introduced, does the manager check that no new fire hazards have been introduced?
6. Is all fire and smoke-stop doors and doors on escape routes regularly maintained?
7. If the hotel has external escape stairs, are these kept in a safe condition?
8. If the hotel has a boiler room, is care taken that no combustible materials other than fuel for the boilers are kept in the room

and, in the case of solid fuel boilers, is the ash which is removed, dampened and placed in specially provided metal receptacles?

First Aid

Everyone should have a basic knowledge of first aid and be able to render it when necessary, but it should be borne in mind that it is only a temporary measure until a doctor arrives. In cases of serious accidents a doctor or ambulance must be called immediately and the reception desk should have a physicians list to handle emergencies. First aid boxes must be provided and staff must be shown the contents and where each box can be located.

All employees of the staff must have first aid training. In hotels, the housekeeper is normally qualified to give first aid, and in the event of accident or illness, it is normally he who could be summoned on the first instance to give help. The person giving first aid must be familiar with any emergency treatment necessary pending the arrival of the doctor. Where the patient cannot be moved, the room should be cleared of people so that those attending can have room to act. The housekeeper or management may need to reassure agitated guests, and whenever possible, efforts should be made to prevent the spread of news or gossip which could prove disturbing to others.

First aid materials and equipment must be kept in hotels and especially in large ones, it is wise to have a number of boxes scattered throughout the building. These may be kept in:

1. Kitchen
2. Housekeeper's office
3. Reception areas etc.

The first aid box should contain:

1. Bandages
   a. ½, 1 and 2 inch roller bandages
   b. Triangular bandages
   c. Cotton wool and boracic tint
   d. Adhesive waterproof dressing
   e. Towel and sterilized gauze
2. Creams etc.
   a. Antiseptic creams (*i.e.*, salron, hibitane etc.)
   b. Bicarbonate of soda
   c. Disinfectant *i.e.*, Dettol, Savlon, etc.
   d. Acriflavine or other cream
   e. Anthisan cream
3. Other Equipments:
   a. Tweezers
   b. Scissors
   c. Safety pins
   d. Clinical Thermometer
   e. Medicine glass
   f. Pen torch
4. Miscellaneous Items:
   Other items may be needed for nursing purposes, and these are best kept by the housekeepr:
   a. Bed pan and urine bottle
   b. Feeding cup
   c. Portable bed table
   d. Polyphone or rubber sheeting
   e. Bedsheets or other linen

Treatment Guidelines

General Sickness

The housekeeper should endeavour to make the patient comfortable and if necessary call a doctor. In the case of certain diseases which are highly infectious and dangerous, the doctor is requested to notify the medical health officer. Close cooperation with the local health authorities is important especially where rooms have to be fumigated following illnesses.

Bleeding

Direct pressure by either the fingers or hand on an open, clean wound will help control the bleeding. Apply a sterile dressing or pad and bandage firmly. Do not apply a tourniquet. If the bleeding is not controlled increase pressure with the hand and apply more pads.

It may be caused by rupture, or cutting of veins, arteries or capillaries. In such cases:

1. Clean wounded area and remove foreign material
2. Cover with antiseptic dressing
3. Where profuse bleeding occurs, pressure should be applied with a pad bandage above the wound in the case of venous bleeding. Arterial ruptures are characterized by a jerky flow of blood and a tourniquet (released every 15 minutes) or pressure applied to the nearest pressure point should be used. An ambulance or doctor should be summoned immediately.

Artificial respiration or resuscitation

If a person has ceased to breathe, immediately lay him on his back. Clear the airway by tilting the head and chin backwards away from the chest. Make sure there is no obstruction by the tongue or foreign matter. Open your mouth, take a deep breath, pinch the casualty's nostrils together, then seal his or her mouth with your lips, keeping the head back all the time, and blow into the lungs until the chest rises. Remove your mouth and watch the chest deflate. Give the first four inflations as rapidly as possible, then repeat this operation as long as is necessary. Remember, time saves live.

There are two methods of artificial respirations:

1. Mouth to mouth or 'kiss of life'
2. Pumping Method

Nose Bleeding

Allow blood to drip into a basin and apply cold pack to the nose or back of the neck. Do not blow nose until wound has had time heal. If bleeding continues send for a doctor.

Bruising

Severe bruising should be informed to a doctor as soon as possible.

Burns and Scalds

If possible, immerse the burn or scald in cold water to alleviate the pain. Do not remove any burnt clothing. Do not apply any oils or ointments, and do not break any blisters. The burnt area should be covered with a dry sterile dressing or some clean fabric. Patients with severe burns should be taken to a hospital or doctor without delay.

Minor burns

Apply a burn cream like Burnol.

More serious burns

Cover affected part with a dry sterile dressing to exclude air. Do not apply antiseptics. Patients with extensive burns should be sent to hospital immediately.

Clothes on Fire

Smother flames – wrap the person in a blanket, coat, rug etc. If burns are serious, apply dry sterile dressing and send to hospital.

Concussion

(Caused by a blow on the head) – Call a doctor immediately.

Convulsions

Keep patient warm and send for doctor.

Diabetes

Where insulin shock occurs, as a result of insufficient food to balance the insulin, the patient should be given sugar or chocolate, and doctor called where this has no appreciable effect.

Fainting

Lay the patient down and raise the lower limbs. Loosen tight clothing and ensure fresh air by not allowing people to crowd around the casualty.

Massage legs with an upward motion and encourage the patient, when able to take a cup of hot sweet tea.

Fractures

Move the patient as little as possible – immobilize and support the injured part. Call a doctor or an ambulance.

Heart Attack

On no account move the patient. Keep him warm. Clear the room and send for doctor urgently.

Foreign Matter in the Eye

Do not rub the eye. Rinse eye with eye-bath and warm water. Alternatively steady patient and with good illumination seek out foreign body and remove with the rolled corner of a clean handkerchief. If foreign matter has become embedded, do not attempt to remove. Cover eye with a soft pad bandage and take to doctor or hospital.

Lifting the upper lid over the lower lid will often bring the foreign body on to the lower lid from where it can be removed. Blowing the nose will help the eyes to water and wash the object out of the eye. Never rub the eye or use tweezers. If the object is clearly visible, a moistened piece of soft paper can be used to remove it. If the object is embedded in the eyeball, leave it for a doctor to remove.

Shock

A person in shock is pale, and the skin usually cold and clammy. The pulse is fast and breathing quick and irregular. The patient should be laid down with head low and legs raised slightly, and covered with a blanket or clothing to keep him warm. No stimulants should be given. Offer hot strong sweet tea on recovery. Keep the patient quiet. Clear room of unnecessary people.

Electric Shock

If the patient is still in contact with electrical equipment, switch off the electrical supply at once. If this is not possible, do not touch him unless protected by rubber gloves or rubber soles on the shoes.

The Coma Position

This is sometimes called the 'recovery position'. If a patient is unconscious turn him on his side in a 'climbing' position (one leg slightly bent), so that if he should vomit he will not choke. Dentures should be removed, and tight clothing loosened.

Choking

This is usually caused by food or some other foreign body obstructing the windpipe. This can be alleviated by getting the patient to bend over and then, with the flat of the hand, thumping him between the shoulder blades. A small child can be held upside down and thumped on the back. If this does not help, tickle the back of the throat with the fingertips and try and make the patient vomit or cough. If neither method helps, get medical assistance immediately.

Poisons

If the patient is unconscious, do not attempt to treat except with artificial respiration. Casualties of corrosive poisons such as acids, if they are conscious, should be given milk to drink. With non-corrosive poisons, including sleeping pills or narcotics, the patient should be made to vomit by touching the back of the throat with the fingertips, or by giving two tablespoonfuls of salt in warm water to drink. Call the doctor immediately.

Accidents Prevention

Under the office, shops and establishment Act minimum standards of safety and welfare have been made obligatory in premises used as offices, shops etc. and this includes catering establishments. In addition, according to statutory law, all employers have a common law. It is their duty to take reasonable care and precautions to prevent any likely harm or injury to staff, residents or guests.

The genuine accident is really very rare; most result from oversight or carelessness. It will never be possible to eliminate accidents completely but if the management takes accident prevention seriously and is aware of the possible hazards then the organization may become a safer place to to work in.

Frayed carpets, torn or badly worn linen, projecting nails, loose floorboards and highly polished floors all bring about falls. Any danger spots such as these should be noted and reported to the management.

Visitors are always unaware of potential hazards such as an unexpected step up or down, swing doors that fly open violently and steep stairs. When a lift is installed in the building, visitors should always be escorted to the required floor by a messenger or by a hotel employee.

Deliveries of stationery and office requisites should not be left lying around the reception to trip the visitor. These should be stacked neatly out of the way until a messenger or porter arrives to remove them. The porter or messenger should not be allowed to carry awkward or extremely heavy parcels as this in itself may bring about an accident.

A safe step ladder should always be used to reach high shelves. Heavy books, box files and ledgers that are balanced precariously on a shelf may fall at the slightest vibration so they need to be stored very securely. When filing cabinets are overloaded in the top drawers, or when more than one drawer is opened at a time then they may topple forward with very nasty consequences.

A great many mishaps are caused by 'bumping' into someone. Personnel become absorbed in a report or some important papers while walking across the reception area. They may push open glass doors without looking to see if someone is on the other side and a person struck by a glass door could suffer serious facial injuries. There is not really very much a receptionist can do here except to draw attention to such a situation by displaying a warning notice or special warning posters.

Plenty of ashtrays should be provided and visitors be requested to use them if they smoke. Cigarettes left smouldering on the edges of tables or window sills are a fire hazard. Ash trays should not be emptied into a waste paper basket without ensuring that all cigarettes are thoroughly extinguished and waste paper baskets should not be placed too near to an electric fire or other heating appliances.

Fire precautions should be known to all personnel. (Details given in earlier chapter.)

Accident Prevention Precautions

1. Mats and rugs should be secure.
2. Carpets should be secure and tight, stair carpets in particular – any cuts and tears should be repaired.
3. Floors should be kept in good repair.
4. Gas, electric and open fires should have adequate guards.
5. Any low doorways, projectiles or unexpected steps should be clearly marked.
6. Dark corridors should be well lit.
7. All equipment should be well maintained.

Electrical cables, switches and plugs must be carefully maintained and not allowed to fall into disrepair. Plugs must be earthed and no sockets should be overloaded, electric machines such as duplicators should have a 'fail-safe' switch and electric fires must be guarded. The socket should be switched off and the plug removed when equipment is not in use.

It is the duty of the employer to consult representatives of the employees with a view to the making and maintenance of arrangements which will enable him and his employees to cooperate effectively in promoting and developing the health and safety of the employees at the workplace and in making sure that the measures are effective.

Every employee also has a duty while at work:

a. To take reasonable care for the health and safety of himself – and of other persons who may be affected by his acts or omissions at work.
b. As regards any duty or requirement imposed by his employer or any other person or under any of the relevant statutory provisions to cooperate with him so far as is necessary to enable that duty or requirement to be performed or complied with.

In other words, it is the employer's duty to provide and maintain a safe environment in which employees may work. It is the duty of the employees to take reasonable safety precautions and to cooperate with the management in making the organization's premises a safer and healthier place to work in.

The Accident Book

The accident book must be kept in every organization which employs more than ten persons. The receptionist should record all details of accidents which have occurred to employees whilst they were engaged in carrying out their normal daily duties.

Whenever an accident occurs, no matter how trivial, it should be recorded in the accident book. These books, in an approved form, can be obtained from the stationery office, and full details of the accident, such as the name and address of the person concerned, an account of the accident and names of any witnesses, should be entered whilst the details are fresh in mind.

The following instructions appear on the front covers of the Accident Book:

'The purpose of this Accident Book, which is the duty of the occupier to keep under the provision of Regulations, is to assist an injured person in giving notice of accident to his employer as required by regulations made under regulation ellipse. An entry in this book, if made as soon as practicable after the happening of the accident, will be sufficient notice of the accident for the purpose.'

The book must be kept at such place as to be readily accessible at all reasonable times to any injured employee or any *bona fide* person or by someone acting on his behalf.

Particulars of an accident may be entered herein either by the injured person himself or by someone acting on his behalf.

The accident book when filled up should be preserved for a period of three years after the date of the last entry.

Note: Every employer is required to take reasonable steps to investigate the circumstances of every accident recorded herein and, if there appears to him to be any discrepancy between the circumstances found by him and the entry made, he is required to record the circumstances so found.'

Safety Rules and Regulations

Safety rules and regulations should be used for all hotel establishments. These should be designed to encourage staff and others to take precautionary measures against accidents, and to give instruction in the event of an emergency. The staff must be told about the importance of safe working condition and following areas should be discussed.

1. General Behaviour

Management should take a serious view of staff and others who misbehave or who are involved in general horseplay or scuffles. Apart from interfering with the general conduct of houses within the hotel, such action may lead to accidents.

2. Hygiene Regulations

Hygiene Regulations and other legislation affecting those who handle foodstuffs should be explained. Clean working conditions are of vital importance. Slack attitudes can lead to insanitary conditions and thus expose food to contamination.

3. Working Condition

Staff should be informed of regulation governing hazardous working.

4. Condition of Building

Faulty services and weakened parts of the building structure should be reported to management immediately, so that repair work can proceed and so avoid endangering the safety of hotel users.

5. Security within the Hotels

Heads of the department and their staff must observe strict security within each department. This involves check to ensure that gas taps, water taps and equipment are switched off each night. Storerooms and clip boards should be locked outside normal working hours. Before the kitchen and other work areas are vacated each night, checks should be made to ensure that windows are properly secured and that the contents of waste bins and sacks do not present a fire hazard.

6. Unusual working hours

Regulation should cover the situation where individual employees may be required to undertake work at unusual times. Special measures should cover working and servicing boilers, ventilation equipment and undertaking other work away from the main areas of the hotel.

7. Reporting Accidents and First Aid

All accidents must be reported to management or the head of the department. Provision should be made for certain numbers of staff to give first aid treatment. Employees should be aware of the location of first aid boxes and the names of those personnel trained in giving first aid. Where outside medical help is required, staff must know how to summon a doctor or to contact a hospital. Under relevant acts, records of all accidents occurring in the hotel must be kept. Where employees are involved in serious accident, personal injury and other benefits may be claimed by the employees. Employees, in this situation, are required to furnish details of the accidents in order that claim be assessed through the department of social security.

8. Smoking and Refuse Disposal

Regulations should identify areas within the hotel where smoking is not permitted. These measures must be framed in accordance with hygiene regulations and also with fire hazards in mind. Ashtrays should be distributed generously throughout all guest areas and in those areas where staff are permitted to smoke.

Special precautions are necessary for rubbish disposal and care must be shown by staff when emptying ashtrays into bins containing inflammable rubbish. Lift shafts should be checked regularly to ensure that inflammable debris is not allowed to accumulate in the bottom well of the shaft. The regular cleaning operation of the shaft of a service hoist safeguards the outbreak of fire caused by the careless disposal of a cigarette butt.

9. The Shop and Establishments Act

The conditions of employment of some workers in the hotel and catering industry are affected by the Shop and Establishment Act of the concerned state, since a shop is defined in this Act as any premises on which a retail business is conducted. Workers falling within this category are those employed in cafes, restaurants, public houses, snack bars and any catering establishment where there is service to residents. The act deals with statutory holiday entitlement, maximum weekly hours of work, meal times, breaks for rest, Sunday work and holidays. Inspectors appointed by the local authorities pay visits to establishments to supervise the operation of the staff.

Legal Control On The Hotel Premises

There are many legal aspects which relate to the hotel premises. An outline is given below of important legal controls on hotel premises.

1. Hygiene

The Food and Drugs Act and the Food Hygiene (General) Regulations control the cleanliness of all establishments concerned with food preparation, and hotel kitchens must comply with these regulations. Prosecution for offences under either the regulations may lead to heavy penalties, and even to the enforced closure of the premises by the Prevention of Food Adulteration.

2. Fire

Fire, should it occur in a place where a substantial number of people gather, *i.e.*, a bar or a hotel, may have tragic consequences. These are heightened in a hotel, since many people sleep within one building. The Fire Precaution Regulation was passed in order to improve fire safety standards at premises frequented by the general public. Fire certificates are required for certain kinds of premises, including many hotels. These certificates are issued by the local fire authority. An inspection of the premises is carried out and a certificate is only issued where the local fire authority are satisfied that adequate precautions have been taken.

3. Working Conditions

Working conditions are regulated by two major acts, Shops and Establishment Act and the Health and Safety Regulations.

(a) The Shop and Establishment Act

The Act applies to office premises, shop premises and other premises where persons are employed under a contract of employment. Certain premises are excluded from the Act, e.g. small family businesses where only the immediate family are employed. Hence, a small family guest house or tea rooms may be excluded from the Act's operation. The term 'shop premises' covers a number of different premises, including premises from which retail trade or business is carried on. Hence, the Act would appear to cover restaurants, wine bars, etc.

All premises within the scope of the Act are required to be kept in a clean state. This covers all furniture and fittings, etc. on the premises. Neither dirt nor refuse must be allowed to accumulate, and all floors and stairs shall be cleaned at least once a week. The Act is directed towards the protection of the workforce rather than the consumer. The Act also relates to the facilities available at premises covered by the Act, e.g. sanitary conveniences, washing facilities, drinking water and seating facilities for staff.

Some of the provisions of the Act relate to the structure of the building, that all floors, stairs, steps, passages and gangways shall be of sound construction and properly maintained. Breach of the requirements set out in the Act is a criminal offence and may lead to prosecution.

(b) Health and Safety Regulations

This requirement is of much broader application. The Health and Safety applies to all places where persons are employed, and makes provisions for the health and safety of such employees. Employers have a general duty imposed by the

Act to safeguard in so far as is reasonably practicable the health, safety and welfare of their employees. Employees should also be given adequate training in safety precautions, etc. Employees are themselves under a duty to take reasonable care not to injure others in the course of their work. The Act is enforced by the Health and Safety Inspectorate, who has various powers, prohibition notices, etc. The Health and Safety Inspectorate may ultimately prosecute the party concerned in the courts and where a person is found guilty, substantial fines may be imposed.

Employees' Health

Regular health check should be encouraged. Hazards can occur as a result of:

1. Physical or mental illness
2. Alcohol and drugs
3. Physical disability

Mental instability is not always easy to establish in a new employee. However, as some tasks within the hotel are not suitable for those with this condition, references should be thoroughly examined and applicants carefully screened.

Alcohol and Drugs

Either of these causes can have serious effects upon the safety of the worker, his fellow-workers and guests. Physical and mental coordination can be affected and again management should be able to recognize the symptoms.

Physical Disability

This can prove hazardous with some forms of work. Physical disability need not bar an individual from employment in the hotel and catering industry, but the disability in individual cases should be considered in relation to the nature of the work to be performed. The relevant acts make recommendation that positions such as lift attendants, car park supervision and similar occupations should be assigned wherever possible to registered disabled persons. The term 'disablement' has wider connotation than loss of limb or the senses and tasks demanding physical agility or fine degree of physical tolerance may fall within the competence of many disabled persons.

Payment of sickness and injury benefits may not directly have an effect on accident reduction within a hotel, but as a part of much wider personnel management policy, this can have reassuring effects upon employees and in certain circumstances could contribute towards a more rapid recovery.

Health of Visitors

Health and safety of all lawful visitors is a common law duty. Laws relating to safety fire, food, hygiene, etc. affect the health and safety issues. In England, there are Acts such as the Occupiers Liability Act 1957, Health and Safety at Work Act 1994, and the Fire Precaution Act 1971 as well as Food Hygiene Regulations.

Essentially safety is a civic duty and negligence is a criminal offence. The implications for staff under the various Registration in India are that they should:

1. Understand the food hygience regulations and that it is their responsibility to act within the boundry of these regulations
2. Notify management of any major illness
3. Perform duties in any area concerned with the handling of food, in a hygienic manner
4. Make themselves familiar with all escape routes and fire exits in the building
5. Insure that fire exits remain clear and unblocked in any way
6. Participate in fire evacuation drills and practices
7. Take reasonable care for the health and safety of themselves and others, and insure that health and safety regulations are followed.

8. Report to heads of departments or duty managers any hazard which may cause injury or ill-health to customers and/or staff.
9. Do not interfere with or misuse anything provided in the interest of health, safety and welfare.
10. Cooperate with employees in order to carry out duties within context of the relevant Acts.

Discrimination

There are premises in various Acts against discrimination on grounds of colour, race, creed or sex. In England, there are the Sex Discrimination Act 1975 and the Race Relating Act 1976. As per Race Relating Act, it is an offence to discriminate on grounds of colour, race or national origins. It precludes advertisements for staff from particular countries on the rejection of a guest solely on the grounds of colour, race or national origins. The Act applies to hotels in the same way as it applies to any other section of the community. While a hotel proprietor may refuse to accept any person who is in an unfit state to be received, this does not permit the refusal to be on grounds of colour, race or creed. When refusing accommodation to any traveller, it is as well to remember that one does so only because there is no accommodation available as discussed earlier.

These Acts clearly define what to discriminate might mean. There must not be:

1. Direct Discrimination

For example, refusing service to customers of particular colour, race, creed or sex.

2. Indirect Discrimination

For example, denying consumer services by the imposition of injustifiable conditions or requirements which have colour, race, creed or sex implications.

3. Discriminating through Victimization

For example,

a. Refusal of provision – Refusal of admission on basis of ethnic origins or sex.
b. Omission of provision – providing services to ethnic customers that are markedly inferior to those available to the public in general or which may only be available at a premium price.

Staff Training

In addition to general training from the point of view of accident prevention, proper training is important. Work which involves the use of mechanical or electric equipment should not be undertaken by new workers until they are fully familiar with its working and can manipulate it safely and efficiently. Staff should be told of the hazards caused by overloading machinery and given advice on the cause of action to follow in the event of break down.

Employees should be instructed in the proper and safe handling of kitchen knives, cooking equipment, office machinery, safes, cleaning equipment, refrigeration equipment, cork and canister beer, carbon dioxide cylinders, central heating and ventilation equipment and all other hazardous machinery and fixtures.

Training programmes should include details of the procedure to be followed when breakdown occurs, it is important to avoid the situation. For example, where a room maid tries to clean the suction fan on a vacuum cleaner while it is still running. Staff should be taught to switch off the electricity supply and seek competent help. Proper training programme will greatly eliminate the rise of workers taking 'short cuts' in their work. The worker who has not been made aware of the reasons for holding and manipulating a boning knife in a particular way, for instance, can jeopardize his own and other people's safety.

Some tasks are more readily learnt than others. But habits are difficult to unlearn. Older employees may find it more difficult to unlearn and hence pose more serious accident risks.

Employees within the hotel should periodically follow a safety-training programme. This should include instructions in the use of fire fighting equipment and practice of fire drills. Furthermore, the importance of the use of protective clothing and non-slip footwear should be ensured, especially where potentially hazardous or dangerous tasks are being performed.

Conditions of Work

Conditions within the work environment affect the safety of staff. These fall broadly in two categories:

1. Staff motivation
2. Working condition and fatigue

The managerial or supervisory atmosphere affects work performance. Staff react against an unfair or prejudicial management and a supervisor who is vindictive towards members of staff may incur their anger and discontent. These feelings on the part of the staff and management alike make them more vulnerable to accidents. A waiter in the hotel restaurant after crossing words with the chef, is more likely to be slipshod in his service duties. He may even inadvertently spill food on a seated guest. A happy working environment which creates among the staff an interest, satisfaction and contentment contributes much, not only to improved job performance but also to a reduced accident rate.

Physical working conditions affect the manner in which we work. Legislation prescribes certain minimum standards of work comfort in the hotel situation. An ill-conceived kitchen layout can create similar annoyance to the chef if simple tasks cannot be performed except through considerable movement within the kitchen.

Other frustrations are common in hotel working situations and staff consequently become more prone to accidents. Where poor illumination is used to create a more intimate or sociable atmosphere in bars and restaurants, the visual clarity of staff may be impaired; more so when illumination or contrasts between kitchen and dining room causes staff to be continually involved in accommodating to well and poorly illuminated environments alternatively.

The smoky atmosphere of a bar may influence the efficiency, fatigue and accident proneness of the barman. Noise in the bar, handling a wide range of items (draught beers, bottled beers, cash and so on), talking to an ever-changing group of faces, feeling concern over the security of cash in the till, rowdyism and his own safety and well-being are all legitimate factors which could affect the barman's performance. Although these and/ or physical influences exist in all types of hotel work, wc may bc ablc to disrcgard thosc which do not overwhelmingly intrude into the work routine. However, where these external stimuli begin to overload the sense of sight, smell, touch, hearing, and so on, fatigue frequently occurs and makes the worker furthermore susceptible to making mistakes. A high noise level in a busy bar can cause fatigue to a barman.

The age of employees is also of some consequence. People generally require greater illumination levels as they become older, and their power of accommodation is affected. This could affect accident rates. On the other hand, a young person may be equally accident prone through his lack of skill and experience.

Boredom, like fatigue, affects work performance. This may have motivational implications.

External Influences

External environment influences can affect work performance quite substantially. The personnel management must play an important role in being sensitive to employees' domestic or personal circumstances. Illness at home or a family bereavement can have repercussions at work. A traffic summons or financial problems can cause a worker's concentration to wander during some delicate tasks. A chef can quite absentmindedly leave pot handles protruding over the edge of a stove, or forget to use a kitchen cloth when attempting to pick up a very hot cooking pot. There are number of other unsafe acts which could occur as an indirect result of external influences.

Part-V
Appendices

Some English-French Terms in Hospitality

A

Additional : Supplémentaire
After dinner speech : Discourse d' aprésdîner
Air Conditioner : Climatiseur
Appetite : Appétit
Appetizer : Apéritif (n.m.); Hors-d'oeuvre (n.m.)
Apple : Pommé
Appointment : Rendez-vous
Apron : Tablier
Armchair : Fauteuil
Authority : Autorité; Discipline

B

Balcony : Balcon
Bar Counter : Comptoir
Bed Sheet : Drap
Best : Le Meilleur
Bill : Addition
Bill Folder : Pique Note
Blender : Mélangeur
Booking : Réservation
Bottle : Bouteille
Bouquet : Bouquet (flowers); Fumet (wine)
Breakfast : Petite-déjeuner
Buffet : Buffet
Business : Commerce; Maison; Ėtablissement

C

Carpet : Tapis
Caviar Knife : Couteau à caviare
Ceiling : Plafond
Chair : Chaise
Champagne Cooler : Seau à frapper
Cigarette Lighter : Briquet
Cleanliness : Propreté

Cloak Room	:	Vestisire
Clock Room	:	Vestaire (Des dames)
Coffee Tray	:	Plateau à café
Cold and Hot Servory	:	Bain Marie
Comfortable	:	Confortable; al'aise, Àsonaise
Consommé Cup	:	Tasse à consommé
Cooking Range	:	Cuisiniére
Cover or Place Setting	:	Couvert
Crockery	:	Vaisselle
Curtain	:	Rideau
Customer	:	Client (Cliente)
D		
Day	:	Jour (n.m.); Journée(f.)
Description	:	Description
Dinner	:	Dîner
Direction	:	Direction; Avis
Director	:	Directuer (n.m.); Directrice (f.)
Dish of the Day	:	Plat Du Jour
Duster	:	Torchon
E		
Elevator	:	Ascenseur
Escalator	:	Escalateur
Establishment	:	Établissement (n.m.); Maison (f.)
Etiquette	:	Protocole (n.m.); Etiquette (f.)
F		
Fan	:	Evantail
Floor	:	Étage
G		
Gentle lady	:	Madâm/Madamoiselle
Gentleman	:	Monsieur
Gift	:	Cadeau
Good Health	:	Àvotre santé
Guest	:	Invité (n.m.); Invitée (f.)
H		
Hostess Desk	:	Pupitre (D' Hôtesse
I		
Infusion	:	Tisane (n.f.); Infusion (f.)
Introduction	:	Présentation

K

Kitchen	:	Chambra à cuisine
Kitchen Dress	:	Tenne de cuisine

L

Linen	:	Linge
Lunch	:	Déjeuner

M

Management	:	Direction
Meeting	:	Rencontre (Réunion)
Morning Dress	:	Tenue de ville

N

News	:	Nourlles
Next	:	Proclain
Night	:	Nuite
Notice	:	Avis

O

Occupation	:	Emploi (n.m.); Situation (f.)

P

Pantry	:	Garde Manger
Plate	:	Assiette
Please	:	S'il vous plaît (interj.); S'il te plait
Practical	:	Practique

Q

Quality	:	Qualité
Quantity	:	Quantité
Question	:	Question
Quick	:	Rapide

R

Radio	:	Radio
Refrigerator	:	Frigo
Regulation	:	Réglement
Reservation	:	Réservation

S

Side Board	:	Buffet, Étagère
Silver Room	:	Pièce d' Argenterie
Slip Cloth	:	Napperon
Sofa	:	Sofa

T

To accompany : Accompagner

To clean : Nettoyer

To clear : Débarrasser

To come again/to come back : Revenir

To come in : Entrer

To come in again : Rentrer

To come out : Sortir

To come out again : Ressortier

Trolley : Table roulante

U

Uniform (n.) : Uniformé

Useful (ad.) : Utilé

V

Vacant : Libre (adj.); Inoccupé

Various : Divers (adj.); Variés

W

Waiter : Garcon

Waiter's Cloth : Nappe de Garçon

Matter in Hoteliering

Here is everything you wanted to know about the hotel industry. Jagmohan Negi, who has been associated with this industry for three decades, outlines all the aspects of hotel management, based on his own experience and interaction with the industry people. Since hoteliering is a service-oriented industry, the book too places a strong emphasis on management of people and takes into account human relations, the nationality factor and cultural differences. How to deal with guests, how to win their trust, is the crux of the book. Hotel management encompasses many areas– from designing to budgeting. The book serves to provide a basic framework to hotel management...

Don't expect a thorough analysis. The author makes a submission in the beginning that it is meant to serve as an outline, from which students will get a broad idea. Based on this, they will definitely be required to do more in-depth study of various aspects like house-keeping, food purchasing, etc.

Legal issues have been rightly given great emphasis in each and every department. After all, law comes in at every stage –be it at the stage of acquisition of land, environment clearance, construction, publicity, food poisoning, alcohol licence, etc. Discussing consumer protection, the author states how the earlier principle of caveat emptor has been largely discarded and replaced by provisions to the effect that it is illegal to make false statements about services, accommodation and facilities. If such statements are made knowingly or recklessly.

But one serious issue that has embroiled many hotels in a legal mess, as one would say, has been brushed aside. Environmental concerns and local unrest should have been given due emphasis, and every problem should have been mentioned– receding water-level, depletion of green cover, garbage management, cultural alienation and villagers' rights to resources. Instead, a pledge of the American Hotel and Motel Association's Committee for a Quality Environment has been thought to be sufficient: "Whenever I plan new facilities, I must acknowledge my responsibility to give approval and direction to architects and building contractors that will minimise contribution to pollution and visual blight. This is an obligation to my neighbours as well as to future progress."

A major area of concern for hoteliers is the safety and security of guests. Not only are the guests to be protected against theft, fire, etc, but also against possible occurrences of indecent behaviour of a staffer or a trespasser. A series of dos' and don'ts have been prescribed, along with new modes of security. The author could have taken up examples of leading hotels in the country to show how each hotel has evolved its own unique security set-up, and projects it as its USP. Thus, a leading hotel in the capital now claims the security of it's women guests as its USP.

A major clientele of large hotel chains the world over is now the business traveller. Arranging conferences has now emerged as a major revenue earner for hotels. Management of conferences is another area that deserves reading.

One would take small services like arrangement of flowers, decoration of biscuits, presence of attractive shampoos and hot water, for granted. But no one cares to give a thought to the hierarchy, or how many people are involved in these seemingly small services. The book describes all these departments, along with charts to show how exactly is every department supposed to function.

In every department, it is the management aspect (and in some departments even the PR aspect), rather than the technical aspect that is stressed.

It' is not necessary, the author avers, that a good cook will necessarily make a good chef. It is his management abilities that will make him successful at his work

The author says he was assisted by industry people in writing this book. Interviews and discussions with them brought to the fore several issues. But he could have added quotes from those in the industry, to make the book more interactive. Instances of libel cases could have been included to add gist to a textbook style description.

Appendix-C

Hotel Management Computerized System

The application of computer in hospitality management requires in-depth knowledge, hoteliering experience and dedication to give you total support. The system is developed with consultancy organization promoted by hoteliers of hospitality industry to fulfill the need of hotel industry for specialist organizations. In this system one get total support from people who understand the hotel business and from people who share your concerns. The system support package typically includes the following:

1. Property survey
2. Project plan
3. Site specifications
4. System installation
5. Procedure/form design
6. Staff training
7. Management education
8. Implementation
9. System audit

The system support can be optionally extend to:

1. Operations consultancy
2. Operation training particularly in front office, food & beverage and kitchen areas
3. Organizational structure, design and personal audit

Figure 'A' indicates an integrated hotel management system based on computerized technology.

Main Features:

1. **Integrated System:** Different modules for both front office and back office are designed to draw information from the same pool of data. There is no need for messy methods of transferring data from one file to another
2. **Comprehensive System:** The system covers all possible areas in the hotel, which can benefit from computerization. It even focuses on areas like food & beverage, cost control, banquets and personnel management. Computerized system integrated the hotel system with other office automation requirements.
3. **Based on Current Technology:** The computerized system gives you the State-of-the-Art in technology, not obsolete equipment.
4. **A Friendly System:** The system has been designed by computer professional who are dedicated to software work for the service industry as well as hotel managers who understand the need for having a simple, easy-to-use system.
5. **A Modular System:** Both the hardware and software are based on a modular design so that the hotel can add applications as and when required. The initial investment to get you started on computerized system can be extremely low.
6. **A extremely Reliable System:** The computerized system should be widely tested for one full year at a large city convention hotel under the most difficult environments, before release.
7. **A Cost Competitive System:** The computerized system can be cost competitively configured with an optional

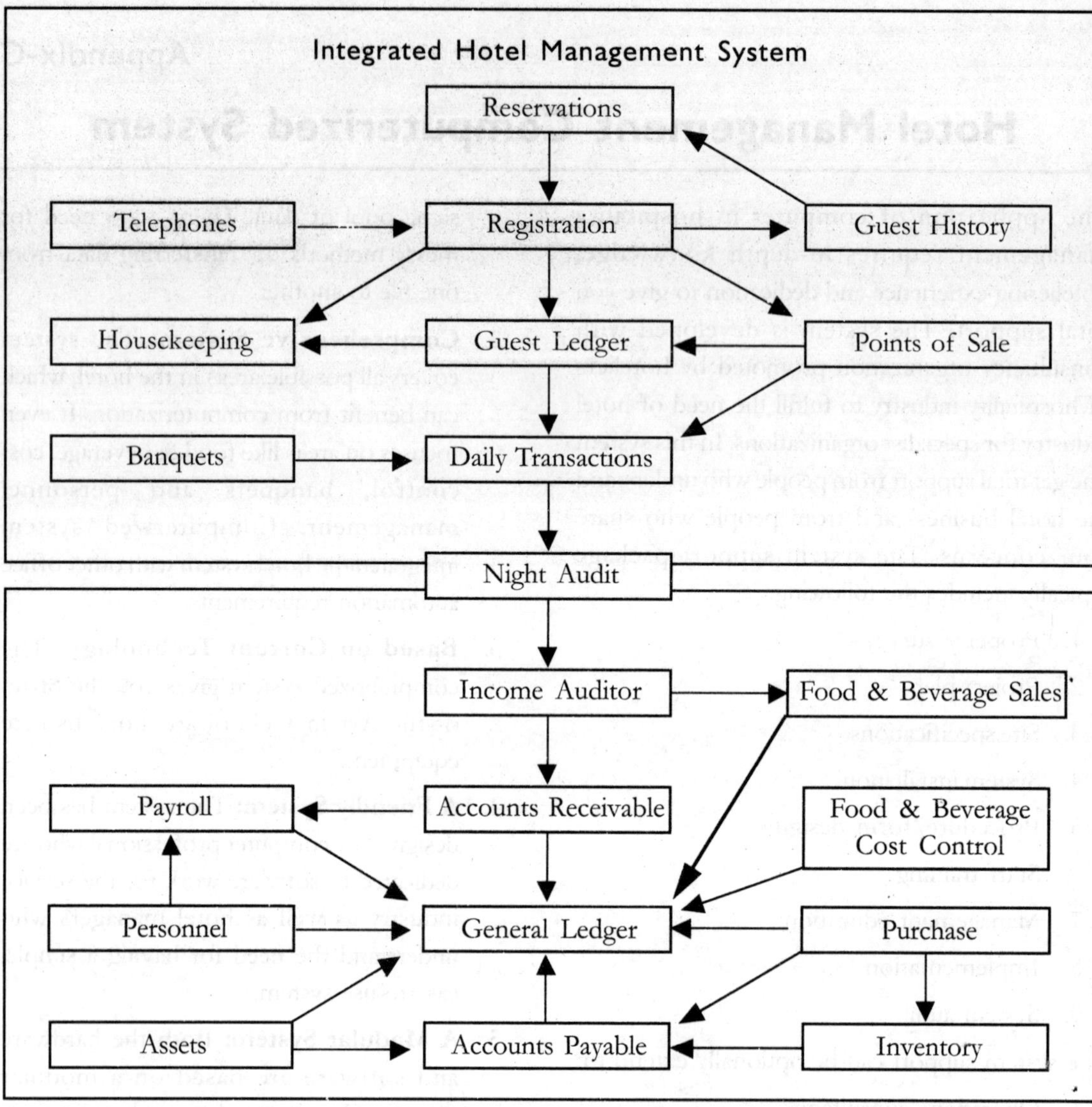

Fig. A: Flow chart of computerized integrated hotel management system

dual system for any hotel from 50 rooms from to 600 rooms.

1. **Front Office System:** An integrated real time system that cater to reservations, registration, guest billing, restaurant billing, guest history, housekeeping, telephones, room service, night audit, income auditing and sales analysis.
2. **Financial Accounting System:** Consists of modules for general ledger, accounts receivables, accounts payables, fixed asset accounting and other finance support systems.
3. **Budgetary Control System:** Information required for management control and incorporate cost center analysis and flexible budgeting.

Figure 'B' gives an overview of computerized hotel management system.

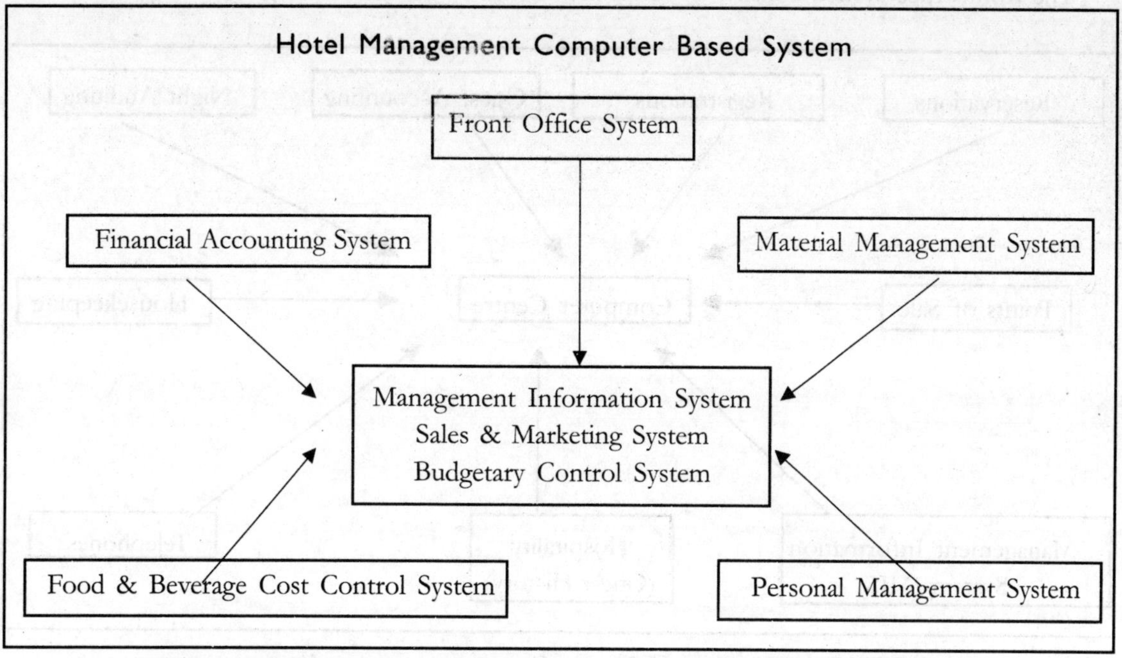

Fig. B: Flow chart of computerized hotel management system

4. **Material Management System:** Combination of on-line data entry/inquiry and batch processing software that meets the requirements of stores accounting, purchase management, menu pricing, kitchen materials requisition and ordering. A system, which provides integration of stores accounting, purchase management and inventory control.
5. **Personnel Management System:** Information requirements necessary for effective manpower administration, planning and control.
6. **Food & Beverage Cost Control System:** Information that allows the comparison of food & beverage cost against standards that reflect the actual consumption, menu items and sales mix. A system that tells you exactly where the variance is, so that specific, timely action is possible.
7. **Management Information System:** A decision support system giving timely, relevant information required for management planning, analysis and control.

In the following pages, these systems are described in greater details.

Reservations

The reservation system handles all reservations and related activities within a hotel. This sub-system allows for individual (F.I.T.), tour group, conference and miscellaneous group booking to be made for any date in the future. Reservations can be retrieved at any time by guest name, arrival date, and group Id or reservation number. The original reservation can be displayed, updated or cancelled. Room availability is checked for every reservation request, depending on room type and number of rooms requested.

Front Office System

The front office system consists of integrated software sub-systems as given in Figure 'C'.

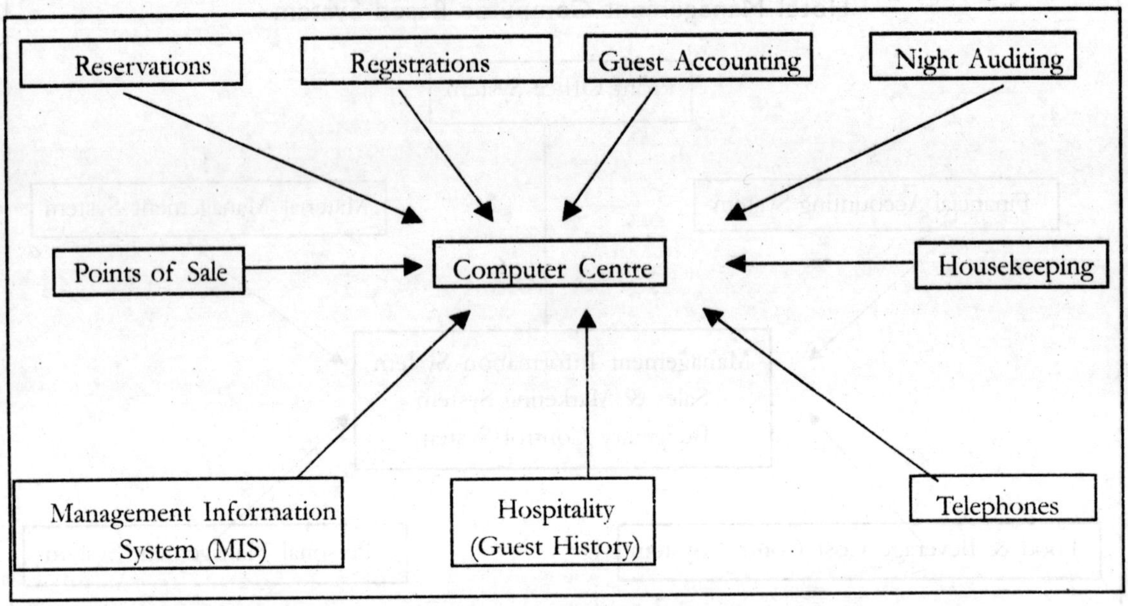

Fig. C: The computerized front office integrated software system

Reservation Handling Function-Main Features

1. Create a reservation (up to a maximum of 700 days in the future) for individuals, groups, conferences and crews
2. Modify an existing reservation
3. Cancel an existing reservation
4. Re-activate a cancelled reservation
5. Display all details about an existing reservation
6. Auto transfer of guest details from guest history onto reservation
7. Auto calculation of room rate while creating a reservation, based on room type, company Id, rate code (*i.e.*, rack rate/discounted/special), number of persons and package code
8. On-line update of rooms availability while creating/modifying/canceling and re-activating a reservation
9. Display of overall room availability, for a given date
10. Display of room availability for a given room type (up to a maximum of 15 room types)
11. On-line inquiry for expected arrivals on a given date
12. Post deposits received/refunded/commission paid to travel agents to a reservation
13. Locate a reservation by specifying either name/arrival date/group Id/reservation number
14. Create special accounts for travel agents/tour operators/commercial houses/airlines/ embassies from whom regular business expected.

Reports generated

1. Daily reservation activity report
2. Future room availability report
3. Future movement forecast report
4. Group/conference report by date
5. Arrival reports
6. Group arrival reports
7. Expected VIP arrivals
8. Guest special service requirements for arrivals.

Registrations

The registration system in an integral part of the reservation system. Guest details once keyed in at the time of reservation have not to be keyed in again upon the guest's arrival. The data is automatically transferred from the reservation to the registration system. It provides for smooth and accurate check in, pre-registration, guest room assignment and on-line room status inquiry facilitates faster check-in, giving the staff more time to concentrate on guest service thereby making happier clients. Very powerful features for inquiry on in-house guest information are available.

Registration Handling Functions-Main Features

1. Pre-register reserved guests/groups, by assigning rooms prior to their arrival – today's arrivals
2. Print registration cards with guest details already filed in
3. Check-in guests with reservation
4. Check-in walk-in guests (without reservations)
5. Display the status of rooms by specifying the status for which inquiry is to be made; *i.e.*, AVL/OCP/OOO/COUNT etc.
6. Modify in-house guest information
7. Inquire about in-house guests by giving name/room number/group Id/guest class/company Id/room type/rate code, etc.
8. Move guest to a new room. The bills belonging to the guest will automatically get transferred to the new room.

Reports generated

1. In-house guest list (alphabetically)
2. In-house guest list (room number-wise)
3. Departure reports (alphabetically)
4. Departure reports (room number-wise)
5. Expected departure list
6. In-house VIP report
7. No-show/walk-ins report
8. Credit limit check report
9. In-house complimentary & staff rooms report.

Guest Accounting

The guest accounting system provides the accurate, on-line posting of guest charges and settlement of guest accounts. Each guest account can be displayed, printed or settled at any time. Speedy group check-out is possible with the group auto-printing, settlement and check-out features.

Features

1. Post charges to individual guest bills
2. Modify charges posted to guest bills
3. Establish multiple bills for an individual guest
4. Display bills
5. Print bills
6. Post settlements to guest bills. Multiple settlements are allowed for the same bill
7. Check-out guest

8. Automatic room and tax charges posting
9. Posting of non-resident charges, when hotel facilities are used by non-resident guests
10. Facility to close a guest's accounts.

Reports generated

1. Cashier's shift summary
2. Shift transactions list; a list of all transactions for a particular account code
3. Credit limit check report
4. A/R collection report; payments taken on behalf of the credit department.

Housekeeping

The housekeeping system allows for a constant update of room status. The precise communication link between housekeeping and the front desk contributes to a smooth, error-free handling of check-ins and faster turn around of rooms.

Features

1. Inquiry on room status by room type, floor, bed type
2. Facility to change status of a checked-out-room to an available room
3. Rom discrepancy check.

Banquet

The banquet system is an unique system that caters to banquet reservations. The extensive enquiry capability of the banquet system gives information on booking positions for any particular hall, function, day or time. Billing and posting of transactions to the sales ledger is also handled by this module.

Night Auditing

The night audit is the most important function in the daily operation of the hotel. The night audit system posts room tariff automatically, prints the final trial balance, which reflects the entire day's sales and collection and close the day's business. A comprehensive audit trial and accounting reports help reconcile all transactions in a short span of time.

Features

1. Automatic room charges, service charges, tax and daily accounts posting
2. Conforms to tax/audit regulations
3. Ability to view cashiers transactions by shift, cashier Id, account Id
4. Automatic change date procedures
5. Sorting of transactions by system name, account date.

Reports generated

1. Room rate variance report
2. Guest outstanding balance report
3. Guest accounting journal list
4. Guest accounting summary
5. Hotel trial balance
6. Account code-wise postings list
7. Room bill posting today
8. Restaurant sales summary.

Telephone Operator

The telephone operator system enables operators to have easy access to information of all in-house guests, expected arrivals and departures. Guest inquiries by name and room number facilitate impressive, personalized service. Wake-call requests can be handled quickly and efficiently. An optional interface with the EPABX system allows for automatic posting of telephone charges to guest folios.

Features

1. Guest look-up by room or name for in-house, today's expected arrivals and departures.
2. In-house guest wake-up call insert/delete/inquiry.

Guest History

The guest history system provides for a personal, thoughtful and efficient guest service and hospitality. Personal histories on each individual guest are compiled, maintained and updated automatically after check-out. This information id available for review by the front office staff.

Features

1. Guests and group history is automatically updated after check-out of the guest
2. Powerful inquiry and display functions of guest and group history
3. Automatic transfer of information from guest history to reservations
4. Provision for selective addition/deletion of guest history records.

Reports generated

1. Mailing list by selected criteria
2. Birthday list
3. Anniversary list
4. List by club.

Management Information System

The management information system provides statistical information to the management to assist in decision making and control. The timely accurate information provides the ability to direct manpower efforts towards quality service, higher occupancy and increased revenues. Comparison of budgets with actual by responsibility centers supports management center systems. Automatic MIS data collection provides you a comprehensive business and sales analysis. The timely accurate information provided ensure increased revenues, higher occupancy and cost savings.

Features

1. Automatic MIS data collection, during the night audit
2. Comparison of budget with actual, highlighting variances.

Reports generated

1. Room occupancy analysis
2. Hotel daily sales report
3. Monthly source of booking analysis
4. Monthly nationality analysis
5. Geographical analysis report
6. Food & Beverage sales analysis report
7. Group materialization report
8. Company materialization report.

Point of Sale System

The POS system is a comprehensive system for handling all aspects of restaurant accounting. The system allows for entering orders received from the restaurant, printing of guest checks, posting settlements, printing sales analysis report amongst other functions. The point-of sale system is designed for the complete overtaking and cashiering functions at any outlet. In-house guest information is available to the cashier, enabling personalized attention as well as timely, accurate posting to the guest ledger. The system incorporates all the functions of a cash register and is particularly effective in room service.

POS Handling Functions–Main Features

1. Post charges to tables
2. Modify charges posted to tables
3. Print guest checks
4. Settle guest checks
5. Cancel guest checks when properly authorized
6. Display tables with outstanding bills
7. Facility to move the guest to a new table
8. Facility to account separately for staff and house entertainment charges.

Reports generated

1. Cashier's shift summary.
2. Detailed transactions list, by shift no., account code, etc.

3. Covers analysis
4. Food & Beverage sales analysis
5. Chance sheet by bill no. F&B types and settlement method
6. Outstanding charges report
7. Missing KOT's report.

Back Office System

Material Management System (MMS)

The entire material management functions-requirements planning, purchase, receipt, stock accounting, issue can be viewed as an integrated activity and provide information for effecting decision making a swell as book-keeping. In the purchase management system it is envisaged that the feedback of the historical consumption information as well as current stock levels will assist in purchase decisions while the purchase order/follow up system will ensure scheduled deliveries. The issue, receipt, stores accounting and pricing functions are covered in the inventory control and stores accounting system.

The system will be implemented for all types of stores, food & beverage, engineering, linen, operating supplies items.

Subsystems

1. Inventory control and stores accounting system
2. Purchase management system.

Features

1. Purchase price/consumption trend analysis automatically maintained
2. Vendor history/appraisal automatically maintained
3. Preparation of purchase orders and automatic reminder for follow-up action
4. On-line entry of issues and receipts
5. Inquiry of current stock level
6. Inventory ABC analysis
7. Automatic weighed average stores pricing of stock and issues
8. Perishable stock analysis
9. Order to be placed warning reminders automatically generated.

Benefits

1. Better ordering and purchase decisions, reduces purchases
2. Effective follow-up of purchase orders pending; timely supplies
3. Proper inventory control particularly for perishable/limited shelf life items
4. Assists administration of purchase and sales department
5. Provides automatic stock counting; allows spot stock taking; reducing reconciliation problems and pilferage.
6. Provides data for G/L and departmental costing.

Financial Accounting Systems

Under this category fall the basic accounting functions in the hotel. Most important is the general ledger system where all expenses and revenues are booked and trial balance and monthly P&L statements are prepared. The posting of expenses also provides the necessary input of budgetary control system.

Account receivables and account payables are subsets of the general ledger but deserve special mention due to their complexity.

Various other systems to facilitate book-keeping and reconciliation are also necessary as part of the system.

Information required for basic accounting functions and financial management in a hotel are incorporated in a comprehensive set of integrated modules.

Subsystems

1. Accounts receivable system
2. Accounts payable system
3. Payroll with general ledger system
4. Cheque reconciliation system.

Features

1. All books of accounts are computer generated
2. All expenses and revenue transactions are entered into the system
3. Extensive audit aids and reconciliation statements prepared.

Benefits

1. Significant aid to accounts administration and audit/reconciliation
2. Monthly trial balance and P&L prepared by the 5th of each months
3. Timely, updated, accurate financial information
4. Faster collections and better information of account receivables
5. Forecasts of cash flows for better cash management
6. Comprehensive audit trials and auto reconciliation
7. Faster statement of accounts for debtors/creditors
8. Comparison of budgeted and actual revenue/expenditure
9. Comparison of historical information for trend.

Budgetary Control System (BCS)

A well management control system is the key to control of cost and performance appraisal. A MCS has to be supported by an appropriate budgetary control and information system. The system solution requires:

1. Definition of responsibility centers; as revenue centers, cost centers and profit centers
2. Collection of costs and revenues by account heads. The account head must be classified into:
   a. Variable costs
   b. Semi-variable costs
   c. Fixed costs
3. Setting of budgets with a flexible budgeting system to take into account variable costs in relation to their dependent relationships
4. Comparison of budgets and actual with proper variance analysis and exceptional reporting.

The design concept provides for posting all revenues and expenses by account heads and responsibility centers (may be coincident with department) and as far as possible once only (by integrating w˙h other systems).

Subsystems

1. Departmental budgetary control system

Features

1. Flexible budgeting so that expense budget relates to actual revenues and volumes
2. Complete departmental costing including overhead expenses
3. Maximum utilization of data from other systems- efficient data usage
4. Interaction with F.O. systems, material management and financial systems.

Benefits

1. Objective performance appraisal
2. Timely, effective, specific control measures
3. Better budgeting and forecasting.

Food & Beverage Cost Control System

The F&B cost control system establishes standards for the raw material usage by exploding the recipes for all prepared food items. Thus, it is possible to know those raw materials where usage is exceptionally high. Tight F&B cost control can be exercised because not only the correct cost figure for day, for the given sales mix is calculated, but also why the variance has arisen. Such F&B cost control is not possible at all in the manual systems.

The system will be implemented for all types of stores, food & beverage, engineering, linen, operat ng supplies items.

Subsystems

1. F&B cost control system
2. F&B menu costing system

Features

1. Establishes standards for raw material usage through recipe explosion
2. Highlights raw materials where variance is exceptionally high
3. Automatic pickup of issues and costing from MMS
4. Automatic pickup of sales detail from Point-of-sale system
5. Automatic pickup of issues and pricing of MMS
6. If POS system is in use, automatic pickup of all menu sales from front office systems
7. Automatic calculation of standard material usage from recepies.

Benefits

1. Effective control of F&B material usage
2. Accurate information of F&B price trends and menu costs.

Personnel Management System

The most asset in a hotel is its people. The personnel management system integrates the requirements for effective career planning, personnel administration and payroll.

The personnel management system caters to the requirements of personnel administration, planning and payroll. It is envisaged that a personnel history for all employees would be maintained that would be invaluable for getting information regarding promotions, career planning as well as personalized care from the management.

Subsystems

1. Payroll systems
2. Personnel history system.

Features

1. Complete data from personnel files on computer to prepare a variety of reports
2. Payroll preparation including printing of pay-slips, cheuqes, provident fund, gratuity, income tax, and statements.

Benefits

1. Comprehensive date on personnel for career planning and administration, happier employees, better manpower development
2. Avoids time consuming paper work for timekeeping and payroll
3. All the statutory requirements automatically fulfilled
4. Extensive reporting capabilities on employment profiles
5. Aids personnel administration
6. Comprehensive payroll system with automatic calculations and printing of pay-slips.

Bibliography

List of Research Projects and Publications

Andrews Sudhir, *Food and Beverage Service,* Tata McGraw Hill, New Delhi, 1990.

Andrews Sudhir, *Hotel Front Office,* Tata McGraw Hill, New Delhi, 1990.

Andrews Sudhir, *Hotel Housekeeping,* Tata McGraw Hill, New Delhi, 1990.

Baldwin, J.H., *Environmental Planning & Management,* I.B.D., Dehradun, 1985.

Bardi, James A., *Hotel Front Office Management,* Van Nostrand Reinhold, New York, 1990.

Beaner, Allan, *Retail Travel Practice,* Beaner & Gardonland Tours Ltd., London, 1980.

Branson, Joan C. and Margett L. Lenneox, *Hotel, Hostel and Hospital Housekeeping,* ELBS.

Chandra, P., *Financial Management,* Tata McGraw Hill, Delhi.

Cooper , C.P., *Progress in Tourism, Recreation and Hospitality Management,* Vol. III, CBS Publishers & Distributors (P) Ltd., New Delhi, 1992.

Cooper Chris, John Fletcher, David Gilbert and Wanhill Stephen, *Tourism Principles and Practices,* Pitman Publishing, London.

Cuthman and Dongall, *Corporate Financial Policy,* ____.

Davis, Barnad and Sally, Stare, *Food and Beverage Management,* Meinmann, Oxford, 1989.

Lillicrop, Dennis R. and A. Cousins, *Food and Beverage Service,* ELBS, 1990.

Fellows, Jame, *Housekeeping Supervision,* Pitman, 1985.

Food Adulteration Act, 1954.

Gaur, Sanjay Singh and Sanjay V. Saggere, *Event Marketing and Management,* Vikas Publishing House Pvt. Ltd., 2003.

Gee, Chuck and Y. Makens, *Professional Travel Agency Management,* New York, 1989.

Holfert, A., *Techniques of Financial Analysis,* Irwin Homewood, Illinois, 1987.

Horne, J.V., *Financial Management & Policy.*

Millar, R., Jeffery, *Legal Aspects of Travel Agency Management,* Albany, My: Delmar Publishers Inc., 1990.

Karma, Krishnan K., Robert, Cmill, S. Kaushal (eds), *Hc pitality: Operations and Management,* Wheeler Publishing, New Delhi, 2000.

Kast, F.E. and Rosenwing, J.E., *Organization and Management: A System and Contingency Approach,* Tata McGraw Hill Book Company, New York, 1985.

Kinton and Casserani, *The Theory of Catering,* Arnold, Heinmann, 1985.

Kuchhal, S.C., *Financial Management.*

Kumar, H.L., *Personnel Management in Hotel and Catering Industry,* Metropolitan, New Delhi, 1986.

McIntosh Robert, W. Goelder and R. Charles (1990), *Tourism, Principles, Practices & Philosophies,* John Wiley & Sons Inc. New York, (6th edition).

Negi, J., *International Tourism and Travel–Principles and Concepts,* 2003, Pages 471

Negi, J., *Foundation for Tourism Development in Developing and Underdeveloped Countries,* 2002, Pages 278

Negi, J., *Marketing and Sales Strategies for Hotels and Travel Trade,* 2002, Pages 374

Negi, J., *Rashtriya Sanskritik Sampada–Sanskritik Prayatan avam Paryavaran,* 2002 Pages 399

Negi, J., *Managing Hotels and Restaurants,* 2002, Pages 390

Negi, J., *Professional Hotel Management–Concept, Principles and Practices,* 1997 Pages 734, edition 2002, Pages 874

Negi, J., *Adventure Tourism and Sports–Risk and Challenges, 2001 Vol. I & II,* Pages 742

Negi, J., *Hotel and Tourism Laws,* 2001, Pages 355

Negi, J., *Human Resource Development and Management in Hotel Industry* 2000, Pages 294

Negi, J., *Food & Beverage Costing* 2000, Pages 450

Negi, J., *Food & Beverage Management and Cost Control* 1999, Pages 397

Negi, J., *Tourism* 1998, Pages 350

Negi, J., *Regional Development: Tourism Hotel and Travel Trade (Vol. I, Vol. II, Vol. III),* 1998, Pages 937

Negi, J., *Tourism and Travel: Concepts and Principles,* 1998, Page 550, revised edition 1995

Negi, J., *Sampuran Sharat Ke Sanskritik avam Prayatan Sthal,* 1997, Pages 319

Negi, J., *Prayatan* Marketing *avam Vikas,* 1997, Pages 208

Negi, J., *Travel Agency and Tour Operation: Principles and Concepts* 1996, Pages 498

Negi, J., *Himalayan Heritage,* 1995, Pages 321

Negi, J., *Vishwa Ke Sahasik Prayatan avam Kiwi,* 1994, Pages 264 (Honoured and awarded by the Department of Tourism, Govt. of India, under *Rahul Sanskrityayan Purushkar Yojana,* 1994)

Negi, J., *Principles of Grading and Classification of Hotels, Tourism Resorts and Restaurants,* 1992, Pages 350

Negi, J., *Prayatan avam Yatra ke Siddhant,* 1991, Pages 315 (Honoured and awarded by the Department of Tourism, Govt. of India under *Rahul Sanskrityayan Purushkar Yojana,* 1991)

Negi, J., *Financial and Cost Control Techniques in Hotel and Catering Industry,* 1987, Pages 360, revised 1998

Negi, J., *Tourism Development and resource conservation, an environmental ecological and cultural approach to tourism in developing countries,* 1990, Page 250

Negi, J., *Hotels for Tourism Development (Financial Management and Economic Planning* 1984, Pages 392, revised 1997

Negi, J., *Tourism & Hoteliering–a worldwide industry,* 1982, Page 450

Negi, Jagmohan, *Adventure Tourism & Sports – Risks and Challenges,* Kanishka Publications, New Delhi.

Negi, Jagmohan, *Air Ticketing and Fare Construction,* Kaniska Publications, New Delhi.

Negi, Jagmohan, *Elements of Hotel Accountancy,* 2004, 7th edition, HKS International Publication & Aman Publications, New Delhi.

Negi, Jagmohan, *Financial & Cost Control Techniques in Hotel and Catering Industry,* (revised 1998), Metropolitan Book Company, New Delhi.

Negi, Jagmohan, *Food & Beverage Costing,* 2000, Himalaya Publishing House, New Delhi.

Negi, Jagmohan, *Food & Beverage Laws: Food Safety & Hygiene,* (with model questions) 2004.

Negi, Jagmohan, *Food & Beverage Management and Cost Control,* Kaniska Publishers & Distributors, New Delhi.

Negi, Jagmohan, *Foundation for Tourism Developments in Developing and Under-Developed Countries,* 2002, Galgotia Publishing Co. New Delhi.

Negi, Jagmohan, *Hotel & Tourism Laws,* 2001, Frank Brothers, New Delhi.

Negi, Jagmohan, *Hotel and Tourism Development,* Metropolitan, New Delhi, 1984.

Negi, Jagmohan, *Hotel and Tourism Laws,* Frank Bros., New Delhi.

Negi, Jagmohan, *Human Resources Development and Management in Hotel Industry,* 2000, Frank Brothers, New Delhi.

Negi, Jagmohan, *International Tourism & Travel Concepts & Principles,* S. Chand & Co. New Delhi.

Negi, Jagmohan, *Managing Hotels & Restaurants,* 2002, Aurthors Press, New Delhi.

Negi, Jagmohan, *Marketing and Sales Strageties for Hotels and Travel Trade,* 2002, S. Chand & Co., New Delhi.

Negi, Jagmohan, *Principles of Grading and Classification of Hotels, Tourism Resorts and Restaurants,* 1992 (Revised Ed. 2003), Kaniska Publishers & Distributors, New Delhi.

Negi, Jagmohan, *Professional Hotel Management,* 1997, Sultan Chand and Sons, New Delhi.

Negi, Jagmohan, *Regional Development: Tourism Hotel and Travel Trade* (Vol. I, II, III), 1998, Rima Publishing House, New Delhi.

Negi, Jagmohan, *Tourism & Hoteliering – A Worldwide Industry,* 1982, Indian Book Service, New Delhi.

Negi, Jagmohan, *Tourism Development and Resource Conservation: an environmental ecological and cultural approach to tourism in developing countries,* 1990, Metropolitan Book Company, New Delhi.

Negi, Jagmohan, *Tourism Development in Developing Region,* Galgotia Publication, New Delhi.

Pandey, I.M., *Financial Management,* Vikas Publishing House, New Delhi.

Peynter, J.M., *Tour Design, Marketing & Management,* Prentice Hall, UK, 1993.

Rutherferd, Denny G., *Hotel Management and Operations,* Van Nostrand Reinhold, New York, 1990.

Seth, Pran Nath, *Successful Tourism Planning & Management,* Cross Section Publications.

Stoner, James, *Management,* Prentice Hall, 1982, New Delhi.

Baun, Tom, *Human Resources Issues in International Tourism,* Butterworth Heinmann, 1993.

Trooboff , S.K., Roberta Schwartz and D.J. Mac Neil, *Travel Sales and Customer Service,* Irwin Mirror Press, Boston 1995.

Weihrich, Heinz and Koontz, Harold, *Management: A Global Perspective,* McGraw Hill, 1998.

Welsh, A.N., *The Skills of Management,* Gover Franborough, 1980.

William, Allen M., *Tourism & Economic Development,* Belhaven Press London.

Wren, D., *The Evolution of Management Thought,* Ronald Press, New York.

Yvonne, Johns, *Hospitality & Catering,* GNVQ, Advanced Text Book, Butterworth Heinmann, 1995.

Index

A

B

C

D

E

F

G